into the Light

Light

a family's epic journey

by
Dave & Jaja Martin

Beowulf Press

cover photographs by Dave Martin
cover and interior design by Doug Lochner, HLI Systems
maps by Stephen L. Davis

First Printing April 2002

Library of Congress Control Number: 2002101537
Martin, Dave and Jaja

ISBN 1-930086-04-0

BEOWULF PRESS
http://www.SetSail.com

For Chris, Holly, and Teiga

Acknowledgements

Jaja and I would like to give special recognition to our editor and friend, Gail E. Anderson. Her energy and sound ideas have had a significant influence on the outcome of this book.

We would also like to thank Thorvardur Gunnlaugsson. He not only shared his computer and printer, skis, washing machine, coffee, and XO Cognac–he also gave us his friendship when we needed it most.

Introduction

*E*VERYDAY LIFE IS LIKE A ROAD with many options: off-ramps, of sorts, that lead you smoothly away from the highway in almost any direction. Sometimes, though, the road ends abruptly. You stop short and look around. Detour! Which way now?

In June 1996, we took a detour–a sharp turn off the highway–and headed down the road to adventure. The highway we left led toward a convenient life on shore. It had tempted us for a while; the highway was smooth and well-traveled, with straight yellow lines. Billboards in the distance advertised creature comforts and long-term security. The road we chose instead was unpaved and full of pitfalls, with few signs to guide us. However, when the crisp line of the ocean's horizon appeared, and the first hint of a sea breeze blew across our faces, we knew what we had to do.

Our "odyssey" began in earnest when we purchased a 20-year-old, 33-foot steel sloop. We named her *Driver* because we hoped the boat would "drive" us to new places, both geographically and emotionally. We rebuilt her on a very tight timetable and budget, then set off with our three children (all under the age of seven) for the high northern latitudes. We cruised and lived in Iceland, the Faroe Islands, northern Scotland, Norway, and the arctic island of Spitsbergen. Our voyage lasted three years, and during that time *Driver* was our only home.

The regions in which we sailed had vicious currents and rough weather, with sea water so cold that survival was unlikely if we fell overboard. It was up to us to maintain *Driver*'s systems and equipment. We had no refrigerator, washed clothes by hand, and heated bath water on the stove.

Why were we willing to rough it and take the risks? What were the rewards? We considered ourselves treasure hunters. We knew we would find adventure along the way, but we also wondered what unexpected riches we might unearth. We weren't disappointed.

Our journey turned out to be both a physical and a mental one. Our self-sufficiency was tested daily, and we grew emotionally. On the surface, this book may appear to be the story of our cruise to places where the northern lights dance in the winter skies. Yes, you will read about our journey to the north, but moving beneath the surface you'll find a concurrent journey, the journey of our minds and souls. We hope that our story will inspire you to take a detour of your own and to discover the riches that await you around each new corner, just out of sight.

– DAVE & JAJA MARTIN

Chapter One

Adventure is what you make of it–
and what it makes of you.

HEAVY SEAS POUNDED our 33-foot sloop *Driver*. Alone in the cockpit, I scanned the wave-torn horizon and ducked flying spray. The tiller was lashed, so at least I didn't need to hand-steer. Another ocean swell peaked and toppled, sending a cascade of cold Atlantic Ocean onto the deck. *Driver* yielded to the abuse by rolling her leeward gunnel into the sea. To keep the boat from being overpowered by the wind, I had lowered the jib several hours earlier–as soon as the storm hit–and had reefed the mainsail as small as it would go. We were making scant forward headway toward land, but at least we weren't drifting farther away from it. I was happy; *Driver* was holding her own against the elements.

After a last look at the sail and the seas, I struggled down the companionway ladder to take refuge in the dry cabin. I pulled off my waterproof gloves, removed my wool cap, and then peeled off my red foul-weather gear jacket. The jacket collar still smelled like vomit, courtesy of my seasick son, Chris. I leaned my shoulder into the cabin bulkhead for support as yet another wave knocked *Driver* on her side. Fireman-style, I pushed my foul-weather pants down around my ankles, stepped out of my rubber boots, and wriggled my feet into sheepskin moccasins.

My wife, Jaja, was at the galley stove cooking dinner, her hip jammed against the sink for support. The lid was off the pressure cooker, and she was adding salt from a plastic shaker.

"Food in about five minutes," she said loudly. Even in the cabin, the noise of the wind was deafening.

I rubbed my stomach in jest.

Out of habit, I lifted the floorboard that covered the bilge. Usually the bilge was bone dry, but this time was different. Several gallons of water sloshed back and forth ominously. I couldn't believe it. Adrenaline rushed through my body. I took a deep breath, dipped my finger in the clear liquid, and tasted it. The bitterness of the sea made me wince.

Jaja's eyes were wide and questioning. I nodded slowly and mouthed the words, "salt water!"

My mind raced with the implications. We were on a small sailboat with a family crew of five, in the middle of a very angry ocean. The nearest land was the sea floor two miles below us. Greenland was the closest dry land, 500 miles to the northwest. Iceland was 700 miles to the northeast. We had already been at sea, en route from Bermuda to Iceland, for 2 1/2 weeks. It would be at least another week before we could make landfall–assuming we floated that long.

Think rationally, I told myself. We need to find the source of the leak– immediately. But a routine check of all the likely sources–shaft log, seacocks, hoses, through-hull fittings, the anchor locker drain–revealed nothing. Did we have a hole in the hull somewhere? Or was it merely a deck leak?

I had checked the bilge frequently since our departure, yet I did not remember exactly when I had checked it last. Jaja pumped the bilge dry, and I noted the time in our logbook. Even though the water didn't come gushing back, there was definitely a leak somewhere.

I closed the log. "It'll be a few hours before we know how bad it really is."

Jaja nodded.

My panic instincts told me to radio a Mayday call, but my rational side asked how we could make the decision to abandon ship when we didn't know the extent of our problem. Could we even be rescued this far from land? If so, how would we make the difficult transfer to a rescue vessel in a gale, with children in our crew? Stay calm, I told myself, and don't allow fear to force us into making an illogical decision.

Once again, I tried to think logically:

Were our lives threatened? Not yet.

Was the boat still floating? So far.

But one line of thought crushed this rationale:

Maybe we should send out a Mayday and abandon ship before the situation gets worse.

I waited. Later that evening, I sponged up a few more cups of salt water in the bilge. *Driver* is a 20-year-old steel boat that we had refurbished ourselves. Any water finding its way inside meant big trouble. I knew that steel has good tensile strength and that any damage was likely to remain localized. But what if the leak was the first link in a greater, impending catastrophe?

Night came quickly. We rested in the cabin's gloom, listening to the howling of the gale and the seas pounding the hull. At the foot of the companionway hatch, my foul-weather gear jacket swung back and forth rhythmically. The metal zipper car clicked annoyingly against the bulkhead, but I was too exhausted to get up and do anything about it.

Another large swell lifted *Driver* high, and then threw her into the wave trough with a hull-shuddering crash. In my mind, I roamed the hull's surface trying to understand where the water was coming from. We were skeptical that it was a deck leak. All the lockers were dry, and the flow of water was regimented–the way water would come in if the leak were below the waterline. There had to be a hole in the hull. But where? And would it get worse? Another breaking wave bowled into *Driver*, knocking her sideways. I made a conscious effort to release the tension in my neck and shoulders.

The hours ticked by, but our position remained nearly stationary due to the severity of the storm. I looked at Jaja, held her gaze, then raised my eyebrows questioningly.

She closed her eyes and laid her head back before answering. "I think we should wait a day and see what happens."

My burning, salt-saturated eyes closed by themselves. I forced them open. "I agree. Get some rest, OK? I'll keep my eyes on the radar screen for a while to make sure we don't add to our problems by getting run down by a ship."

"Wake me in an hour, and I'll spell you," Jaja replied.

I listened to the wind for a while, then got up to check the bilge again. My joints were stiff, and my fingertips were sore from a day on deck handling lines and sails. I lifted the floorboard. Swirling water danced in the beam of the flashlight, taunting me. *Where* was the water coming from?

MY MIND STRAYED to how we got here. I remembered Bermuda–how the varied tones of blue had hung in the air surrealistically on the day we departed for Iceland. The shadows in the lush green foliage ashore were inky black, and the pure sunlight made the pastel houses and buildings look like cartoon creations. A strong breeze churned the surface of the harbor. It was difficult to leave such a scene.

"I guess it's good to be slightly apprehensive before a long ocean passage," I said.

Jaja and I were sitting in *Driver*'s warm cockpit drinking coffee.

Jaja laughed. "Think how great it will be when we arrive in Iceland."

The inspiration for the voyage on which we were about to embark had been planted two summers earlier when our friend Rick asked about our future sailing plans. We were in Oriental, North Carolina, where we were finishing our 18-month-long refit of *Driver*.

"We're going to circumnavigate Iceland," Jaja had answered offhandedly.

Amused, I grinned and shook my head. "We are?"

"Think how exciting it would be," Jaja said. *"Anyway, it's just an idea."*

That idea germinated and took root, and now the shoot was about to break through the soil. Bermuda would be our last taste of dry land for many weeks.

After breakfast we hoisted the dinghy on deck, lashed it carefully, and then raised the anchor. Our three kids–Chris (8), Holly (6), and Teiga (2)–ran around the deck in their life jackets, excited to be going to sea. Evidently, our attempt at pumping them up had been successful.

With a hearty, "Let's do it," we powered to the middle of St. Georges Harbor to hoist the sails. The mainsail flogged defiantly. Before the sail reached the top of the mast, the jib blew off the foredeck into the water. I let go of the mainsail halyard and clamored forward to drag the jib back aboard. At the same moment, Teiga slipped in the cockpit, hit her head, and began to cry. Holly thought Teiga was seriously hurt and also began to cry.

Looking up at the half-raised mainsail, I noticed that a batten was coming out of its pocket. I lowered the sail to restitch the pocket before we lost the batten. Jaja set the engine at idle, hugged Teiga, and soothed Holly. With her foot on the tiller, she held *Driver* stationary in the middle of the harbor. Chris helped me to hold the mainsail.

Eighteen months of thoughtful preparation and anticipation were being challenged by a windy day and two inches of loose stitching. I caught Jaja's amused eye. We were about to sail across the Atlantic Ocean, and before we even saw a clear horizon, minor chaos had set in. I went below to get a sail needle and thread.

The cabin was hot. All the hatches were shut tight, ready for sea. I opened the locker beneath the chart table, took out a small bag, and rummaged through it to find the spool of waxed twine and the pack of big needles. On my way back to the companionway ladder, I glanced at the fresh white cabin paint that gleamed in the sunlight and at the teak trim that sparkled like amber. I remembered how atrocious the cabin had looked when we purchased the boat.

WHEN WE BOUGHT *Driver*, her gear and accommodations were outdated, obliging us to inject hundreds of hours of time and labor to prepare her for our journey. I worked a "real job" all day in a boatyard repairing other peoples' problems, came home for dinner, then worked on *Driver* until midnight. On weekends I worked on the boat from sunrise to sunset.

Jaja had her hands full at our rented house in Oriental. She home-schooled Holly and Chris while holding Teiga on her hip. She prepared meals, cleaned, and did the shopping. I knew I was devoting too much time to the boat when I overheard Chris talking to Jaja.

"Will Daddy be home on Christmas?"

Driver sat on land for eight months. The cabin was inadequately laid out for our growing family of five, so we tore it all out and started from scratch. We made all the modifications ourselves, and they took twice as long as anticipated.

I had told our landlord that we would be out of the house by the end of summer. He was a sailor himself, with no wish to evict us if we needed more time. It was tempting to let the project carry into late autumn. But we wondered if staying in the house longer would allow us to get more done on *Driver*, or if it would mean getting the same amount of work accomplished at a slower pace. Staying longer in the house meant paying more rent and utility bills. We also planned to sell our car to help with our growing expenses. But giving up the car would be impractical while we still lived in the house.

The only way to squeeze more hours out of my day and get *Driver* finished quickly was to quit my job. But that meant less income. We wanted to get away from land at all cost and return to the cruising life. We tried to keep in mind that once we left the dock, everything would fall into place. Not because we wanted it to, but because it had to. The most crucial step in any voyage is leaving. As with every major decision in our cruising lives, we reevaluated our priorities. I quit my job, and we devoted all our energy to finishing the boat.

At *Driver*'s christening party, our friends stood close and watched as Jaja poured a liter bottle of Budweiser over the anchors. Custom demands that you smash a bottle of champagne against the hull, but I had devoted too many hours to the boat to justify chipping off a great whack of paint for the sake of formality.

Our friends wondered why we planned to sail to Iceland rather than the Tropics. I explained that we wanted a cruising ground that was remote, somewhere free from the clutch of mass-market tourism, somewhere off the beaten track. The Tropics were great, but the splendor of the high latitudes beckoned. Snow-covered mountains, prolific wildlife, and most importantly, few cruising boats. We wanted to become time travelers and discover what voyaging might have been like 50 years ago, at the dawn of the cruising scene. Jaja's chance remark had changed our whole way of thinking.

When the christening party ended, I went aboard to lock up before spending our last night ashore. I peered into the dry bilge and flicked off the battery switches. As I made my way through the dark cabin, I reflected that adventure comes in three stages: Contemplation, action, and reflection.

"Contemplation" is the most pleasurable because it is the most naïve. Dreaming about conquering the world transports your mind to plateaus of thought unchallenged by inconvenience or sacrifice. "Action" requires day-by-day courage, strength, and introspection for coping with the uncertainties and the unknowns. "Reflection" comes at the end of the voyage, after your personal strengths and weaknesses are revealed, after some myths are shattered, and after you achieve greater understanding. Fortunately, Jaja and I are inclined to positive reflection, which causes us to play down the hardships and to eke out the ironies.

UNDER THE BRIGHT SUN in St. Georges Harbor, I finished stitching the batten pocket, then double-checked the other three battens for signs of wear. I rehoisted the mainsail, and we slid down the harbor toward Government Cut. With Teiga still on her hip, Jaja steered with the tiller between her legs. Chris switched off the engine, and I raised the jib.

At the Break Sea Spit buoy, off the eastern shore of Bermuda, the first swell hit *Driver*. She commenced a rolling gait that would not cease until we arrived in Reykjavík. With the motion came the reminder that Holly and Teiga had lost some glass marbles on the boat while we were in port. A few chinked back and forth under the cockpit grating, providing quite a resonance against the steel floor. I wondered where the rest of the lost marbles were.

As soon as we felt settled, I put the jib out on the whisker pole, and *Driver* took off at hull speed. Six knots. Nightfall was only a few hours away, and already the sun was casting long shadows. The sky was dark blue in front of us, turning a paler blue toward the sun. Very soon, the hues would turn to yellows and oranges, then reds, more subtle violets, and finally, black. As the sun sank, the humidity in the air rose, making our clothes, hair, and skin feel damp.

Teiga was the first to vomit, followed by Holly, then Chris. Before setting sail, I had threatened Chris with capital punishment if he vomited all over the cabin again. The lowest point of our passage to Bermuda from Florida, three weeks earlier, had occurred on the first evening. Chris awakened, crawled out of his bunk, chatted with Jaja who was lying with Teiga in the main cabin, then made cautious steps up the companionway ladder where I was on watch in the shelter of the canvas dodger. Chris glanced at the moon, which was half-hidden behind low-flying cumulus clouds, then turned to go back to bed.

At that second, *Driver* gave a sudden, stomach-grinding lurch. Bracing himself solidly, Chris unloaded a spray of vomit inside the cabin. Because of *Driver*'s steep angle of heel and because he was perched high on the companionway ladder, Chris achieved great velocity with impressive saturation. He covered a six-foot arc that included the vegetable drawers (where vomit oozed into the vent holes) and the head (where it coated the lockers behind the toilet). The worst casualty was my brand new foul-weather gear jacket. He hit the furry pile collar with laser-derived precision. Working together, it took Jaja and me half an hour to clean up the mess, at the end of which time we were both making repeated dashes to the cockpit for air.

"*Chris!!! You were out in the cockpit only seconds before. Why didn't you barf there?*"

Chris shrugged his shoulders, "I couldn't help it."

This time, on our first night out from Bermuda, Chris wisely used the family throw-up bowl. Jaja lay on a settee tightly holding Teiga, who was still emptying the contents of her soul. Jaja's aim was to catch all the vomit to avoid having our bedding and cushions soiled for the remainder of the passage. My role was barf-boy, disposing of the bowl's sloshy contents until the fun and games were played out.

At the end of my duties, I was queasy, too, so I escaped on deck to see how *Driver* was getting along. Twenty minutes later, Jaja sneaked out to join me, and we watched our closest star become obscured by the earth's rotation. By the time it was dark, Bermuda was well over the horizon and no longer influenced the ocean swells. We were alone on the Atlantic, a floating tribe, bowing low and worshiping Toss, the god of vomit. I thought of the infinite number of waves we would encounter on the 2,700 miles separating us from Reykjavík. I checked the log reading to verify our progress: 26 miles. I groaned. Was that it? *Only* 26 miles?

THE SHORTEST AND MOST DIRECT course from Bermuda to Iceland is 2,400 miles. That route follows a line that crosses the Grand Banks and provides a stopover about halfway, at St. John, Newfoundland. Logically, it is the most sensible route, but the shortest isn't necessarily the safest. There are fog, fishing boats, heavy shipping traffic, and sometimes even icebergs on the Banks. Plus, the shoal waters and swirling currents can be dangerous during a late spring gale.

The safest route is the longest. If we sailed to the Azores first, we could make our easting in the lower latitudes and avoid the Banks. But going that way would increase the overall distance by 850 miles. And between the Azores and Iceland, we would probably face an 1,800-mile beat to windward.

The route we chose was a compromise between the two. We designed a course that skirted the Grand Banks by 150 miles. It would keep us in the warmer and deeper waters of the Gulf Stream and presumably, would avoid the fog, fishing boats, and ice. The route would add 300 miles to the rhumb line, but by keeping away from the cold Newfoundland waters, we could also expect more favorable and steady westerly winds. We decided it would be faster and less distracting to keep a clear horizon toward our goal. In the short summer season, we needed to use our time wisely every step of the way.

Route planning is like gambling. We were playing the weather odds to gain the best advantage. If the transition from spring gales to summer calms came late, we might have a boisterous journey. If the high-pressure weather systems of summer came early, we might have slow going. There was no way to know. Keeping in mind that calms usually occur between the passage of frontal systems, we made a conservative guess at *Driver*'s daily progress. We hoped to make Iceland in 22 days, putting our arrival somewhere around June 11th.

Originally, our inspired plan included circumnavigating Iceland, but since then, we had pared down our schedule to realistic proportions, given time constraints and crew limitations. We decided to cruise along the southwest coast near Reykjavík, then perhaps continue to northern Europe for the winter. Our goal was to make it to Iceland in one piece. After that we weren't too focused. We had a long way to go.

JAJA AND I RECALLED the beginnings of so many ocean passages. Prior to buying and refitting *Driver*, we had spent seven years sailing around the world aboard our first boat–a small, fiberglass Cal 25 sloop named *Direction*. Jaja and I began that voyage as wandering gypsies, going where the whims of nature blew us. Later, when we became the astonished parents of Chris, our eight-pound baby boy, we knew what path to take. We sailed on. Over the years we had covered more sea miles with children than without.

Philosophically, we reminded ourselves that the first few days out are usually the worst. Motion sickness is a paradox. It focuses your field of vision on misery at the precise moment when you need a broader perspective. Until everyone becomes acclimated to the motion, life onboard is hard. Sailing with kids is not as easy as living in a house, but the solidarity we strive for as a floating family is not usually weakened by a few days of vomiting. Each time the children are seasick, Jaja is their slave–the caregiver, the comforter, the mother–until they feel better. My role as the father is to stand by helplessly, wishing I could do more.

Just when we thought peace had descended on *Driver*, Jaja heard Holly call out. She dove below, grabbed the throw-up bowl, and shoved it under Holly's chin just in time.

I applauded from the companionway.

"Well done!" I went below and fetched the bowl, emptied the contents into the head, flushed it down, washed the bowl out in the galley sink, and gave it to Jaja for the next emergency.

"Back in action," I said.

At that moment, Teiga rolled over and puked all over the pillow. I quickly removed the case, salvaging the pillow, and chucked the sacrificial case overboard. I grabbed a new one from the stack that was placed conveniently on the V-berth.

"One down, nine to go." Teiga was also wearing sacrificial clothes, bought at the Salvation Army. Over they went.

Jaja cleaned up Teiga with a baby wipe, put her in a fresh set of old clothes, then laid down with her to breast-feed. Resigned, Jaja began reading *The Secret Garden* aloud to the kids. I was bewildered as to how she could read a book without getting sick herself.

I took the opportunity to slip back out in the cockpit to scan the horizon for ships. *Driver* was roaring along, with the self-steering windvane guiding her course. She was in charge of the situation, allowing us humble land dwellers a chance to assimilate. The stunning colors and green foliage of Bermuda were just vague memories on our bleak ocean plain. Our bodies were in turmoil, and we counted on *Driver's* stout hull to protect us. We pushed on into the darkness.

A FEW NIGHTS LATER, I sat under the dodger on watch listening to a CD through headphones. The crisp tones of 1970s rock-and-roll complimented *Driver's* motion. In the cabin, Jaja lay awake on the port settee with Teiga, who was getting a midnight snack at the milk bar. Holly and Chris were sacked out in their bunks. I went below to put the kettle on for coffee. Jaja caught my attention by waving her book in the air. I removed my headphones.

"As soon as Teiga is finished with her feed, I'll take a watch. In about 30 minutes."

"Thanks. Do you want a cup of something now? Or would you rather wait?"

"I'll wait."

I returned to my perch in the enclosed dodger and stared into the enveloping darkness. I hooked the handle of my coffee cup with my right index finger and winced involuntarily. I had nicked my knuckle while scraping barnacles off *Driver's* hull in a Florida boatyard, and ever since, my finger had been swollen. I had disinfected the minor wound with iodine, then dressed it carefully with tape and gauze. Despite my precautions, a mild infection developed en route to Bermuda. After our arrival, the swelling disappeared, so I forgot about the problem. By day two of the passage to Iceland, my finger became painfully swollen again. I began a course of antibiotics to kill the infection, but even after three days, there was no indication that the infection was subsiding.

I felt a nagging wave of apprehension. Would the infection spread or became life threatening? In the dark of night it was easy to take the "what-ifs" to extremes. At the moment, my finger was just uncomfortable with no sign of the infection's spreading into my hand. It seemed apparent that using the finger aggravated the swelling, so I resolved to go easy on it. We decided I should continue the drugs for a week, then reevaluate the situation.

I held the cup with my left hand, took a sip, then let my tired mind wander. How many cups of coffee had I drunk in my lifetime? How many parties had Jaja and I attended? What was the dumbest thing I had ever said? Jaja said she sometimes passed the long hours during a sleepy night watch by picking a year out of her past and trying to remember everything about it. We both liked following the thread of the past–the seemingly inconsequential decisions that steered the transitions in our lives. From our musings, Jaja and I both agree that spontaneous acts produce better memories than cautious ones.

I grinned in the darkness as I recalled one of the dumbest things I had ever said. A decade earlier, my uncle remarried, and he asked me to be his best man. The invitation had surprised me (we had not seen each other for years), but I eagerly accepted, rented a tuxedo, and flew to his hometown. During the flight, I engineered a "clever" best man's toast that involved my long and privileged association with him as an only nephew. When it came time for the toast, the guests assembled in my new aunt's living room and beamed while someone went around topping off glasses with champagne.

I cleared my throat: "When I was four years old, I was the ring bearer at my uncle's first wedding." I prattled on about life, how we mature, and how we wander along false paths until we find the right one. I raised my glass to my newest aunt and put my arm around my uncle's shoulder.

"Furthermore," I said, "my uncle and I have both attained new plateaus. I have progressed from ring bearer to best man and despite my uncle's long journey, he has finally found his treasure!" My speech was met with drunken applause and general tittering.

A year later, during a family reunion, my newest aunt hit me with extraordinary news. She told me that because of my toast, it hadn't taken her long to deduce that she was wife number three, *not* wife number two as she had been led to believe. I nodded my head dumbly as I recalled two details that had always puzzled me about their wedding. The first was why my newest aunt calmly asked me my age immediately after the toast while everyone was still tittering. The second was wondering why my uncle suddenly became uncharacteristically tense.

The CD ended just as Jaja switched off her light and began extracting herself from Teiga's clutch. As I went below to reheat the water, I glanced at Teiga, who was lactose drunk and sleeping soundly. After my coffee, I lay on my back fully clothed, closed my eyes, and fell asleep instantly.

DULL GRAY CLOUDS HID THE SUN, but calm seas and slow going enhanced the kids' enthusiasm. For the first time since leaving Bermuda, we let them venture on deck to stretch their legs and view the world. No longer seasick, Holly liked being in the middle of the ocean with just the thin line of the horizon to define our boundaries.

"It makes me feel like I'm high above the ground, flying," she said.

Chris started to climb the mast until I reminded him that EMTs don't come this far into the ocean and that our only cure was prevention.

"Please keep your feet on the deck," I said.

"Both feet?" Chris asked slyly. "Does that mean I have to shuffle back to the cockpit?"

I laughed. Smart aleck.

During the late morning, Jaja made a big batch of pancakes smothered in maple syrup, and Chris ate his faster than she could cook them. Later, Jaja sat between Holly and Teiga with a plate balanced on her knees and fed the girls their sticky meal.

After breakfast I unrolled the chart to update our position. The inch-by-inch path that *Driver* made across the chart toward Iceland–which on paper measured over two feet from Bermuda–could appear futile if we allowed it. The ocean, represented on the chart as a white void besprinkled with depths, could easily seem vast and unconquerable. I plotted our most recent position, drew a line between it and the previous day's position, and passed the chart around for all to see. The kids were unimpressed and went back to playing with their Legos. They accepted the pace of life at sea more readily than Jaja and I did.

At the beginning of this long passage, all we thought about was arriving. The thought of traveling any slower than *Driver*'s maximum hull speed, stood like a mental wall between us and our destination. But when we're cruising, everything good seems to unfold slowly–like a gorgeous sunset. Focusing solely on the end of a trip takes the fun out of getting there–even if getting there is not always fun. Do all of life's adventures have to be fun? We can never decide if ocean sailing demands sagacity or blind patience.

Driver's position was roughly 650 miles northwest of Bermuda. With our global positioning system (GPS) receiver providing constant analysis, it was tempting to update the paper chart frequently. But with no threat of land in our path, updating our position several times a day was a pointless exercise that cluttered the chart and emphasized our reptilian speed. I jotted the GPS positions in the logbook every four to six hours, along with our speed and compass heading, to serve as a backup in case we suffered electrical failure.

ON OUR FIRST BOAT, *Direction*, we navigated most of the way around the world with a sextant. On calm days in midocean, Jaja would sit in the cockpit, balancing toddlers, while I stood on the stern deck balancing the sextant. After I hollered "OK!" to indicate I had a sight, Jaja would note the time on a scrap of paper then copy down the sextant angles as I called them out. During the rough times at sea, when Jaja had to remain in the cabin with our young crewmembers, I would scream "OK!" at the top of my voice, then poke my head in the companionway to relay the figures. During the intervals between sights, Jaja drew cartoons on the sides of my worksheets illustrating the funny things that happened that day. The kids usually added their input by asking Jaja to draw a bird pooping on my head or a fish biting my bottom.

After the rituals of taking the morning and afternoon sights, I would combine the figures into a running fix, and we would gaze in wonder at our latest position, a dot derived by mathematical magic. The addition of GPS killed this family tradition.

When I installed GPS aboard *Direction*, I distrusted its automated precision at first. Working a sextant sight with a pencil and a clean sheet of paper was a cerebral process that interfaced the mind with all of the geographical possibilities of getting lost. GPS was a mystery box that required faith in delicate circuitry and roaming satellites. Obtaining a morning and afternoon running fix with a sextant represented about two hours of work and gave an accuracy of plus or minus five miles. Plotting a course with a GPS took 30 seconds, yielding an accuracy measured in boatlengths.

Rain or shine, day or night, GPS is ultimately safer and more reliable, which is why we use it. But it reduces the need for spatial thinking, for conceptualizing the celestial heavens and the sea as one entity. With GPS, your mind only has to journey between the magic electronic box and the compass.

Voyaging beyond sight of land requires certain levels of self-reliance that an unconscious dependence on electronics can undermine. Crossing an ocean with only a sextant demands a large dose of gut instinct and inner confidence. Except for a few practice sights to prove that I could still do it, I had not derived a sextant position in years. We had become complacent about navigating with a GPS, and I wondered if our level of deep-seated self-reliance–not only about navigation but about all aspects of cruising–was still as sound as it once was. We were close to finding out.

THE WIND CONTINUED LIGHT throughout the morning, and *Driver's* forward progress remained slow. During the calm, we rested and recharged. There was no telling when the next opportunity might come. As the day warmed, I went on deck to adjust the dorade vents for maximum air flow to the cabin below. While bending down to twist the starboard vent, my eye caught an odd blemish on a fitting–part of the mast's rigging. Although *Driver* was two decades old, the mast and its components were less than a year old. We had replaced everything as part of our refit program before leaving the States.

At the lower ends of the wire stays, or shrouds, that support the mast, there are stainless steel end-fittings. The fittings connect the stays to adjustable turnbuckles that, in turn, are attached to the boat's hull. With the tip of my finger, I wiped away the salt crystals from one of the shiny end-fittings. I stared incredulously. A half-inch-long vertical crack, as thin as a hair, ran through the fitting.

Our rigging is flawed, I thought. *Our mast is unsafe. We are hundreds of miles away from land. We're screwed...*

This could mean we might have to abandon our journey north. How long had the rigging piece been broken?

Except for birth control, this rigging problem was the most serious gear failure Jaja and I had suffered during our years of bluewater cruising. I cursed my arrogance for thinking the boat was indestructible. I went below, full of disbelief, and broke the news to Jaja. She took a deep breath after I relayed the problem.

"Are you sure, Dave? The timing couldn't be worse."

"Just another of life's unexpected thrills."

"Can you fix it?"

"We have two spare fittings," I said.

Jaja was thoughtful. "Do you think other end-fittings are broken?"

"I'm going to go inspect them now." There were 25 to examine.

Years ago, when I had dismantled our salty binoculars for cleaning, I found that the eyepiece optics are similar to a jeweler's loupe. We'd had fun looking at our magnified skin and at the scratches in our gold wedding rings, but now I had a more practical use in mind. I unscrewed an eyepiece and headed for the foredeck to inspect every rigging component. Thankfully, the sea was calm.

I spent an hour free-climbing the mast (adrenaline is a wonderful energy boost) and crawling on my hands and knees on deck. Then I returned to the cabin where Jaja was making lunch and the kids were listening to a book cassette on the tape deck. Roald Dahl was reading his story, *James and the Giant Peach*. His delectable and rumbling voice was as provoking as the actual words.

"We've been waiting for you...You are one of us now...You are one of the crew."

"What'd you find?" Jaja asked casually.

"There's only one other cracked fitting."

She sighed visibly. "Want a coffee?"

We pondered our options. Iceland was still 2,000 miles away, and we could expect plenty of rough conditions before we arrived. St. John, Newfoundland, was the closest port, but to get there demanded that we cross the Grand Banks, an area where incredible loads could be placed on the mast if we were hit by a gale. Bermuda was dead to windward, so we had no hope of returning. The Azores seemed the most likely place to duck in for repairs. The main harbor on Faial Island was 1,200 miles away, but we could count on downwind sailing conditions and a low probability of gales. It would be easy on the rigging–and easy on our peace of mind.

Two years of preparation and planning took a chair in the debate. We knew instinctively that if we made a detour to the Azores, we would never make it to Iceland this year. There was no way we could order new rigging from the States or England and have it shipped and installed in time to make the trek north. We questioned whether or not our Icelandic plans could hold up through a yearlong delay. We also wondered if we were overreacting to the problem by thinking we needed to replace all the rigging. It was difficult not to feel vulnerable in midocean.

"If we replace the two fittings, do you think there will be more problems later on?" Jaja asked.

"The million dollar question."

After our coffee, I dug the two spare fittings out of our plastic rigging supply box and held them in my hand like talismans. I assembled tools, put them into a bucket, then put the two new fittings into my pocket. I recalled the nights at our rented house when we laid out rigging wire from the living room, down the hallway, and into the bedrooms. To measure the lengths correctly I snaked the tape measure through two doorways. Jaja kept the wire and the tape taut, side by side. We spent several evenings assembling *Driver's* rigging while sitting on the couch in the living room with the same tools that were now in the bucket. The two-piece, screw-together end-fittings seemed indestructible then; the rigging wire seemed flexible and strong. Knowing that rigging failures were possible, I stocked the spare parts as a precaution. I never imagined we would need them.

"The heck with quitting," I said, going with my gut feeling. "I think we should assume the two broken fittings are bad apples and that the others will be fine."

"I'm all for continuing." Jaja was enthusiastic.

"Onwards then?"

Jaja smiled. "Like a herd of wild turtles."

To REPLACE THE TWO BROKEN FITTINGS, I had to disconnect the stays from the turnbuckles. The idea of removing any wires that held up the mast while in the middle of the ocean was contradictory to reason, but there was no choice. We lowered the jib to reduce our speed but left the mainsail up. The wind would push against the sail. This would put pressure only on the rigging on the windward side of the boat–on the opposite side from where I was working.

I walked carefully to the leeward side of the boat with the tools, tied the bucket to the lifelines, then began to loosen a turnbuckle using a screwdriver and an adjustable wrench. When the turnbuckle was loose and the stay was slack, I pulled the pin out of the turnbuckle, disconnecting the stay. Using my hefty wire cutters, I nipped the flawed end-fitting off the stay. Installing the spare end-fitting was an easy procedure that took about 10 minutes. While I worked, I knew that if I fixated on *not* dropping the spare fittings into the water, it was sure to happen. To keep my mind diverted, I contemplated a very odd coincidence.

Twelve years earlier, I sailed transatlantic with a friend aboard his brand new 44-foot sloop. We were pounding to windward bound for Chesapeake Bay from the Azores when an inner forestay on the mast broke with a loud CRACK! We rushed on deck to find the middle of the mast bent aft from the recoil, pulsating dangerously and ready to collapse. We turned the boat away from the wind to let the pressure of the mainsail push the mast back into column.

The culprit, we soon learned, was a stainless steel rigging fitting that had sheared off, a victim of metal fatigue. We had no spares for this part, so we made a temporary repair by wrapping line around the mast then tying it to a cleat on deck. We used a block and tackle to exert enough tension on the line to hold the mast straight. We completed the final 1,000 miles of the arduous passage to windward without further mishap. Ironically, that rigging failure occurred in nearly the same geographical position in which *Driver* was located when I discovered our cracked end-fittings.

My thoughts returned to the work at hand. I finished installing the first replacement fitting. One down, one to go. The second flawed fitting was also at deck level, but on the opposite side of the boat. So we tacked the mainsail to the other side, and I completed the second repair. When I finished, I left the cotter pins out of the turnbuckles. That way, I could tighten the turnbuckles and tune the shrouds more precisely while the mast was under load.

If we hadn't had the spare fittings, we could have replaced the flawed shrouds with chain, or with the Kevlar rope we carried for emergencies. But it was satisfying to have stocked the right parts.

Nevertheless, a nagging doubt remained. Would there be any more rigging failures? If something broke when the mast was under tremendous load, I knew from experience that the recoil could send the mast crashing to the deck. If the rigging broke in a gale, instead of during the settled conditions we had, an emergency repair could be dangerous, and more likely, impossible.

Jaja and I were both happy to be headed toward our goal once more, but I harbored a secret disgust for myself. Overconfidence can be as great a pitfall as neglect. An hour spent inspecting the rigging back in Bermuda might have saved us from a potentially disastrous, midocean nightmare.

After I cleared the deck of tools, I hoisted the jib, Jaja let out the mainsail, and we resumed our course of 95 degrees magnetic for the "Land of Fire and Ice."

Our confidence may have returned too soon, however. The next threat to our small craft on a big ocean was to come from below the waterline.

Chapter Two

*There is a narrow distinction
between feeling vulnerable and accepting one's vulnerability.
The first is a state of mind; the other is a fact.*

IN BERMUDA, we had bought a trim, do-it-yourself weather handbook called *Instant Weather Forecasting*. It was full of cloud illustrations, and we were supposed to match the photos in the book with what we observed overhead. We had put 200 miles under our keel since the rigging repair. Because there were no more apparent rigging problems, we decided it was time for a diversion. We would compare the current radio forecast to the weather forecast we formulated using the book. A more scientific approach might have been to make our own weather prediction *before* listening to the radio, but we were not feeling scientific that day. According to the book, a northeast blizzard with hailstones and lightning was due to hit within 12 hours.

Instead of storms, we spent long hours, day after day, lounging in the sunny cockpit. The endless progression of low-pressure systems slid eastward under Newfoundland and missed us with flawless precision. A gale center would pass just out of reach in front of us, and another would fizzle behind, leaving *Driver* unscathed and moving purposefully in moderate winds. Thankfully, our fears of battling storm-force winds the entire way to Iceland were being cheated.

The kids relaxed and fell into a comfortable routine. One game we played frequently was Twenty Questions. After hours of guessing, Jaja and I would beg for mercy and ask for a break. Chris and Holly would continue to play tirelessly on their own, providing Jaja and me with unparalleled entertainment.

"OK, Chris," Holly said. "I'm thinking of something."

"Is it a mineral?"

"No."

"A vegetable?"

"Sort of."

"Is it an animal then?"

"Sort of."

"It's both an animal and a vegetable?'"
"Yes."
"That's impossible, Holly."
"No it's not. It's a giraffe eating a carrot."
"That's silly, Holly," Chris said. "It has to be just one thing. Now it's my turn. Let's see. OK, I have one. I'm thinking of a number between one and a million."
"Um, fifty thousand?"
"Nope."
"Fifty thousand and seven?"

One night, a weather front moved over us, and we spent the dark hours speeding downwind with just the mainsail up. The squally conditions were gone by breakfast, but so was the semitropical weather we had enjoyed since Bermuda. No more warm days in the cockpit. Dense fog sat balanced on the rim of the horizon for several days, and the damp, chilly dew infiltrated the cabin.

We fired up the diesel stove each morning to drive the persistent gray out of the cabin. And we strung a clothesline over the diesel stove to dry our drenched gloves, wet towels, and soggy hats. The temperature in the cabin soared to a tropical 70 degrees Fahrenheit, while on deck the temperature remained at 45. Our clammy skin and damp bedding became as dry as hot sand. All we needed was a shower, clean clothes, and a piña colada.

We ran the radar on foggy days, and one morning we picked up a ship on the screen. We made contact on our Very High Frequency (VHF) radio and learned that it was delivering engine parts to Louisiana. The skipper politely made a slight course correction to give us a safer margin before he steamed by. Like music to our ears, he told us over the VHF that he had seen us on his radar from 12 miles away. Whether it was due to our steel hull or the two radar reflectors at the top of our mast, it was comforting to know we had been "seen."

It reminded me of an incident aboard our previous boat *Direction*. Sitting becalmed in dense fog, we heard the ominous vibrations of an approaching ship. After a few minutes, it was obvious that it was coming right for us. I tried to hail the ship on the VHF to beg the captain to alter course, but he did not reply. At the time, we didn't know that our VHF microphone was broken. What's more, *Direction* did not have a radar reflector because I had acciden-tally dropped it overboard while trying to improve the way it was secured to the backstay. I remembered someone telling us they had made a makeshift radar reflector by filling a green garbage bag with empty beer cans and hoist-ing it to the masthead. Great idea. Regrettably, all we had on board were glass bottles filled with rum.

As the sound of the ship grew louder and louder, I contemplated digging the outboard motor out of *Direction*'s aft lazaret and using it to power out of harm's way. But to extract and set up the motor would take at least 10 minutes–time I knew we didn't have.

We stood on the foredeck transfixed, staring into the gloom. Thump, clang, rattle–the ship's engine played a dissonant dirge. Only our ears could detect the ship's proximity, and our hearing was doing a wonderful job of relaying panic messages to our brains. As we stared into the wall of white fog, the sound began to change. The ship was clunking safely past in front of us. After a slow five-count, the first wave from the ship's wake appeared out of the murk and rolled *Direction* on her beam-ends. Fog is the curse of every mariner.

THE FIRST LOW-PRESSURE CENTER nailed *Driver* on day 16 of the passage to Iceland. Over a period of six hours, we shortened sail by increments until we were hunkered down for the night with our triple-reefed American-made mainsail, our French-fabricated staysail, and our New Zealand-built storm jib. We ate up the miles in relative comfort, happy at the chance to be moving forward again after a week of slow going. Before it got dark, I roamed the decks, tidied lines, checked the lashings on the dinghy, and inspected the rigging. All seemed well. Luckily, the fog had blown away.

As I worked on deck, I made plenty of noise so that Jaja, who lay below with Teiga, would know that I was still on board. Each of us lived in fear of the other's falling overboard while we slept. Jaja told me that when she woke from an off watch-sleep, the first thing she did was to get up and look for me. Her constant, paralyzing fear was that she might not find me. The notion of falling overboard was a serpent that lived in a dark corner of my subconscious. I did not dwell on falling in, but I was aware of the possibility, and it added limits to my outward carelessness.

After finishing my duties, I sat on deck with my back to the howling wind, staring at the dark horizon. There was no place on earth more desolate than a black night in the middle of the ocean. I remembered another black night, before Jaja and I were married, while I was sailing *Direction* across the Atlantic alone.

I was resting in the cabin when the rising wind prompted me to go on deck. I climbed into the cockpit and stood for a few minutes to let the freshening breeze blow the drowsiness from my brain. Then I bounded on deck automatically. My hand found the jib halyard and released it. The sail slid down the forestay. With only the mainsail providing lateral balance, *Direction*'s motion changed from semipredictable to just wishful thinking. As I started across the heaving foredeck to collect the flogging jib, I realized I was no longer on my feet. I was falling headfirst toward the water.

There was no transition from walking to falling. There were no theatrics with pinwheeling arms or mock looks of disbelief. As the inverted deck flew past my eyes, my reflexes kicked in. I caught the lower lifeline by the tips of two fingers. The lifeline wire cut grooves into my salt-soaked skin, but my tenuous grasp was enough to put the brakes on my descent. My feet pivoted in an arc and slapped the ocean. As my sea boots filled with the leaden weight of the North Atlantic, my sore fingers slid along the wire like worn-out pulleys.

Just when my grip was almost gone, my safety tether came up tight. Although the tether whacked my nose, its added support allowed me to find a better handhold. I crawled back on deck and finished reefing the jib. As soon as I raised the reefed jib, *Direction* resumed a purposeful and lively motion. I retreated to the cabin, soaked from the waist down. That three-second scenario shocked my 24-year-old bravado. Until then, I believed that falling overboard was something that only happened to other people. It also strengthened my resolve to wear my safety harness and clip on every time I ventured on deck.

Afterwards, I had two weeks alone before landfall to ponder the experience. My conclusion was that I could live an idle life ashore, mummified by caution, or I could keep sailing and just be a little smarter about it. I blamed fatigue for the reason I fell overboard and promised to allow myself more quality rest.

While solo sailing, I was so fanatically worried about getting run down by a ship that I could not doze for longer than 20 minutes at a time. I felt half-asleep during the day and half-awake during the night. After going overboard, I forced myself to sleep a solid three-hour chunk once a day. As justification for not keeping a responsible, continuous deck watch, I reasoned that I might be run down by a ship, but lack of sleep would surely kill me.

As *Driver* crawled across the vast Atlantic toward Iceland, Jaja and I were sleep deprived–but for a different reason. When it came to sleeping and waking, the children ran the show. Jaja and I napped during the day whenever it was convenient for the other to stand watch. During the dark hours, we took it night by night, each scenario between sunset and sunrise proving slightly different. Teiga dictated our actions. When rough seas disturbed her sleep, Jaja was obliged to lie with her, wide awake and frustrated at not being able to leave the berth. Meanwhile, I stayed dopey with fatigue on a late-night watch, dozing intermittently, frustrated for not being able to help with the childcare.

As soon as Jaja could extract herself from Teiga's clutch, she would happily take over our little ship and enjoy the night hours–which, after all, were supposed to be free from mothering duties. But ours is an imperfect world. Jaja stayed stressed knowing that Teiga could wake up at any minute and infiltrate the night with loud crying. I was often only an hour into a sound sleep when Teiga woke. I always tried sneaking into bed with her, pretending I was Jaja, but that subterfuge never worked. Not once.

We fantasized about our prechildren years when a stack of books, afternoons of leisure, and a casual watch schedule at night made the days at sea fly by. With three children demanding more attention than the boat, going to sea became less about sailing and more about providing food and entertainment. Children change your life no matter what you are doing.

I WENT BACK ONTO DRIVER'S FOREDECK in the wee hours to modify our politically correct sail combination. The French staysail was the first to come down. After I furled and lashed it on deck, I sat down to observe the scene. We were forereaching at seven knots, with spray flying spreader high. Frothy white horses were the only things showing on the dark, windswept, ocean plain.

The commotion I made on deck had awakened Jaja. She was sitting under the dodger, waiting her turn on watch. Before I went below to sleep, we sat together observing the world around us, while our "other world" slept soundly in the cabin below. *Driver*'s heavy displacement allowed her to travel over and through the seas with an iron–or, given her hull material, perhaps I should say, *steely*–will, and we moved toward Iceland on course. Only 800 miles to go.

After 36 hours, the wind petered out, leaving us becalmed. The barometer had fallen steadily and remained bottomed out at 999 millibars. Usually the barometer went up after a blow, signifying a return to more settled conditions. By staying down, the barometer indicated that the low-pressure system had probably stalled right over us. When the low moved again, it was impossible for us to predict whether the wind would be stronger, the same, or weaker than what we had already experienced. It was unlikely to be weaker. The radio weather forecast gave an indeterminate position for the low and predicted associated cold fronts of varying magnitudes. We had to wait.

The clearing skies slowly filled with haze, then with heavy clouds. We wallowed in a cauldron of restless seas for 12 hours. A boat with forward motion is a living entity with emotion, but a boat that bobs like a Styrofoam fishing float is a disgrace.

The slack sails beat themselves uncontrollably against the rigging, and the cacophony sent tension through the hull into the cabin. We became one with *Driver*, rejoicing in her triumphs and suffering in her misery. Now we suffered. I dropped the jib to save it from being chafed to death against the spreaders. Despite the lack of wind, I put a double reef in the mainsail so less sailcloth would be exposed to snap unmercifully as the boat rolled.

While lowering the jib and fighting the motion on the foredeck, I wrenched my sore index finger. Intense pain telegraphed up my arm. Although I had tried two different types of antibiotics, the swelling in my hand was steadily getting worse.

At sunrise, the barometer was still rock-bottom at 999 millibars. The sky was brown and gray, and there was a new feel in the air. At 53 degrees north latitude, the only remaining traces of the Tropics were our tans, which slowly faded beneath our long underwear.

At 10:00 a.m., the wind filled in gently from the northeast. I raised the jib. By 11:00, I doused it again. The wind was screaming. We made scant forward progress with only a small triangle of reefed mainsail showing. It provided just enough steerage so we could keep *Driver*'s bow aimed close to the eye of the wind and the onslaught of the seas. The tiller was lashed, so we could all stay belowdecks. At noon, the surface of the sea was a white veil of foam, and the wind strummed the rigging with virtuosity, creating unheard-of strains. Here was a real storm–45 knots, 50-plus in gusts.

After 19 days on the ocean, we were one with the storm and actually drew power from it. We had planned for midocean gales and were in awe of their force. What a contrast to our departure from Bermuda when we were fighting a sunny breeze far less challenging than this! Now the worst part was wondering how bad conditions would get. Once the storm peaked and stabilized, we relaxed a little and took the opportunity to critically observe one of nature's spectacles.

The kids were having a blast. Earlier in the passage, they began a game that involved sliding down the slanted cabin floor, or sole, on a piece of slippery sailcloth. The game evolved into a contest to see who could walk the 14-foot distance from the galley to the V-berth up forward without touching anything. The catch was you had to negotiate the recklessly tilted cabin sole wearing socks. As *Driver* slogged along in the watery tumult like a lame whale, Chris and Holly roared with laughter, trying to balance on their tiptoes. Teiga enjoyed the game, too. Her version was to cover the distance on her fast-moving hands and knees.

The power of the storm charged us up, and we entertained happy fantasies about what we would do when we reached Reykjavík. There were the usual desires: A hot shower, fresh fruit, a calm harbor. On top of our list was climbing into our bunks all at the same time to sleep the night away knowing that no one had to stand watch. With the demands of childcare and those of the boat, Jaja and I become strangers during ocean passages. All our energy is focused on maintaining equilibrium for the family unit–which includes us and *Driver*.

As the storm continued to rage, the kids grew weary of their cabin-sole calisthenics. Like animals returning to their cages, they retired to their customary positions on the settees in the main saloon. The 18-inch-high, canvas lee-cloths that we rigged in bad weather kept the kids from falling off the settees.

Life at sea for a child can be sedentary, but according to statistics, their peers on shore spend more hours per year lounging in front of televisions than being active. We did not have a television or videotape player on *Driver*. Our boat life was like a play where all the props had to ring true for the illusion to work. How could we become a close-knit unit if our thoughts were diluted with fast-paced, commercialized images? Living on a boat is a unique art form, we did not want to dilute that uniqueness with mass-market visual input.

While Holly entertained Teiga on the leeward settee, Jaja worked in the galley. It was feeding time. Soon the pressure cooker was full of boiling pasta. Jaja gave instructions to the kids to keep clear of the stove lest they get burned by scalding water. Most "safety aboard" books advise against boiling water during rough conditions at sea, yet it is during cold weather and storms that our bodies need warm, high-carbohydrate nourishment. I distributed peanuts and raisins to keep the kid's small mouths occupied until dinner was ready. Suddenly, Chris spilled his cup of rations, sending his treats into the blankets. Jaja and I smiled. We knew that if we ever faced starvation at sea, a foray under the cushions would provide ample provisions.

I crawled into my damp foul-weather gear and fought my way up the companionway. Before my feet left the ladder, I clipped my safety harness onto the tether that lay waiting in the companionway. My harness is a belt of webbing that is an integral part of my foul-weather jacket. The tether is a 20-foot-long piece of 1/2-inch-thick rope, or line, with a snapshackle at one end. The other end of this safety line is attached to a stainless steal eye bolt that is through-bolted to the boat beside the companionway. To "clip on," I simply fastened the snapshackle of the safety line to my jacket harness. Then I could move around on deck and still be tethered to the boat. It was my safety line that had saved me when I went overboard on *Direction*.

In the cockpit, I watched the storm rage, double-checking that all was well on deck. My eyes scanned the rigging, the lashings on the dinghy, and the lashings on the sails. To windward, a gargantuan sea rose high above our mast. Just when it seemed we would be pummeled by a deluge, *Driver* hobbled up the wave face, limped over the breaking crest, and fell headlong with a crash into the trough behind. Occasionally, the crest of the wave would break and rumble down the face of the swell. The white water would pound our hull with a ferocious WHOMP, and *Driver* would skid sideways down into the trough.

The wind had decreased a notch from the initial blasts–I guessed the speed at around 35 knots, with gusts in the 40s. The barometer rose slowly. We figured conditions would mellow within 18 hours. Visibility was less than a mile in the driving rain and spume. Spotting shipping traffic was nearly impossible, but we weren't too worried because we hadn't seen another vessel in over a week.

The only other evidence of civilization were the jet contrails we observed overhead on clear days. It was strange to think that while we bobbed along on the surface of the sea, there were a few hundred people just seven miles away who were impatient for their six-hour transatlantic flight to be over. We thought of them, lounging with their shoes off, complaining about airline food. One day, a sonic boom shook our habitat from keel to masthead and nearly sent us all into cardiac arrest. We thought we had been struck by a submarine.

I took a 360-degree swipe of our visible world, then opened the dodger flap to go below. Moving around in wet foul-weather gear and big rubber boats was like trying to swim in a vat of honey. I struggled back down the companionway, caught the aroma of spaghetti sauce, then stripped off my rain gear. The roar of the wind and the sound of rushing water were deafening, even inside the cabin. I had to speak loudly.

"Jaja, I don't know how you can cook meals during a gale."

Jaja smiled. "I don't know how you can go on the foredeck and not get washed overboard."

IT WAS THEN THAT I LIFTED the floorboard at the foot of the companionway and stared transfixed at the liquid invasion. I licked my salty finger and looked up at Jaja. Her face mirrored mine.

Chris was watching Jaja and me intently. "What's the matter?" he shouted.

"Nothing," I said.

Chris sprang off the settee and looked over my shoulder. "Why is there water in the bilge?"

"Chris," Jaja said firmly, "let us think. Go back and lie down."

Ten minutes later, after our first fruitless search for the source of the leak, we pumped the bilge dry. The screaming wind, which had been part of the background all day, began to get on my nerves. I wished it would just be quiet for an hour so I could concentrate. Where was the water coming from?

"Are we sinking?" Chris asked.

"No," I said, "We're not sinking."

Chris was quiet for a minute. "Are we going to be OK?"

"Yes," Jaja said calmly. "We'll be fine."

I downed a bowl of spaghetti, then spent an hour on my hands and knees with a flashlight, playing it over the dark recesses of the bilge. I saw a lot of idle water running back and forth, but I could not spot anything obvious like a hole or a cracked weld. Jaja checked every locker for evidence of a deck leak, but everything there was dry.

Although we didn't appear to be in grave danger, I played worst-case scenarios in my head. We only had a minor leak, but if the water coming in was due to a structural calamity, how many more pounding waves would it take before *Driver*'s hull split wide open? An hour's worth? A day's worth? Two years?

In the event that we began to sink, Jaja's role was to put life jackets on the kids and tie them to her bodily. My role was to launch the life raft and grab the emergency overboard bag, which was wedged under the companionway ladder. The bag was stocked with food rations, a manual desalinator, fishing tackle, a 406 MHz Emergency Position Indicator Radio Beacon (EPIRB), a dedicated 227 MHz EPIRB, a strobe light, six parachute distress rockets, hand flares, and a hand-held VHF radio. We also had a medical kit with painkillers, penicillin, sterile dressings, tampons, and potions for diarrhea, constipation, earache, sinuses, chapped lips, saltwater sores, burns, and muscle aches.

We felt as prepared as possible, but I wondered how we would feel if we saw a ship. Would we be tempted to radio it and abandon *Driver*? There might not be another ship as close for weeks.

When Jaja and I began sailing around the world on *Direction*, we did not carry safety gear. No life raft, not one life jacket, no fire extinguishers. We lived by the proclamation of youth: *Hey, it won't happen to us.* Jaja and I sailed *Direction* halfway around the world depending heavily on self-reliance and a strong boat.

Having children changed our thinking. Dying tragically as lovers was one thing, but sacrificing our firstborn for a romantic vision was a theme that only had credence in very old books. When we contemplated pumping up *Direction*'s inflatable dinghy in an emergency while treading water and holding newborn Chris, we came face to face with responsibility. We bought a self-inflating life raft and an EPIRB.

With the addition of safety gear aboard *Direction*, our self-reliance was suddenly burdened with contradiction. We ventured away from land by choice, to be independent from outside intervention, yet we carried a satellite-dependent EPIRB to call the Coast Guard if we had problems. In our present situation aboard *Driver*, hanging on until the last minute to call for a rescue just might be postponing hypocrisy. Why not send a Mayday call immediately and get it over with?

Despite the array of electronic gadgets undermining our values aboard *Driver*, our dignity and integrity were intact. The leak represented the unknown. It did not *necessarily* represent life-threatening danger. We may only have perceived it that way. Until we could figure out exactly what the problem was, we had to keep our heads clear. To do that, we needed rest.

We lay on the settees under heavy blankets. Jaja hugged the girls for warmth; I clutched Chris. The wind continued to rage hour after monotonous hour until time stood still. The atmosphere on deck infiltrated the cabin, making everything cold, damp, and soggy. Although I tried lighting the diesel stove, the strong wind and high waves prevented the smoke from drawing up the stack. Noxious diesel fumes cast a pall in the stale air, testing our forgotten queasiness. I finally gave up.

We thought back to the time on *Direction* when Chris was two years old, and Holly was five months. Gale-force winds battered us for half of a 16-day, salt-sprayed passage between New Zealand and Fiji. Jaja and I spent the better part of a stormy week lying in *Direction*'s sopping wet cabin, each of us clutching a child, wondering about our sanity–or lack of it. We watched the seas as they covered the portholes with a dark blue evenness, and we became nonplused as the sea sprayed through the cracks of the companionway doors, turning our bedding into a swamp. We subsisted on cookies and crackers because the motion was too violent to prepare anything else. Never in our wildest imaginings would we have believed that six years later we would be battling a storm aboard a leaky steel boat, 700 miles south of Iceland.

FINALLY, THE BAROMETER BEGAN to climb rapidly, confirming the arrival of a big high-pressure system. As the wind subsided during the night, the breaking wave crests lost their vigor. Eventually, *Driver* was left starving for wind in the grip of a titanic ground swell. Although we rolled violently, our deck dried off. Unfortunately, water continued to infiltrate the bilge at a constant rate of two gallons a day. Since our decks were dry, we became convinced that the leak was lower down, probably below the waterline.

After many, many hours on my hands and knees with a flashlight and a mirror, I located a two-inch-long hairline crack in the hull, about three feet away from the keel. Finding a hole in our boat was hardly cause for a celebration, but I was thankful that I had finally discovered the source of the water in the bilge. Technically speaking, the leak wasn't that bad. The water's obstinate accumulation was its only real drawback. But for us to be the victors in this battle, we needed to exercise our superiority and stop the flow. I tried squashing waterproof epoxy over the rent, but the glob of fast-curing putty failed to adhere.

We thought of several other options. One was to through-bolt a piece of wood over the crack on the outside of the hull. But we didn't want to add more holes below the waterline. Then we decided that it wasn't necessary to stop the leak; we just needed to contain it from the inside. But fixing the crack from the inside was complicated because the crack ran under one of the steel T-bar hull frames, or stringers, making it impossible to simply push something flat over the crack.

I had an inspiration. I built a complicated plywood box measuring roughly six inches square by one inch high. It fit intricately over and around the stringer and isolated the crack. I planned to seal the pieces of the box together and fasten the box to the inside of the hull with polysulfide sealant, which cured well when immersed in sea water.

To alleviate pressure inside the box while the sealant cured, I inserted a small relief hose in the top of the box. As Jaja handed me materials, I worked like a surgeon. I dried the hull with rubbing alcohol and a clean rag. Then I quickly smeared the pieces of the box with sealant and assembled it around the crack. I had predrilled holes in the box so I could screw it together easily. We watched apprehensively. Soon sea water began to trickle from the relief hose into a bottle, but no water leaked through the seams of the box. Without internal pressure from a buildup of seawater, the sealant was not "blown out" before it cured.

Twelve hours later, the sealant was rock hard, so I pinched off the hose. The box, which was two feet below the waterline, contained the pressure of the ocean without a single leak. Our bilge was dry once again. It was time to celebrate. We opened several cans of fruit and smothered peaches, blackberries, and apricots with gobs of canned, sweetened condensed milk. The kids said that under the circumstances, it was the next best thing to ice cream.

For several days, we sailed slowly with light tail winds on a sea that undulated like liquid plastic. The enormous high-pressure system spanned the waters from Canada to northern Europe, smothering every hope of a breeze. *Driver*'s sails slatted annoyingly. Although we were still 370 miles from Iceland, we decided to fire up the diesel engine, determined to get to terra firma before the next onslaught of bad weather could test the integrity of our temporary repair. After all, we had enough diesel in *Driver*'s tank to motor 700 miles.

Motoring on the calm ocean was disappointing and noisy. It would have been great to sail the entire way from Bermuda and think of ourselves as seafarers of yore (despite our radar and GPS). But as the wind died and the seas calmed, I reflected that prudent seamanship and ego could be foolish rivals. We motored, and we were happy about our ability to do so.

I have never been able to fathom why some sailors feel guilty every time they use their engines. Perhaps in the age-old war between sailors and powerboaters, we sailors fear that we will be considered frauds if we use our engines occasionally to bring us to our goals more easily and quickly. A few hundred miles off Iceland, we felt that using the engine was also safer. Not only did we have a hull problem, but I had slipped on deck during the gale and jammed my sore finger. I made a splint from scrap aluminum, taped my middle and index fingers to it, and took ibuprofen every few hours to ease the pain. Whatever the infection was, two full courses of antibiotics hadn't even touched it. We needed to get to shore.

We crossed 60 degrees north under power, leaving all traces of night behind. The sun dipped below the horizon for several hours each evening, but a substantial amount of twilight remained. Standing night watches became effortless. The cabin was never dark. Teiga slept better now that *Driver* was not heeling. And the engine seemed to lull her. Jaja was able to spend more cherished hours alone under the dodger without Teiga at her breast, and I was able to spend more hours sleeping.

As we neared Iceland, the northeast swell continued to fade until it disappeared completely. The twilight each "night" became brighter. On our last night at sea, the sun hovered barely out of sight below the horizon, sending its rays of arctic light upward into the puffy fair-weather clouds.

AFTER THREE WEEKS AT SEA, I raised my eyes to the horizon and blinked in the twilight. Still over 60 miles away, Snæfellsnes Glacier, an icy cap that covers a 4,000-foot mountain, hovered mystically in the clouds. Land!

I dove below, roused Jaja from a deep sleep, and begged her to come on deck. We stood in the cockpit, our arms around each other's waists, drinking in our first glimpse of Iceland. *Driver* steamed on purposely, the autopilot steering and the engine running faultlessly. It was difficult not to let my excitement dominate more practical thoughts that argued: *We're not in yet.*

Because of the settled weather conditions, we cut across the shoal waters south of the Reykjanes Peninsula–Iceland's most dangerous headland–saving a few miles. The area is renowned for violent seas during southwest gales, but for us, the sea remained impossibly flat with neither ripple nor swell.

Sunrise at 2:00 a.m. filled our world with bright light and life. Birds of all kinds glided on the still air, and the sea came alive with fish, whales, and porpoises. In the cabin, our diesel heater warmed the 45-degree dawn air to a cozy 70. The kids slept under light blankets. I estimated our arrival in Reykjavík Harbor at around 11:00 a.m. Jaja and I took turns trying to sleep, but each of us was too distracted to settle down.

When the kids awoke at 8:00, we casually mentioned that if they went on deck, they might see something. Chris and Holly bolted up the companionway ladder and screamed with delight at the mountains that encompassed 180 degrees of the horizon. They could see lighthouses, buildings, fishing boats, airplanes, and cars and buses on distant roads.

I radioed ahead to the port captain. He gave us berthing instructions and agreed to notify customs and immigration of our anticipated arrival. While we motored, we tidied lines, folded the headsails that had lain idle for two days, dropped the mainsail, prepared fenders and docklines. Best of all, we took off our sea boots and put on sneakers. Our hearts pounded in anticipation.

Jaja teased me. "Are we allowed to get excited yet?"

Coming back to land after a long voyage creates new cycles of anxiety and anticipation. During a passage, "getting there" is our motive for nearly every action. But as the moment approaches for us to step ashore, we are seized with anxiety. *Driver* is our world, our habitat. At sea, Jaja and I are in tune with one another's thoughts and moods. The magic of our isolation would be watered down after we touched Iceland. We had endured long days to achieve our privileged, isolated plateau, and it was sad to contemplate its passing. Each ocean passage develops its own personality. Whether a passage was a good experience or not, its exact mood can never be recreated.

The bright sun and blue sky made the Day-Glo-orange lighthouses look like caricatures. We followed the entrance buoys as if they were road signs until we spied the entrance to the breakwater at Reykjavík Harbor. I put the chart aside as we slid past a large Coast Guard rescue ship tied to the main wharf. Then I throttled back the engine. Jaja stood on the foredeck, ready with a dockline. The kids were going crazy.

"Get ready to cast on!" Chris shouted.

I edged *Driver* alongside the floating visitors' pontoon, and we jumped onto its solid surface feeling like uncoordinated spastics. We secured our lines and adjusted the fenders. Chris shut down the engine. The storms, the seasickness, the leak, the broken rigging, my sore finger all faded with the vibration of the engine.

We had made it!

An older gentleman sauntered up to *Driver*–our first contact with an Icelander. He looked at our American flag flying from the transom, and speaking perfect English, he asked the familiar questions.

"So, where have you just come from?"

"Bermuda."

"How many days? If I may ask."

"Twenty-four."

"Was it a good passage?"

"Yeah," I said easily. "It was great."

Chapter Three

Ocean passages are like babies.
During the delivery, you swear you'll never do it again,
but after a while, you begin to plan for another one.

*T*HE CUSTOMS AND IMMIGRATION OFFICIAL came and went quickly. The only evidence of his visit was the yellow copy of a signed and stamped clearance document that we eventually lost. Months later, we tore the boat apart searching for it, but that's another story.

Set free, we headed for the center of Reykjavík. We still hadn't reclaimed our land legs, so each of us shuffled along, convinced that one of our legs had grown longer than the other. The kids found their rhythm first, and they jumped in sequence like performing dolphins.

"Ice cream!"

We looked at *Driver* across the small boat basin, unable to believe we had done it–made it to Iceland. All the planning, the hundreds of hours of preparation, the thousands of miles of sailing.

"If we had to board a plane right now and fly to the States," I observed, "my sailing desires would be sated forever."

Jaja laughed. "That's a good one."

An old iron steam engine was on display near the cruise ship wharf. Chris and Holly climbed aboard, drawing on a month's worth of unused energy. Jaja lifted Teiga into the cab then came over and sat with me on a low wall. Our kids still had dark tans and white, sun-bleached hair–the very essence of health and vitality. Jaja and I might have looked the same except for our fatigue and lightheaded stupor. We needed a good week's rest.

A busy four-lane street separated us from the city center. I looked at the cars and buses buzzing back and forth spewing blue exhaust into the pristine sunlight. I contemplated crossing.

"We'll never make it," I said.

"Why not?" Jaja wanted to know.

"Too dangerous."

As Jaja got up to retrieve Teiga from the engine cab, a cruise ship tourist approached her.

"Do you speak English?" the woman asked. She had a rich English accent.
"Yes," Jaja said.

"Do you mind if I take a picture of your children?"

"No, not at all," Jaja smiled. "Good luck getting them to stand still."

The lady took the picture. "Iceland is a beautiful county," she said. "And all the Icelandic children I've seen during my holiday are so healthy looking."

"This certainly is an amazing place. We feel lucky to be here."

"Where in Iceland is your home?"

"Here in Reykjavík," Jaja answered.

"Wonderful city! Well, thank you for letting me take a picture. And, by the way," the lady added kindly, "you speak English almost perfectly."

We finally rallied enough courage to cross the busy road, taking care to use the crosswalk. Then we let ourselves be devoured by the winding city streets. Compared to the carnival atmosphere of Bermuda, Reykjavík was calm. An aura of history oozed out of the cobblestones. Ancient stone buildings, century-old wooden dwellings, glass-and-aluminum structures all coexisted–proof of Iceland's varied economic times. We saw chic adults walking the street purposefully, talking into cell phones. In a small square, we saw elderly people sitting with their faces toward the sun, worshiping mortality, while reckless youths rode skateboards nearby–tempting it. Everyone seemed at ease and secure, making us feel almost as if we had walked uninvited into someone's backyard.

A Thomas Cook office cheerfully took advantage of the weekend by keeping 10 percent of our currency exchange transaction. Crooks! We took our foreign money outside into the sunlight. It was called kronurs, and the bank notes resembled Latin money because there were a lot of zeros after each digit. We had 7,000 units of Icelandic money in our pockets instead of the original US$100 we had offered in exchange. We felt like big spenders. Unfortunately, the zeros were the only resemblance that the kronur had to Latin money. Iceland is one of the most expensive countries in the world.

We wound our way along the streets looking for ice cream. We found a big public garden where people were sitting on bright green grass, their faces aimed at the sun like sunflower plants. We bought five ice cream cones in a nearby shop then headed back to the city "pasture." How strange it was to be sitting on shoots of chlorophyll, surrounded by humanity, when only a few hours before we had been gliding along on the surface of salt water. Neither scenario seemed real.

Before long, Teiga's ice cream ran down her arm, and she began to cry. Holly also started to cry when she dripped a big blob of strawberry swirl on her favorite shirt. Chris finished his treat first. "I'm bored," he whined.

Retreat!

On the return trip to the harbor, we bought a bag of vegetables, a smoked salmon fillet, milk, bread, cheese, yogurt, and fruit juice. Then we were broke again. One hundred U.S. dollars don't last long on a Saturday in Iceland.

Back on *Driver*, the kids settled down as if we had given them Valium (we hadn't). Home sweet home. Jaja and I opened a bottle of duty-free Grand Marnier and munched greedily on the salmon and cheese. The kids devoured the yogurts and ate bowl after bowl of sliced apples and pears. When we were satisfied they had ingested enough nutrition, we gave them cookies and hot chocolate.

With our second glass of liqueur, we began to fade into oblivion. It was grand to sit idle without the boat's demanding our attention. After listening to the engine off and on for three days, and to the sails' slatting, the cabin was blissfully quiet. That is, until Chris and Holly developed a raging case of the "tired jollies." With renewed vigor, they began jumping around and laughing hysterically. Unable to bear the onslaught any longer, Jaja, Teiga, and I flaked out in the V-berth up forward on our clean, flannel sheets. With instructions to Chris and Holly not to leave the cabin under any circumstances, the three of us dropped off into a groggy and delicious sleep.

I woke once, many hours later, and noticed the kids were in their bunks. The wind whispered in the rigging. I closed my eyes again. The region behind my eyelids was bombarded by the glare of an empty horizon and the sparkle of waves. Jaja rolled over.

"Everything OK?" she asked.

"Yeah. Chris and Holly are in their berths."

"I put them to bed hours ago," she replied.

"Hey, when I close my eyes, all I see is the ocean. How about you?"

"When I close my eyes, all I see are the stacks of children's books I read out loud during the passage."

I laughed.

"Actually," Jaja added, "the image in my mind is arctic light. I've forgotten what a dark night is like."

Although it was 2:00 a.m., the cabin was brightly lit. "Coming here was the coolest thing we've ever done." I said.

"We made it," Jaja confirmed. "I knew we would."

THE NEXT MORNING at 11:00, Olafur Sigurdsson, the gentleman who had greeted us on arrival, came aboard for coffee and rolls. Olafur is a retired Coast Guard commander and Master Mariner. He was curious about our voyage. We told him that our plan was to cruise Iceland's west coast for six weeks before turning south. We said we might winter over somewhere in Great Britain.

"Yes, of course," Olafur said. "Naturally, you would not want to live on your boat during an Icelandic winter, especially with three children."

"Are winters bad?"

"The days are short, and nights can be long, dark, and damp. Reykjavík gets very little snowfall, but the wind blows, and driving sleet can make life uncomfortable."

"How dark does it actually get?" Jaja asked. "Is it pitch black 24 hours a day?"

"No, not quite. By Christmas, a low gray sun lights the sky for six hours. With persistent cloud cover, it can be very depressing. Many people hide indoors."

"It's so beautiful now," Jaja said. "The perpetual light is like a drug to us. We can't get enough of it. It's hard to imagine the darkness."

Olafur laughed. "Everyone likes Iceland when the sky is blue and the sun is shining. Have you noticed how the local people are always sitting or standing with their faces to the sun? This is the first taste of clear weather we've had in many months. People are going crazy. They can't sleep because they don't want to miss a moment of it. We have had many summers when the sun never penetrates the thick clouds. You are experiencing a rare glimpse of Iceland."

When we first met Olafur on the dock, he had inquired why my fingers were taped together in a splint. I explained about the infection and said I planned to visit the hospital in the coming week. I knew there was something seriously wrong with my hand, and we didn't want to go to sea again until we found out what it was.

After coffee, we took Olafur's offer of assistance. We trooped into his car, and he drove us to the hospital emergency room. The hand specialist scratched his head when I related the history of my hand–how I had nicked it on a barnacle in Florida, and how it began to "seize up" within a week of our departure for Bermuda. The doctor said it didn't appear to be an ordinary infection because the surface swelling was negligible.

"Doing any sort of hauling or hanging on aggravates the stiffness," I explained.

"Don't use your hand then," he offered.

"But what's wrong? Is it an infection of some variety? Arthritis? Cancer?"

"It is impossible to know without doing some expensive blood tests. Why don't you let your hand rest for a week then come back and let me look at it again."

I let the doctor immobilize my right hand and forearm in a plaster cast. I argued that I lived on a boat, that the thing would turn into a soggy mess within a few hours, but he persuaded me to "just try it." I paid with my Visa card and made a sloppy left-handed signature. When I emerged from the emergency entrance with a cast, the kids were concerned.

"What's wrong with your hand, Daddy?"

"It's attached to a tourist."

On the trip back from the hospital, Olafur drove the long way to give us a tour of the city. We stopped at a tiny marina designed for small motorboats, and we inspected the concrete launching ramp that doubled as a tidal grid. Olafur thought we could careen *Driver* there–bring her in at high tide and let her sit on her keel while the tide went out. We could walk around her and repair the leak.

"I will loan you my welding machine if you like," Olafur suggested. "With our 14-foot tides this month, you should have plenty of time to work and avoid electrocution." He smiled.

I laughed. "Are there any hauling facilities?"

"You could hire a crane, but it might be expensive. Otherwise, there are only the marine railways for fishing boats."

"We need to think about it."

"Yes, of course."

IN MIDOCEAN, I had made a silent promise to service the engine as soon as possible after making port. So I changed the engine oil and transmission oil, replaced the seawater impeller and all the filters, adjusted the valves, and tested the thermostat. Jaja wisely took the kids for a walk. I dislike working on the engine, and it usually makes me grumpy.

When we bought *Driver*, I knew very little about diesel engines. Years before, I had a job installing them, but my duties only involved designing and fiberglassing the engine beds. At that time, I took a course in order to understand basic engine mechanics. However, the more I learned about diesel engines, the more I realized it was best to avoid them. *Direction*, for example, was powered by a six-horsepower, gasoline outboard.

We admire cruisers who choose not to clutter their boats and budgets with an engine, but we don't envy them. We would consider it foolish not to have an engine on our boat. We have used our engine to get into tight harbors and down many narrow, current-ridden channels. And we were learning that in the high latitudes in summer, the wind is frequently dead calm. Jaja and I preferred to motor to our destination and spend our precious time at anchor or ashore, than to drift in midocean becalmed without an engine.

When Jaja and the kids returned a few hours later, I had the diesel chugging away. Regardless of my dislike for engines, I consider it vital to perform the routine maintenance myself. There are no engine repairmen in the middle of the ocean or in isolated anchorages. Even if there were, the cost of hiring one could be demoralizing and economically catastrophic. I feel that it is poor seamanship to rely on a diesel engine if I can't at least make basic repairs. After all, the majority of engine problems *are* basic. The engine manual gives most of the information I need, and the rest I acquire from friends. Anyone with any engine experience is usually more than willing to share what he knows.

I dusted my hands in a mock fashion when Jaja came below. "Good as new."

Jaja laughed, "You're in high spirits, Dave. Everything must have gone smoothly. Do you mind if I ask why you couldn't have postponed servicing the engine until your plaster cast was off?"

"You'll laugh."

"Why?"

"I made a paganistic deal after the storm. I promised the engine that if it got us to Iceland without a hitch, I would service it at the earliest possible convenience."

"Oh."

"It worked."

"No argument there. Uh, your cast now matches your oily shirt."

"No worries." I took the shirt off. Then, using a serrated bread knife, I began to saw off the cast. Teiga stood transfixed.

"Mommy? Why is Daddy cutting off his arm?"

In five minutes the cast was in the trash. "Should have done that sooner. I'll stick to using tape."

THREE DAYS AFTER OUR LANDFALL, we rented a car. Since my hand needed rest, we decided on a road trip instead of sailing up the coast right away. I took a final look into the bilge before locking the companionway. Dry as a desert. Our temporary box was holding.

We began our car journey by getting lost in Reykjavík. Our brains were still motoring at five knots in the middle of the ocean. We found it difficult to assimilate the fast pace of the traffic and to read the foreign road signs that flew by. When we finally found our way out of the city, we headed in the general direction of Eyja Fjord on Iceland's north coast, about 250 miles away by road. We were all excited by the novelty of being off the boat for a few days.

Jaja navigated. She had collected a stack of travel brochures and free booklets at the information center and had marked pertinent pages with paper clips. Our objective–aside from not getting killed in an auto accident–was to avoid the organized tourist attractions and anything else that required spending money. Gasoline cost the equivalent of US$4 per gallon, and the car rental was around $150 a day. We were warned that car rental prices in Iceland bordered on highway robbery.

It was another stunning day. The sky was dark blue, and the sun stabbed the landscape like a finely tuned laser beam. Perfect traveling weather. The two-lane main highway was one of the few paved roads in the country. Somehow, we never seemed to travel on it for any great distance. Instead, we rattled down gravel tracks for miles and miles in our low-budget rental sedan, happy it wasn't our own car being shaken up.

We made many unusual detours to view hidden vistas. On first inspection, the landscape seemed plain. In fact, we were slightly disappointed. For the most part, the terrain we saw was barren and rocky. Basalt mountains and solidified lava flows dotted the periphery, the road was often the only sign of man's intrusion. The scenery reminded us of a land version of the ocean. It was remote, but awe inspiring in its vastness.

As the hours wore on, however, we began to sense a secondary beauty that superseded what first met the eye. In ocean sailing, each wave is a variation on the same theme–but with intricacies that are forever changing. Similarly, the Icelandic landscape changed with the angle of light, the weather conditions, and with our state of mind. We soon became mesmerized and captivated by what we saw; there was a pulse, a hidden message that transcended ordinary sensory input.

I rolled down my window to savor the fresh, dry inland air.

"How about that!" I said loudly over the roaring wind blasting into the car. I took a deep, theatrical breath. "Not one iota of salt!"

"Daddy?" Holly called out. "I'm cold. Could you please roll up your hatch?"

The kids got antsy as the day wore on, requiring frequent stops. We didn't worry about darkness obliterating our travels. If we had wanted to, we could have driven round the clock without missing a thing. Around 9:00 p.m., we crested the mountains and caught our first glimpse of Eyja Fjord. We drove southward along its shoreline until we reached Akureyri, Iceland's second largest city after Reykjavík.

We coasted through Akureyri's traffic lights, praising our little rental car for delivering us safely across the rugged landscape. We thoroughly enjoyed the journey, but I was careful to rein in my enthusiasm. Automobiles are an enigma. In our regular workaday routine in the States, we convinced ourselves we needed a car and then engineered our lives so that we were unable to function without one. My fondest memory of going cruising again was selling the car.

Jaja had owned many cars prior to our relationship. Her last car had holes under the floor mats, obliging her to drive with the windows rolled down to avoid asphyxiation. Too bad she lived in Maine that winter. I was a vehicle virgin until I was 34. So innocent. My first car was a 16-year-old Honda Accord that we purchased for $200 when we arrived in Oriental, North Carolina. Even by Jaja's standards, it was a beauty. The tires stayed inflated, and we didn't have to park it on a hill in order to start it later—which was a good thing because there are no hills in Oriental.

We drove the beloved mustard-brown Honda for a year before a vital component linking the steering wheel to the front wheels broke while I was doing 50 miles an hour. Out of control, I stamped on the almost useless brakes (which I had been meaning to have fixed) and came to a peaceful and happy halt in tall weeds. I was pleased. I hadn't spilt a drop out of my full coffee cup—a result, no doubt, of my having spent so many years at sea on a small boat. Instead of fixing the car, we traded it for a three-gallon, stainless steel day tank for *Driver's* diesel stove.

We spent an entire, disorienting week without any form of motorized transportation. It felt as if both our oars were broken and the current was ebbing. The car was the means. Without it, we couldn't drive to, and work on, *Driver*, the dream ship that was going to take us away from the insanity of needing a car. Cars have a mysterious way of controlling our lives.

Looking out the car's windows at Akureyri, we were surprised that a modern city of 15,000 inhabitants existed in such a remote part of the world. The guidebooks spoke of a university, an art museum, a music school, a theater, good shopping, fine dining, and elegant hotels. Our immediate concern was cheap lodging. We found the Icelandic version for $100 a night. After a picnic dinner in the common room, we did what any tourist sailor would do. We walked down the hill to the waterfront to look at the boats.

The low sun exaggerated the colors around us and gave everything a sparkling brilliance. The surface of the fjord reflected the blue sky, and the snow-covered mountain peaks shimmered like a hologram. A 40-foot steel sailboat was tied securely to the town jetty. Across from it rode an 80-foot wooden gaff-rigged schooner, beautifully restored. The varnished brightwork on the schooner shone, and the miles of running rigging swayed downwards from the mastheads in gentle arcs. In the same protected basin, there was a small, empty concrete pontoon used by launches for discharging passengers from summer cruise ships. It was a quiet and fairly well protected waterfront.

In the morning, we went swimming at the geothermally heated outdoor swimming complex. The kids played on a two-story-high tube slide, and we lounged in the hot tubs, gazing at the mountains. When I closed my eyes, I saw distant glaciers and lava flows. Jaja remarked that the image of the sun still glowed whenever she closed her eyes.

Feeling cleaner than we had in weeks, we set off in the car toward a lake region not far from Akureyri called Myvatn. We stopped at waterfalls, climbed an extinct volcano, and reveled in the unspoiled landscape.

Jaja was inspired. "Wouldn't it be great to live in Iceland?"

"We could come back someday and rent a summer cottage."

"Or we could stay a year and live on *Driver.*"

"Through the winter? It would be too cold."

"True," Jaja agreed, "but I've been thinking. We've put so much time, energy, and money into getting to Iceland. Doesn't it seem stupid to stay only a few weeks?"

"It does. The logistics of staying longer are impossible, though. How would we cope with the winter temperatures?"

"Maybe we could rent a place."

"I suppose."

"Anyway, it's just an idea."

Familiar warning bells began ringing in my head. I looked over at Jaja, but she was gazing out the side window. In the back seat, Chris and Holly were sleeping. Teiga was sacked out in Jaja's arms.

I looked at Jaja again, and she smiled.

WE WOKE AT 3:00 A.M., poured coffee down our throats as if it were medicine, started *Driver's* engine, then powered out of Reykjavík Harbor onto the smooth, ripple-less bay. The three kids continued to sleep, which gave Jaja and me the chance to enjoy the cool, overcast morning together without distraction. To the north, a thick slab of mist was spilling over the high peaks like a never-ending avalanche. To the east, the Reykjavík skyline sat low and sprawling, colorful and diverse. We were alone on the bay.

The tide was an hour from high water. With time to spare, we idled up to the cement tidal grid and secured our lines methodically. At 8:00, Olafur arrived in his car. We unloaded the welding machine, found an electrical outlet that worked, then went aboard for a cup of coffee. *Driver* was already sitting rooted to the bottom, but we had another half-hour to wait before the keel would be completely out of the water.

We recounted our car trip to Olafur. "Iceland's landscape is a paradox," I said. "The scenery is constant, yet it is always changing."

"Just like our economy," Olafur chuckled.

"We fell in love with Akureyri," Jaja said. "We only spent two days in the region, but it was enough to captivate us. We wondered how everyone up there survives the cold winters."

Olafur took a sip of coffee. "Akureyri does not get that cold. If I recall my facts, the average winter temperature is 25 degrees Fahrenheit."

"Is that all?"

"The Gulf Stream is a wonderful influence. I've spent my whole life on the coast, and it is a rare winter when icebergs are spotted on the horizon."

Jaja was thoughtful. "So, Akureyri doesn't get that cold."

"No," Olafur reiterated. "They may get a few single-digit low temperatures during the winter, but it seldom lasts for longer than a day or two. One of Iceland's greatest secrets is that the climate is not as harsh as the world imagines."

I looked over the side. "Tide is out, time to get moving."

Not long after tying *Driver* to the ramp, I used a hammer and a chisel to remove the temporary plywood box from inside the hull. Once the box was off, I scraped away the surrounding paint and epoxy, then drilled a 1/16-inch hole through the middle of the crack in the hull to help me identify it easily from the outside. When I was able to stand outside in rubber boots next to the keel, I inspected the culprit. The crack was not a clean slice; it was more of a beveled tear.

I cut a three-inch square from scrap steel, rounded the edges, then pounded it into a slight curve to match the shape of the hull. My plan was to weld the patch over the crack on the outside, like a waterproof band aid. The "proper" way to make the repair was to cut the damaged section of hull away then insert a new piece of steel flush with the hull, like a windowpane. I didn't want to do that because I was worried about cutting a large hole in the bottom of *Driver* with the tide licking ominously at the end of the ramp. What if the welder broke? What if the power went out? We would be stuck with an even worse problem. The patch was a temporary measure, but it would suffice until we could get to a boatyard and do it properly.

When we bought *Driver*, her deck was covered with 20 years' worth of outdated hardware. I removed it all and welded up the holes. I also welded new steel chainplates for the forward lower shrouds, reworked the dual anchor roller system at the bow, moved the steel brackets for the big jibsheet winches, and made a life-raft rack. I took a basic welding course at Pamlico Community College near Oriental, and although the course did not teach precise marine welding techniques, I learned how to use the equipment. I considered myself a novice, but my minimal skills were about to pay off. One of the advantages of a steel hull is the ease with which it can be repaired.

With Olafur, Holly, and Chris close by, I untaped my stiff fingers, shoved them into my welding mitts, lowered Olafur's welding hood over my eyes, and began. First, I ran a bead along the crack itself, to seal it off. Then I welded the 3/16-inch-thick patch over the crack. Jaja stayed above with Teiga to make sure I didn't inadvertently set the boat on fire.

When I finished, I wire-brushed my sloppy welds before spreading a thin coat of epoxy primer over the warm steel. Inside the hull in the bilge, I sanded away the residue of epoxy that was burned by the heat of the welding and applied fresh epoxy. Then I went back down to the concrete ramp and smeared a second coat over the patch on the outside of the hull. While I painted, Olafur generously carried tools to the top of the ramp away from the incoming tide. Before long, the 39-degree harbor water began climbing up the keel. I finished the job on the outside of the hull by brushing antifouling paint over the patch.

At noontime, the sun emerged from behind the clouds, and we all sat in the cockpit waiting for the tide to rise. Olafur was at ease with us, the greatest compliment a friend can pay. He told us about different sections of the coast, cautioned us to pay close attention to the weather, then mentioned the harbors we shouldn't miss.

"You must try and visit the Snæfellsnes Peninsula," he suggested. "You can find good protection at Ólafsvík harbor."

Snæfellsnes Peninsula, 65 miles northwest of Reykjavík, had provided us with our first glimpse of Iceland from the sea. I mentioned this fact to Olafur.

"Yes, many mariners have that same experience," Olafur replied. "Actually, the Snæfellsnes Glacier and the surrounding mountains are famous in Icelandic legends. It is said that trolls and monsters once lived in the region."

"Monsters!" Chris exclaimed.

"Yes, it's true. In fact, my wife is from the peninsula. So you see, I am speaking from a position of authority." Olafur smiled kindly. "Speaking of authority, she is expecting me home for lunch at this very minute. I will return later."

After he had gone, Jaja casually said, "If what Olafur says is true about the weather, we could tie next to the concrete pontoon."

"What concrete pontoon?"

"The one in Akureyri."

I nodded. "If the weather really is that mild, I'm all for wintering over."

"Are you?"

"Why not? We'll be dockside in the middle of the city. If we have problems, the worst-case scenario would be to haul out *Driver* and rent an apartment, or fly back to the States, or something. The winter Teiga was born in Oriental, we had nighttime lows in the 20s. It wasn't that bad."

"I think it'll be great if we stay," Jaja declared. "We'll be able to experience living aboard in Iceland and still enjoy the grocery stores, the library, and especially the hot pools. The perks of civilization.

"We have to do something in life," I agreed. "Why not this?" I chuckled. "It's a great opportunity for adventure. We would be fools to let this one go."

"The perpetual light fascinates me," Jaja said. "But it would be interesting to live through a dark winter. Then we would understand how it feels when the sun comes back. We could witness the entire cycle. I can guess what it's like, but we'll never really know unless we live through it."

We motored back to the guest pontoon on Reykjavík Harbor. The steel patch was proving watertight, although I was still skeptical about it. I had done plenty of welding on deck, but this was my first attempt at welding below the waterline. Maybe it was only the epoxy primer that was keeping the water out. Who could say? At least the crack itself, which had probably been caused by metal fatigue, was being held in check. Once again *Driver* seemed safe.

AT THE INFORMATION CENTER in Reykjavík, we researched annual Icelandic temperatures. Olafur's recollections were accurate. Even though it was hard to believe, the coast remained ice free year round. *Iceland*–so much for a name. According to the statistics, Iceland experiences milder winter temperatures than the U.S. Midwest. The catch was that winter in Iceland lasts from September to May with summer highs only around 55 degrees. Snowfall in Akureyri averages five feet. The previous winter, we learned, was almost snowless until January.

Excited by our research, I called the Icelandic immigration office to ask if we could stay in the country for an entire year.

"No."

"May I ask why?" I was crestfallen; we didn't think there would be a problem.

"You were given a two-month tourist visa on arrival," they said. "You may not extend it unless you return to your home country and apply from there."

"We sailed here on our own boat," I argued. "Going back would be difficult."

After a moment, we were told to come to the main office with our passports, ship's papers, and with a current bank statement to prove we could support ourselves during our intended visit. Jaja and I dressed in our cleanest tourist clothes. We also dolled up the girls but only managed to get Chris to change his socks. The officer in charge made photocopies of our documents, then gave me five forms to fill in. I smiled at Jaja–*piece of cake.*

"Fine, Mr. Martin. Before we can process your case, you and your family need to be tested for tuberculosis, hepatitis, and your general state of health."

"Uh...excuse me," I stammered. "But, can't you decide the case first *then* let us take the tests if we are allowed to stay?"

"No."

"I see." They handed me a typed list giving the names of several doctors who were accustomed to the procedure.

It took 10 days to set up the appointments, have the tests, and await the results. Our summer of sailing was evaporating quickly in a mindless paper chase. During the interval, we visited the zoo, swam in the thermal swimming pools, went shopping, and took scenic walks. In between, we worked on

Driver. I dismantled every fitting in the rigging and inspected each with care. We repaired sails, epoxied the odd deck ding, and greased the winches and blocks. We put *Driver* back into ocean trim. My dad mailed a few spare fittings for our rigging box to replace the ones we had used.

When the results of the medical tests came back, there was only one glitch. I tested positive for tuberculosis. The next step was a chest X-ray. Paralyzed with apprehension, I stood alone in a dim, white sterile room with my bare chest pressed against the cold glass of a monstrous X-ray apparatus.

"This isn't happening," I said to myself. "I did not sail to Iceland to be diagnosed with TB." Jaja sat fretting in the waiting room.

The X-ray proved negative. The doctor explained that the erroneous test results might have been caused by my childhood inoculation for TB.

I pretended to cough. "So I don't have to go to a sanatorium?"

The doctor gave me a stern look.

Up at immigration, I handed over our large manila envelope. Included with the completed application forms and medical data was our typed cover letter. It explained that we had ample savings to support ourselves without the need to seek work in Iceland and that we supplemented our budget by selling photos and stories to sailing magazines.

The reason we wanted to stay, I wrote, was to gain a better understanding of the Icelandic culture, which greatly intrigued us. I also mentioned that we would be living aboard *Driver* and wouldn't need housing ashore. I wanted to make it clear that we would not be a burden to their economy or to their limited, man-made resources. We were told the decision could take a month.

By the time we were ready to cruise up the coast, we had burned three weeks sitting dockside in Reykjavík. It was already the first week of July. If we didn't get the visa extension, we would have to leave in another three weeks to head toward Scotland, a distance of 1,200 miles. If we were allowed to stay in Iceland, we could move slowly up the coast toward Akureyri, a distance by sea of about 500 miles, and savor each new place along the way.

Spontaneous planning is good for the soul but hell on logistics. Not knowing until the last minute if we could stay was frustrating, but if we hadn't applied for the chance to stay, we would have always regretted not trying. We resolved that the next time we did something spontaneous, we would try to take care of the paperwork ahead of time.

Idle words.

Chapter Four

On the scales of life, chores balance indulgence.
If you are always having a good time,
you must be wasting it.

GUSTS OF WIND fanned out over Faxaflói Bay. *Driver*'s sails caught the puffs and transferred the energy into forward motion, bringing us closer to Akranes, 12 miles northwest of Reykjavík. Below the icy blue sky, the water was grayish black, torn by whitecaps. The atmosphere was so sharp that visual images looked artificial.

Even though it was midday, the sun perched low in the sky, creating long shadows on the crumbly, brown mountains where hardly a trace of green could be seen. This rarefied day reminded us that after a long and eventful "climb," we had reached the apex–the "summit" of our cruising goal. The *Direction* voyage should have cured us of doing extreme things, but the confidence we acquired on that voyage expanded our definition of excitement. Sailing to Iceland had fulfilled our increased sense of adventure–for the time being.

We like exploring the diverse regions of our planet, and we especially enjoy meeting individuals who have strong geographic identities. For example, the Pacific islanders we visited while we cruised on *Direction* had evolved on warm shores where fruit practically fell from the trees. The easy way of life in those islands was satisfying, and we greatly enjoyed our time there. But after several years of tranquil, tropical cruising, we had grown restless with the languid culture.

On the other hand, Icelandic farmers have coaxed crops and struggled to raise animals on seemingly lifeless terrain for 1,000 years. Earthquakes, mini-ice ages, and volcanic eruptions have punctuated Iceland's history. Languor does not promote longevity in the Land of Fire and Ice. We were eager to immerse ourselves in the culture–to learn more about these hearty people. Iceland is modern now, but the people still have strong identities that are influenced by traditional values and etiquette. We hoped we would be given the chance to stay the winter to really get to know the people.

A 40-foot-high breakwater protects the man-made harbor at Akranes. The height of the breakwater testifies to the force of winter storms, and it honors the fishermen who work year round. Inside the protected harbor, the floating pontoons were overcrowded with fishing boats, so we tied to the main wharf. Neatly hung truck tires prevented *Driver* from coming in contact with the slimy cement wall. To reach the top of the wharf, Jaja climbed a 15-foot-high, barnacle-covered ladder. She looped our docklines over the giant bollards, and I paid out slack from on deck–enough to compensate for the tide, which was predicted to drop another four feet.

Following our tourist maps, we navigated through town. The modest entrance fee to the thermally heated outdoor swimming pool was the equivalent of US$2 apiece. We proceeded to the men's and women's locker rooms respectively and showered with hot water and soap. Custom strictly forbids anyone to enter Icelandic pools without bathing first. At most of the pools, a shower attendant enforces the rules among untrained tourists, lazy locals, and kids.

Chris and I slipped into our bathing suits and ran through the breezy, 50-degree-Fahrenheit afternoon toward the outdoor hot tubs. Moments later, Jaja and the girls ran out of the women's changing room, and we settled slowly into the 104-degree water. The kids purred their delight and began yakking excitedly–proof of their contentment. Jaja and I lay back in the delicious water, facetiously contemplating how we could install a hot tub on *Driver*.

The next morning, we sailed for Ólafsvík on the northern shore of the Snæfellsnes Peninsula. By late afternoon, the forecasted southerlies were replaced by unforecasted drizzle and light, variable winds. I took down the jib, and we motorsailed over the sedate swell with the mainsail hanging slack much of the time. We were locked in a gray void, the numbers on the GPS display acting as the only verification of favorable progress. The Snæfellsnes Glacier remained hidden from view, even though it was only 10 miles away. We chuckled. We'd had a better glimpse of it some 60 miles away during our last night at sea.

When we saw the glacier that first time, we felt fulfilled. However, our long rest in Reykjavík had rekindled our desires. Jaja's idea of circumnavigating Iceland still tempted us, and our enchantment with the midnight sun gave us a new yearning to sail north of Iceland. We wanted to cross the Arctic Circle and go into the polar region where the sun never sets during the summer months and where it never rises in the winter.

But we would need extra time to do that. Unless our visa extension came through, our quest would have to be curtailed. We would sail up Iceland's west coast as far as possible before turning south for Great Britain. The Arctic Circle was only 150 miles away, but we were on a coast where the weather changes hourly and where the currents run swiftly and unpredictably. It was prudent to move cautiously and slowly, especially with a crew of three children and just two adults.

At midnight, the ambient light dimmed, and the rain came down more steadily. Jaja stood watch while Teiga slept. But not for long. After only two hours, Teiga woke up crying, demanding her mamma.

"Sometimes," Jaja said wistfully, "sometimes, I wish guys could breast-feed babies."

While I slept, the wind had increased to 20 knots from astern, and the visibility had decreased to less than two miles. The shoreline was a black smudge in the mist, but three knots of favorable current pushed us along. This compensated for the lack of scenery. As we came under the lee of the land and began the final seven-mile journey up Breitha Fjord to Ólafsvík, the wind began swirling in aggravating gusts. One minute the sails would fill; the next minute, they would luff. Suddenly, the wind backed 180 degrees and blew–cold and wet–down the fjord in our face at a steady 25 knots.

My good humor found nothing good nor humorous in the prospect of slogging to windward at 4:00 a.m. I doused the jib, sheeted in the main, and fired up the diesel, determined to motorsail the remaining distance to the harbor. With my head encased in a balaclava and my nose buried deep in the collar of my foul-weather gear jacket, I stood resolutely in the cockpit. I was forced to duck behind the dodger frequently to avoid the bursts of spray that exploded at the bow and blew aft with the wind.

An occasional glance at the radar was enough to confirm our heading. I thought back to the "white knuckle" days aboard *Direction* when our only navigational aids were a sextant, a radio direction finder, and a compass. Without a vast array of electronics, we had always found our way safely from place to place. The recollection was nostalgic. The good old days. I dared myself to turn off *Driver*'s radar and GPS to relive that nostalgia, but I was reluctant to replace my warm feelings for the past with the cold realities of dead reckoning without electronics.

The wind eased up as we neared the harbor breakwater. Jaja managed to extract herself from Teiga and went on deck to drop the mainsail. The strong odor of fresh fish filled the air. We were getting used to the cologne of Iceland's waterfronts–a good smell that meant prosperity and a safe harbor. We found a space at the main wharf just big enough for us, and we edged *Driver* against the ubiquitous tires. Before retreating to our warm cocoon below for some much needed sleep, I let out enough scope in our docklines to compensate for the 16-foot tide.

WE WERE AWAKENED later in the morning to noises on the pier high overhead. Cars and trucks came and went, their wheels chattering on the loose jetty timbers. The vehicle sounds, combined with the metallic clang of heavy fishing tackle, signified a busy waterfront at Ólafsvík. But something wasn't right. *Driver* was heeled away from the wharf about 10 degrees, and our fenders, hanging between *Driver*'s hull and the wall, were scrunching in agony. I put on my damp foul-weather gear jacket and poked my head out of the companionway. The depthsounder readout in the cockpit read 11 feet. At first, I had assumed our keel must have touched bottom, but there was plenty of water depth.

My next paralyzing thought was that the steel patch had begun to leak and that *Driver* was sinking. I darted below and lifted the floorboard, but the bilge was dry. Puzzled, I went back on deck. Then I looked up and realized that our docklines were too short for the falling tide. *Driver* was hanging from the massive bollards on the pier like an old suit of armor, her docklines as taut as steel lances. Carefully, I released a dockline that was fastened around one of *Driver*'s oversized cleats. I released just one wrap and used the friction of the remaining wraps around the cleat to ease the line slowly so my hands would not be "burned" by the rope.

When *Driver* was floating on her waterline again, I threw out an extra handful of line for good measure, then returned below with frozen fingertips. I cursed the large tidal range, but then I cheered up when I remembered an advantage of visiting Icelandic ports.

Olafur had told us that few yachts visit Iceland each year, so a system of docking fees had not been devised. All docks were free for visitors. The jetties and floating pontoons were run on a co-op system. Reciprocal agreements among Icelandic ports, large or small, allowed fishermen to come and go as they pleased without having to fill in forms or clear in and out. Iceland was the only country we had ever visited where you could clear customs and immigration for free, then tie to all the docks at no charge. One of the pleasures of cruising is discovering hidden financial advantages. Of course, the other side of the coin is inadvertently stumbling across little financial disasters.

Coin-operated laundromats did not exist in Iceland, and the cost of doing laundry ashore was the equivalent of a few days' stay in a modest U.S. marina. After our passage from Bermuda, we had two duffel bags stuffed with dirty clothes. In high spirits after the successful voyage, and easy with our money, we left the bags at a commercial laundry without bothering to ask the price. We cringed when we saw the bill.

Generally, Jaja refuses to squander our budget on a task she can perform herself. During our years on *Direction*, she washed all our clothes by hand, as well as the cloth diapers for Chris and Holly. One positive outcome from having to soak and scrub the diapers was that Chris was fully potty trained when he was 18 months old, and Holly finished having accidents by the time she was 14 months old. Teiga's training fitted somewhere in between.

Aboard *Direction,* after that wet, miserable, 16-day passage between New Zealand and Fiji, every item inside the boat needed to be washed. Even the children's Duplo plastic toy blocks had begun to mold. One afternoon, an Australian tourist approached Jaja as she was rinsing a bucket of stuffed animals. He asked if he could take her picture. The clotheslines strung all around *Direction* sported everything from towels to cushion covers. It was obvious she had been busy.

The guy was sincere. "My wife and I are planning to go cruising. She thinks that as soon as we step foot aboard, the drudgeries of life will vanish. She thinks that every day is going be a picnic." He pointed to the laundry that was drying in the hot sun.

Jaja laughed, then pushed her hair away from her face with a rubber-gloved hand. "Well, I guess it all depends on how much money you have."

Early in our cruising life, Jaja and I realized that chores were the payoff for the simple lifestyle we enjoyed and for the togetherness we sought. Washing clothes in the Tropics was painless because the fresh water was warm, and the sun was hot for drying. Hand-washing in the higher latitudes, however, was a chilling experience because water running out of the taps in Iceland is around 45 degrees.

In Ólafsvík, Jaja stood on the high jetty wearing yellow rubber gloves and scrubbing our dirty clothes. I wrung them out, much to the elbow-jabbing amusement of the fishermen who thought we were both nuts. But we were happy because we had a hose and free water. In the Tropics, those are two very rare commodities. Afterwards, we dashed off to the local pool to soak ourselves in the hot tubs.

Later, we took a bus trip around the base of the Snæfellsnes Mountain, but to Chris's chagrin, we did not see any monsters. Nevertheless, in such a landscape, it was easy to imagine wild and wonderful things. The not-so-ancient lava flows had cooled into weird rock formations, and the desolate, seemingly lifeless terrain inspired dark mystery. The author Jules Verne immortalized the Snæfellsnes Peninsula in a book where his characters had journeyed to the center of the earth.

The region was also used as a setting by Icelandic writers. In the town of Hellnar on the south side of the peninsula, author Haldur Laxness pitted his characters against the whims of the church and the spirits of the glacier. Jaja and I were entranced by the atmosphere, but the main "struggle" of the bus

trip was to keep the spirits of our three children satisfied as they pitted themselves against the availability of public restrooms.

By the time we returned to *Driver*, the weather was socked in. Rain
poured down, giving our laundry a second rinse cycle. Fortunately, the tide
was high, making it easy for the kids to come aboard. The primary argument
after our homecoming centered around who got to use the head first. Jaja
won.

A FULL-GROWN HUMPBACK WHALE glided down the face of an enormous swell. The sun, which was making a rare appearance in the pale blue
sky, lit the creature dramatically, creating a blinding reflection across its
metallic looking back. When it exhaled, the sun created a rainbow in the
misty vapors. Later in the day, we passed so close to a domineering 20-foot
whale that Jaja involuntarily praised our choice to buy a steel boat.

We had left Ólafsvík early that morning and headed for the next series of
fjords, 60 miles up the coast, in a region called Westfjord. The day started out
calm. As the breeze filled in, we sailed along easily under the full main and
jib.

The wind died by the time we got to Ønundar Fjord, halfway up the
Westfjord region, so I yanked down the jib and fired up the engine. We
motored the remaining 10 miles up the fjord to the town of Flateyri and once
again, nestled against black tires. We received a warm and immediate welcome from a woman in a car. The tide was high, which made eye contact
easy.

Her name was Gudrún, and she was bursting with excitement. "Where
have you come from? How long will you stay in Flateyri? Where are you
headed?"

I grinned. "Ólafsvík. A few days. And, we're not sure."

Gudrún smiled broadly and immediately invited us to visit her house for
coffee. As we spoke, a fishing boat pulled up to the wharf, and Gudrún's son
Birkir casually threw his lines around a cleat and sauntered over. Later, he
proudly showed us the 25-foot fishing boat he had chartered for the season. It
was filled to the gunnels with large cod. Using three automatic cod-jigging
machines, Birkir had singlehandedly hooked 1,700 pounds of fish. Half of
the catch went to the owner of the boat, and the other half was Birkir's to sell
at about $1.40 a pound. Fishing is the economic backbone of Iceland.

Birkir was 22, spoke good English like his mother, and dreamed of making enough money to buy a sailboat and go cruising. His family had fished
for generations, and the sea ran strong in his imagination. One summer,
Birkir bought a 14-foot sailing dinghy and tried to learn to sail. On the
maiden voyage, he capsized in the middle of the fjord and nearly died of

hypothermia. The boat, which was holed while Birkir was being rescued, still lay abandoned on the beach.

At his parents' house, we were treated like family and fed like nobility. The invitation for "coffee" included platters of smoked lamb, smoked fish, dried fish, homemade pastries, smoked flat breads, and at least four different types of cakes. In the center of it all was a huge bowl of fresh whipped cream and several varieties of jams. We were overwhelmed by such a generous welcome, especially by the powerful feelings of goodwill–feelings that almost seemed tangible. Our hosts made us so comfortable it felt as though we had known them our whole lives.

The next morning, Gudrún and her husband Einar gave us a tour of their business. Using their own boats, they caught haddock, catfish, and cod. They filleted the fish and packed it in an enormous freezer. During winter, they removed the fish from the freezer and hung it outdoors on covered racks to "dry." After two or three months, when all the moisture had evaporated, they put the fish back into the freezer. The dried fish is a delicacy eaten plain, like beef jerky, or reconstituted by soaking in fresh water. Mountain climbers in many parts of the world order the dried fish for expeditions because it is pure protein, high in complex carbohydrates, requires no wasteful packaging, and lasts for months unrefrigerated. It is also light–about 1/7th its original weight.

Iceland has rich fisheries, the income from which has helped the nation create a state-of-the-art telecommunications system, good roads, and a wealthy social welfare program. National identity is at the root of Iceland's success. People work hard for the good of the country. When Icelanders learned that we had worked and traveled overseas for a dozen years, many asked if we thought we were letting our country down by not lending a hand to help improve the U.S. economy. The people who asked this question did not understand the "every man for himself" mentality of American culture.

The next day, a deep, low-pressure system moving across from Greenland brought 40-knot onshore winds and massive seas. The northwesterlies rushed over the mountains behind the town and hit the harbor with accelerated gusts that reached 60 knots. Miniature white-water tornadoes zigzagged down the fjord, throwing salt spray across the spit of land on which the town was built. *Driver* remained safe and sound, tied to the wharf. We spent the day at the indoor pool swimming laps and horsing around with the kids on floats. Free coffee was available on a table near the hot tub. There are worse ways to sit out a gale.

On the way back to the harbor after swimming, I placed a call to the immigration department in Reykjavík. I was anxious to know our fate because it was already the middle of July. We had only been on the coast for two weeks, but it was becoming more and more difficult to contemplate leaving. If immigration gave us thumbs down, we would have to turn south when the first fair weather system arrived.

Jaja and the kids sat in the warm post office foyer hiding from the gale, while I stood at a public phone and punched in the numbers: Wait, wait, wait. On hold. Next office. Out to lunch. Please wait. I hate it when my destiny hinges on a single event–such as one telephone call. The anticipation was agonizing.

"Mr. Martin? Yes, your visa application has been approved. Where shall we send it?"

BIRKIR'S ACCOUNT OF TREADING WATER in August without a wetsuit when his dinghy capsized cured us of wanting to sail *Driver*'s dinghy on the fjords. Even during settled weather, strong gusts–like the one that flipped Birkir's boat–could come out of nowhere. The air, passing over the warming and cooling land, constantly sought equilibrium.

Instead, we loaded a daypack with food and fruit juice and set out on a calm day to climb the mountains that formed the backdrop of the town. Chris and Holly moved easily through the long grass near the base of the hillside, trying their best to sneak up on wary sheep. Teiga rode high in her babypack while Jaja and I took turns puffing and blowing under her weight. We had not quite shaken our ocean lethargy.

As the hillside became steeper, the grass gave way to detritus. Our destination was a wide saddle between two peaks. But the closer we got, the steeper it became, until it was too dangerous to proceed with the children. We descended a short way back to the grass and reclined comfortably in a hollow against some large, mossy stones. The sun streamed down, reminding us of the Tropics. Far below, we could easily spot *Driver*'s solitary mast amongst the squat rigging of the fishing boats. We were the first cruising sailboat to visit the harbor in over a year.

We pondered a sad tale. Two winters before, a devastating avalanche coursed down the hillside, crushing homes, killing three families, and mauling a dozen individuals. Because of the severity of the storm, no one in town heard the assault. After receiving a panicked telephone call from a buried survivor on a cell phone, Einar was the first on the scene. He found tons of snow 20 feet deep around the destroyed homes. Within an hour, the soft snow solidified, trapping the unlucky families in a death grip. Teams of rescue volunteers with search dogs flew in from all over Iceland, but the scattered remnants of glass, timber, wallboard, fiberglass insulation, and household debris confused the dogs and diminished their ability to sniff out people. The glass in the snow also cut the dogs' feet.

The workers dug with pickaxes and shovels for days. Gudrún and her neighbors took charge of feeding the volunteers, and eventually, everyone was driven to exhaustion. Due to an unusually heavy snowfall that year, houses that had narrowly missed being annihilated were evacuated as a precaution. Homeless and scared, many people left Flateyri for different regions, while others fled to escape painful memories. Almost overnight, the population fell from 500 to 220 people.

"That was two years ago," Gudrún told us, "but it feels like the avalanche happened only yesterday. I may never forget the trauma. We were a thriving town, and now we are faced with oblivion."

Gudrún took us to the church where a memorial stands for her 20 lost friends. Like a stone in a stream, the church was left unharmed, even though ice and debris had rumbled past it on either side for another 200 yards. In the churchyard, a three-foot rock, deposited randomly by the avalanche, stood as a reminder. You often hear about miraculous acts of "natural selection," but the example of the church made us wonder. Why had the empty church been spared when families were crushed in nearby homes?

BRILLIANT WEATHER DESCENDED ON FLATEYRI, but we didn't feel any urgency to depart, now that we had an entire year to explore the country. *Driver* became the focal point of nightly entertainment. Birkir would come to the boat accompanied by friends or his older brother and sister-in-law. We drank coffee, yarned, and seldom ended our conversations until 1:00 or 2:00 a.m.

One day Birkir and his family drove us to their summer cabin near the headwaters of the fjord. Cows and sheep stood placidly on the narrow gravel roads, a sight that made our kids laugh hysterically. Einar shooed them playfully with his hand but to no avail. This made Chris and Holly laugh even harder. He finally edged the stubborn animals out of the way with the car's bumper.

At the cabin, we were greeted by an astounding view that extended from the fjord all the way to the ocean. The summer sun cast long shadows on the fertile green pastures, and the feeling of Iceland's calmness and enormity seeped further into our beings.

Less than a quarter-mile away, an old, crumbling one-room house stood like a monument. Einar proudly announced that he and his 16 brothers, sisters, and cousins were raised in that house.

"We spent a lot of our time outdoors," Einar recalled.

Without darkness to mark the passing days, our summer in the north began to feel limitless. The hours flew by, and we finished our chores without conscious thought. After all, procrastination is only satisfying when time has meaning.

While rebuilding *Driver* in Oriental, we let ourselves get so pressed for time that a single hour had intricacies that wouldn't fill a half-day in Iceland. At the other end of the spectrum, time became overextended during our long passage to Iceland from Bermuda. Each minor task had profound significance. Even brushing our teeth was a major event. Despite the belief by some individuals that 24 days at sea on *Driver* must have seemed like purgatory, it actually wasn't. The relatively passive life at sea was tolerable because the reason for being there was to move resolutely towards a specific destination. Ocean sailing is goal oriented.

We walked along the edge of the fjord, picking our way slowly across rocks and grasses. A narrow strip of ocean was visible in the distance at the entrance of the fjord. Otherwise, we were surrounded by steep mountains. It felt as if the walls were closing in, that we were losing sight of our objectives.

"I think it's time to be moving on," I said.

Jaja nodded in comprehension. "I have an idea that might help speed up our pace," she said. "Instead of getting to Akureyri sometime in late October and home-schooling the kids, what do you think about enrolling Holly and Chris in an Icelandic public school at the beginning of the term? Gudrún says the school year starts the first week of September. Think of the experiences that Chris and Holly would gain. They would..."

Holly interrupted. "But Mommy, we don't speak Icelandic."

"You would learn," Jaja encouraged. "You would become bilingual."

Chris said, "Isn't bilingual when two men get married?"

"Where did you learn that?" I asked, mortified.

"I heard you and Mommy talking at sea one night about some people you knew."

I tried to recall the exact conversation but couldn't.

Holly asked. "What school will we go to?"

"I don't know exactly."

"Are we going to stay in Flateyri? I like it here."

"So do we," Jaja said, "but our plan is to go to Akureyri."

"What's for dinner tonight?" Chris wanted to know.

"Fish."

"Oh, not fish again..."

We visited Einar and Gudrún at their workshop to let them know we would be going. Making friends ashore, then leaving them, is never easy. Meeting people on other cruising boats is different because we are all transients going to many destinations. The chance for meeting the same cruisers again is usually high because eventually many of us will visit the same ports. When we sail away from relationships on shore, however, the departures have a bittersweet quality–one of finality.

"We knew you would be going soon," Gudrún said. "These past 10 days have been very special to us."

Special to them!

"We'll probably never see you again," Gudrún said sadly.

Jaja said, "A part of us will always remain in Flateyri, thanks to your kindness. And a part of your spirit will always travel with us on *Driver*."

Birkir sailed with us to Bulungarvik, the next harbor, 22 miles to the north. It was his first excursion on a "big" sailboat, and his calm, usually unfazed Icelandic face could barely contain his excitement. When the wind heeled *Driver* over, his placid eyes brightened. We could see that sailing made the gears spin in his head.

"Yeah!" Birkir said, nodding slowly. "Yeah!"

CROSSING THE ARCTIC CIRCLE aboard *Driver* was our next milestone–an imaginary line against which we could measure our achievement. We waited many days for good weather before our patience was rewarded: Moderate winds with the nearest low-pressure system over 48 hours away. Who could ask for more?

Iceland has many notorious capes. The three most dangerous are the Reykjanes Peninsula on the southwest coast (which we rounded in calm weather on the last night of our passage from Bermuda), the Langenes Peninsula on the northeast coast, and the one we faced now–the Straumnes Peninsula on the northwest coast. Back in Reykjavík, Olafur advised us to stay as close to shore as possible when rounding headlands. The dangerous tide rips that are found there generally fan out from the promontories in the shape of a V. The smallest part of the vector, he said, is closest to the beach.

A few weeks earlier, we had ignored his advice when we rounded the Bjargtanger Peninsula en route to Flateyri. We regretted it immediately. At the time, we were more concerned with avoiding a potentially dangerous lee shore. We stayed two miles off the headland to keep *Driver* a safe distance from the pounding surf. Conditions were settled offshore, and there was no indication of dangerous tidal overfalls. Approaching the headland, we suddenly entered a churning, boat-swallowing tide rip. For two agonizing hours, *Driver* was abused by angry waves that crashed on deck like shore break.

At Straumnes, we hugged the shoreline like a long-lost friend. We thought we were cutting it close, but several small fishing boats were going even closer. *Driver* chugged along under power on a calm ocean. Coastal fog soon obliterated the shoreline.

There are all sorts of rituals designed for crossing the equator for the first time. What are the rituals, we wondered, for crossing the Arctic Circle? Because large continents cover most of this imaginary line, there are only two areas on the globe where ships can cross it: The Bering Strait between Alaska and Russia and the waters between Canada and Norway. Compared to the equator, which crosses vast open stretches of water, "only" 1,500 miles of open water is available for crossing the Arctic parallel at 66 degrees, 33 minutes north latitude.

Jaja was thoughtful. "You could go swimming, Dave."

"We could do that."

At 11:00 a.m. on August eighth, we were 10 miles north of Iceland when the GPS indicated the Arctic Circle was 100 yards in front of us. Our moment of triumph was near.

The wind was negligible, and we motored along at five knots with the full mainsail up to help steady the boat. All three kids were playing happily in the level cabin, but Jaja and I called them on deck to witness our crowning achievement. I counted down the minutes of latitude displayed on the GPS as if it were New Year's Eve.

"We're on the Arctic Circle!" I shouted.

"OK," Jaja teased. "Strip."

"*You* strip. Swimming was your idea."

The kids stood in the cockpit wondering what all the fuss was about. Even though the bright sun above penetrated the mists, the horizon was only faintly visible. To the south of us, the mighty cliffs on Iceland's Horn Peninsula rose above the fog like a kinfe-edge, in sharp contrast to the snow-covered ranges that hovered even farther in the distance. The sea was a mirror with only a slight swell coming down from the north.

Teiga's feeding instincts kicked in, and she tugged at Jaja's shirt.

Chris gave his stock observation. "I'm hungry."

Holly was thoughtful. "You know, Daddy, it looks pretty much the same out here as usual. Doesn't it?"

When I pored over the Atlantic pilot charts way back in Bermuda, the thought of reaching Reykjavík raised the hairs on the back of my neck. The idea that we would make our way to the north coast on *Driver* had been beyond comprehension. Phrases such as, "it's too far," "it's too dangerous," "it's too remote," and "it would be too much for our pint-sized crewmembers," stood in the way. Some people climb mountains to conquer them. We find fulfillment by sailing around them.

All through the day as we motored due east on a tranquil sea, we kept reminding ourselves that we were cruising in the Arctic, north of Iceland.

North of Iceland!

We were bound for a small island called Grímsey, 30 miles off the Icelandic north coast. Jaja and I stood the night watch together for a change, enjoying the undemanding hours of solitude. One advantage of motoring on a calm sea was that our kids slept deeply, especially Teiga. Although *Driver*'s position was north of the Arctic Circle, summer was too far advanced for the sun to remain visible above the horizon throughout the night. Instead, a brilliant twilight warmed the midnight sky.

When the sun rose at 3:00 a.m., the silvery sea resembled smoothed-out aluminum foil. By 7:00 a.m., a slight breezed filled in from the east, dead on the nose. Then the clouds took on an ominous dimension, and the barometer plunged. I called the shore station at Seydis Fjord on our VHF radio and learned that the low-pressure system over Greenland was moving faster than anticipated. A gale warning was issued for the waters on the north coast, and the wind was predicted to increase within 18 hours. Our pulses skipped a beat when we heard the radio–audible in the cabin even over the roar of the engine. I thanked the radioman profusely and wished him a good morning before clearing the channel. It was hard to get used to the unstable weather.

Now Grímsey was only 20 miles away, and we pushed toward our destination. We never regretted having made time by motoring through the night.

GRÍMSEY ISLAND IS a three-mile-long, half-mile-wide treeless speck. The harbor is minuscule. The outer basin is exposed to the south and is barely large enough for the biweekly ferry to back in and tie up. The inner basin, where we tied *Driver*, is less than 150 feet in diameter. It is a land-locked haven created by a system of overlapping breakwaters. We tied to a concrete pier, leaving enough scope in our docklines to compensate for the six-foot tide.

Our geographic position in the inner basin was a mile south of the Arctic Circle. We walked to a sign that was erected on the actual line, near the gravel airstrip, before continuing up the sloping, grassy hills to the northern tip of the island. Finally, we were walking in the Arctic.

Grímsey is home to 90 permanent residents and is a nesting site for half a million migratory birds. The Icelanders and their families live in modern houses near the harbor, and the birds reside on the bold sea cliffs for which the island is famous. Puffins, which lined the cliffs by the tens of thousands, dropped awkwardly into flight whenever they saw us. Arctic terns hovered overhead, protecting their nests, and the kittiwakes and guillemots flashed on and off the cliffs with grace and dignity.

We kept a tight reign on Chris, Holly, and Teiga, forbidding them to leave our sides. The tall green grass looked benign and inviting, but the grass extended right to the tops of the sheer cliffs. There are no warnings, no signs, no ropes to mark the edge. The storekeeper on Grímsey had looked at our kids, then told us about a five-year-old triplet who plunged to his death near the harbor while his two brothers helplessly watched. He warned us to be careful.

As the sun moved north and began to descend, I took the kids for a walk on the low flat rocks near the harbor where they could roam at will. Jaja stayed aboard for a welcome kid break. The wind began to blow from the east, and it was accompanied by an increasing swell. Wherever the swell met the impenetrable shoreline, surf exploded into the air.

By midnight, the wind was screaming over the island. Driving rain pelted the deck like marbles. Fortunately, there was only a slight surge in the harbor–a gentle up-and-down sensation–even though the wind grabbed the mast and made *Driver* heel over.

We learned that in the winter, deep low-pressure systems could cause the sea level at Grímsey to rise by as much as six feet–high enough to cover the wharves. Most fishermen on the island took their boats out of the water for the winter or else roped them in place, away from the docks. We were also told about the effect of gales on the lighthouse, which stands atop a 60-foot cliff on the south side of the island. During one severe storm, driftwood logs had been deposited 50 yards inland from the light, and spray had been carried over the entire island.

I lay awake listening to the wind, contemplating the force of the winter gales. I wondered what we were getting ourselves into by planning to stay the winter in Iceland. I crawled out from under our warm blankets, walked barefoot across the cold cabin sole, and poked my head out of the dodger to double-check that our docklines had enough scope. Then I reclosed the flap on the dodger and sat in the companionway looking at the small fishing harbor that endures such brutal weather.

Grímsey cast a spell on us because of its location, its unique physical characteristics, and the geographical achievement it represented for us. The remoteness of Grímsey reminded me of Cocos Keeling, an island we visited during our circumnavigation aboard *Direction*. That atoll lay on the Indian Ocean, 900 miles west of Australia.

Cocos is rimmed with reefs and studded with coconut palms. The climate is tropical, and the vast lagoon is ringed by fine white-sand beaches. We visited islands in the Pacific that were equally pristine and certainly less populated, but Cocos gripped us in a way that was hard to shake. Thinking back, I concluded that the island held an extra attraction because we were already committed to crossing 3,500 miles of gale-plagued Indian Ocean. It was to be the most difficult leg of our circumnavigation. Cocos was just a handy midocean stopover; staying forever was not an option. We knew that raising the anchor would annihilate this time-and-place nirvana for us and replace it with certain hardship.

The idea of leaving the harbor at Grímsey caused us to experience similar foreboding. Akureyri, our destination for the winter, was only 60 miles away. It wasn't the meager distance that heightened our desire to stay put at Grímsey. What caused us to waver was the knowledge that arriving at Akureyri would represent the end of our summer of sailing–even though the summer was sometimes difficult–and would mark the beginning of a long, relatively uncertain winter. I wondered what the heck we had committed ourselves to this time.

I clamored back down the companionway, checked the bilge, then crawled under our warm blankets again.

Jaja stirred. "How is it out there?"

I took a moment before answering. "Remember the 11-day gale we endured after leaving Cocos?"

"I'll never forget it."

"Hold that thought."

THE FISHERMAN WHO GREETED US on our first day in Grímsey invited us to his house for lunch. His wife saw Jaja washing clothes by hand in the freezing water that came out of the hose on the wharf, and she implored Jaja to bring our laundry. Jaja yielded happily.

It was raining heavily when we knocked on their door. We were pulled inside like drowning swimmers and resuscitated with coffee. Icelanders know how to make good coffee, and we received generous cups of thick, well balanced, high-octane brew. Only real coffee lovers can make it that way.

In the main sitting room, which would have offered a magnificent view of the Icelandic coast if it weren't raining, the fisherman's 12-year-old son was playing a game on the computer. He said hello to Chris, Holly, and Teiga, abandoned his game, and slammed a video into the VCR. Before long, some neighborhood children sauntered in, and they all began to play noisily like regular kids. Jaja and I sat comfortably around the kitchen table with our hosts, getting high on coffee, eating small sweet cakes, homemade breads, fruits, and the smoked fish and meats for which Iceland is famous.

One of the delicious smoked meats was dark red and tasted slightly gamy. We couldn't guess what it was, but we weren't surprised to learn that it was smoked puffin. Icelanders have eaten puffin for centuries, and Grímsey is one of the few islands where people can still catch them legally. Our host asked if I wanted to try netting some.

"Sure," I said. "Why not?"

Two hours later, Jaja took the kids back to the boat, and I rode with the fisherman in his battered four-wheel-drive vehicle to the eastern side of the island–the side with the highest cliffs. I swore involuntarily when I saw the rope that we would use to begin our descent to the beach, 120 feet below. We lowered ourselves hand over hand for about 30 feet to the end of the rope and landed on a three-foot-wide grassy ridge. Then we crept cautiously along the narrow, uneven ridge, which angled down the side of the cliff like some weird, inverted walkway. As we crept downward, I was keenly aware that if I lost my footing I would slide off the edge of the ridge on my slippery foul-weather gear. According to the shopkeeper, whom I suspected was also the undertaker, slipping on the grass and flying over the cliffs was a time-worn cause of death on Grímsey. Finally, we reached the huge boulders heaped at the foot of precipice.

Down at beach level, the puffins swarmed like insects. It took considerably more effort than I had imagined to hurl the 12-foot pole with its three-foot-diameter net upwards in the path of the innocent, soaring creatures. After I watched the fisherman drag a squirming, stubby puffin out of his net and ring its feathery neck in one quick motion, I lost interest in the sport and successfully avoided catching any birds. My host was apologetic when he saw my failed attempts.

"I guess it takes a little practice," he said.

When I returned to *Driver*, muddy and bruised, Holly ignored me. Jaja caught sight of my confusion and laughed.

"Holly is wondering if you killed any puffins."

"Mommy! I am not!"

I held up my hand in defense. "Not one, I swear it."

Holly gave me a smile that stretched ear to ear.

THE WEATHER FORECAST WAS MARGINAL, but the extended outlook was worse. So we left Grímsey for the mainland before the really bad weather hit. The sea conditions were uncomfortable, but not dangerous. Heavy rain and dense fog obscured the horizon. Our mental picture was also clouded by uncertainty. After 10 days on the island, we were tired of thinking about the upcoming winter. We were ready to settle in port and to conquer some of the unknowns. Would we be allowed to live alongside the concrete pontoon at Akureyri? Would our kids be allowed to attend the school? Would the townsfolk accept us?

The entrance to five-mile-wide Eyja Fjord appeared on our radar screen like a doorway. Once through the "door", we would sail on to Akureyri, 35 miles down the fjord. The wind, which had been blowing hard from the northwest, became gusty–influenced by the mountains. We kept a cautious eye to windward for unpredictable, hurricane-force downdrafts that can knock down a sailboat. As the water began to shoal, swirling currents distorted the large, more regular ground swells. The confused waters tossed *Driver* around like a discarded fuel drum. Jaja remained below with the kids, trying to sooth their queasiness and ease their boredom. I steered the boat towards Dalvík, a fishing village tucked three miles inside the fjord entrance.

As we neared the large fishing harbor, the low fog lifted, and we could see that the lower hills behind the town were covered with the first snows of autumn. Because of the wind chill, the temperature on deck during the passage from Grímsey was below freezing. Once again, our thoughts turned to the coming winter.

And it's only August!

The wharves in Dalvík's protected basin were crowded with small wooden fishing boats, big steel trawlers, and faded fiberglass runabouts. The wooden boats were quaint, the steel ones were ugly, and the rest were utilitarian. We saw a well maintained local sailboat tied to the small-boat pontoon, but we didn't think there would be enough room to raft up. So we prepared to tie to a rusty trawler at the main wharf. Luckily, a fellow aboard the docked sailboat saw *Driver* and signaled for us to come alongside his 35-foot sloop, *Niña II.*

Halli was our age and had a thick, full beard–a quintessential Viking. He worked as an engineer aboard one of the large trawlers, and in a few days, he was scheduled to head back to sea for a month. Halli warned us about the potential for winter ice the farther we ranged up the fjord. Dalvík's harbor remains ice-free year round. But, he said, the harbor at Akureyri freezes easily. There, rivers empty copious amounts of water into the fjord, and fresh water freezes sooner–at a higher temperature–than salt water.

In Reykjavík, we had met a German couple aboard a 30-foot steel sloop. The construction of their hull was similar to *Driver*'s, and they told us about their experience on the waterways of Denmark, locked in 18 inches of ice. They had survived without mishap.

"How thick does the ice get in Akureyri?" I asked Halli.

"Never more than about eight or 10 inches in a bad year."

No problem.

Later, while dining at Halli's house, his wife Katrin shook her head at our plans.

"Why?" she asked. "Why do you want to live on your boat for the coming winter?"

"Because we think it'll be a fun experience."

"Aren't you at all worried?"

"Only a little."

Katrin was a schoolteacher in Dalvík. She told us there were three grammar schools in Akureyri, and she recommended Brekkuskoli, the school on the hill. When she offered to call ahead for us, to let the headmaster know we were coming, we accepted gratefully. We had never enrolled our children in a foreign school, and we needed all the help we could get.

A fleet of small fishing boats came chugging into the harbor at 8:00 p.m. An old-timer rafted alongside, nodded a curt hello in the Icelandic fashion, and then crossed our decks on his way to shore. If we hadn't been accustomed to this type of subdued greeting, we might have thought he was angry. After all, *Driver* was hogging a considerable portion of the dock. The next morning at 5:00 a.m., I heard his careful footfalls on deck and listened as he quietly untied his lines. After that–silence. Curious to know why the fisherman hadn't started his engine, I crawled up the companionway ladder. He was drifting away from us with the wind, toward the middle of the harbor. When he was a few dozen feet off, he fired up his diesel and steamed away with the rest of the fleet. He didn't even awaken the kids.

After breakfast, we untied our lines and headed up the fjord to Akureyri, the town that had inspired our plans for the winter. We were almost there.

Chapter Five

If adventuring were easy,
everybody would be doing it.

We SAT ON DECK and grimaced. Fast-moving cars and noisy trucks roared by, spewing exhaust less than a stone's throw from the dock. We remembered Akureyri as a quiet, isolated hamlet. Now it seemed like a vast, high-rise metropolis, a veritable cosmopolitan destination. Surely this wasn't the same place we had visited back in June.

"Jaja! Pass me the navigation chart, will you? I think we've come to the wrong town."

"We'll get used to it in a few days."

"That's what worries me."

Compared to the carnival atmosphere in Bermuda, Reykjavík had felt like a calm haven. Compared to Reykjavík, the Akureyri we had discovered during our car trip felt like a quiet mountain oasis. On our sail northward from Reykjavík, our perceptions of noise and population density had changed again. We found solace in towns such as Flateyri, and in remote places such as Grímsey, where birds outnumbered people thousands to one. Returning to Akureyri proved that our perceptions were relative. We wondered how we would feel about Reykjavík if we were to return there.

Holly was desperate to live on Grímsey. She loved the birds and the open horizon that surrounded the island. She saw herself walking in the tall grass of summer, picnicking in the sun. Jaja and I were also tempted to try wintering on board at Grímsey, but after examining the facts more closely, we changed our minds. In September, all the birds would leave the island. Attacked by winter storms, the tall grass would be flattened by ice and snow. Most importantly, the tiny harbor would not be safe for *Driver*.

Flateyri touched our hearts, but we wondered about activities and services. There was a small grocery store with a limited selection. Although food was not high on our list of priorities, the price we paid for it was. Most people in Flateyri drove 45 minutes to Ísafjordur for supplies and medical services. If we stayed in Flateyri, we would be dependent on the bus schedule or on friends' cars.

The town dock in Akureyri put us within walking distance of grocery stores, hardware stores, the post office, the library, the school, and sundry shops. Best of all, there was a pediadent across the street from the concrete pontoon. Teiga had a unique problem with the development of her teeth, and she needed to see a dentist every three months. In Reykjavík, we took her to a dentist to have a malformed tooth filled. There we learned about several other pediadents in Iceland, including one in Akureyri and another in Ísafjordur.

After lunch, we ventured ashore to reacquaint ourselves with the town we had spent all summer dreaming about. The kids skipped along, happy that we had stopped cruising for the season. Holly continued to mourn the solitude of Grímsey, but she soon saw the benefits of town life in the shape of a large ice cream cone. Teiga sat in her backpack smearing vanilla pecan in my hair, while Chris bumped up and down, one foot in the street, the other on the curb.

As we walked, Jaja and I talked. We often have our best conversations while in motion. The real problem with the apparent noise and confusion of Akureyri, we decided, was the knowledge that our summer of sailing was finished. The roller coaster ride was over, and we had just come to a shuddering halt. The thrill of cruising had ended, and we needed to shift mental gears, elbow our way through the crowds, and prepare for "the next thing." That didn't mean the next thing–in this case stopping at Akureyri–would be bad; it would just be different. We knew we couldn't go through life on a rush. If that were all we ever did, even the rush would become a routine.

A number of uncertainties lay before us, made more complicated because we did not speak Icelandic. We knew that most people in Iceland speak English, but we were shy to force our language on people in their own country. At the top of our "to do" list were visits to the port captain, the school, and the post office. First priority was asking the port captain for permission to live alongside the floating concrete pontoon for the winter.

We climbed the wide stairs inside the Eimskip Shipping building, which sat on the main wharf, and waited patiently while the port captain was summoned. He came into the room smiling, but he frowned when we laid our request at his feet.

"No," he said emphatically.

"Why not?"

He pointed to our three kids, then highlighted succinctly what he thought were the dangers.

"During the winter it will be cold, it will be dark, and the harbor will freeze. That is not an environment for children."

We detailed our previous adventures, explaining to the port captain that we had years of experience living in extreme situations with our children and that we weren't exposing ourselves to any real danger by living dockside. I told him our boat was built of steel, that it was well insulated, and that it had a reliable heater.

"If there is a problem," I added, "all we have to do is walk off the boat and take a taxi to the airport. Spain is only a few hours away by plane."

The port captain was noncommittal. "I will have to think about it."

We offered our cheery thanks–even though we did not feel cheery–saying we would await his decision. Officials generally prefer written requests. That way, they can refuse more easily–impersonally, in writing. But our lifestyle is not mainstream, and following mainstream protocol usually does not work for us. We prefer knocking on the door of officialdom, offering a big smile and a firm handshake.

Feeling despondent, we hit the cold air outside the Eimskip building. Our plans were close to collapsing under the weight of authority. Was the port captain right? Were we fools? Jaja and I felt like children who had a bright, elaborate plan that was about to be shot down by a cynical and unimaginative parent. We would have to be patient.

WE CROSSED THE MAIN ROAD, zigzagged between the city buildings, and began to ascend the 110 steps to a modern concrete-looking church. At the top of the long staircase, we took a breather and admired the view. Eyja Fjord was a wide, blue ribbon that stretched for miles toward the coast until it became obscured from view by mountains. The town center lay below us. We could even see *Driver.* After a short respite, we mounted more steps–and yet another small hill–before reaching the school. We told the kids that not only would they learn a new language, they would be in great physical shape.

Chris sounded concerned. "But I thought the port captain said we couldn't stay. Why are we bothering to look at the school?"

I secretly admired my son's practical view.

"The port captain didn't refuse us," Jaja replied. "He said he'd think about it."

"Whenever you and Daddy say you'll 'think about it,' it always means 'no'."

There were a dozen more steps leading to the main doors of the school. Because the building was four stories high, there were even more stairs inside before we reached the top floor. It finally made sense to us: In Icelandic *Brekku* means "hill," and *skoli* means "school."

The office staff at Brekkuskoli had received Katrin's call a few days earlier, and they were awaiting our appearance. Holly and Chris were placed in second- and third-grade classes, respectively, with teachers who spoke English well. We learned that in four days we should return to the school with the other parents and students for orientation.

Chris and Holly were getting nervous. On one hand, they were excited because neither of them had attended public school before. Holly, in particular, wanted to take part in the classroom social scene–something she had only read about in books. Chris liked the idea of recess. The thought of being away from home for the first time was unsettling to them, but the kids' primary worry was the language barrier.

Icelandic is complicated, and it is radically different from the Latin-based Spanish and French that Jaja and I learned in school. Icelandic has many formidable grammar rules. Adjectives and verbs–as well as nouns–are conjugated to distraction. A person's given name has different spellings depending on whether the person is being spoken to, spoken about, introduced, or given something. Numbers one through four are spelled differently depending on the gender of the noun. Six is my favorite number in Icelandic because it is spelled s-e-x, and it is pronounced the same as in English. Every language has its perks.

Jaja began home-schooling our young crewmembers in simple math onboard *Direction* during our 51-day passage from Cape Town, South Africa, to Barbados in the West Indies. Chris, who was four years old, and Holly, who was three, learned quickly. Jaja continued the home-schooling after we moved ashore in Oriental. At that time, Holly was only four, but she did the same first-grade correspondence course that Chris was studying. With newborn Teiga in her arms, Jaja turned the kitchen of our rented house into a miniature schoolroom. The aromas of food mingled with the children's delight over academic discoveries.

Holly was easy to home-school. Chris was stubborn. After moving aboard *Driver*, Jaja tried everything to motivate Chris–to help him complete his schoolwork–but he fought every step of the way. He did the work in the end, and he did learn, but it was a hard slog to windward. Chris was easily distracted, and there were plenty of distractions on the boat. Holly sailed through her courses, eager to please, eager to succeed. By teaching two types of students side by side, Jaja experienced both the frustration and joy of home-schooling.

Enrolling our kids in the Icelandic school would prevent them from being isolated from other children all winter. Holly would do well with the foreign curriculum, and we hoped that Chris would find learning more enjoyable in a classroom. We thanked the office staff at Brekkuskoli for letting our kids attend.

KNÚTUR KARLSSON, the owner of the 40-foot sailboat moored across the basin from us, asked if we were the couple who had sailed the 25-footer around the world. Knútur had been reading about our travels aboard *Direction* in sailing magazines for many years. He wasn't surprised to learn that we planned to spend the winter in the harbor.

"That is," Jaja added, "we'll stay if the port captain will allow us. He thinks we're crazy for wanting to live aboard and is trying to discourage us."

Knútur laughed. "Yes, yes. The port captain is a friend of mine. I shall tell him that you and Dave are well accustomed to a lifestyle that involves suffering."

"Thanks," I said. "We really do want to stay."

"Yes, yes, of course. I will see what I can do to help you."

"Will you leave your boat in the water over the winter?" I asked.

"Yes. A little ice collects in the basin, but it is never dangerous. Your boat is steel like mine, so it should not be a concern for you."

The last thing on our list was to set up a mailing address. By some coincidence, many of the towns in which we have lived over the years built new post offices while we were there. There was a post office under construction in Tauranga, New Zealand, the town where Holly was born. And it was the same at Chris's birthplace, Bundaberg, Australia. There was even a new post office built in Oriental shortly after Teiga's birth. While waiting in line to mail some letters in Akureyri, we learned that a new postal facility was under construction.

"A good omen," I whispered to Jaja.

"Thank God you've had a vasectomy," she whispered back.

THE SUN BLAZED; the colors in the landscape glowed. There was a coolness to the slight breeze that blew over the fjord, and it felt more like October than the last day of August. We panted up the church steps to Brekkuskoli, then continued even farther up the hill to the Middle School for the parent-student orientation meeting. We entered on the lower level before proceeding up a flight of stairs to the auditorium.

The room was jammed with adorable blond children, all of whom were dressed in bright clothes. Most of the parents were dressed the same way as Jaja and I–in jeans, cotton shirts, and sneakers. We felt at ease until the headmaster, who was wearing a tie, walked to the podium and began speaking in Icelandic. Suddenly, we were disoriented. The other parents were nodding their heads attentively while Jaja and I sat in dumb disbelief. What was he saying? What was going on? What had we gotten ourselves into?

Holly asked Jaja what was happening.

"Oh, he's just telling us about the coming year," Jaja said casually. "You know, things like that."

"Things like what?"

"I'll tell you later," Jaja whispered.

The headmaster began calling out names. One by one, the kids lined up near the podium. After about 18 children had assembled, the group left the room with their teacher. The parents followed closely behind. We listened carefully to the roll call, which consisted of a steady barrage of unusual sounding names, hoping we would recognize Chris's and Holly's names when they were announced.

"Sigrún Björk Svienbjörnsdóttir, Sólveig Huld Jónsdóttir, Gísli Hróar Gíslason, Holly Christine Martin, Orri Sigmarsson..."

"Here we go," Jaja said, hoisting Teiga on her hip and taking Holly by the hand. "Good luck, Dave. See you later."

Chris and I waited for several more classes to be called before we followed his teacher down the stairs, out of the building, over to Brekkuskoli, and up two flights of stairs to Chris's classroom. For 25 minutes, I sat with glazed eyes as Helga, Chris's teacher, bombarded my brain with a steady attack of Icelandic.

"What's she saying?" Chris quietly asked.

"I'll tell you afterwards."

I gazed around the clean, white classroom, at the tidy, kid-sized desks, at the chalkboards–and at the clock. It was the same as any classroom I had occupied when I was a kid in Seattle. When I was bored with the inside of the room, I used to look out the window. Here, I noticed that a substantial breeze was bending the trees violently. I began to worry about *Driver*, hoping the docklines were rigged correctly for the breeze and that the fenders were riding well between the boat and the dock.

No reason worrying, I said to myself. Everything is probably fine.

The room was warm, and I became drowsy as I stared at the sun streaming in the windows. I wondered how many hours I had spent daydreaming in a classroom.

Starting in the fourth grade, I began to fantasize about sailing around the world. Mom gave me Robin Graham's picture book for kids, about the young man's solo circumnavigation aboard his small boat *Dove*. I would flip through the pages at recess, entranced with names such as New Hebrides, Samoa, Tonga, and Fiji. Like every other kid in the world who read that book, I dreamed of following in Graham's footsteps. I wanted to be like him–

which is ironic, because Graham grew to despise sailing by the end of his voyage. He allowed himself to be corrupted by the record books and by financial commitments.

Many years later, when I was 24, I was aboard *Direction* in the Virgin Islands at the start of my own circumnavigation. I was short-tacking across Charlotte Amalie Harbor when I found the 24-foot *Dove* at anchor. Graham had switched to a larger boat on his way to Panama. The little boat I saw was a victim of neglect, not the dream machine that had changed my life. Nevertheless, it revived memories in me that were still pristine. As a boy, I vowed to sail the globe. I also hoped to find a girl, if I could, and take her with me.

Chris nudged me. I came out of my reverie and realized that Helga was trying to get my attention. Speaking in English, she asked if I had any questions.

"No."

She resumed speaking in Icelandic. Then a student handed out two papers to each parent. Although there were no obvious words of dismissal, everyone began filing quietly out of the room. In public, Icelanders speak very softly to each other, or not at all. I asked Helga about the papers and learned that one was the class schedule and the other was a list of the classroom supplies we needed to buy at the bookstore in town. When Chris and I found Jaja, Holly, and Teiga, we felt as if we had just sighted land after a year at sea.

"How was *your* Icelandic experience?" I asked.

"Apparently, about the same as yours," Jaja replied.

"Did you understand anything?"

"Not really."

As we walked away from the school, we wondered if we were doing the right thing. We had heard about an embassy school in Reykjavík that had an English speaking curriculum, but we wanted our kids to meet local children. We were in Iceland. We wanted them to meet Icelanders. We tried to convince Chris and Holly that only the first few months at school would be difficult and that the overall rewards would far outweigh their initial confusion. Sometimes, we said, you have to move toward an empty horizon and have faith that good things await you just out of sight.

They didn't believe us.

When we descended to the top of the 110 church steps, the full effect of the 50-knot gale slammed into us. The surface of the bay was white and angry. Frequent gusts cascaded down the mountains, hitting the water violently and lifting curtains of spray. Like a dust storm, the spray flew across the fjord, plastering the buildings on the foreshore with spume.

In the town center, the buildings created venturis that accelerated the wind. The gusts ripped posters from signposts and overturned advertising sandwich boards, sending them on errant journeys up the hillside. Doors slammed. Choking grime whirled on the roads, forcing us to pull our jacket collars over our faces.

A light chop from the south was rolling into the inner basin. *Driver* pitched and sawed. Her fenders were squashed flat against the dock. Worried that the wind might blow harder, I spent a half-hour rigging a breast line to the breakwater. But as quickly as the wind had begun, it subsided, leaving the air clean and silent. We shifted *Driver* to the other side of the pontoon. If the mountain winds geared up again, we would be blown away from the dock instead of onto it.

Several nights later, Knútur arrived with good news. The port captain had changed his mind: We could stay in the harbor for the winter. The bad news was the port captain insisted that we move to the main wharf next to Knútur's boat because our floating pontoon did not have electricity or water. We sighed. At the top of the ramp to our pontoon, there was a wide sidewalk that ran alongside a small parking lot and an open field. Once the children were off the dock, there was little danger that they would fall in the water. There was also a large area in which they could play. The main wharf on the opposite side of the harbor had a wall like a high cliff. We would have to hold tight to our kids every time we stepped ashore. Worse still, the wharf bordered on a busy traffic intersection so there was no place for them to play. I told Knútur that it would be safer for us to stay tied where we were.

Knútur agreed. "I'll tell the port captain that your heater doesn't require electricity and that you have reliable 12-volt batteries. I can see that your children will be much safer here."

THE FIRST SNOWS OF WINTER dusted *Driver*'s deck on October 17th. Within a week, three feet of the stuff covered the town like epoxy-saturated microballoons. This much snow in October was unusual, we were informed, but winter weather was extremely variable from year to year. We began to wonder what the winter had in store for us.

Near the end of the month, the temperature plunged to zero degrees Fahrenheit. Winter had begun. The sky was dark blue, and the sun, which rose low over the mountains, provided visual stimulation but little warmth. Jaja walked Chris and Holly to school as usual, and I could hear their voices clearly as they shuffled down the footpath toward town.

"It's too *cooold*!"

"I want to stay home today!"

"My nose is numb!"

Below in the cabin, Teiga and I played her favorite game. I made elaborate sculptures with play dough, and she smashed them with a toy rolling pin, laughing uncontrollably.

Jaja's cheeks were bright red when she returned. She urged me to get out and see the day while the sun burned orange. As I stepped on deck, a thick layer of ice crunched underfoot like pieces of broken glass. The condensation from my breath froze on my scarf, and I could feel icy fingers of cold reaching under my down-filled parka. Out on the fjord, the 34-degree harbor water–which was much warmer than the air–steamed like liquid in a boiling cauldron. The vapor blew ashore on the slight breeze, giving the town a dreamy look.

On the waterfront footpath, the tightly packed snow squeaked with every step. I could smell the horse stables miles away at the back of the fjord. I also could clearly see and hear a plane, idling on the airport runway over a mile away. The stench of jet fuel mingled with the scent of horse manure. When the propeller-driven aircraft roared overhead, I was forced to cover my ears. Sights, sounds, and odors took on exaggerated qualities.

I crawled back into *Driver*'s cabin. We were accustomed to keeping the cabin temperature close to 68, but this morning, the temperature only reached 60. Although I increased the fuel flow, the stove didn't get any hotter. I opened the lid of the burn pot. A thick skin of carbon at the bottom was restricting the flow of diesel fuel. I would have to shut down the stove and clean it. How long, I wondered, would the heat in the cabin last with the stove turned off?

It took 20 minutes for the scorching metal to cool enough so that I could touch it. By then, the temperature in the cabin had dropped to 50. I chipped the scale out of the burn pot with a screwdriver, extracted sooty sludge from the feed line, and replaced the fuel filter for good measure. The cabin temperature dropped to 45. I primed the stove, and after 15 minutes, the stack warmed up and was drawing. Only then could I increase the flow of diesel to "full." By the time heat began to replace the intrusion of polar air, the cabin temperature had plunged to 40. It took four hours to raise the temperature to 68.

This episode proved how dependent we were on the stove. We hadn't winterized the engine, and we couldn't winterize the water tanks because we needed them. *Driver* was well insulated, but if the stove stopped working, all our systems would be frozen solid within hours.

The cold snap lasted three days. Then temperatures rose to the mid-20s. Snow fell regularly, and stiff breezes blew down the fjord. Fortunately, the wind in Akureyri was tame in comparison to the full blast of storms that screamed down the exposed Icelandic coast. During one gale, the weather buoy between Grímsey and Eyja Fjord reported 70-knot winds with 41-foot waves. In Akureyri, the only evidence of the large seas was an imperceptible harbor surge that made the roller on our dock ramp squeak annoyingly. We were glad we weren't wintering at Grímsey.

WHILE CHRIS AND HOLLY WERE AT SCHOOL, Jaja, Teiga, and I explored our environs on foot. We pulled Teiga behind us in her sled, and she dragged her hands in the snow happily. One morning, Jaja suggested a new route. She guided us on a circuitous path to the hospital where we ducked conveniently into the waiting room so Teiga could warm up. Jaja casually suggested I have a doctor examine my right hand.

"As long as we're here," she added quickly.

"I've been tricked!"

Jaja just laughed.

I had stubbornly resisted the idea of a consultation. I preferred to suffer the inconvenience of a lame hand rather than pay for another lame prognosis. I stood my ground for a few minutes, then reluctantly agreed to see a doctor. The fingers on my right hand were so stiff that I was unable to make a fist.

After an interminable wait, an intern pulled me into an examination room, asked his stock questions, and filled out his stock forms. His superior suggested an X-ray, and even I could tell by looking at the image that there was nothing unusual going on inside my hand.

They were stumped. "Let your hand rest for another month then come back."

"It's been resting for several months already, and it's not getting better." I was exasperated.

"Give it more time."

I paid the fee in cash.

Meanwhile, life on *Driver* moved on, sore hand or not. Filling our water tanks became a wearisome chore—mindless hauling that wasn't doing my hand any favors. At first, getting water was relatively easy. We filled our jugs using a tap not far from our pontoon. When the temperature dipped below freezing during the second week of September, the water was shut off, and we were forced to range further afield. There was a hose at the gas station several blocks away, but even using Teiga's stroller as a cart for a pair of five-gallon jugs, we found the daily water ritual to be monotonous and back-breaking.

Using my brain instead of my back, I designed and built a 3' x 2' x 2' rectangular plywood box. I lined it with clear plastic sheeting, hammered on a lid, and mounted the box on two stout hand-truck wheels that I had rescued from the dump on Grímsey. The water box held a generous 37 gallons. It was simple to push it to the gas station and fill it. Wheeling it back to the pontoon took considerable effort, but one fillup lasted us five days. The trick was to wait for low tide when *Driver* floated below the level of the sidewalk. Then we could feed the water into *Driver*'s tanks using a long hose and gravity.

The "Box," as we fondly named it, performed well until it began to snow in October. According to average weather statistics, I should have been able to wheel the Box on bare ground until December. I fantasized about installing skis under it, instead of wheels, but there were too many bare patches on the roads for skis to be practical. Our new friends Jón and Disa, who lived a short distance away, invited us to fill the Box using a hose in a shed behind their house. We could get there on side streets without having to negotiate the busy four-way intersection near the gas station where snow-plows had clogged the sidewalks.

A full load of water in the Box weighted 320 pounds. Rolling the con-traption on the hard-packed snowy roads was difficult, but the parking lot in front of our dock ramp was a nightmare because it was seldom plowed. The lot belonged to a fitness gym, and the constant comings and goings of patrons' cars made irregular ruts in the deep snow. When Jaja and I struggled and heaved to get the stubborn Box moving across the frozen tire tracks, we felt like polar explorers trying to coax a sled over jagged ice formations.

The fitness fanatics who walked on their treadmills inside the heated gym nudged each other playfully. *Look at the Americans now!* We tried to appear nonchalant, as if we had pushed water boxes every day of our lives. I suppose they were trying to look macho, as if tight Lycra and calorie com-puter analysis were the keys to a happy life. We all find challenges in differ-ent ways.

One of the greatest ironies in history is the shortage of drinkable water often experienced by liveaboard cruising sailors who are literally surrounded by water. While cruising on *Direction*, I spent countless hours hauling water, not only for drinking, but also for washing clothes and diapers. I became a water-hauling expert.

On our voyage around the world, we sometimes took *Direction* to the dock to get water, but usually I filled jugs and ferried them from shore in the dinghy. I estimate that I hauled 15,000 gallons of water over a seven-year period. Roughly speaking, that's 130,000 pounds.

People who never hand-washed diapers on a boat often told Jaja that she should wash Chris's and Holly's diapers in salt water.

"It would save a lot of water hauling," one guy told her, nodding at me sympathetically in a man-to-man sort of way.

Later, Jaja asked me, "I wonder if that guy would wash his underwear in salt water?"

In an effort to improve the quality of life on *Driver*, I installed a desalinator to help meet our fresh water needs. The harbor water in Akureyri was actually clean enough for the watermaker, but there was a glitch. The water temperature was too cold for the unit to work efficiently.

So we hauled.

During a water run in late November, while casually forcing the miserable Box through a slushy snowdrift in front of the health club's large plate-glass windows, I overstressed my right hand. The next morning, my fingers were painfully swollen, worse than they had ever been. Jaja persuaded me to make another journey to the hospital. After a half-hour wait, a clipboard-slinging intern greeted me. I explained my condition and described how I had recently aggravated the problem.

"I've watched you," he said. "What's in that box, anyway?"

"Water."

He whistled under his breath, then began the same spiel about letting my hand rest. Unable to restrain my anger, I demanded that a specialist look at my hand.

The next morning, I had an appointment with an arthritis specialist who introduced himself as Bjørn. Not *Doctor* Bjørn Gudmansson, just Bjørn. Iceland has a unique system where everyone goes by first names, avoids titles, and skips the "Mr." and "Mrs." formalities. The Icelandic telephone directory was complicated because it listed everyone alphabetically by *first name*. The library was impossible.

Bjørn examined all my joints and asked me a few questions. After drawing a blank, he called in the senior hand surgeon. Arí listened attentively as I relayed the history of my hand for the 10th time, going all the way back to the first injury I received while scraping barnacles off *Driver*'s bottom in Florida. Both he and Bjørn were fluent in English, but Arí asked me to clarify one point.

"What's a barnacle?" he asked.

"It looks like a miniature volcano and sticks to the bottom of a boat."

Comprehension spread over Arí's face as he dredged some detail of information from his mind.

"I think I know what this is," he said with an alarming grin. "I *think* you may have a form of marine tuberculosis living in your hand. This is very interesting. May I see your hand again? Yes, this is going to be exciting. We don't see many patients with tropical ailments in Iceland."

UP AT BREKKUSKOLI, the kids had accepted Holly. On the first day of school, for example, a group of pigtailed girls took her by the hand and led her to the swings. She also liked her teacher, who was very sympathetic.

Nevertheless, Holly was having more difficulty adjusting to school than Chris, and she wanted to resume home-schooling with Jaja.

Being away from home for the first time was Holly's main problem. The language barrier didn't upset her. She was just a small six-year-old who was used to being at her mother's side 24 hours a day. We sensed that Holly needed more time to adjust, so we gently persuaded her to push on. We told her to keep trying until Christmas. If she didn't want to go back to school by the end of the holidays, she could stay home and study.

Chris didn't seem to mind being away from us, but it took a superhuman effort to get him out of bed, to make sure he was clothed and fed, and to prod him to march up the hill. Chris didn't mind the classroom part of the day because he liked his teacher. And the other kids fought to play with him at recess.

Chris's teacher Helga and Holly's teacher Áthora had both lived overseas with their own children, and they understood the difficulty of learning a new language. In the classroom, they sometimes spoke to Chris and Holly in English, knowing that it was good for the other students to hear it. For homework, Chris and Holly were expected to read and write in Icelandic. They made minor complaints about not always knowing what was going on in the classroom, but we told them they were lucky because they were learning how to communicate by observation. We told them that the words would eventually make sense. We tried to instill patience.

When Holly's class had a midterm get-together for parents and students, we attended eagerly. It was our first social. We assembled in Holly's classroom at 5:30 p.m., nodding silent hellos to the other parents. No one spoke to us, and we suspected they were shy to speak English in front of their friends. We could relate. We were shy about trying our few words of Icelandic for fear of saying something stupid and embarrassing.

After a few announcements, the kids filed into the room, and one by one, read a short poem. We applauded each performance. When the poetry reading was over, bingo cards were handed around. The kids all bubbled excitedly. Jaja helped Teiga get organized, while Chris and Holly grabbed a pile of markers for themselves. Having nothing to do, I grabbed a card and began filling in the numbers. Knowing *which* numbers and letters were being called posed some problems, but a sympathetic parent kept whispering them to us in English.

I hadn't played bingo in 25 years. The room was silent as the kids concentrated on trying to win. Much to my surprise, I filled in the "B" column with six quick moves. It was a personal record.

"Bingo!" I shouted. A few of the parents sniggered. Jaja tried to get my attention, but the lady in charge had already come over to examine my card and to double-check that I wasn't cheating.

"You're a winner, all right." With that announcement, the parents and kids applauded. The room mother brought a small cardboard box over and insisted I draw a prize. "Sorry the gifts are all geared for kids," she said politely in perfect English.

As soon as I pulled a colorfully wrapped present out of the box, it hit me. I looked at Jaja for help. She was biting her lower lip, and her shoulders were shaking convulsively. I felt my face turn crimson. I thought my ears were going to burn. I quickly gave the present to Holly. She unwrapped a miniature paint set with three colors and a tiny brush. Everyone clapped again; then a new game started.

After a few more games of bingo, we took a break. I was sweating and sat rooted in my chair, terrified of meeting any of the parents in the hallway.

I whispered to Jaja angrily. "Why didn't you tell me the game was only for the kids?"

"I thought you knew!" She put a cup of coffee to her lips, but I could tell by her eyes that she was still grinning.

When everybody filed back into the room, the lady in charge muttered more unintelligible Icelandic words. I looked at the clock. Another hour to go. God help us!

A father stood in front of the class. Without a word, he began strutting back and forth in a caricature of a prima donna. He fluffed his hair, winked at the other parents, and gazed at his fingernails admiringly. No one in the room moved or made a sound. *What the hell was going on?* I looked at Jaja who was still trigger happy. She began to giggle into her coffee cup again. The man repeated the performance, leaving everybody spellbound. I was happy the spotlight was finally on a local. Someone in the class shouted something in Icelandic, but he was ignored. Then someone else shouted a word, followed by another.

I whispered to Jaja knowingly. "Charades."

Jaja nodded in comprehension, but before I had the chance, she beat me to a more startling conclusion. "You do it, Dave. You've already made a fool of yourself."

When it was my turn, the room mother translated the word that was written on the slip of paper that I drew from the coffee can. I stood in front of the parents and acted out my role. People began to yell incomprehensible words to me in Icelandic, and I had to check my slip of paper several times to see if the word matched what I thought I heard: *Njósnari.* Someone finally guessed

I was a spy, but I felt more like a traitor to intelligent life. I would never make it in the P.T.A.

We walked back to *Driver*, looking at the stars that shone brightly.

"Maybe we'll see the northern lights tonight," I mused.

As soon as we were back onboard, Holly began playing with her new paint set. Chris complained that he hadn't received a prize.

"Maybe Daddy will win one for you at your party," Jaja teased.

"Keep it up," I joked, "and I will torture you after the kids fall asleep."

"Will I have to pretend to resist?"

"H'm...only if you want to."

WE SAT IN THE CABIN playing cribbage by candlelight. We still had some duty-free Grand Marnier left from Bermuda, and we breathed in the liqueur's sweet aroma. We preferred sipping small quantities of expensive alcohol rather than guzzling large quantities of more reasonably priced drink.

After losing the cribbage game, I stuck my head out of the dodger to scan the heavens. A thin band of green neon light that looked like an oversized jet contrail was frozen directly overhead, extending west to east.

"Northern lights!" Jaja and I donned hats, mitts, boots, and warm coats before crunching into the frozen cockpit. Staring straight up, we stood transfixed, shifting back and forth on our feet to keep warm. The green band turned tubular. Then it pulsed like a massive umbilical cord snaking across the sky until it became a wide smear highlighted by yellow and violet. The shimmering movement slowed; the colors swirled like an oil drop on calm water. As suddenly as the motion had begun, the swirling subsided, reverting back to the green band.

"Did that really happen?" I was in awe.

"I think so. Want to go in to warm up?"

Holly was awake when we entered the cabin, and she wanted to know why we had been stamping our feet in the cockpit. I looked outside again to be sure the northern lights were still there, then asked her if she wanted to see something neat.

"What's neat?" came Chris's muffled voice from the depths of his bunk.

"All right," I whispered. "Everybody topside to see the spectacle. And keep it quiet. We don't want to wake Teiga."

The aurora borealis boiled silently overhead, causing Holly and Chris to make continuous exclamations of wonder. The wandering clouds of light changed again, taking on the appearance of greenish shards of ice that were vibrating silently to a cosmic signal. The lights suddenly faded, returning to the original bandlike configuration across the sky.

We were captivated, oblivious of the 14-degree night air that penetrated our clothing. I found myself marveling that *Driver* was moored next to a floating dock, dozens of miles up a mountainous fjord on the north coast of Iceland. What were the forces that had provoked us to give up a comfortable, midlatitude existence so that we could breathe the thin air of a high-latitude night?

We weren't the only ones to wonder. Our families and close friends still couldn't understand why we chose a remote, cold winter in lieu of a warm one in the Tropics. But there has to be more to life than the conscious pursuit of predictable comfort. Does everything have to be safe and warm for it to be inherently good?

Humans are thinking animals that have flourished because we are good at survival, good at adaptability. Adventure-type vacations are popular these days because most of us want to test ourselves, to tweak the survival nerve centers in our brains. Humans thrive on taking chances. There are casinos, roller coasters, fast cars, and stock markets. We climb vertical rock walls, jump out of airplanes, and swim underwater with air bottles strapped to our backs. For centuries, explorers have made epic journeys across oceans on wind-propelled vessels.

It's easy to belittle individuals who engineer hardship into their lives, to say they are crazy or stupid, that the risks and inconveniences they've taken for the sake of adventure are not worth it. But self-imposed hardship is a rare currency that increases the value of a chosen lifestyle. Jaja and I accepted the drawbacks that came with living aboard during a high-latitude winter because we wanted experiences that were beyond market value. Enduring an extreme climate and absorbing a unique culture are experiences that cannot be purchased easily with hard cash. Sometimes you have to give blood.

Chapter Six

It's tempting to use
conventional wisdom as a crutch.

$\mathcal{N}$EARLY ALL THE SNOW that covered the town in early October melted by December. Weather fronts brought moist "warm" air from the south, and we basked in temperatures just above freezing.

As both the sun and the melting snow sank lower, the exposed brown mountains and bare streets in Akureyri reflected less ambient light. By 3:30 p.m., the daylight was gone, followed by 18 hours of darkness. It rained frequently. What little sunlight peeked over the mountains seemed like a wasted effort. The dark days of winter, a phenomenon we wanted to experience so much, descended on us like a wet, wool blanket.

In our quest to be independent of shore power, I had overlooked the fact that the long hours of darkness would require extensive use of our cabin lights. By late November, there wasn't enough natural light in the cabin to see anything, even at midday. Our 12-volt power consumption soared.

I engineered *Driver's* electrical system using 12-volt wiring and batteries. My aim was to keep it simple. To charge the batteries, we used a wind generator and solar panels, which were normally hooked up. We could also run the engine, but *Driver's* engine-driven alternator was not adequate for charging our deep-cycle batteries quickly. In fact, in order to recharge a completely "flat" battery, we would have had to run the engine for three days. We didn't want to listen to the noise for that long, nor did we want to waste the engine's life on the lame task of spinning an alternator.

Fortunately, we *had* made one wise decision. Our natural draft, diesel heating stove had a gravity-feed fuel supply, and it did not require one iota of electricity for its operation. Our cabin may have been dark, but it was warm and dry.

In the lower latitudes, our solar panels and our wind generator always provided ample power to recharge the batteries. The solar panels also worked well during the high-latitude summer because of the long days and the many hours of sunlight. By the end of October, however, the solar panels provided scant amperage. By mid-November, they were completely nonproductive. Sheltering the cockpit from snow became their only function.

The wind generator kept the batteries charged during the autumn gales, but by December, the gales were replaced by long periods of calm. Meanwhile, our two, 120-ampere batteries became discharged to the point of oblivion. To conserve power during the dark days, we relied on candles, two small kerosene lamps, and a solitary fluorescent light in the main cabin. Too bad we hadn't bought the big kerosene lamp before we left the States. Like mariners caught in the doldrums, we prayed for wind.

The inner basin was not protected from easterly winds, and earlier in the season I had voiced my concerns to Knútur. He and several others told us not to worry; the wind only blew from the east once every 10 years.

The day of the 10-year storm dawned like any other that week–with low clouds, drizzle, and dead calm. By lunch time, a stiff breeze was blowing. We were happy. The wind generator was in high gear, driven by the onslaught and telegraphing amps to the battery at a fantastic rate. We praised Mother Nature.

By the time the kids came home from school, a severe chop had developed, causing *Driver* to seesaw uncomfortably. Although we were being blown safely away from the pontoon, the docklines were coming up short, creating violent jerking motions. The wind increased. When it reached 50 knots, *Driver* started bouncing viciously. Jaja and I added extra docklines. Ten feet away from our bow, the rocky foreshore was deflecting spray high into the air.

The rain compressed the snow on the floating dock into four inches of ice. Walking on the pontoon was slippery in the best of conditions, but trying to move on top of a mini-glacier in storm-force winds was treacherous. I kept my footing by treading along the six-inch-wide dry strip at the edge of the pontoon. From *Driver*'s icy, pitching foredeck, Jaja let out the docklines. She was having problems of her own.

The parking lot at the top of the ramp to our dock was also a sheet of ice. When people drove up to see how the Americans were faring, their cars were blown sideways. The wind generator eventually became overloaded in the ferocious gusts, so I turned it off. We cursed Mother Nature.

The storm winds peaked at 60 knots. A constant barrage of stinging spray blew over the low breakwater, and the choppy harbor surge continued. The motion on *Driver* was grotesque, causing the kids to lay below in queasy despair. I also despaired when I wondered how well the pontoon was anchored to the bottom. I knew if the mooring chains parted, *Driver* would drift onto the rocks and would be pounded by the weight of the heavy dock.

I stood in the parking lot hugging a lamp pole, snapping photos with my waterproof camera. I had to shout to be heard by the people who slid by in their cars. Many of them invited us to their homes for the night. Unfortunately, it was too dangerous to transfer the kids off the boat. *Driver* was three feet away from the icy pontoon, heeled over by the wind and pitching. The docklines were as taut as steel rods. I couldn't get back aboard.

An hour later as the wind began to diminish, Jaja brought the kids to the companionway. During a lull, she handed them over the rail to me. I carried Chris to the parking lot and made him hold onto the lamp pole for dear life. Next came Holly. Then Teiga and Jaja. We left *Driver* and went to the library for a few hours until the wind and waves quieted down.

A few violent gusts gave us the bum's rush as we walked up the hill through town. The gray clouds hung low, but the worst of the storm had retreated, taking the rain with it. At the library, we drank coffee and watched a video. After the kids' stomachs settled, we ate dinner in a restaurant. Getting away from the wet, pitching boat is something every sailor dreams about while in a storm at sea. We were lucky to be tied to land so we could leave.

The next morning, the clear sky glowed pink, and the tops of the mountains revealed fresh snowfall. The wind on the fjord was dead calm. The batteries continued their determined decline, and I regretted not taking the time in the States to replace the engine's alternator, which was undersized. To replace the alternator in Iceland and to buy one more suited to our deep-cycle batteries represented a cash investment that bordered on insanity. Another financially debilitating idea was to replace the wind generator with one that could produce more amperage in a shorter period of time.

I grudgingly disconnected the batteries and one by one, pushed them in Teiga's stroller to the local Shell service station for charging. It was an easy solution, and at first my only concern was accidentally damaging the batteries in transit. By the second trip, I was anxious for a different reason; I did not like relying on outside help in a situation where we ought to have been self-sufficient.

There was one last solution. Tucked in our cabin was a portable, 1,000-watt gasoline generator that we had carried around the world on *Direction*. The machine was 10 years old and on its last legs. I had resisted using it to charge *Driver*'s batteries because I wanted to save it for operating power tools in an emergency. But now we were faced with dead batteries, and it seemed foolish to save the generator for "someday" when it could save the day right now. I disconnected the cables that ran to the lifeless solar panels and connected them to the portable generator. It took 18 hours of continuous running to charge one battery, but the charge lasted five days. We were back in business.

CHRIS AND HOLLY CAME HOME from school and excitedly told us about an Icelandic Christmas tradition that would be observed beginning on December 12th. It had something to do with shoes, they said. Intrigued, Jaja and I asked around and learned about a legend that had gripped the imaginations of Icelandic children for centuries.

During the winter solstice, 13 troll brothers roamed the Icelandic countryside. Their mother was very mean and never gave her sons enough to eat. Each winter, when the brothers could stand their hunger no longer, they raided distant farmhouses for food. The trolls were naughty and played pranks on the families from whom they stole. Each of the brothers had a specialty: There was a door slammer, a candle eater, a meat hooker, and a sausage stealer, to name a few. The worst troll was Stiffleg. He would jump on children while they slept and spit sour goat's milk in their faces. Winter was a dark time on the farms, and tales of these pranks brought terror to the hearts of children.

Cold and hungry, the brothers were trudging through a snowstorm one night when they were knocked flat by something that fell from the sky. When they shook the snow from their eyes they found a decorated sleigh with eight reindeer harnessed to it. In the sleigh was a sack loaded with toys and good things to eat. A little farther away, they found a big black boot sticking out of the snow. The boot was attached to a person's foot, and when the trolls dug him out, Santa Claus praised the brothers for rescuing him.

"Where am I?" Santa laughed. "I seem to have lost my way!"

"You are in Iceland," the brothers answered, "the Land of Fire and Ice. And what are you doing with that big bag of toys and treats? Have you been raiding the farmhouses, too? You are so big and fat you have probably left nothing for us!" The trolls told Santa how they stole food every year around the solstice and how, just for fun, they scared the children with pranks.

"I have taken nothing." Santa said. He was shocked to discover that children lived in such a desolate land. "This is Christmas Eve," he explained. "Every year on this night I surprise children with toys and candy. It's terrible that you lads go around stealing food and playing tricks."

The trolls argued that they were always hungry and that Santa was lucky because he obviously never lacked for a meal. "You are so jolly, you must have plenty to eat."

Santa was distressed that the trolls were causing children to suffer on Christmas Eve instead of helping the children to anticipate Christmas morning. He gave the trolls a large bag.

"The weather in this land makes it too dangerous for me to visit in the winter," Santa said. "Here is a magic sack that will fill itself with toys and treats each year. Rather than going to the farms to steal and play nasty tricks, you can give presents instead."

The trolls were skeptical, "Will the magic bag also fill our stomachs?"

"No," Santa declared. "But by giving instead of stealing, your hearts will be filled with joy. If you are happy, you will be able to acquire food without having to take it."

The trolls eventually agreed, and they decided they would go in turn to the farmhouses, one troll on each night, beginning 13 nights before Christmas. It was Santa's idea that they put the presents in the children's shoes, in memory of how the trolls had found him.

Happiness descended on the Land of Fire and Ice.

WITH THE CHRISTMAS SEASON came invitations for dinner. Soon, our social calendar snowballed. The townsfolk in Akureyri decided that since we had made it halfway through winter, we must be tenacious. We were well acquainted with hospitality in Akureyri, but we hadn't made much headway in the social scene.

The school had helped us tremendously by letting our kids enroll. Thóra, the head janitor at Brekkuskoli, saw Jaja's frozen laundry hanging stiffly in the breeze in September. She got permission from the headmaster for Jaja to use the school's washing machine and dryer free of charge. The port captain had also been kind. After accepting the fact that we were determined to live at the pontoon for the winter, he provided a wooden staircase that made it easier to get on and off *Driver*. At the library, we had access to videos, free coffee, the Internet, and books and magazines in English. We always received a warm smile whenever we entered.

Over time, we made friends with Adda and Gudni, the parents of Chris's classmate María. Both Chris and Holly spent hours after school playing with María and her younger brother Valur. Adda was a pharmacist, and following a pleasant Sunday meal at their house, I related the story of my hand to her.

After a series of blood tests to determine whether or not I had arthritis or any other disabling diseases, I was diagnosed in perfect health. My right hand, however, continued to contradict my privileged status. Arí's guess that my right index knuckle was infected with the bacteria called *Mycobacterium Marinum* was finally proven correct. The disease is a not-so-rare form of marine tuberculosis. It was a mistake on my part to douse my barnacle cuts with iodine–something I had always done to disinfect wounds. Iodine is a favorite food of the tuberculin, and they had thrived immediately, creating a ring of necrosis that shielded them from common antibiotics. Arí said he should operate on my hand to remove the necrosis ring so that drugs could work on the bacterium.

I placed a long-distance call to our good friend Buddy Floyd, a highly respected pharmacist in North Carolina. He consulted with his doctor friends and faxed us some medical data. The information matched the suggestions of Bjørn and Arí, so Jaja and I agreed to the operation without further concern. We were in a foreign land, and it was comforting to have support from a trustworthy friend back in the States.

Arí made a four-inch-long incision along my right index finger and knuckle, removed as much of the necrosis as possible, then sewed me up expertly. As my mind floated on a raft of Valium, I gazed at the theater of bright lights around me and at the sterile atmosphere. The operating room nurses moved silently doing this and that, and occasionally Arí would chat to me. It was a hypnotic and alien scene compared to the life I was accustomed to on the boat.

Adda listened to the recounting of my hospital experience with a professional ear.

"They say Arí is a superb surgeon."

I looked at the wicked scar on my hand. "He said in a year the incision will become invisible."

Friderik Yngvason, head of pulmonary medicine, took over my case, and he put me on the same drugs used to fight TB in human lungs. There were less severe antibiotics available, but we decided to go for the guaranteed cure. I did not want the infection to linger. I wondered if my hand infection was the reason that I tested positive for TB back in Reykjavík, but Friderik assured me that it was only a coincidence. I remembered faking a cough to the doctor and joking about going to a sanatorium. Now the joke was on me.

"Will your insurance in America cover anything?" Gudni asked.

"No. We don't have medical insurance. Nor do we have boat or life insurance. Most of the people we know think we're foolish gamblers to go without insurance, but we had a choice: Stay at home and work to support the insurance premiums or take a chance and see the world."

Our Icelandic friends, who were accustomed to their socialized medical system, were as bewildered as we were by the cost of insurance in the United States. To protect ourselves against medical costs, we have kept a reserve account over the years with a modest balance.

Bjørn billed me for the blood tests, but like Arí and Friderik, he refused to charge for his personal services. They all said they were interested in our nomadic lifestyle and that they wanted to help perpetuate our experience by donating their professional time. I paid the equivalent of just US$1,000 for the drugs, the blood tests, and the operating room expenses.

We also did not have maternity insurance, and all three of our kids were born C.O.D.–cash on delivery. During Chris's hospital birth in Australia, the nurses knew we were paying out of pocket, and they geared their procedures to inflict the least financial pain. We paid less than $300. In New Zealand, the midwife who delivered Holly in the back bedroom at our friend's house was also sympathetic to our lifestyle. She engineered a birth that cost next to nothing.

Jaja was four months pregnant with Teiga when we returned to the States on *Direction*. We knew a birth in our home country might be pricey, but the cost was not the first shock. A well-respected doctor opened our eyes to the real "costs" of medical care, U.S. style.

"Hello," Jaja said to the O.B. during a consultation. "I'm pregnant."

"Who's your previous doctor?" he asked.

"I don't have a doctor. This is my first visit. We've been traveling and..."

The doctor interrupted. "So at this point, what you're telling me is you have an unconfirmed pregnancy?"

Jaja laughed. "My husband and I have two children. I think I recognize the symptoms."

The doctor waved his hand in the air impatiently. "Without a record of your prenatal history, I cannot examine you."

"Why?"

"Because, you are uninsured. You also haven't seen a doctor yet. I cannot discount the possibility of previous substance abuses that might cause birth defects. My insurance company would never accept the risk."

I was sitting in the office with Jaja, hugging Chris and Holly who were the essence of health and vitality.

"So," Jaja clarified, "you won't provide prenatal care because I'm already pregnant."

"That about sums it up."

After settling down for the winter aboard *Direction* at a marina in Oriental, we discovered some odd North Carolina laws. Home births with a midwife were illegal, but an "unattended" birth at home was acceptable. Holly's home birth in New Zealand was a joy, and it fueled our desire to have the same experience when Teiga arrived. We contemplated flying back to New Zealand to have the baby because even with airfare, it would be cheaper than paying for a birth at the hospital in North Carolina. The decision to deliver Teiga ourselves aboard *Direction* came to us slowly, but naturally.

We did have the money to pay for a hospital birth in the States, but dollar cost was not foremost. The hospital was run according to the old school, and we disagreed with its inflexible procedures. Jaja didn't want some slick doctor treating her like an invalid. We had just spent seven years sailing around the world, relying heavily on ourselves. We were attuned to our inner voices. We had faith in our instincts.

By choosing to deliver Teiga ourselves, we felt as if we were leaving shore for an extended ocean voyage. Out of sight of land, the worry of a medical emergency is omnipresent, but it had never stopped us–or countless others–from putting to sea. In the past, when we took complete responsibility for our actions, events were more apt to go our way. In Oriental, we were 45 minutes from the hospital by car. Compared to crossing an ocean and being weeks away from land, we had a viable safety net. In a strange way, the close proximity of the hospital undermined our confidence instead of increasing it.

We kept our intentions secret and told only a few individuals who might be able to help us; we did not need do-gooders stomping down the dock and interfering with a decision that had no relevance to their lives. We confided in our friend Linda, who was studying midwifery. Through her, we discovered a midwife network that proved we weren't alone. The "network" lent us textbooks, a fetal scope, a sphygmomanometer, cord clamps, sterile dressings, and herbal concoctions for hemorrhaging. Jaja had delivered both Holly and Chris without any form of painkillers, so that aspect did not worry her. We studied the books, made notes, and asked questions. We were apprehensive, but our course was set, and there was no turning back.

On a cold, foggy morning in late January, Teiga opened her eyes for the first time under *Direction*'s dim cabin lights. Chris and Holly stood silently and watched with wonder at the new life tugging on Jaja's breast. When the time was right, Holly cut the umbilical cord with our sterile scissors. Teiga Calypso was free at last.

Later that same morning, we carried our four-hour-old daughter down the dock to the Whittaker Creek chandlery to show her off to our friends. Thinking the boat-birth had been an "accident," everyone urged Jaja to go to the hospital at once. But there was no reason for it. Both Mom and Baby were doing fine. Using a hand-held fish scale and her baby blanket as a "net," we weighed Teiga. A whopping 11 pounds. She was a keeper.

CHRIS, HOLLY, AND TEIGA WERE ECSTATIC to learn that there were 13 Santas who left gifts for children in Iceland. Jaja and I reflected that the tradition would make any American retailer jealous. Beginning on the 12th night of December, Icelandic children put one of their shoes on a windowsill before going to bed in anticipation of the trolls who would come bearing gifts. Aboard *Driver*, we modified the tradition slightly and encouraged our kids to put one of their boots in the dodger. It worked! They awoke on the morning of the 13th and found a small present wedged inside each boot. Using a flashlight, they looked for footprints in the freshly fallen snow.

"He wasn't here that long ago," Chris observed. "His tracks on the pontoon are still fresh!"

I winked at Jaja.

Chris, Holly, and Teiga were very careful during the 13 days prior to Christmas. They had heard that naughty children often received rocks or rotten potatoes from the mischievous trolls. Jaja and I approved of any tradition that inspired good behavior in children.

Up at the school, the students and parents assembled to make Christmas crafts. Each classroom had a different project. After buying the necessary components at the door, we went into the rooms and taped, glued, cut, sponged, colored, folded, and licked. We made angels using Styrofoam balls and paper cones, we decorated sugar cookies, we made colorful Christmas cards with construction paper, but best of all, we made an advent candle display. Chris, Holly, and Teiga each filled a red ceramic flower pot with clay, garnished it with very dry pine branches, then adorned it with dried berries, fake mushrooms, and a small wooden star. A tall, thin, purple-and-gold candle was stuck in the middle of it all. It was the most marvelous fire hazard I had ever seen, and every kid in school was walking around with one.

Every year at Christmas, we debated having a real Christmas tree. And every year we decided that putting a tree on a boat was highly impractical. During our years on *Direction*, we put Christmas presents on the cabin sole in front of the kerosene stove. We usually hung a few ornaments around the cabin, but we didn't go overboard on decorations. When we arrived back in the States after our circumnavigation, we took Chris and Holly to see Santa Claus at a store in New Bern, North Carolina. When Saint Nick asked Holly what she wanted for Christmas, she answered, "a real Christmas tree with lights." I could see tears welling up in Jaja's eyes.

We celebrated our first Christmas aboard *Driver* at anchor in Stuart, Florida. Inside *Driver*'s cabin, the steel compression post that supports the mast had "Christmas tree potential" written all over it. That year we decorated the "Pole" with colorful paper. For our Icelandic Christmas, we wanted more authenticity, so we priced real Christmas trees at a lot in town. Three-footers, imported from Denmark, cost the equivalent of US$120. Cut branches were $5 a foot, and loose pine needles were priced by the gram. In nearly treeless Iceland, we were careful not to get our kids excited about having a real tree. Fortunately, they accepted our decision not to buy one as *status quo*.

In our rented house in Oriental, we bought a genuine Christmas tree, one that touched the ceiling in the living room. We adorned it with so much tinsel and so many lights and ornaments that the tree could have been fake because you couldn't see it anyway. It smelled good, though.

Gently falling snow accompanied us from Akureyri's downtown tree lot to Blómval, an indoor garden center that sold Christmas decorations. Fake trees were tempting, but the cost was also ridiculous. The kids were begging for lights, but without shore power, there was no way to electrify them on board. A 10-foot-long piece of plastic pine garland that looked real from two paces was the answer. We wound it up the Pole in a spiral. Inside *Driver*'s dark cabin, the garland looked real from two inches away. We decorated the garland using wooden carvings we had collected over the years. The kids were ecstatic. The down side was that anyone who brushed past–which was about every 30 seconds–knocked ornaments off the "tree" onto the cabin sole. The best part of the tree illusion was that 2 1/2-year-old Teiga couldn't knock it over.

After the Pole was decorated, the kids lit their incendiary candle displays, and the extra candlepower drove the nearly perpetual night from the cabin. With the fluorescent light turned off to save power and with Christmas music playing on the tape deck, *Driver* become a force in the night, a bubble of warmth and good feeling on an otherwise cold and dark fjord.

Chris and Holly had given the 13 Santas some deep thought. "If the real Santa doesn't come to Iceland because of the weather, does that mean we aren't going to get any presents on Christmas morning?"

"Bad weather was a problem that Santa faced many, many, years ago," I said. "He has GPS now."

A look of relief spread across their faces.

ADDA INVITED US FOR DINNER a few days before Christmas, and Gudni provided a lamb raised on his father's farm. Leg of lamb was the most conventional body part on display, but the most recognizable was certainly the sheep's head. It was boiled in hot water, split in two, and its teeth gleamed in the candlelight. Adda had only permitted the sheep's head into the house for our benefit. She thought it was crucial to our "Icelandic experience" to try everything. Otherwise, if Gudni craved sheep's head, he had to travel to his parents' farm in Grenavík to eat it.

Another dish contained a marbled looking pâté that our hosts tried to pass off as *pâté de fois gras,* but we knew darn well it was ram's testicles. The other platter on the table contained a smoked sheep roast called *hangikjøt,* or hanging meat. We had eaten it before, but Gudni's roast had been home-smoked by his father in the traditional way. It was delicious. The flavor of the meat entered our sinuses, swirled in our heads for a while, and conjured images of turf huts, Viking warriors, and dark stormy nights. The smoked meat was boiled first, then eaten cold with pickled purple cabbage. Something we did not know until *after* dinner was that traditional hangikjøt is smoked using dried sheep's dung. Gudni facetiously apologized for omitting that minor detail.

The leg of lamb was barbecued on a spit over a charcoal fire. With cups of strong coffee in our hands, Gudni and I stood out in the snow on the front porch turning the lamb and filling our lungs with the succulent aromas. We snacked on the smoked salmon and dried fish that we brought from Gudrún's and Einar's workshop at Flateyri, while Chris, Holly, and Teiga ran wild with María and Valur. At the table, Jaja and I tried the sheep's head and the ram-testicle pâté, receiving applause with every mouthful we braved. Adda's 13-year-old niece Elva ate half a sheep's head on her own. Even she wouldn't touch the pâté.

To thank Adda and Gudni for an enjoyable evening, we wrote a saga for them in the Icelandic tradition:

> *We came to Iceland for six weeks,*
> *But stayed on through the seasons.*
> *Out on the street a local seeks*
> *Our motives and our reasons.*

> *The northern lights, the long dark nights,*
> *The snow and isolation.*
> *The puffin's plume, their awkward flight,*
> *The molten conflagration.*

> *"My gosh!" our new friends said. "That's great!*
> *But next you'll have to try,*
> *The food that one and all once ate,*
> *We'll promise you won't die."*

> *The lamb, the veg, the fish we tried,*
> *We emptied all the bowls.*
> *"But wait!" our host said, then he cried,*
> *"Bring out those testicles!"*

> *The dung-smoked lamb, the singed sheep skulls,*
> *We liked most every bit.*
> *But then we ate those testicles*
> *And groaned: "These taste like shit!"*

ON CHRISTMAS MORNING, Chris, Holly, and Teiga whispered quietly together. They wondered if Santa had found his way to *Driver*, and they dared each other to turn on a flashlight and look under the Pole for presents. Jaja and I lay in the dark listening, holding each other silently and pretending to be asleep. Our own childhood memories came to mind. The feeling of joy on Christmas morning had stayed with us through the years.

What would our kids remember? Our Icelandic Christmas? The dark morning, with fresh-fallen snow covering the hatches and cabin windows? Or maybe they would recall our Christmas in northern Australia aboard *Direction*. We awoke to a bright, hot and breathless, 90-degree-Fahrenheit morning, then spent the whole day swimming in a billibong, the Aussie word for swimming hole. Maybe they would remember snatches of our conventional "house Christmas" in the States–the big tree, relatives, and plenty of lights.

For Jaja and me, wondering *where* we were going to be at Christmas was similar to our kids' anticipation of *what* they would receive. Would we be on the boat? In a house? In the Tropics? We shook the contents of our imagination, trying to speculate on the intricacies that might shape our future Christmas seasons. It was just as well we didn't know what the fates had in store for us the following Christmas.

We pulled the covers over our heads and whispered sentimental thoughts to each other. Without warning, six elbows and six knees suddenly attacked us. Chris, Holly, and Teiga giggled excitedly.

"We knew you were awake!"

A FEW DAYS BEFORE WINTER VACATION, the headmaster of Brekkuskoli came to *Driver* for a visit. Bjørn wished us a Merry Christmas, said he hoped that the school year wasn't too trying for our kids, and then fished a key from his pocket.

"This is to the school's back door. During the holidays, it would please me and my staff if your family would go to the school whenever you wish. Let your children run free in the halls. You may use the kitchen, and we have set up a television and video player in the day-care room. It you want to, you may bring your sleeping bags and live at the school. It's up to you. And of course, you may continue to use the washer and dryer."

It was never the intention of an altruistic individual such as the headmaster to make us feel guilty. But we often felt embarrassed when we were offered such unrestrained kindness because we were seldom in a position to reciprocate on equal terms. Refusing offers of help bordered on being ungrateful, yet always saying yes made us feel selfish. In each situation, we tried to give whatever we could of ourselves, even if it was only friendship. We tried to remember that one day we might be able to bestow kindness on others in turn, and that would help keep the gates of goodwill unlocked.

We accepted the key.

The week following Christmas was "favored" by frequent onslaughts of sleet and wet snow. The temperature hovered a fraction of a degree above freezing. Damp air from the south hung over the fjord in a gray pall, and the five hours of daylight did little to brighten the scene. We spent our mornings at the school. We rented videos from the library, horsed around in the day-care room, and encouraged our kids to run up and down the school halls and scream and yell to their hearts' content.

Chris frowned. "Running isn't any fun if you're *allowed* to do it."

Most afternoons we walked the short distance to the swimming pool to soak in hot water. Some evenings, we had invitations to dinner, but every night we returned to *Driver*'s welcoming cocoon. People could not under-stand why we preferred sleeping on our boat when we could have slept at the school. *Driver* was our home, the kids' home; there was nothing better than sleeping in our own bunks. That way, we woke to familiar routines, familiar sights, and the day began predictably.

Most Icelanders had difficulty accepting our pronouncement that *Driver* was our only residence. They could not believe that we did not have a house sitting empty somewhere awaiting our return. Everyone thought we were on an extended camping trip, that at the end of a predetermined amount of time we would go back to where we came from and fall back into a landbound rou-tine. But *Driver* was our mold, a pointed steel box that shaped our lifestyle and aimed us skyward like a rocket. We were out to see the world with as few ties as possible. We liked it that way.

Our long-winded oration on why we chose to live on a boat was often met with disbelief. Why did we want to live on a cold boat? We invited locals aboard frequently to show them how comfortable our home really was. From the outside, *Driver* was caked with ice and snow and looked like an iceberg with a mast. Belowdecks, our miniature abode was complete in every way. When people stepped into the cabin for the first time, they all said the same thing.

"Hey! It's warm in here!"

ON DECEMBER 31st, KNÚTUR HELD his annual New Year's Eve party. His wife, Gógó, made a cauldron of fish stew, and friends and family brought cakes and cookies. There was a hot spiced wine drink called glögg plus plenty of beer and coffee. For the kids, there was candy, soda, fruit, ice cream, and real hot chocolate. Jaja baked a batch of pecan sugar cookies, and we brought Gógó a bouquet of flowers.

At 8:00 p.m., after sumptuous eating, we drove from Knútur's house to the edge of town, then tramped with our kids through a foot of slush–along with throngs of other alcohol-impaired parents–to watch the annual fire-works. With long hours of darkness, New Year's Eve provided a fine chance to celebrate. The Red Cross rescue organization sells fireworks to the public and also orchestrates the big fireworks displays in the towns. Several days before the New Year, pyrotechnics went on sale at the rescue center. The booms and whistles, plus the shoosh of rockets, began filling the air. Kids ran around wearing hats, gloves, and heavy coats trying their darnedest to destroy the world. It was a winter version of America's Independence Day.

As a child in the States, I remember running with my barefoot friends on July 4th in the warm twilight of summer vacation. None of us had any money, but we always managed to acquire bottle rockets, Piccolo Petes, and a book of paper matches. Parents warned us not to put out an eye, neighbors complained that we were scaring their dogs, and we all dared each other into acts of foolishness.

One of the dumbest things I did on the 4th was to take a dozen rolls of red cap-gun caps and cut the unraveled strips into single squares. Each red square had a blister of gunpowder on it. Using nearly half of a roll of masking tape, I shaped the hundred or so squares into a crude round bomb, about the size of a golf ball. I recall kneeling on my driveway, with my homemade bomb in front of me and pounding it as hard as I could with my father's claw hammer. I walked around the rest of that day saying, *"Huh?"*

At 10:30 on New Year's Eve, Icelandic TV broadcasts a one-hour show satirizing the year's political and social events. Since we could not understand the show, we said farewell to Knútur's family and departed. Although someone offered us a lift, we preferred to walk.

We inhaled the fresh air of a 20-degree polar night. The roadside slush, which had melted in large rivulets during the early evening, was frozen solid making it easy for all five of us to slide down the hills toward the waterfront.

The town was deathly quiet. We were the only people in sight. No cars were moving, and even the cacophony of fireworks that had continued in Akureyri for the past three days ceased temporarily. As we walked, we could see the blue glow from television screens lighting dark living rooms. We could imagine families gathered around, watching the yearly program that they scorned in public but clearly enjoyed in private.

At 11:30, the town came back to life. We sat on *Driver*, looking up the hillside toward town, waiting for the last and most exciting phase of New Year's.

The fireworks sold by the Red Cross in Iceland would make the officials in any American city look for a bomb shelter. "Safe and sane" is not a phrase that describes Iceland's import "restrictions" on Chinese pyrotechnics. Soup-can-size rockets glued to five-foot-long wooden sticks were popular, as were large cardboard boxes loaded with self-firing continuous-barrage-style explosives. The fireworks were expensive, but Iceland is a wealthy nation, and its citizens enjoy a night of fun. If you knew the right people at the Red Cross, you could get your hands on the fairground-quality stuff. The town display at 8:00 was impressive, but our friends told us to wait until midnight when the private arsenals were unleashed.

At 11:45, the tempo accelerated as larger and larger rockets hit the skies. The government requires that all commercial vessels replace their emergency parachute flares annually, so fishermen use New Year's as an opportunity to fire their out-of-date ones. Parachute flares were going off steadily all day, drifting slowly earthward, but by 10 minutes to midnight, we counted at least 40 in the air at any given moment. Only a fool would put to sea on New Year's Eve. With so many "distress" flares being set off, no one could possibly discern a real emergency.

We had six out-of-date parachute flares of our own that we had bought from a cruise ship four years earlier. We fired the oldest to see if it still worked. It whooshed up. Then like magic, the flare ignited, the little parachute popped out, and we watched it float back to earth. It was still burning when it landed in the harbor just three feet from Knútur's boat.

At five minutes to midnight, the entire town was ablaze with flashes, booms, and soaring rockets. People were launching them from gardens, street corners, rooftops, and verandas. The largest rockets went up at midnight, making the first moments of January look like a night on the Western Front. On the other side of the fjord, a team of volunteers stuck hundreds of hand flares in the snow to form the numbers 1998. At precisely midnight, the volunteers changed the eight to a nine. The digits 1999 burned on the hillside for a quarter of an hour.

From the harbor, we had a splendid view of everything. The choking smell of gunpowder hung in the air, and residual smoke hung like fog over the windless fjord. Pieces of blown-to-bits paper fluttered like snow, burning parachute flares got hung up in trees and on rooftops, and the now powerless wooden rocket sticks fell without purpose, stabbing the snow like dull knives. By 12:15, the show was over. Except for the odd, small rocket and the red glow of lingering parachute flares, peace was restored.

Holly, Chris and Teiga had sat on deck, clapping and yelling excitedly over the din. Holly was beside herself with joy.

"This is the best night of my life!"

Chapter Seven

If you want hometown prices,
you should stay home.

*T*HE EUPHORIA OF New Year's Eve faded, and the bleak days of January followed one another with gray monotony. Chris and Holly went to school every day, their breath billowing in front of them. Besides walking them to school and meeting them at the end of the day, Jaja marched up the hill three times a week with the laundry bag on one arm and Teiga on the other. She thrived on the exercise. We shopped for food, used the Box to fill our water tanks, checked the new post office for mail, visited the library, swam laps in the heated outdoor pool, battled the Icelandic language, and waited for the sun to return.

The steady attack of chilly air and the cold ocean currents gradually lowered the water temperature in the fjord. During calm weather, the end of the fjord where we were berthed froze. Most of the time we liked the ice because it prevented small, choppy waves from infiltrating the inner basin. The only motion we felt onboard was created by the wind. Gusts would nudge *Driver*'s mast, making her tip slightly.

Unfortunately, the harbor ice came and went frequently–broken by strong northerly winds that sent waves surging down the long arm of the fjord. Sometimes a big slab of ice in the inner basin would break loose from the shoreline. This was the worst scenario for us. The piece could be as large as 200 feet in circumference and four inches thick–a veritable battering ram. We worried that the ice would damage our rudder. Sometimes, it would push into *Driver* with such force that it wedged itself beneath the hull where we could hear it scraping close to the propeller. Luckily, these slabs always seemed to snap off before inflicting any damage. We were relieved that our boat was built of steel.

If wind-driven waves didn't do the job, the rising and falling tide would eventually cause the ice in the basin to self-destruct on the rocky foreshore. After the rocks whittled down the ice slab, the tide would carry it through the opening between the breakwater and the wharf. Then the wind would suck it into the fjord. Good riddance. After each slab departed, the inner basin was frequently ice-free for several days.

The next type of problem would occur when the cold, northerly winds shifted back to the prevailing southerlies. The warmer, south winds would push the broken ice chunks back into the basin where they banged against our hull menacingly. The first time this happened, we lay awake all night worrying. We soon realized, however, that the small ice chunks weren't threatening the integrity of the hull–only our nerves.

The surface of the fjord outside the basin didn't freeze until January. This delay was due in part to the temperature of the fresh water that is discharged from the city. Iceland is an active, geothermic island. Its volcanoes, warm springs, and other hot spots belie the country's icy name. Akureyri is heated by 200-degree-Fahrenheit water that is piped from an inland hot spring. It trickles continually through radiators inside homes, stores, and offices. When it leaves the buildings, most of the water runs through storm drains into the harbor. In the city center, the sidewalks and pavement in the main square don't freeze because the water discharged from the buildings runs through an elaborate system of underground tubing. Piped warm water even keeps the 110 church steps free of ice.

Icelanders considered themselves very lucky to have this rich, nonpolluting, natural resource. And the hot water was cheap. Knútur heated his modest-size home for less than it cost us to heat *Driver*.

AFTER THE CHRISTMAS BREAK, Jaja and I hiked up the dry steps to return the key to the school and to thank Bjørn the headmaster profusely for allowing us to use the facilities. While chatting in the hallway, we complimented Bjørn on the unique and successful way the school operated.

Every child and adult entering the school removed his shoes and boots at the entrance and placed them on shoe racks. In the halls, most kids wore socks, but some wore indoor shoes. Even on the rainiest, muddiest days, the floors remained dry and shiny, the classrooms clean. Only during school assemblies, when entire families were at the school, did the system become overloaded. Then, understandably, the entrance foyer became swamped with thousands of shoes. Long traffic jams occurred during departures as everyone balanced expertly on one foot, slipping on boots or doing laces.

Five janitors, who doubled as hall monitors, kept the 250 students circulating during school hours. One of the monitors stood at the main doors in the morning and greeted each child by name. The others roamed the halls helping kids out of one-piece snowsuits and into line by their classroom doors. Recess was pandemonium as hundreds of kids squirmed wormlike on the floor, putting on their suits and boots.

On snowy days, a monitor stood at the door with a long-handled broom to sweep the snow off the kids as they entered. Chris called them the "child brushers." The hall monitors also knew who owned each hat and pair of gloves. If a student lost an article of outdoor clothing, it was returned promptly. One day in November, Chris came in from recess muddy from head to toe. The head janitor, Thóra, knew that it would be difficult for us to clean Chris's snowsuit on *Driver*, so she washed and dried the suit while Chris attended class. The hall monitors are highly respected in the community.

On the last day of Christmas break, Holly decided to continue attending Brekkuskoli. It had been touch and go. Although Jaja would not have minded home-schooling Holly, we were happy that she wanted to be with her friends and to persevere with learning the Icelandic language. Instead of learning American history and U.S. current events, our kids were learning about, and adapting to, a different culture. We felt the experiences our children were gaining outweighed what they might be missing.

After school on Tuesdays, Chris and Holly took art classes. On Thursdays, they went to music school. Other days, they were invited to play at friends' houses, or we had their friends aboard *Driver*. Our dark cabin quickly became overcrowded with two or three extra bodies and snowy clothes, but the laughter and the sense of adventure that our young visitors experienced always made it worthwhile.

By January, Holly and Chris had learned enough Icelandic to get by, and their friends knew enough English so that the children could speak a sort of "Ice-English." Jaja and I, on the other hand, suffered trying to learn Icelandic. We had placed Chris and Holly in a difficult situation, and they came through with flying colors. When all the kids in *Driver*'s cabin laughed hilariously at some joke in Icelandic, Jaja and I hoped they weren't laughing at us.

Holly had fun showing our collection of English-language children's books to her friends. Adda's and Gudni's daughter María was the most interested. She and Holly sat together for hours reading aloud from beginners' books, such as *One Fish, Two Fish* by Doctor Seuss. María practiced the odd sounds, giggling over the silly rhymes and the funny words.

"*Bump! Bump! Bump!*
Did you ever ride a wump?
We have a wump with just one hump."

We gave the book to María as a gift, and she took it home, eager to learn. One day when Jaja and I went to Adda's and Gudni's for coffee, Adda picked up *One Fish, Two Fish*, which was lying on their kitchen table.

"Thank you for giving the book to María. It has really helped her reading."

"It's our pleasure." Jaja took a sip of coffee and smiled. "Holly and María have had great fun with that book."

"Yes, they have. Do you mind if I ask you a question, though? I've searched in my two Icelandic-English dictionaries, and I have gone crazy trying to locate a word. What's a *wump*?"

Jaja tried to stop grinning long enough to explain, but she was saved by a knock at the front door. When Adda came back she had an exasperated look on her face.

"It was someone from the girls' club again," Adda said. "Tell me, in America, they only sell cookies and candy door to door, right?"

"Yes," Jaja said. "Usually. Do they do the same thing here?"

"Not lately," Adda laughed. "Now they're selling toilet paper to raise money. That's the third one to come by today."

Jaja started giggling again. "Toilet paper! What a strange thing to sell door to door. I guess it's practical." We looked out the window and saw a small girl hefting a ridiculously large sack over her shoulder.

We filed the incident in our minds under "cultural oddities," then forgot about it for the moment.

IN REYKJAVÍK, we became well acquainted with the dreaded exchange rate–the illusive percentage that always seemed to reduce the buying power of our currency instead of increasing it. During our first weeks in the Land of Fire and Ice, Jaja and I roamed the supermarket aisles amazed at the prices. When we found a particularly expensive item by U.S. standards, we would exclaim and hold it high in the air. Price awareness was our form of cheap thrills.

"Jaja, look at this! A two-pound frozen chicken: The equivalent of US$12!"

"Dave, check it out! One gallon of milk: $6."

A dozen eggs: $4. Sliced bread: $3.50. Iceberg lettuce: $3 a head.

To add insult to injury, stores charged heavily for each plastic bag, then made you pack your own groceries. Before paying, the smiling cashier would ask how many bags you wanted.

One afternoon in Reykjavík, I got in trouble with Jaja over one of my private, cheap thrills. I wheeled our shopping cart up to the prettiest Icelandic cashier. When she asked the inevitable question, "How many bags do you want?" I smiled coyly. I answered the question using the only Icelandic word I could remember.

"Sex please?"

"Sure."

"Thanks!"

Before we left Florida, we stocked *Driver* with as much food as we could carry. When Sir Francis Chichester sailed *Gypsy Moth* around the world in the 1960s, he devised a good system for provisioning. He kept track of everything he ate during his summer shakedown cruise. When he provisioned for his circumnavigation, he used extrapolation to determine how much food to bring for his yearlong voyage. Our provisioning technique aboard *Driver* was much less exact, but still quite effective. We kept track of how much money we spent. When it was gone, we stopped buying food.

After shopping in a few Icelandic grocery stores, we became bewildered by the cost of basic living. How did people manage? From a financial point of view, we questioned the sanity of wintering over. Compared to the cost of food in the States, we could expect to spend three, even four, times as much per month. But we couldn't forego the once-in-a-lifetime opportunity to winter in Iceland just for the sake of balancing our budget.

Fortunately, we discovered that eating cheaply in Iceland was possible; it just took a little work. Rice, pasta, and potatoes provided the base for nearly every meal on *Driver*. Using canned staples such as tomatoes, condensed soups, water chestnuts, olives, tuna, and various canned or dried vegetables, we created easy and relatively inexpensive one-pot stews. Adding long-lasting freshies such as onions, garlic, or cabbage provided natural vitamins. We took multivitamin tablets when vegetables were in short supply.

Jaja despised the old-time cruisers' standby, canned corned beef. She argued that factories producing the canned meat used one recipe and two labels–one label for people, another for pets. When we first began cruising together on *Direction,* Jaja made derogatory barking sounds whenever I fished out a can of corned beef from a food locker.

But canned corned beef is a symbol of my youth, and Jaja usually allows one or two cans aboard for sentimental reasons. There is something about that trapezoidal lump of animal composite (and the cheap little key glued to the bottom of the can) that reminds me of the time when my goal was to absorb protein with as little fuss as possible. In my bachelor days, I ate canned corned beef cold with a spoon. At sea on *Driver*, we get protein from nuts and fish. I don't care for dried beans and lentils.

When we rebuilt *Driver*'s interior, we choose not to install refrigeration–not even a simple icebox. An icebox or a freezer allows you to improve and vary your diet at sea and in remote anchorages. On a small boat, however, an icebox devours valuable space that we feel is better used for storing water as well as canned and packaged food. In addition, you can lose hundreds of dollars of perishables if your refrigeration fails. We have learned to lead a well-adjusted existence without suffering ice addiction or refrigeration mania.

In the high latitudes where the seawater is cold, the bilge worked well as a refrigerator. Meat lasted for days. We also kept fresh milk, butter, and vegetables cool under the floorboards. When cruising in warm waters near stores, we could usually keep frozen meat overnight if we wrapped it in our diver's wetsuit for insulation. Margarine could last months in a warm locker, although some brands separate. On *Direction*, Chris and Holly were raised on margarine and powdered milk. The first time they tasted real milk and real butter, they thought the flavors were odd.

Sampling food and drink from around the world is one of the pleasures of cruising. Some of our favorite foods are dried fruits from South Africa, canned tuna from the Cape Verde Islands, powdered milk from New Zealand, fresh fruit from Indonesia, Bundaberg ginger beer from Australia, and Mount Gay rum from Barbados. In Iceland, we added smoked lamb to the list.

THE CONTRAST BETWEEN THE COLD temperatures on deck and the warm air in the cabin caused condensation to form aboard *Driver*. We had kept the insulation that was in place when we bought the boat. The cabin walls and overhead are insulated with one-inch-thick Styrofoam covered by quarter-inch plywood. In Iceland, the foam kept the cold out of the cabin, but heavy condensation formed in the air space between the foam and the steel hull. This condensation ran down the inside of the hull, and about three quarts of fresh water per day collected in the bilge. We used a small hand-pump to extract the accumulation.

When I rebuilt the cabin in Oriental, I was aware that the steel hull might "sweat." I took pains to design the interior so that it would channel condensation along the inside of the hull unimpeded into the bilge. The interior was intended to act as a "roof" over the cabin so that condensation was deflected and didn't drip on our heads or ruin our belongings. I paid extra attention to the quarterberths, which are located under the cockpit in the stern part of the cabin. Quarterberths are often the wettest places on a boat because they are the farthest away from the drying heat of the stove.

To help prevent condensation from forming on our cabin windows, I created a two-inch air space between two panes of Lexan. No matter what the temperature difference between the outside and the inside of the boat, the windows never fogged or sweated. I applied the same theory to the deck hatches that have alloy metal frames, which are prime candidates for condensation. I taped clear plastic sheeting under the hatches in the cabin using double-sided sailmaker's tape. This created an air space under the hatches.

We were happy to see that snow on the outside of the hatches and windows did not melt.

The worst condensation occurred when the outside temperature hovered just above freezing. Miraculously, we were only bothered by two predictable condensation leaks in our living space. One of the drips fell with guided precision into the speaker of our single-sideband (SSB) radio. The other landed in the middle of Jaja's pillow. I dangled strips of cotton cloth under these drips. The cloth absorbed the moisture, which later evaporated.

When the temperature on deck went below 15 degrees Fahrenheit, the condensation between the foam and the hull froze. Inevitably, warm fronts would arrive, sending temperatures soaring overnight to the 30s. Then, even our carefully designed, "water-shedding" interior could not keep up. The sudden thaw would send a torrent of melted condensation through the cabin. Drips fell like rain in our living space, giving the illusion that the deck was full of holes. Only the drying ability of our diesel stove prevented our cushions and bedding from becoming saturated sponges. However, our books and electronics did suffer from the deluge, forcing us to protect them with towels for about 12 hours until each torrent ended.

By February, the warm fronts that brought moist air from the southern latitudes were history. The outside air temperature remained in the teens and 20s. At sea level, our world became white and solid, creating beautiful Arctic marine scenery. *Driver* was trapped in eight-inch-thick ice. Even though our cabin temperature remained at 68, the temperature in the bilge fell below freezing, causing the accumulated condensation to freeze.

Snow fell nearly every day, and the sound of snowplows scraping the roads became as familiar as the sound of wind humming in *Driver*'s rigging. We longed for a sunny day in the 50-degree range. We recalled fondly the first sun soaked weeks in Reykjavík. All five of us came down with cabin fever.

As THE SEASON ADVANCED, the sun returned to the pallid skies. A two-hour glimpse of the sun in January quickly became four hours long in February. Each morning, the sun rose earlier. By March, direct sunlight lit the town for most of the day. Temperatures continued to hover in the teens with regular snowfall, but even the indirect sunlight had a new intensity to it.

Clinical depression has long been associated with cloud cover and high-latitude winters. Contrary to rationale, however, the most debilitating levels of depression were shown to affect the people who are prone to it after the sun returns–not during the time when it is gone.

In a way this makes sense. Without the sun illuminating the skies and brightening our cabin, we began to enjoy living under the cover of darkness.

With the cabin in shadow, we weren't obliged to clean it as often or as thoroughly, because we couldn't see the dirt and grime. When we went outside, we didn't feel it was necessary to wear clean clothes or comb our hair because no one could see us anyway. With the darkness, we felt comfortable lounging on the boat or at the pool in the middle of the day. We were complacent and went to bed early. On weekends, we got up at noon, when the light was brightest. Adjusting to the impending gloom in November was difficult, even depressing. By December, we had adjusted to the dark like any Icelander. We went into a cozy hibernation.

As the sun began to reemerge, our circadian rhythms tasted the sweet thrill of natural light and called for more. Like searching the horizon for a point of land after a long ocean passage, we became fixated on the spring equinox–*willing* it to arrive. We grew more and more impatient for sunlight.

Getting the kids out of bed by candlelight and marching them up the hill in the dark to school became a less-than-festive event. My choice of music reflected my longing for the joys of sunny youth. I played 1970s rock-and-roll on our tape deck; the rhythms conjured up memories of my teenage years.

Jaja dreamed of sunlight–tropical hues of yellow and green. In her dreams, she lay under leafy trees, staring at shafts of sunlight filtering down. The kids talked about our previous winter in the Bahamas and about our other low-latitude adventures. We probed our psyches during the dark months and found rewards and fulfillment from within. With the returning light, we sought outward fulfillment. Our cabin fever "broke," and we were ready to join the world again.

When a ray of sunlight first pierced *Driver*'s windows during a blue afternoon in March, the cabin seemed like a hostile and primitive land that we were seeing for the first time. We noticed that the hard-to-clean corners were crammed with muck; the white vinyl overhead was black with candle soot; our burgundy-colored cushion covers were soiled and picked. On deck, a winter's accumulation of automobile and truck exhaust left a black film, and the discharge of fluids from fishing trawlers in the harbor left the waterline of our hull greasy. Instead of tuning out the dirt and grime, we were inspired by the sun. Spring cleaning fever gripped us. We scrubbed and polished.

Gone were the days when we could hide under the cover of darkness. When the predawn glow began nudging our cabin at the relatively early hour of 7:00 a.m., we felt we were wasting the day if we stayed in bed. In town, we felt exposed, open to public scrutiny. Like moles emerging above ground after a long winter, we had weak eyes. The stabbing sun forced us to wear sunglasses for the first time in five months.

On clear days, we spent as much time as possible outside absorbing sunlight, like the dormant trees around town. We avoided shadows, fearful of missing a single drop of ultraviolet energy. We began to see more of our friends as they, too, ventured out. We waved our gloved hands cheerfully to acquaintances who drove past in their heated cars.

When Chris and Holly were two and three, we lived aboard *Direction* on Australia's northern coast where the temperature didn't drop below 85 degrees for seven months. The white sand beach was an inferno that provided only visual rewards. We couldn't go swimming because the harbor was infested with stinging jellyfish and deadly crocodiles. We sweated buckets under the oppressively humid atmosphere of the summer monsoon. Mosquitoes swarmed in clouds. It was the first time we truly understood that to endure an extreme climate you need to "give blood."

Raucous flocks of corellas and hoards of blue-tongued lizards accompanied us on our frequent back-road excursions. Usually, the motion of walking provided the only source of moving air. We made long detours to find relief in the scant shade of frail gum trees. The nights were as hot as the days, but darkness made it seem cooler. Each afternoon, cooked to the bone, we counted the hours until sunset.

One day, we happened upon a battered station wagon full of silent aborigines. The hood was up, and a tall thin-legged chap wearing cutoffs and a singlet was hitting the engine halfheartedly with a short stick.

"What's the problem?" I asked.

"The motor stopped working."

Leaning over the engine was like leaning over an open fire. I checked the oil. None. The dipstick was smoking. Very cautiously, I opened the radiator cap using my T-shirt as a "potholder." Inside, the radiator was as dry and parched as the ground we stood on.

"Put some water in here," I pointed at the radiator. "Fill'er up all the way." Then I pointed to a cap on the engine's valve cover. "Might add some oil while you're at it."

A week or so later, I saw the same station wagon screaming down the road leaving a cloud of dust a mile high. The driver lay the on the horn as he approached, and the half-dozen passengers stuck their thin, black arms out of the open windows and waved. We waved cheerfully to our new acquaintances, then quickly covered our faces until the red dust drifted away. We dreamed about snow that summer.

APRIL. OUR BODIES AND OUR IDEALS had withstood the dark days of the Icelandic winter. Like the soaring sun, our spirits were flying. We were excited to be facing another season of cruising. The best part was that the vast expanse of the Atlantic Ocean was behind us. We faced relatively short hops between countries, which would give us more time to explore ashore.

A decade earlier, before we had kids, Jaja and I were anchored on the south coast of England contemplating our sailing itinerary. We wanted to take *Direction* to high latitudes: Scotland, the Faroes, Denmark, and Norway. Even then, we were eager to go north, but *Direction* wasn't insulated and didn't have a heater. We were too broke to make the alterations. The approaching winter along Britain's expensive south coast loomed like a dark squall, so we went south to stay warm. We reluctantly placed the northern countries on a high shelf in our imaginations hoping to visit them another time.

From England, we crossed the Bay of Biscay to Spain, a passage that marked the beginning of our tropical circumnavigation. By taking *Direction* south, instead of north, we avoided the hardships associated with the high latitudes. We substituted the discomforts of taking babies to sea for the vicissitudes of cold-climate cruising. We are all free to paint art into our lives, but at the point we turned south, destiny seemed bent on providing us with the colors.

Where did we want to go after Iceland? Although we were reluctant to make plans that were too specific, we felt it was prudent to have a general itinerary when we left–a framework from which to operate. The trick was to balance our desire to explore each place thoroughly with the necessity to keep moving. The northern summer is short, and if we dawdled, it could dissolve like snow in spring.

Originally, we planned to stay in Iceland six weeks. Look what happened! How could we possibly project the circumstances that might effect our summer journey? The most important decision was to determine where we would spend the following winter. If we established the location of our winter haven before we left Akureyri, we could focus on the journey, not where the journey might end. We wanted to avoid another time-consuming paper chase such as the one we experienced in Reykjavík.

We brought down Scotland, the Faroes, Denmark, and Norway from the high shelf of our imaginations. The dust on those dreams was thick, but with renewed springtime energy, it was wiped away easily. Scotland was the most logical place to winter over. A common language and a less debilitating exchange rate were pluses. Denmark was also attractive because of its proximity to Norway–our intended cruising ground for the following spring.

But first we had to sail down the Icelandic coast. After leaving Iceland, we would cruise for a month in the Faroe Islands and for six weeks in northern Scotland, before making the North Sea crossing. Satisfied with our rough itinerary, I sent our passports to the Danish embassy to apply for winter visas.

I had many discussions with trawler captains regarding the earliest time we could leave Akureyri and safely cruise down the Icelandic coast. Like stockbrokers wondering when to buy and sell, we analyzed how early in the year we could begin our cruise and how late in the season we could stretch it out.

Storms threaten Icelandic waters year round. The gales in spring can be severe and unpredictable, and the lulls between the weather systems are usually short. In summer, the threat of bad weather never disappears, but the lulls are longer, and the winds are less intense. May in Iceland is a transitional month. It was almost too early in the season to leave, but if we departed in May, we could take our time, watch the weather, and move when conditions were right. If necessary, we could duck into the many protected harbors on the Icelandic coast. If we were holed up in port waiting for a good forecast, we would not feel anxious that our summer was evaporating. If we waited until June to leave Akureyri, we still had to monitor the weather closely, and we could still easily get stuck in port. But in the latter case, we would watch our summer plans dissolve. We set the first week of May as our tentative date of departure.

Waiting for weather was a familiar routine for us. While laying in northern Australia, we waited eagerly for the arrival of the winter trade winds, a signal that we could start cruising again. In the Northern Territories of Australia, the summer weather is unstable, punctuated by severe lightning and torrential rain followed by fluky winds. The winter weather patterns bring steady, westerly trade winds, fair skies, and less humidity. Storms are practically unheard of during the winter trades.

The oppressive Aussie summer finally climaxed with two solid weeks of rain and strong winds. The day before the rain started, we had hauled *Direction* for a bottom job. Jaja and I spent more hours hanging plastic tarps to keep the rain off the hull than we actually spent sanding and painting.

One morning, the winter trades arrived–just like that. One minute the weather was unpredictable, the next it was fine–and going to be fine for six months. In Iceland, there would be no such assurances.

From Akureyri, we planned to return to Grímsey Island, wait, pick our weather, and then continue along Iceland's north coast. The most difficult section of coastline would be the extreme northeast corner, the Langenes Peninsula. It is Iceland's second most dangerous cape. Ocean currents merge at the peninsula, creating horrendous tide rips. The weather gets caught between mountain and ocean influences and becomes unpredictable. A permanent gale rages off the peninsula during the winter months. Langenes can be a formidable headland in the best of circumstances. From Langenes, we would sail to Seydis Fjord on Iceland's east coast. We would wait there until we had a good forecast for going south to the Faroe Islands.

Several years earlier in June, our friend Halli had sailed his 35-foot sloop *Niña II* to the Faroes. He cruised in company with some friends who were aboard a 27-foot sloop. Both boats rounded stormy Langenes and continued southward with a reasonable weather forecast. Their plan was to sail nonstop.

A few days later, they were hit by a 60-knot storm. They were blown into the shoal waters south of the Faroes. The 27-footer was rolled upside down by the horrendous seas, knocking everyone overboard. Fortunately, the crewmembers were young, strong fishermen, and they clamored aboard easily after the boat righted itself.

"Try keeping your time at sea to a minimum, Dave," Halli emphasized. "That storm came out of nowhere."

APPREHENSION BEFORE A PASSAGE can help you focus on preparation, but it tends to discourage sound sleeping. When the next spring gale surged down the fjord, Jaja and I lay in bed listening to the wind. Our stomachs tensed at the thought of leaving. Although we were excited to be going sailing again, we were anxious about cruising the north coast and rounding Langenes.

While thoughts of putting to sea challenged our nerves, we gained a new appreciation for our shoreside surroundings. We saw the town afresh, and we gazed at the mountainous panorama above *Driver* with a fondness bordering on proprietorship. We loved the view, and the idea of leaving it behind forever increased the value of each observation. Sadness crept into our hearts.

During our long months in Akureyri, we explored every nook and cranny within walking distance. We always found things to do with our free time. There was the river trail on the outskirts of town, the horse farms, and the outdoor skating rink. We walked on the frozen marshes at the headwaters of the fjord, borrowed Adda's and Gudni's equipment to go downhill skiing, and were regulars at the thermal swimming pool. One thing we hadn't done was to drive inland and see the snow-covered lava and the frozen lakes and waterfalls. We often talked about it, but the $150-a-day car rental rate dampened our enthusiasm.

During the Easter school break in early April, a large high-pressure system sent the temperature plummeting. The sky cleared and became a deep, dark blue. We sat at the top of our dock ramp basking in the morning brilliance. Recent heavy snowfall covered the mountains down to the high-tide line, creating a white world that was inspiring and unsurpassable. The sun seemed to blaze from every direction at once.

We were antsy to do something new, to take advantage of the longer days and the fine weather. Eight-inch-thick ice prevented us from sailing around the harbor. We wondered if we would be able to leave in May.

Jaja turned her face to the sun, and in one of her typical pragmatic visions, she outlined the big picture.

"This is the most beautiful day in six months," she began.

I agreed, wondering how she was going to talk us into renting a car.

"If we don't go inland, we will always regret not doing so."

"Point well taken."

"We need to live for today. I figure if we blow our money on a car rental, the effects of the bite will wear off in a few days when the next financial crisis arises–whatever it happens to be."

I laughed. "That's the most brilliant justification for spending money I have ever heard."

At 8:00 the next morning, we walked a quarter-mile through squeaking snow to the car rental office. Icicles hanging from gutters glistened, and smoke rising from chimneys settled low over backyards. The smoke created texture in the shafts of sunlight that sifted through bare tree limbs. Many cars still lay buried at the side of the road, victims of the snowplow. A few people were exhuming their automobiles with shovels, while others worked at scraping ice off windshields. Whenever Jaja and I witnessed the morning car routine, we were glad that we didn't own one, especially in a winter climate.

We headed out of town in our rented car toward the Myvatn lake region where we had driven the previous June during our auto trip from Reykjavík. We drove down the same stretch of road where Jaja had first suggested spending the winter in Iceland. Chris, Holly, and Teiga sat in the back seat, wide awake and happy. The newness of the trip had not worn off yet.

"Just think, if we had gone on to Scotland last summer instead of wintering over," I said. "Imagine what we would have missed."

"It makes you wonder what other opportunities in life have passed us by."

"We can't do everything, I suppose." We drove on and mused that every time we make a choice, we eliminate a thousand other possibilities.

"That reminds me," Jaja said. "You know what it's like in the dark to sense an object in your peripheral vision, and then if you look right at the thing, it fades away? I've been looking straight at out summer plan, and there's something about it that bugs me."

"Do you think we shouldn't go to Denmark?"

"No, it's just that our itinerary seems too pat."

I drummed my fingers on the steering wheel. One of the reasons we seldom stick to a plan is because events often unfold and evolve as we go along, creating circumstances that were unforeseeable before departure. Somewhere along the way, we usually make a 90-degree turn and radically change our plans. We also tend to bite off more than we can chew.

The scenery outside the car's windows held us spellbound. The summer before, the land had been garnished with green bushes, yellow grasses, and brown rock. Now the prevalent colors were just white snow and blue sky. The road was well plowed, but it supported a thick layer of hard-packed snow that merged with the shoulder of the road and spread out to the mountains in an unbroken, white sheet. The widely separated farmhouses stood like beacons on the snowy plain, the thin trails of smoke from their chimneys giving evidence of life within.

I stopped the car at Godafoss Waterfall, which we had visited the summer before. The frozen falls were visible from the main road, but Holly wanted to get a close-up view. The two of us trudged through knee-deep powder to see the 100-foot-high wall of ice. The temperature roamed in the single digits, and a slight breeze added a face-numbing wind chill. It was too cold outside for Teiga, so she and Jaja remained in the car with Chris, drinking hot chocolate.

Lake Myvatn was a white, flat disk. The summer before, it had been blue liquid with the sun sparkling on wind-driven ripples. The lava in the area had been black and ancient looking, covered with mosses that glowed in subtle reds and yellows. Now, everything was white. There was not a cloud in sight, and the sun shone unchallenged through the clear, northern atmosphere.

We drove northward over the rolling hills to the coastal town of Húsavík, the location of the first Viking settlement 1,000 years ago. We stopped near a ski area, picnicked in the warmth of the sun, and let the kids sled until they were dopey with breathlessness. We explored all day, taking roads that led nowhere, roads that led somewhere. We remained in awe of the winter scenery that unfolded before us. We returned to *Driver* exhausted and sated.

THE FOLLOWING WEEKEND, we went with Adda and Gudni to their summer cottage in the mountains. It was another brilliant day. We lounged in the sun, the kids had a sledding competition down a very steep hill, and during the dark hours after dinner, we stood on the veranda watching the northern lights. Holly nursed a bump on her head that she received when she whizzed out of control on her sled and ran into a bush. Chris continued to talk excitedly about his death-defying jump. He had zoomed down the hill and hit a low embankment bordering the narrow, side road. His sled literally flew over the road into the ditch on the other side. We were angry with him for being foolish, but the fact remained that it had been an amazing jump.

Our days in Akureyri were coming to an end. On our last weekend, Gudni took us to his grandparent's unused homestead near Grenavík. He parked the car off the main road and unloaded his snowmobile from its trailer. Using the snowmobile as a land-dinghy, he ferried kids, adults, and picnic supplies up the quarter-mile-long, unplowed driveway. Northern Iceland had received one of the highest snowfalls in many years, and the old house stood in snow that reached to its second story windows.

It was another blue-on-white weekend. Adda's brother Anton came with his family, and all the kids ran wild, charged by the life-giving light. Spring was poking its head through the ice, and the world was thawing out. Dark nights had become a thing of the past. A rich twilight lit the skies each night.

I sat behind Gudni on his snowmobile as we raced up the powdery slopes of 3,600-foot Kalbakur Mountain, one of the highest in the area. We gained elevation at a tremendous rate. It was familiar territory for Gudni, who had grown up hiking the mountains in summer and snowmobiling over them in the spring. We stopped on a high ridge where we could see all of Eyja Fjord spread out below. Akureyri was a dot to the left, and to the right, the ocean was a blue ribbon. The sea looked smooth and inviting from so high an elevation. Below us, we could see the homestead.

We dropped over the back of a ridge, screamed at high speed down a long valley, used our momentum to go up the other side, then stopped at the top of a steep, narrow gully. The mountain was covered evenly by snow with not one bush visible for miles. The hard, white line of the ridge behind us looked as if it were cut out against the dark blue sky.

Gudni called, "Ready?" I lowered the visor on my helmet and locked my hands around his waist. We accelerated quickly, dropping into the gully at 50 miles an hour. Turning slowly, we edged up the wall of the ravine. When we began to stall on the steep incline, Gudni turned us back downwards toward the middle of the gully. Once again, we accelerated, leaving our stomachs far behind. Back and forth we ranged, up one wall, down the other, as fast as we could go. I was involuntarily shouting my excitement, yodeling and whooping wildly, convinced we would die at any second, yet uncaring because it was such a thrill. Any roller coaster was sordid and predictable by comparison. I trusted Gudni. He was a champion snowmobile racer.

When we idled up to the homestead, my voice was raw, and my fingers and feet were numb from hanging on. That ride is similar to our life at sea on *Driver*. Both experiences possess a genuine element of mortality. People frequently ask Jaja and me why we purposely put ourselves in uncomfortable shipboard situations. We continue to sail because we like challenges and thrills.

Grinning like a maniac, I staggered off the snowmobile. I told Gudni that Jaja would love the experience. I gave her my helmet and watched them zoom away. When they came back a half-hour later, Jaja's face looked like mine when I had returned–frozen in a grinning position.

The night before our departure, we went to Adda's and Gudni's house for a going-away party. Saying goodbye was difficult; our friends had become an integral part of our lives. We drank coffee, ate Adda's famous homemade cheesecake, and exchanged gifts under a cloud of melancholy. We gave María and Valur felt-tip pens, books in English, and stickers. We saved Adda's and Gudni's present for last. It was the size of two large suitcases with rounded edges, and it weighed a ton. María and Valur pounced on the package and tore off the paper. When the gift was revealed, the room fell silent.

"Uh, it's a giant pack of toilet paper," Adda said.

"Seventy-five rolls," Jaja admitted. The kids started giggling first, then the laughter spread as Adda and Gudni realized it was a gag. We had shared many chuckles over the previous weeks since members of the girls' club had come knocking.

I chuckled. "We gave you toilet paper," I said, "so that you will remember us every day after we've gone."

Gudni left the room smiling and returned with a 44-pound sack of homegrown potatoes. He dropped them at our feet.

"Yes. And you can think about us while you're peeling these."

Chapter Eight

The hardest part of any voyage is leaving.

OUR FEELINGS WERE in a muddle. We were sad to leave Akureyri, yet anxious to be moving on. It was difficult to differentiate among our emotions–lethargy, apprehension, real desire, fanciful wishes, common sense. *Why* did we have to move on? In recent weeks, Chris and Holly had become steadily more proficient in Icelandic. We knew that their fluency would vanish without continued practice.

Laying dockside in Akureyri was comfortable, warm, and familiar. We felt as if we had just awakened on a weekday and wanted to steal one more snooze before getting out of bed. Untying our docklines and steaming up the fjord would be the definitive act, but we feared that leaving would put us in an apprehensive, lightheaded stupor. Jaja is fond of saying that the difficult choices are often the right ones. Departing would be the hardest choice, but would it be the right decision? Battling options and gray areas is what adulthood is all about.

Driver had survived the season intact. She required almost no last-minute preparation. During the winter, I rebuilt the water pump in the engine, cleaned out the fuel lines, and checked all the hoses. In recent weeks, I went aloft to clean and oil light-bulb contacts, check masthead halyard sheaves, and inspect every inch of rigging.

When the ice on deck melted, I gave the sails a once-over–oiling the piston hanks and checking seams. We bent the mainsail back onto the boom, rigged reefing lines, and inserted the battens–being sure to double-check the stitching on the batten pockets. Preparing all systems for sea was not only crucial to our safety, it also drove the cobwebs from our brains. Very soon we would be at sea where hesitation and uncertainty could be dangerous.

May 9th, our last morning in Akureyri, dawned clear, sunny, and relatively warm. When people had asked, "What time are you leaving?" we would reply, "Around 10:00 or so." We would have preferred slipping out at midnight to avoid an emotional goodbye, but that wouldn't be fair to our friends who wanted to wish us well. Our stay in Akureyri was successful because of them. We felt ashamed of our caginess, wishing that we had given them a definite time. Sometimes, Jaja and I wondered if we would ever grow up.

We were having a contest with a 12-foot-high pile of snow in the gym parking lot. For three weeks, the pile melted steadily in the sun, and we wondered whether we would depart before or after the pile did. The recent cold weather slowed the melting, and on our last day, the pile was still three feet high and about 10 feet in circumference, solid as a rock. We won, but it was a hollow victory compared to the "heady" days of competition.

At breakfast time, the thermometer read 36 degrees Fahrenheit, an improvement over the previous morning's 25. Snow had fallen continually during the past week, accompanied by strong northerly winds. We could just imagine the weather conditions on the exposed coast. We wondered if we were leaving too early in the season. What was the hurry? Why not stay until June, allow the snowpile to melt, let the temperatures climb, and enjoy socializing with our friends ashore? Why not immigrate to Iceland? Sell the boat, give up the anxieties of cruising offshore with small children. Live an easier lifestyle.

By 9:30 a.m., about 20 people had assembled on our pontoon. The sun was brilliant, glowing on the tops of peoples' heads and glistening on their coats. Everyone wore–or wished they had worn–sunglasses. The port captain presented us with a polished brass plate mounted on a varnished plaque. The inscription indicated that the sailing vessel *Driver* had spent the winter in Akureyri Harbor in 1998-1999. Friends brought candy for the kids, boxes of chocolates for Jaja and me, and fruit. Only one person was missing. Knútur had suffered a mild heart attack and was recovering in the hospital.

Earlier that week I visited his private room for a chat and admired the splendid view of the harbor out his hospital window. I confessed that his sons had revealed his secret plan. He wanted to organize a flotilla to accompany us up the fjord, led by his own boat *Gógó*.

He smiled kindly. "I would have enjoyed doing that."

At 10:00, I started the engine, and Jaja raised the mainsail. Icelanders are deep-thinking people who do not express their emotions with frivolous public displays of gaiety. Everyone was silent. After hugs and handshakes, we cast off our lines. When *Driver* began moving forward, the realization that we were actually going fell on our shoulders like an avalanche. We fought the urge to turn the boat around and tie up again. We waved cheerily, although we did not feel cheery. Even though I longed to alter course and return to the dock, I held the tiller steady.

Jaja was the first to speak. "My God, Dave, are we really going? I feel like I've left a piece of me behind."

Chris and Holly were in tears. Even little Teiga had her face buried in Jaja's neck. María, and Holly's other friend Inga Rakel, ran to the end of the breakwater to wave. They shouted the informal Icelandic goodbye:

"*Bless, bless*! Holly, Chris, and Teiga. *Bless bless!*"

Instead of turning left outside the basin to go north, we went straight to the back of the bay, which was now free of ice. When we were beside the hospital, I stood on deck and waved to Knútur who was standing at the window in his white hospital gown. We each held our arms high, in an acknowledgement of shared emotion, then I swung *Driver* around to begin our journey out of the fjord.

Adda and Gudni followed us in their car as far as Grenivík, 18 miles away. They paced our snail-like progress for a time before they sped off. A half-hour later, we spotted them for the last time standing on a stony beach, waving and taking pictures. We sailed straight for the land, shouted another farewell, then tacked away at the last minute to avoid running aground. It was a close one. Fog soon obscured the blue horizon, and we steamed for several hours using the radar as our eyes.

A STIFF BREEZE SPRANG UP and began to blow the fog away. When we sailed between the rocky breakwaters that protect the harbor at Dalvik, Halli was standing on the deck of his boat, waiting to take our lines.

"Jón and Disa called me when you left. You've made good time. Would you like to come to the house for dinner?"

Halli's house was built by his grandparents. He was born and raised there. It was a comfortable home. Halli named the house *Svalbardi* after the group of islands in the Arctic.

Katrin greeted us warmly. Halli thrust a beer in my hand, a glass of wine in Jaja's, and we stood out in the thin sunshine barbecuing steaks. The house was still surrounded by 10 feet of snow. Our kids and Halli's and Katrin's children went sledding and fed some horses. During dinner, Katrin congratulated us for surviving the winter afloat.

"At first, everyone in town thought we were crazy," I said. "But we were eventually accepted."

"I still think you're crazy." Katrin laughed. "Tell me, was it fun?"

"We're not sure yet," Jaja answered. "We're too sad."

Halli said, "Now you must sail to Svalbard."

"Svalbard!" I said, "No way. I know our limitations. A trip up there is beyond our capabilities."

"Where's Svalbard?" Jaja asked.

"It's a group of islands in the Arctic, north of Norway." Halli replied, "at 80 degrees north. It's also known as Spitsbergen. A few private boats go there each season when the pack ice melts. Spitsbergen is isolated. It has active glaciers; steep, snow-covered mountains; and diverse wildlife. I'm planning to take *Niña* there someday."

"We'd never make it with our kids," I said. "It's too far and too remote."

The next morning, visibility on the fjord was obscured by dense fog. Instead of leaving, we went to Dalvik's outdoor thermal swimming pool. Afterwards, we sent a postcard to Adda and Gudni thanking them for a wonderful send-off. On the card was a black-and-white picture of a toothless old lady sitting in a rocker scowling at the world. We put a word-bubble above her head which read, "Finally got rid of the Americans!"

The next day we bid farewell to Halli and Katrin and struck out for Grímsey Island. We left in patchy fog, but by the time we reached the mouth of Eyja Fjord, the sky had cleared. The sea was lumpy, even though there was not a breath of wind. We motored along in the sunshine, content to be under way. Moving forward was a good way to numb our sadness and to encourage positive thoughts. The temperature hovered at a seasonable 36, and the unusually deep snowfall blanketed the mountains down to the water. It was difficult to remember that summer was right around the corner. It still looked like February.

We tied to the same wharf in Grímsey that we had used the previous August. The island was cold, windswept, and lifeless. The flocks of birds and the bright green grass on the foreshore were nowhere to be seen.

We walked across the Arctic Circle, past the high cliffs, and down to the sloping field at the north end of the island. There was little snow left on the island, and the patches of exposed grass were brown and flattened. Not much snow accumulates on Grímsey. The wind blows it all away.

Our faces were numbed by the chilly breeze, so we walked in silence. We were anxious about our trip down the Icelandic coast, and the bleakness on Grímsey did not inspire conversation. The air was raw. I remembered the magic of the previous summer–how we had lounged in the high, emerald grass under the rarefied Arctic sky, speculating on the coming winter. Now we just wanted to go south to warmer climes.

Chris, Holly, and Teiga ran ahead of us a short way and stopped. They pointed at the ground, then waved us over. They had discovered a solitary, black fleece glove. Once furry, it was now stiff, slightly bleached, caked with dirt, and home to a family of small white worms.

"Mommy! We found your lost glove!"

We stared at the thing for a moment.

"Come on," Jaja said, "Let's keep moving or we'll get cold."

Chris reached down to take the glove.

"Let's leave that one," Jaja said. "It belongs here now."

Back at the harbor, the new storeowners were curious about how we had managed to survive the long winter on our boat. They had read about us in the newspapers. (Our arrival in Akureyri the summer before had sparked great interest.)

We said that living on a boat in winter is probably not much different than living on Grímsey. Time can hang heavy if you let it. It all depends on how you use your waking hours. As the winter had approached, we welcomed the chance to experience the dark, the cold, and the isolation. After we experienced those things, we felt fulfilled. There was no reason to consider them hardships. The most difficult part of our winter, we told the storeowners, was saying goodbye. In private, Jaja and I jested that the next time we lived in a town, we would avoid making friends.

After a three-day wait, the weather forecast seemed mild enough for us to leave. We took a morning walk to the lighthouse at the southern end of the island where the driftwood logs sat atop the cliff. The logs seemed to shriek the word *"shipwreck!"*

Seeing those logs–which gave testament to the force of the ocean–might have been enough to deter some people from leaving the safety of land on a boat. On the other hand, it was tempting to think that shipwrecks happen only to other people. *It'll never happen to me* is the immortal chant of mankind. The threat of an auto accident, for example, does not stop motorists from leaving their driveways. In the end, the logs did not deter us. They did, however, provide a sobering reminder to keep a close eye on the weather.

The sea was lumpy as we skirted the southern point of Grímsey, but *Driver* punched through the chop on a broad reach. With all sails flying, we headed due east toward an overcast sky and a gray horizon. The last we saw of Grímsey was the bright orange lighthouse, a symbol of reassurance in an inhospitable region. There were no small fishing boats bobbing around, nor did we hear the distant hum of invisible trawlers. We felt alone on the planet.

The coast of Iceland was 20 miles south of us, and the somber atmosphere made the distant, snowy mountains on the mainland look ashen. Raufarhöfn lay 80 miles ahead, a safe harbor where we could get an updated weather report and some rest before continuing toward the infamous Langenes Peninsula. We wanted to be as fresh as possible before rounding that headland.

The winds soon petered out, the sky became a dull beige, and the temperature dropped to a fraction above freezing. I started the engine, set the electronic autopilot, and let *Driver* carry on toward our destination at 5 1/2 knots. The sea was calm.

I went below to warm my feet. The kids were lounging comfortably in the 70-degree cabin. While I was below, Jaja donned warm clothes and slipped into the cockpit for some air. She had loaded the galley oven with Gudni's potatoes. I ate them plain; their scalding heat warmed my insides. They were the best potatoes we had ever eaten–sweet and firm. Their steaming aroma, rich with the scent of soil, enhanced my mood. We doubted Adda and Gudni were getting as much enjoyment from the toilet paper.

At 8:00 p.m., we motored out of the Arctic, certain that we would never sail over that magic line again. With each mile, our goals were slipping astern in our wake. Rounding Langenes in one piece and sailing down the east coast of Iceland were formidable short-term challenges. But what about the rest of the summer? Was there anything in our itinerary that would compare to what we were leaving behind? Jaja's observation that we were missing something began to infiltrate my thoughts. I wondered why we always feel the need to be overchallenged.

We entered the unfamiliar harbor at Raufarhöfn in the welcome, near-perpetual light of summer. We tied to a floating pontoon at midnight and slept until 10:00 a.m. The lowering sky had cleared somewhat, and the day looked promising. There was even a fair breeze. We weren't in the mood for sitting, and we hoped the forecast would remain satisfactory.

I phoned the weather service from the grocery store while the kids licked ice cream cones. There were no public phones in town, so the store manager let me use the one in his office. Fifteen-to-20-knot northwesterlies were still forecast with a shift to the south after 36 hours. The time was ripe. If we left immediately, we would have favorable tail winds down the coast. If we lounged in town for another day, we would miss the short weather window. Then we would have to battle headwinds–our worst fear.

I talked to a trawler captain who believed the wind might be stronger than the weather bureau in Reykjavík was forecasting.

"How strong do you think?" I asked.

"Twenty-five knots, maybe."

"What about Langenes in seven or eight hours? Do you think it will be safe to round?"

"Should be. If things pick up, it won't be for another 12 hours when the small high-pressure ridge passes over. Hug the point as close as you dare. It's deep right on in. Don't go wide."

"Thanks for the advice," I said sincerely.

He looked at *Driver*, looked at Jaja and our small crew, and shook his head.

Oh well. There were probably aspects of his life that I would disagree with if I knew about them.

WE SET SAIL at 3:00 p.m. The low, broken clouds of the past few days had lifted. The sun cast a pale glow on our sails. The Langenes Peninsula is 24 miles long with high cliffs and a perfectly flat top. From a distance, it looked like a giant candy bar.

Driver was on a broad reach, flying the working jib and the mainsail with a single reef in it. We sailed parallel to the foreboding cliffs. Powered by the wind, *Driver* carried on with a determination that seemed almost human. The 20-knot northerlies, which would provide favorable downwind sailing after we rounded the headland, were pushing us right onto the peninsula. If we had a sudden problem with the mast or sails and couldn't make headway, we would be driven onto the rocks. In an emergency, we could have tried the engine, but I doubted that we would make much headway under power because the sea was too choppy.

We were very vulnerable. If we went farther offshore, we risked being caught in adverse currents and heavy seas. We had to have faith in our abilities and our gear and "just go for it". Whenever possible, we try to avoid sailing on a lee shore such as this. The greatest satisfaction we get from doing so, however, is the feeling of relief when it's over. Langenes was no exception.

"Stay in close. Don't go wide," the trawler captain had said.

We had planned this passage for so long that arriving at Langenes felt like a dream. My stomach tensed. We could see the end of the peninsula, and we pushed *Driver* toward it like a thoroughbred racehorse bound for the finish line. Just a little farther. Just a little farther. Jaja gripped the tiller, keeping us firmly on course.

Chris poked his head up the companionway. "Mommy? Can we have a snack?"

"There's some peanuts in the starboard food locker."

"Where in the locker?"

"Top shelf."

From out of nowhere, a gust of wind overpowered us. I raced onto the foredeck to tie another reef in the mainsail. This would reduce our sail area and would help prevent *Driver* from being knocked down. I had just released the mainsail halyard when I heard Chris holler from down below.

"Where on the top shelf?"

With one hand on the tiller, Jaja used her other hand to let out the mainsheet and spill wind from the sail. She poked her head under the dodger.

"Be there in a *min*-ute." To break the tension, she sang the words playfully, emphasizing the "min."

On deck, I battled the flailing mainsail, watching the coast as it approached all too rapidly. To port, I could see a clear horizon. To starboard behind the jib, all I could see were rocks. Jaja was driving hard for the end of the peninsula. Her face was set with concentration.

The seas were backwashing–rebounding off the land. The ocean churned as the wash fought with the wind-driven waves and with the two-knot current that pushed us along. An underwater shelf juts a quarter-mile to seaward off the end of the peninsula. The shelf tamed the waves somewhat. Farther out in deeper water, it was a different story. There, I could see the telltale peaked waves of vicious tide rips. If we stayed very close to land over the shelf, we would avoid the worst of the seas.

At 9:00 p.m., we drew abreast of the mighty Langenes. The swirling currents grabbed our hull. Jaja threw her weight into the tiller to keep us on course. Rocks on one side. Open sea on the other. Then the entire land mass of Iceland pivoted on our beam as Jaja turned the boat southward.

Instantly, the seas and wind calmed in the lee of the peninsula. We knew that conditions would pick up again as we moved away from land and into deeper water, but for the moment, it was a welcome respite. Chris poked his head out of the companionway.

"Can we have those peanuts now?"

I CHECKED THE SET OF THE JIB and the whisker pole, put a preventer line on the mainboom, then adjusted the windvane self-steering. I looked at our compass heading, then dropped below to warm up. We were a dozen miles from shore, and I couldn't see any fishing boats or other hazards.

Jaja was reading a bedtime story to the kids. Chris and Holly were holding their own. Teiga, however, had fallen into the mixed-up world of seasickness where energy is sapped, ambition destroyed, and your outlook becomes morbid. Motion sickness wouldn't be so bad if your mind weren't involved. We gave Teiga a Phenergan suppository, which made her drowsy enough to nod off. This allowed Jaja to get some air on deck. Chris and Holly retired to their bunks. Peace and tranquility descended on the cabin.

The chill wind from the mountains kicked up the sea, creating frothy whitecaps. Jaja and I huddled together for warmth without the need to talk. The relief of having conquered Langenes fed our spirits. I knew what Jaja was thinking. Our winter in Akureyri was receding with every wave, and the distance wasn't making our sadness any less acute. We had built a support system of satisfaction and friendship. With the simple acts of slipping our docklines and starting the engine, we had annihilated it all.

During our years on *Direction*, we were always eager to move on. Curiously, if we had sentimental attachments, they were usually for the place, not for the people. Leaving was more difficult this time around. Maybe we were getting old.

While the kids slept, Jaja stood watch. Before I fell into my bunk, I looked at the snowy mountains and at the long rays of the sun sneaking out from under high, black clouds. The east coast of Iceland looked uninviting and forlorn. It seemed to be telling me that any mistakes I made could be fatal, that any thought not geared toward survival was frivolous. Belowdecks, the cabin felt comforting and real. The flame in our heating stove was a light in the wilderness, keeping the demons of melancholy at bay. I fell asleep instantly.

JAJA WOKE ME IN THE HALF-LIGHT at 1:00 a.m. She insisted I come on deck. I sat up, groggy from sleep. Nevertheless, I comprehended the urgency. *Driver* was out of control, flying along with the wind behind us. The windvane steering struggled, making violent and jagged course corrections. I stepped into my foul-weather pants and boots that were still stowed together. I threw on my foul-weather gear jacket and added a hat and waterproof gloves. Before my feet left the companionway ladder, I clipped on my safety harness.

On deck, I found a gnarly world of menacing clouds, graphite seas, platinum wave tops, and cold salt spray. The swells were hitting us from behind. A large sea rose under *Driver*, tipped her bow downwards, and sent us surfing at nine knots. At the foot of the wave, our speed slowed. The continued momentum of the swell lifted our stern and pushed it sideways, causing us to broach wildly. The jib back-winded on its whisker pole; the mainsail flogged. The next wave slammed into our hull, which was pushed broadside to the seas, and sent a cascade of water over the foredeck. Slowly, the windvane steering pulled us back to course. When the jib filled with wind again, it cracked like a gunshot, propelling *Driver* along at breakneck speed.

"The wind is rising by the second," Jaja hollered. "I need your help getting the jib down."

I untangled my safety harness line, which lay in a pile next to the companionway, and bounded onto the foredeck. Before I could release the jib halyard, a large swell lifted the stern high and nudged us off course. *Driver* accelerated and began to broach ever so slowly. Jaja grabbed the tiller to assist the self-steering. She tried to bring us back to course, but our angle of heel and our high-speed sideways motion prevented the rudder from having any affect. *Driver* traversed the face of the steep wave. The jib was partially back-winded; the mainboom dragged in the water. Another breaking sea lifted our bow and set it down with a shuddering crash. I clung to the mast as if my life depended on it–because it really did.

When the angle of heel decreased and the boat leveled out, I yelled "Now!" Jaja released the jibsheet and let it run. Simultaneously, I released the jib halyard, then clamored onto the foredeck to drag down the jib. With only the mainsail flying, we were able to resume control and continue on our southerly course. I lashed the jib securely to the deck, where it would be ready if we needed it in an emergency, and stowed the whisker pole against the mast.

Within minutes, the wind was blowing still harder, so I tied a third reef in the main to reduce the sail area even more. Remembering the violent knock-down, I struggled below as nimbly as I could in my heavy boots and clumsy foul-weather gear to inspect the hull patch. Would I find water flooding into the bilge? I lifted the floorboards cautiously. Not one drop of water had seeped in around the patch.

The seas were too short and steep for the windvane. Jaja was hand-steer-ing, fighting with the tiller to keep *Driver* on course. I sat beside her, then took over the helm.

"I'm beat," Jaja admitted. "Mind if I get some rest?"

"I'll shout if I need you. Could you turn on the radar before you lie down? It looks like a rain squall is coming."

The wind peaked at 35 knots ahead of the squall. Instead of raining, it snowed. The flakes flew horizontally, lending unnecessary texture to the already coarse seascape. The wind veered and started blowing from the north, straight down the coast. We lost what scant shelter the land had provided. The seas were ferocious–short, steep brutes, determined to knock us over. Steer-ing with my back to the snowstorm, I anticipated the waves by feel. The tran-som would lift, and depending on which way the mast heeled, I would push or pull the tiller in the opposite direction. These adjustments kept us on course, but if I anticipated the following seas incorrectly or let *Driver* wander excessively, it was a battle to regain control.

Four hours went by. Jaja came on deck every hour or so to steer, giving me the chance to stretch and drink some coffee. Afterwards, she sat under the dodger or went below to rest. She needed to stay warm and reserve some energy for coping with Chris and Holly when they woke up. Teiga, who was up and down all night, seemed to need Jaja constantly.

By 6:00 a.m., the sun had been above the horizon for hours–one of the perks of high-latitude sailing. The long hours of daylight lessened some of the grinding fatigue associated with "night" sailing. Despite having radar and a GPS receiver, our ability to see the coast around the clock removed some of the stress.

At 7:00, the snow flurries stopped, the wind eased to 20 knots, and the sky cleared. The temperature remained at 34 degrees, but just seeing the sun made the air feel warmer. There was neither ice on deck, nor in the rigging. My feet were the only things that had "iced up." With effort, I went on deck to raise the jib. My joints felt leaden. I was extremely cautious.

Jaja came on deck to take a line. When I returned to the cockpit and sat down, Jaja said, "I'm beat. How about you?"

"I feel wasted." A minute later I added, "Hey, wasn't that one hell of a stimulating passage?"

"Stimulating?"

"I never doubted our ability to cope with the situation. We've been through a lot of sticky moments over the years. What could be more satisfying than drawing on the reserves of our own potential?"

"Laying at anchor in Tahiti?"

We sailed at hull speed, riding the waves and rejoicing after the demanding night. The snowy mountains and the clear air played tricks our with perspective, making the shoreline appear continuous and impenetrable. The narrow entrance at Seydis Fjord revealed itself only when we were almost there. At the mouth of the fjord, the wind petered out completely.

We fired up the engine, dropped the sails, and motored 10 miles to the protected basin at the end of the fjord. We saw one or two farms along the way and several abandoned stone buildings. Most of all, we saw boulders, 800-foot-high mountains, and snow. We felt alone.

The harbormaster met us at the dock, so we invited him aboard. He spoke good English.

He climbed below. "Hey, it's warm in here!"

"It's home," Jaja said.

"Aren't you the family who was living in Akureyri? Of course you are. I saw you on TV last winter. What are your plans?"

"We'll leave for the Faroe Islands as soon as the wind cooperates," I said. "Meanwhile, we're happy to be in Seydis Fjord."

The port captain beamed and invited us to lay alongside for as long as we wanted. He congratulated our intrepidness but hastily added that it took all types.

Chris and Holly had slept soundly through the night, oblivious to our high-latitude struggle. When my sister Michelle and I were kids, we used to pile into our parents' camper on Friday evenings after my dad came home from work. Then we would roll out of the California suburbs, headed for the High Sierras. In the morning, like magic, we would wake up in a mountain campground, smelling the fresh-perked coffee. The closest I ever came to being a time traveler was during my childhood.

I asked our kids, "Do you guys remember anything about last night's passage?"

Chris said, "I woke up once, and the sails were shaking the whole boat. Another time, I got up to pee, and I was thrown off the toilet!"

Teiga thought that was very funny and started giggling. Jaja opened the locker door under the sink and grabbed the Clorox.

Holly said, "I dreamed that I was in an airplane doing flips in the sky."

The kids were eager to go to town. A five-minute walk from *Driver* landed us in a small diner. We ordered three ice cream cones and two cups of strong coffee. That night, we went to the indoor swimming pool, swam laps, soaked in the hut tubs, and braised our flesh in the sauna. Afterwards, we called Adda and Gudni to chat. They asked about our trip down the coast.

"It was great."

WHILE SITTING IN THE SAUNA, Jaja and I couldn't decide which is more fun: To cruise in a cold place, wishing it were warm, or to go where it is too hot and complain. Certainly, Akureyri was the coldest place we had ever lived aboard.

Visions of the frozen fjord at Akureyri, our icy decks, and the clothesline in the cabin loaded with snowy gloves and hats would be etched in our minds forever. Suiting up the kids like astronauts several times each day took time and patience. Cold hands and feet had tried their endurance and tested ours.

"Why do kids' socks always fall down in their boots," Jaja wondered, "and at what age does it stop?"

We pondered our distant past, comparing it to our recent experiences. The summer *Direction* lay anchored on Australia's northern coast certainly was our hottest cruising experience.

Every morning after Chris and Holly had pointed out their latest bug bites, we dished out the calamine lotion with the Cream of Wheat. Jaja and I lived for coffee. The first cup was the best because it banished the sensation that our eyelids were lined with Velcro. The caffeine jolt also released the muscle cramps created by sleeping in the hot, sweaty weather. Unfortunately, that first cup of the day also caused a fresh torrent of perspiration to trickle down our backs and to run off our foreheads into our eyes.

Beachcombing in the tropical places wearing only sun cream is an existence close to perfection. The strip of white, sandy beach, the sensuous curve of coconut palms, the clear waves licking the shoreline. These are the things that have inspired cruisers for decades.

In northern Australia, it was tempting to go for a swim. But swimming could be life threatening because of the crocodiles and the poisonous reef creatures. The waters around Iceland could also be deadly–not because of sea animals, but because of hypothermia.

The warm, subtropical weather in Bermuda produced blue skies, little rain, cool white sand, and no bugs. That's perfection in anyone's book. A cruiser's nirvana. But what had we learned about the locals? Anything? Did they befriend us on terms that did not include financial gain? Did we try to dig deeper for a spark of friendship that wasn't service oriented? Tropical places have much to offer on the surface, but the effects of rampant tourism often cause the locals to lock up their emotions.

For us, passagemaking in the Tropics was the ultimate pleasure. Under the stars, barefoot in the cockpit, we found that the easy motion of warm seas could inspire romantic, soul-satisfying visions. The cabin was often hot and stuffy at sea, but we would leave the bugs behind. Sleep was a peaceful activity, not a time for murdering mosquitoes.

In Seydis Fjord, we scaled the mountains behind the boat basin and reached a broad saddle with a view of the fjord. We basked in a warm hollow on dry rocks that the sun's rays had exposed from under the melting snow. We absorbed the scenery and the light.

Going for a walk in Iceland, even in May, means wearing hats, gloves, jackets, heavy socks, and boots. At the top of the hill, we each shed some layers until we achieved our individual comfort levels. Chris stripped down to jeans, a wool hat, a T-shirt, and rubber boots; Holly wore a sweater with her jeans rolled up above her hiking boots; Teiga wore her mittens, coat, and waterproof pants. Jaja and I marveled at the extra clothes lying around. To have started our hike without these clothes would have been dangerous. The day was clear, but passing clouds could produce freezing rain in a flash. Jaja and I lay back in the sun with our eyes closed, imagining that the snow was white sand.

Which *was* best? Balmy beaches and warm skies, or chilly high-latitude splendor? We had learned that there is no such thing as perfection. If there were, it would be boring. It's the contrasts in life that make situations special. We already missed the northern lights, the snug feeling when sheltering from a blizzard–and we missed our hearty friends. Dealing with the cold was part of the experience. Without the chilly temperatures, the things we missed most could not exist.

WE HAD MADE A SPEEDY PASSAGE to Seydis Fjord, and we were rich with time. It was only May 14th. Adda and Gudni planned to drive eight hours from Akureyri to visit us, but snowfall and high winds closed the central mountain passes. The winds between Iceland and the Faroes remained unfavorable obliging us to stay put for a while. We were very sorry that Adda and Gudni couldn't visit.

To "spend" some of our well-earned extra time, we rented a car. There were no sedans available, so the rental agency upgraded us to a four-wheel-drive vehicle for the same price. Neither Jaja nor I had ever driven such a vehicle before. We were tempted to rent one in Florida while provisioning

Driver. We joked that a four-wheel-drive could have saved us hours of frustration by allowing us to drive over curbs and cut across flowerbeds every time we got lost in a mall parking lot.

On a back road near Seydis Fjord, eager to get our money's worth, I took the family on an off-road excursion. While I was busy pretending that I knew what I was doing, the vehicle suddenly tilted sideways at a dangerous angle as we crossed a stream.

I braked to a halt. "I think we're stuck. No one move a muscle."

Jaja gingerly opened her door, which was on the high side. She stepped out carefully to make sure the truck wouldn't flip without her weight. She spent 10 minutes giving me hand signals until we got the vehicle turned around. As we extracted the truck, I was aware that lack of experience coupled with high ambitions could create a dangerous adventure. Wisdom is frequently bestowed at the oddest moments.

We woke up one morning to the scattery sound of snow falling on deck. It dumped heavily all morning creating a wet, slushy mess. When the sun came out late in the day, most of it melted. I called the weather bureau in Reykjavík, talked with familiar voices, and divined that the coming days might be favorable for setting sail. They encouraged me to phone again in the morning. We had been in Seydis Fjord nine days.

The next morning was clear and promising. A low-pressure system was developing west of Iceland, and with any luck, it would continue on its predicted path north of the country. My friends at the weather bureau confirmed that we would have a 48-hour weather window for sailing south to the Faroes. Good news, but it was cutting it close. It would take us a minimum of 36 hours to complete the passage. At noon, we filled our water tanks, made a last trip to the store for vegetables, and set sail down the fjord, bound for the open sea.

When the empty horizon came into view, we knew that our 11 1/2-month Icelandic odyssey was at an end. Long ago, Jaja's chance remark, "We're going to circumnavigate Iceland," had been a solitary snowflake that set off a spectacular avalanche of events.

Our last glimpse of Iceland was a majestic landscape: Jagged snow-covered ridges and crumbling cliffs that dropped into the surf. Then dense fog swallowed us whole.

Driver moved in concert with the waves, her sails caught the wind, and we slid southward bound for the Faroes. We thought the "real" adventure was over. Little did we know that it had only just begun.

Chapter Nine

Nothing compares to being in port–
safe and sound–during a storm.

S UNBEAMS PENETRATED THE cabin ports like knives. They stabbed my eyelids, killing my sleep. I looked at the other settee in the main cabin. Teiga was on her back sound asleep, her chubby arms alongside her head. Jaja stood watch in the warmth of the dodger. I waved good morning silently, and she smiled. Our voices would have waked Teiga in an instant. I looked at my wristwatch–daylight at 2:00 a.m.

I went to the galley, lifted the kettle off the stove, and held it under the water spigot. Using the foot pump, I filled the kettle, careful not to bang it into the stainless steel sink. I placed it quietly back on the stove and lit the propane burner. Then I tapped Jaja on the knee and mouthed the question: "*Coffee?*"

She nodded.

While I waited for the kettle to boil, I pressed a few buttons on the GPS. It told me the Faroes were 33 miles ahead of us and that Iceland was 207 miles behind. Just like that. Wake up, put the kettle on, get an exact position. I really didn't miss using my sextant. On *Direction*, it took hours and many cups of coffee to figure out where we were and how far we had to go.

I looked at the chart. The Faroes are a group of 18 steep islands spread over 50 miles of deep ocean. They are separated by narrow channels and by bottleneck straits through which currents run swiftly, sometimes dangerously. Rich in history, the islands were a pawn between the Danish and the Norwegian monarchies in medieval times. Now they are under the jurisdiction of Denmark. The harbors are quaint, and the hiking is good. The architecture on the islands–stone construction, turf roofs, and colorful paint–suits the breathtaking, rugged landscape. The design of the fishing boats has also been adapted to the rough seas.

We were headed for Djúpini Pass–a strait at the northern end of the island group that is bordered by steep, 1,500-foot-high mountains. If conditions remained calm, we would have no problems. If the wind kicked up, conditions in the entire northern sector of the island group could be 10 times worse than what we had experienced at the Langenes Peninsula. Tides run at up to eight knots around the many headlands in the Faroes. They create vicious seas in bad weather–conditions that even the birds avoid. Halli had warned us against making a landfall in the northern Faroes during strong onshore winds.

The kettle boiled, and I turned off the gas. To allow our young crew-members to sleep, we had removed the piece inside the cap that made the kettle whistle. I put instant coffee, one spoon of sugar, fresh Icelandic milk, and hot water into two mugs. I handed both to Jaja. Sharing a quiet moment together over coffee gives us reassurance. I thought about the significance of coffee in our lives. It brought us together with people ashore and gave us an excuse to invite people aboard. Coffee meant friendship and warmth or just a burst of energy when we needed it.

I put on a jacket and gloves and headed for the cockpit. The sky was clear, dotted with low cumulus clouds that still glowed orange from the slow-motion sunrise. Except for the cool temperature, we could have been making a tropical landfall. In the distance, we could see the tops of the Faroe Islands. Life at sea is civilized when it isn't rough.

Jaja whispered, "Unreal, isn't it?"

A decade had passed since we first thought of going to the Faroes. I remembered sitting in *Direction*'s tiny cabin on England's south coast, listening to the weather bulletin on BBC radio. There had been a 65-knot autumn gale near the Faroes in the forecast sector called "Southeast Iceland." Chills of apprehension surged through us at the thought of sailing there. The Faroes were too far north. They were way beyond what we thought we could handle. We headed south for Spain.

We now drifted peacefully in that Southeast Iceland sector, enjoying a chilly sunrise. Eleven years seemed like a long time to wait for a favorable weather forecast, but here we were, sailing to the Faroes–and sailing away from a place that was even farther north. Our perspective had changed; we were in the present looking down at an old goal instead of looking up at a new one.

Southward.

CHRIS, HOLLY, AND TEIGA WOKE at the same time. Pandemonium. Suddenly, there was a line at the head. Minor quarrels. Lost socks. The kids acted like the three bears in the fairy tale:

"The oatmeal is too hot."

"The oatmeal is too thick. "

"The oatmeal is disgusting."

"Pass the brown sugar."

"The milk tastes bad."

"My spoon has a hair on it."

"At least everyone slept well last night," Jaja said doubtfully.

Grunts and slurps as the food disappeared.

"Should have," I offered. "It was the calmest passage of this voyage."

"When are we going to be in, Daddy?" Holly asked.

"In about two hours."

Pandemonium again as Chris and Holly dropped their bowls and fought to be the first up the companionway ladder to look at the islands. By now, our kids knew a few things about making a landfall. They knew that if we were 30 miles from land on a clear day, they would probably be able to spot it. They also knew that if it was overcast, they might not see anything.

Chris, Holly, and Teiga were involved in almost everything we did. They overheard the trains of logic that we used to make nearly every major decision. Living on board had instilled them with the confidence, patience, and tolerance needed to reside in a relatively cramped space. Jaja entertained them often by reading and playing games, so they were rarely bored. When they needed to stretch and couldn't run horizontally–on an open field, for example–they would channel their energy vertically and climb up. If we were near land (that is, near a doctor) Chris was allowed to climb to the first spreaders, which are about 15 feet off the deck. Holly liked to stand on the boom. The deck of the boat was their environment. They understood the dangers, and they understood how to be safe. We trusted them.

When prospective sailing families ask us for advice on how to extract their kids from a shore-based life, we can't answer. The sailing life is so ingrained in our kids that we have the opposite problem–if it *is* a problem. During our 18 months ashore while we rebuilt *Driver*, all the kids talked about was our previous time aboard *Direction*. Every day they asked when we would return to cruising.

When we first sighted the Faroe Islands, we saw just the tips of the mountains. They gave the illusion that we were approaching low-lying reefs. As the morning matured, the islands rose from the sea, giving Jaja and me a time-lapse view of creation. The gray shapes took on three-dimensional clarity, birds seemed to multiply in number, and the color of the grass changed from neutral to varying hues of green. Small fishing boats dotted the horizon. When we came close to shore, we saw grazing sheep–proof of an organized society. A million years of evolution unfolded before our eyes in a half-day.

The current in Djúpini Pass was slack, testament to the good luck that favored our passage from Iceland. By the time we made our final approach, however, storm clouds filled the skies. Halfway down the 10-mile-long channel, light drizzle forced us to retreat inside our foul-weather gear. According to the weather bulletin, another gale was on its way.

We edged against the small wharf in Fugla Fjord at around noon. Some fishermen wandered over to see what the tide had brought in. They stood silently, watching our three rain-gear-clad children swing from the rigging like a troop of circus monkeys.

One of them spoke. "Come up from Scotland?"

"No," I said. "Down from Iceland."

He raised his eyebrows in surprise. Camaraderie instantly sprang up between us. We were one of them, at home on the sea, willing to take risks. He told us we were the first cruising boat of the season.

We completed customs and immigration formalities, then moved to the town's floating pontoon. There was no charge. The two fishermen came by later and presented us with a plastic bag containing six frozen mackerel and two strong Danish beers.

"Welcome to the Faroe Islands!"

We opened the beers and saluted.

RAIN SHOWERS POURED DOWN intermittently for several days. After the snowy slopes of Iceland, the dark green hills of the Faroes were soothing to our color-starved eyes, even in the rain. We longed to walk on green hillsides, to step on spongy moss, and to goosh our boots in slippery mud. Here, the earth had thawed and was alive. We were in excellent physical condition from walking the hills in Akureyri. Chris and Holly were in particularly good shape, having climbed the church steps every day carrying backpacks filled with books. The rain didn't bother us as we explored the mountains surrounding Fugla Fjord. It was a welcomed respite from snow.

On the other side of the island, behind a small village called Ejde, we hiked through a nobbly green pasture. The incline increased until we were forced to crawl on our hands and knees up the nearly vertical hillside. Well-worn sheep trails crisscrossed the hill, creating a series of rough, steplike terraces. Chris and Holly raced to the top, stood with their hands on their hips, and yelled encouragement to us. Jaja and I took turns helping Teiga. She had outgrown her babypack.

The summit leveled out into a broad, grassy plain about a half-mile in circumference. The seaward edge terminated in a sheer cliff, 800 feet above sea level. We weren't alone. Sheep were grazing and gazing at the world through their oval eyes. Known in the Faroes as "wandering barometers," the sheep are said to move instinctively to protected valleys before the onset of bad weather. During settled weather, we saw sheep at 1,000 feet on seemingly vertical mountainsides. They stood on six-inch-wide paths, eating contentedly. Another interesting fact about sheep: Why do we always feel compelled to "baa" when we see one?

Chris, Holly, and Teiga loved to run after the sheep, trying to pet them. On top of the cliffs above Ejde, we cautioned the children against accidentally running into midair. We told them they would drop like stones to certain death. Best to spell it out plainly.

Jaja and I took turns approaching the cliffs cautiously to look down at the sea, while the other held the kids in check. It was thrilling to be so high on what felt like the edge of the world. Jaja admitted that standing at the cliff edges didn't effect her physically. She enjoyed the thrill in the same way that she had once enjoyed skydiving and flying solo in small airplanes. Alone in the sky, soaring.

Fearless.

I discovered a unique nerve devoted to connecting my eyeballs to my toenails. My toes curled up inside my boots with an intensity that was directly proportional to the height above sea level. I liked the cliff-edge thrill too, but for me, it was a more calculated experience.

From my lofty altitude, I looked toward the northern horizon. A large cargo ship trailing a long, white wake was traversing the broad expanse of ocean. Watching its progress was like watching the moon overhead. I knew the ship was moving, but from this distance, it seemed nearly stationary.

Traveling at sea level on *Driver* is different. Compared to other modes of transportation, *Driver* moves slowly. (Her hull speed–the maximum speed she can sail without an extra push from the waves–is six knots, which is about seven miles per hour.) However, when we are on board watching the water move past us, we feel as if *Driver* is sprinting.

Conquering Iceland left a gap in our aspirations. What were we sprinting toward now? We had reached the summit of our abilities, and we felt a vague detachment as we wandered south down the latitudes. The Faroes were stunning, exciting, and full of mystery, but what was the next challenge? Back when Jaja and I left England for Spain, our goal was to find warm sunshine. As if we were climbing down a ladder from a rocky, windswept precipice, we hadn't stopped until our feet landed in hot, white Caribbean sand. Were we headed for anything symbolic now?

Choosing to have an undefined destination can be a goal in itself because you never know what is coming next. All possibilities are open. After our five-minute marriage ceremony in Barbados, Jaja and I set sail westward toward the Pacific. Our ambitions were to spend as much time together as possible and to see how far we could get before we ran out of money. We lived like children. The ocean was our backyard, and a succession of empty beaches became our playground. We discovered many things about life that year. Most significantly, we learned that romance is free, but hedonism keeps a tab.

We became parents. Our memories began to revolve around the ages of our kids. Their birthdays became our milestones; their height measurements on the main bulkhead of the cabin were measures of distance traveled. Now our kids were sharing our dreams. For the rest of their lives, whenever they look at a world map, Iceland and the Faroes will have textures, sounds, and smells. Our children will have a benchmark against which to measure other cultures.

I walked away from the cliff and uncurled my toes. If we always kept a safe distance from the edges of ambition, we would never appreciate the rewards of the climb. Now we needed to find a new peak to scale.

CHRIS, HOLLY, AND TEIGA ROAMED the floating pontoon in Ejde fishing for cod with hand lines. They screeched with laughter every time they hoisted a fish onto the dock.

"Daddy! We have another one for you! Bring the winch handle and hit it on the head."

In a rare moment of reprise, Jaja was alone in the cabin, her feet up, reading a book. I was in the cockpit making some plywood shelves for the galley pan locker. Our portable generator took a beating in Akureyri, running for several hundred hours on the snowy dock to charge our batteries. Nevertheless, it was still going strong and provided ample power for my 120-volt jigsaw. In between cuts, I clubbed dinner.

At gutting time, the kids gathered around while I dissected a few of the fish. Following Holly's inquisitive suggestions, we opened the stomachs, examined the partially digested crabs and smaller fishes, then picked apart the gills and eyeballs. The kids learned about lateral lines, buoyancy, and blood circulation. The dock became an outdoor schoolroom. Jaja sat on deck and helped identify the organs.

Chris asked, "Do fish get bored? You know, just swimming around in circles?"

"No," I said.

"But what do fish *do*?" Holly asked.

"They eat, they spawn, and they try to survive for as long as possible." Jaja said. "The same as all animals. Staying alive is automatic; it's built into our brains. Humans are different because we want to have *a reason* for trying to stay alive."

"What do you mean?"

I replied, "It means that we humans get bored just walking around in circles."

The next morning, a full-blown northwesterly gale kept us on board. Jaja made the kids write in their journals. They balked at first but enjoyed it once they got going. Even Teiga had a journal. She dictated, and Jaja wrote. Afterwards, the kids played with Legos and colored. At intervals, Jaja and I played Battleship with them, and Uno, and Crazy Eights, and dominoes.

During the blustery day, Jaja and I took turns walking along the coast, watching the thundering seas and the vicious tide rips offshore. The harbor at Ejde is well protected from the churning seas, but hurricane-force gusts roared over the nearby isthmus into the harbor, lifting curtains of white spume. These gusts continued down the inlet then blasted the cliffs on the opposite side. They even blew the falling water in a waterfall straight up, high above the cliff like a geyser. We added extra docklines to *Driver*, thankful that we were not trying to make landfall that day.

After the gale, I called Tórshavn, the capital of the Faroes, on our VHF radio to get an updated forecast. Light northerlies were predicted, but when I conferred with a local fisherman, he looked skyward and insisted the wind would be from the south. He laughed when I mentioned the "official" forecast. The Faroese government can't afford its own weather bureau, so it downloads satellite data from the weather bureau in Denmark without bothering to add interpolations based on local phenomena.

I asked the fisherman for his opinion about going south to the next island called Vaago. I needed all the information I could get because the tide rips are no joke. There is a famous story about a 4,000-ton steamer that set out from the main shipping harbor at Tórshavn in the 1920s. It was an average day until a moderate breeze challenged an adverse current. The ship encountered phenomenal conditions. Her lifeboats and funnels were swept overboard by huge breaking seas. She returned to port for four months of repairs.

Years of subsequent study resulted in a slim volume entitled *Tidal Currents Around the Faroes*. We purchased the book in Fugla Fjord. This volume depicts the movement of the currents in the islands hour by hour and details the severity of the currents as affected by wind from various directions. I mentioned the book to the fishermen, but he waved it off as if I had insulted him.

"Remember," he said. "This is the 'Land of Maybe'. Maybe it will be calm; maybe it will be rough. Maybe there'll be sun. Maybe rain. Conditions can change from hour to hour. But I'd say if you go tomorrow about an hour after low water, you'll have a good time of it. Or maybe, you'll get your decks cleaned. Remember, Son, this coast is unpredictable."

I regarded the old fisherman's arrogant wisdom with respect. The information he gave me about the current matched the tide book perfectly.

We had encountered a five-knot tidal stream while sailing to Ejde. Fortunately, the current and the wind were both pushing us the way we wanted to go. We literally had flown around Rivtangi, a rocky headland at the mouth of the Djúpini Pass. There are so many channels and headlands in the Faroes, however, that getting the timing right in one location does not guarantee that you will get it right just a few miles farther along. I used the tide book like a train schedule picking our time of departure to the half-hour and hoping to make all the right "connections" at each headland.

The tide rips that had nearly sunk the steamer are located in an area of shoals and narrow channels near the southern islands. The headlands on the northern islands are obstacles to be respected, but in the north, the water is deep, and there are few shallow obstructions on the sea bottom to create dangerous waves. As long as the windspeed remained below 12 knots, there was no reason that a well-found boat such as *Driver* should not survive on the north coast. This was not true in the shoal water to the south–as we would soon learn. We had to cross those southern shoals before we headed for Scotland.

UNDER POWER, *Driver* drove purposefully into the harbor at Tórshavn on Streymoy Island. We saw boats, apartment complexes, buildings, houses, trucks, cars, and telephone wires–but our engine drowned out the shoreside noises. This gave the scene an unreal quality–like watching TV with the volume on "mute."

At the visitor wharf in the heart of the city, we turned off our diesel and then cringed. We were used to the small villages in the Faroes–cobbled lanes, turf roofs, wandering old ladies, quiet grocery stores, and slow-moving vehicles. Tórshavn presented constant noise. In addition to the steady hum of automobile traffic, we heard the din of a large commercial shipyard where workers were sand blasting and chipping rust. Fishing boats spewed exhaust and left annoying wakes as they came and went from the busy marina. We heard ferryboat horns, the drone of buses, and the clink of bottles at a sidewalk café. The air over the harbor smelled of fish, urine, paint, and engine exhaust. What little clean air remained was infiltrated by cigarette smoke. It was going to take a day or two to adjust to city life.

If colors and textures could be used to describe a destination, Tórshavn was tarnished silver. It is an old waterfront with a respectable history. To us, Reykjavík was a pleasing, pale gold experience. Landing at Reykjavík, we felt as if we had just reached the thin air of a high-altitude summit. There, our initial disorientation was almost fun. Akureyri, on the other hand, was opal–white on the surface with hidden depths. Grímsey was pure crystal.

We remembered our most severe case of sensory overload–the day we completed our circumnavigation aboard *Direction*. We sailed into Florida's Lake Worth Inlet during a Sunday afternoon in August amid fast speedboats, sport-fishing boats, cabin cruisers, daysailers, aluminum skiffs, jetskis, sailboards, kayaks, brave swimmers, and amphibious dogs. The scene gleamed like orange and red plastic. The sun, our cherished ally, beat down on us with traitorous ferocity. It took us six months to adjust to the hectic pace of the United States. We had just put a lifetime dream behind us. The desire to sail to Iceland rose from the ashes of our burning unrest.

In Tórshavn, we buttoned up *Driver* and headed to shore quickly. The cloudy afternoon made the city look drab, and we felt out of place treading on concrete surrounded by glass, threatened by automobiles, and scrutinized by too many unfamiliar faces. The city streets devoured us, but we knew that "confrontation" is the best remedy for culture shock.

The next morning, we attacked town with a shopping list. Spending money is a good justification for being in a city. The two concepts suit each other. We bought new sneakers for the family, got our film developed, browsed, ate lunch in a restaurant, went to museums, ravaged the grocery store, bought new life jackets for the kids, and spent a lot of time taking money out of cash machines. We became friends with the city of Tórshavn. We had a need–an appetite–and the place fed us.

LATER IN THE AFTERNOON beneath a warm, hazy summer sky, Holly and Teiga played on deck with their two cherished dolls, Buttercup and Cute Baby. Chris played on our bosun's chair, the wooden "swing" on which I go up the mast to make repairs or inspect the rigging. Chris attached the chair to the end of the spare main halyard and then preset the height so that his dangling feet would clear the girls' heads as they played on the foredeck. The chair became a swing that would satisfy the whims of any kid.

First, Chris just pushed off the mast with his feet–in preparation for more serious "flying." Next, he rappelled from the mast to the inner forestay wire, then from the inner forestay to the headstay at the bow of the boat. At the headstay, he positioned his feet carefully against the wire and launched himself with a big, springy push. His swinging path took him out and aft, around the mast. Like a trapeze artist, he came to rest expertly at the stern against the backstay. For two hours, he flew fore and aft–forestay to backstay, backstay to forestay. When he gained confidence, he added a slow, 360-degree twist to the flight. Chris became a cross between Tarzan and Spiderman.

We couldn't have called more attention to ourselves if we had posted a blinking neon sign that read, "Come Stare at Us." Soon, a crowd of spectators–the kids called them "gawkers"–gathered on the wharf to watch Chris. We knew he would not do any stunts that were beyond his capabilities, but he was very fluid in his actions. This gave the illusion that his antics were dangerous. Some people oohed and aahed. I spent my youth climbing the towering Douglas firs and red cedars in my backyard, and I knew firsthand that children possess a remarkable ability to hang on. We did caution Chris against hamming it up. Pride goes before a fall.

Jaja and I smiled at the crowd. (Who can resist being the center of attention?) We politely answered queries from the gawkers.

"Did you sail that boat all the way from America?"

"Did you have any bad storms?"

"Did you see any pirates?"

"What do you do for money?"

When I asked a few of the gawkers what *they* did for money, most of them got angry at my impertinence. So I tried to be more philosophical.

"Priorities," I would explain. "It's not how few dollars we spend that matters. It's what we choose to avoid spending money on that really adds up."

By the time the 20th gawker asked us the same questions in rapid-fire succession, Jaja and I retreated below to protect our sanity. Through the open hatches in the cabin, we heard questions being directed at our children.

"Where are you from?"

"Do you like living on a boat?"

"Do you get scared?"

"Do you get bored?"

Chris gave monosyllabic grunts between flights, Teiga shyly ignored the queries, and Holly tried her best to be polite.

The most challenging question for them was, "Where are you from?" We had coached Chris and Holly because the question confused them.

The children wondered, "Does the person want to know where I was born? Or does he want to know where we last lived?"

Jaja and I said that people are generally interested in where the children were born.

Minutes later, right on cue, we heard a gentleman asking Holly, Chris, and Teiga where they were from. Through a cabin port, we could see the man clearly. His eyes were challenging the children, but his mouth was agape as he watched Chris "fly." He waited patiently for answers.

Between transits Chris shouted, "Au-stral-ia!"

With her pure American accent, Holly quietly said, "I'm from New Zealand, and my little sister was born in an Oriental marina."

The guy looked at *Driver*'s American ensign and walked away grumbling. "Wisenheimers!"

Jaja and I have a difficult time answering the question about our origins. I was born in Los Angeles and raised in Seattle. I left L.A. at age six, and I had been away from Seattle for 14 years. Was I from Seattle? Or was I a Californian? My ancestry is a mix of Scottish, Cherokee, and German. Jaja's ancestry is Scottish, English, Italian, and French. She was born and raised in New Jersey. When we first met, she used to lie and tell people she was from Big Lake, Alaska–a town of her own creation. Jaja had never been to Alaska, but she liked the image the name Big Lake conjured up.

The last place we lived ashore was Oriental. To most people, the coastal region of North Carolina means pine trees, sand dunes, and the Wright brothers–which isn't so bad. The Seattle I knew growing up no longer exists. The low-tech, low-stress, economically stagnant 1970s are gone forever. Seattle's "culture" has been transformed by new freeways, taller buildings, a soaring population, and a famous micro-technological yuppydom. How can I say I'm from a place where I get lost driving around?

Jaja and I envied our Icelandic friends' sense of geographical identity. They would be forever from the towns in which they were born. The Icelandic population is relatively small and unchanging. The energy individuals put into their own communities improves the general good. Ideals are perpetuated through the generations.

While living in Akureyri, we learned the meaning of community spirit. But somehow, once we understood that spirit, our own sense of not belonging became more acute. Despite the overwhelming hospitality we received, we realized we would never "belong". That was something you had to be born to. However, we had tasted the Icelanders' strong nationalism, and it was sweet.

We awoke one morning in Tórshavn and discovered that another foreign sailboat had tied to the wharf. It was a red ketch from Holland named *Terra Nova,* and the couple on board were the first cruisers we had seen in 10 months. We had almost forgotten that other cruisers existed. Sailing alone in the far north taught us a great deal about self-reliance and how to deal with isolation, but the ketch reminded us of the good times traveling with other boats. Each mode of cruising has its compensations.

Anyone who departs in his own boat to go cruising has won a mental battle of sorts and has made the decision to cut the ties that bind him to land. This includes saying goodbye to friends ashore. However, most bluewater cruisers soon form automatic bonds with other cruisers. Friendships spring up easily, and "anchorage communities" form quickly. Social pecking orders develop naturally, and scoundrels either adhere to the group's codes or are snubbed. Everyone who wants to be included takes his or her place and tries to perpetuate good feelings within the group. Belonging to an organized cruising "society" promotes safety and reassurance.

We have also found that it is fun to have entire coastlines to yourself.

WE SET OFF FROM TÓRSHAVN just after noon, eager to be sailing away from the hubbub. Our destination was Suderoy, the southernmost of the Faroe Islands. A gale was due to hit the region later that night, but we had plenty of time to make the 30-mile passage. Despite the moderate northwesterly breeze, the sun felt warm. Its energy softened our impressions of the city from which we had just departed.

We entered the main channel south of Tórshavn at hull speed and caught the six-knot favorable current as if we had jumped onto a passing train. The GPS indicated that our true speed over the bottom was an astonishing 12 knots. We were belted by strong gusts of wind whistling down from the mountains, and I ran to the foredeck to shorten sail. In the lulls, the reefed sails weren't adequate to maintain hull speed, but I resisted shaking out a reef because the frequent gusts were violent. When we entered the next bottleneck channel, we encountered a long ground swell and an increasingly strong breeze. Our excitement gave way to anxiety. We were in the exact location where the ill-fated steamer had run into difficulty.

Conditions deteriorated quickly. The brilliant, clear skies hazed over. The northwest wind began backing to the south–a sure indication that the next low-pressure center was approaching sooner than expected. We had less than five miles to go when the wind increased to near gale force. To maintain our course after the shift in wind direction, we reefed the sails even more and trimmed the sheets in tight. Suddenly, the current began setting us away from the island at an alarming rate. Ever so slowly, we made progress toward our intended haven on Trongisvágs Fjord. The clouds thickened, and it began raining.

The wind funneled down the fjord and screamed in *Driver*'s rigging. Rain beat against our cold faces. Chris and Holly were below on the settees in the main cabin playing a story game that involved characters of their own invention called Pot and Mary. Teiga was queasy, and Jaja stayed below with her as much as possible. Just a routine day-sail. By the time we tied to the high concrete wharf at the town of Tvøroyri at 6:00 p.m., white-water gusts were ranging down the fjord.

The wind remained at gale force the next day, but fortunately, the rain held off. We stayed in port. Tvøroyri is a quintessential Faroese town. Colorful houses and low buildings that look like children's toys stand on a steep hillside. Beside narrow roads and on wandering paths, we saw sheep lazily munching on lush green grass. Groups of boys kicked a ball on the well-kept soccer field. Women pushed baby carriages and chatted with their friends. Small children laughed in playgrounds. Tough-acting teenagers loitered, flirted with the opposite gender, and looked too young and ridiculous to be taken seriously.

I went to the harbor office for a long-range weather forecast. Our next stop was Scotland, 200 miles to the south. The man behind the counter was eager to oblige. He made a telephone call, and a minute later, a dozen feet of paper streamed out of the fax machine. The Danish weather charts provided good detail, and we could see that several days of favorable conditions were imminent.

Using a pay phone, I made a long-distance call to the weather center in Reykjavík and spoke to the senior forecaster, who still remembered me. He confirmed the arrival of a weak high-pressure system and gave me his conservative opinion that, once again, we could expect 48 hours of favorable winds before the next low came through with strong southerlies. To be caught by a southerly and have to beat into the wind would be rough, frustratingly slow, and possibly dangerous. With luck, we would only need 32 hours to make it to Stornoway at the northern end of Scotland's Outer Hebrides Islands.

We waited expectantly for the arrival of the next high-pressure system so that the wind would clock to the northwest, giving us a favorable tail wind. When we went to bed, low clouds were still coming from the south. When I awoke at 4:00 a.m., the sky was clear, and puffy, cumulus clouds had arrived from the north. The barometer had slowed its ascent, another indication that good weather had finally arrived. Jaja and I were dressed by 5:00 a.m. While the kids still slept, we motored out of the fjord to take full advantage of the weather window.

We hoisted sails and set a course that would take us well clear of Flesjarnar, a dangerous group of rocks and shoal water two miles south of Suderoy. Strong currents set across the area. What would seem like an adequate safety margin of a mile or two could be eaten up in a few short minutes. If a small boat is caught in such a strong tide rip, forward progress could be impossible. We gave the rocks a generous berth of six miles. Better safe than sinking.

It was a relief to be under way. The only thing worse than starting a potentially rough passage is waiting to go. In our haste to depart, we had forgotten our favorite Faroe Island myth. I scanned the green hills on the south end of the island with binoculars and grinned.

Sure enough, sheep were heading for the mountaintops.

Chapter Ten

*Boredom and impatience can infect
cruising sailors-tempting them
to go to sea in foul conditions.*

THE 36-HOUR SAIL between the Faroes and Stornoway on the Isle of
Lewis in the Outer Hebrides was almost perfect. The breeze held trade-wind
steady, the skies remained clear, the seas were moderate, and Teiga only
threw up once. But it was cold on deck–somewhere around 40 degrees Fahrenheit–with a damp, chill wind. I wore a hat, gloves, and full foul-weather
gear. After a year in the high latitudes, we longed for hot weather.

We were headed south. Why not keep right on going until we found real
summer weather? In Spain, we could go ashore wearing shorts and T-shirts.
We could sit barefoot at sidewalk restaurants, drink coffee and nibble on
freshly baked bread. We could anchor at Isle de Cies, climb the hills, and
wander on the white sandy beaches. Our kids would love it. From Spain, we
could continue south to Portugal and stop at Peniche where we had bought
our gold wedding rings. Was it really 11 years ago? If we kept moving, we
could be in the Caribbean by Christmas. Bathing-suit sailing. A tan line.
Salty skin and a scratchy T-shirt. Hot sun.

Jaja opened the zipper flap on the dodger. "Why are you smiling?"

"I was remembering the Grenadines."

"You mean the time the charterboat next to us played the stereo all
night? As I recall, the next morning at 6:00 a.m., you started our generator on
purpose, and everyone on the charterboat came on deck screaming."

I chuckled. "I'd forgotten about that. There's nothing worse than suffering someone else's poor taste in loud music."

I took a sip of lukewarm coffee. With the sails set for downwind sailing,
Driver rolled along at six-plus knots. I let out the mainboom on the port side
and rigged a dedicated line called a preventer from the end of the boom to
the deck. This rope "prevented" the boom from swinging back over the boat
unexpectedly, which could injure–or even kill–anyone who stood in its path.
The jib flew from the whisker pole on the opposite (starboard) side of the
boat. "Wing 'n wing" was the technical name for this sail combination. The

self-steering windvane did a superb job of keeping *Driver* right on course. Many cruisers find that their windvanes have difficulty steering with the wind blowing from behind. The windspeed, and its affect on the vane part of the self-steering, is reduced when you are sailing away from the direction of the wind. Fortunately, our windvane was extremely sensitive, even downwind. That, coupled with *Driver's* extraordinary ability to "track" in a straight line through the moderate seas, meant that on this passage, we could enjoy smooth sailing and spend less time checking our course.

Wrapped in a blanket, Teiga sat on Jaja's lap in the companionway. The fresh air coming through the open flap of the dodger revived her. She stood up and poked her head out of the dodger to let the cool breeze blow directly on her. At that moment, an errant waved slapped the side of *Driver*, and a few drops of spray dotted Teiga's face.

"Mommy! I just got ocean in my mouth!"

Twenty-four hours later, we sailed parallel to the pale green, peat hills on the Isle of Lewis. *Driver* surged toward the harbor entrance at Stornoway. Our entire crew was on deck enjoying the thin sun and eager to be in port. How wonderful it would be to step ashore and speak our native tongue! Of course, the joke is that Americans and Scots are separated by a common language. But it would be a heck of a lot easier to understand a heavy Scottish brogue than to catch the feathery intonations of Icelandic.

In Iceland and the Faroes, most adults speak English. But we missed being able to understand the idle chat of kids, and we missed catching the meaning of offhand, colloquial remarks directed at us by locals who thought we understood. We also missed reading the newspaper and listening to regional radio. You miss so much of a culture when you don't speak the language very well. In Scotland, we also looked forward to food prices that were closer to the farm, and drink prices closer to the grain.

After dropping and furling the sails, we motored slowly toward the Stornoway waterfront. The kids jumped up and down.

Holly pointed toward the shoreline. "Mommy! Look at the castle! Can we go in it? I've never seen a real castle before."

"Look at all the stone building blocks," Chris mused. "How much do you think the castle weighs?"

"At least a million pounds," I said.

"You made that up."

"Well, what do you think?"

"At least two million pounds," Chris said knowingly.

Teiga looked at Jaja and whispered. "I wonder if a king lives there."

On the town side of the harbor, brownstone buildings with peaked slate roofs dominated the skyline. Each roof had several yellow chimneys sprouting from it.

"It looks like Mary Poppins lives here!" Holly said.

We tied to the commercial jetty against slimy wooden pilings. The harbormaster assigned us a berth in the small marina, then presented us with the bill to be paid in advance. We hadn't paid for a berth in over a year–not since leaving Bermuda. We feared that in Scotland the relatively low food prices might be negated by the dockage fees. There was a free anchorage, but it was exposed to persistent commercial traffic and would be rolly.

It was warmer on land than on the water. We walked to town in the bright summer sun wearing light sweaters, jeans, and sneakers. Out of habit, we brought a backpack crammed with hats, gloves, heavy sweaters, and raincoats. Our brains needed reprogramming. There wasn't a cloud in the sky, and the boat was only 10 minutes away.

First, we stopped at a cash machine to load our wallets with "pounds" of money. The next stop was a bookstore. Months earlier, we had exhausted our supply of English-language books, and the kids were starved for reading material. This would also be the children's reward for their patience and endurance during our northern adventure. Holly selected the seven books of the *Narnia* series by C. S. Lewis, and she began reading *The Magician's Nephew* before we even left the store. Chris selected books on modern science. Teiga chose titles from the Postman Pat collection and emulated her big sister by walking around with her face in an open book.

At the grocery store, Jaja and I held products in the air, marveling not at how expensive things were, but how relatively cheap. In the center of the market, two full isles of wine, beer, and spirits called for attention. Like gum and candy at the checkout counters, the liquor was put there to tantalize all who were open to temptation. If a country wants to increase its tax revenue, all it needs to do is sell heavily taxed booze in the grocery stores. However, it may not encourage a sober population.

When visiting Great Britain, I've always enjoyed choosing among the many brands of beer. This time, I filled my shopping cart with a dozen samples. Grocery shopping hadn't been this fun in a long time. To balance my indulgence, I added a bottle of Grand Marnier for Jaja.

Back on *Driver*, we unloaded our haul. There was more food than we could conceivably eat in a week, everything from vegetables to chicken to steaks. It was a careless debauch that overcompensated for our yearlong "abstinence." And as if that wasn't enough, we closed up the boat that evening and went out to dinner.

That night, we slept with the diesel stove turned off, something we hadn't done in port since the previous summer. It was strange to wake up in the chilly, damp cabin. Crawling out of the warm sheets and putting on cold clothes reminded me of summer vacations, visiting new places, and a break in routine. The promise of another warm day nurtured my childhood memories.

Across from *Driver* on the other side of the narrow estuary, Lews Castle stood like a rocky island amid a sea of mowed grass. Century-old trees stood guard around it. A blue heron walked majestically on the mud flats searching for food. On our side of the river, Stornoway came to life with the rumble of trucks and the *thud-boom-thump* of high-powered stereo systems blasting from dilapidated automobiles. Civilization. Noise. Instant gratifications.

We wondered what we should do on our first day in Scotland. Precious sunny days should not be wasted. Should we work on *Driver*? Do the laundry? Go sightseeing? We decided to be tourists and boarded a local bus—eager to see the interior as well as the western shore of the island.

Outside of the city, all traces of trees on the low, rolling hills vanished. The Isle of Lewis is a great mound of peat besprinkled with the roaming stone walls so typical of Great Britain. Here and there, a tongue of the sea infiltrates the coast, creating sandy coves and rocky foreshores.

Flocks of sheep and housing developments vied for superiority. The scant motion of dirty wool lent beauty to the desolate plains, and the unpainted stone and mortar dwellings accentuated the emptiness. We spent half the day entombed in the local bus, enjoying mindless sightseeing. Perhaps we should have chosen a more stimulating activity, but if we skipped the bus trip, we knew we would always regret it.

After the toe-bending cliffs in the Faroes, Jaja said the fields on the Isle of Lewis looked like big, green ground swells rolling on the surface of an ocean. I said it looked like a mall parking lot. Jaja saw beauty in the bare hills colored by subtle shades of green and brown. I saw only dreariness. We agreed that the scenery was visually undemanding.

We planned to sail south through the Outer Hebrides, then cross to the Scottish mainland near the Isle of Skye. There were dozens of anchorages—more than we could ever hope to explore in six weeks. From Skye, we would sail to the Caledonian Canal and transit the locks and lakes that cut across the Highlands—countryside made famous by Robert Louis Stevenson and Sir Walter Scott—to the North Sea. Soon we would compare the actual landscape to the mental images we had created while reading books. We had "banked" enough time that we could spend several weeks exploring.

IN STORNOWAY, a cruiser had told us about two-mile-long Loch Mahar-abhig on the east side of the Isle of Lewis. He described empty anchorages and bucolic scenery–a chance to escape the hubbub of town. He also loaned us his charts for photocopying. Now we were looking for the seemingly invisible entrance to the loch. Our faces collected salt spray and cold rain as we searched the shoreline anxiously. The chart showed numerous underwater hazards around us–all demanding extreme caution. Our navigation had to be precise. We should have spotted the narrow cut by now, but all we could see were breakers tumbling over the rocky shoreline. If we couldn't find the entrance soon, we would need to abandon our plans and sail another few hours to the next sheltered bay.

Just as we prepared to turn away, I caught a glimpse of what looked like an extremely narrow channel. My common sense rebelled. How could we take *Driver* in there? Was it worth the risk? After all, it was not crucial that we visit Loch Maharabhig. Had it not been for the local knowledge of the cruiser in Stornoway, we would have passed by without hesitation. Still, we doubted his assurances that the unbuoyed entrance was deep and safe. Conversely, his opinion that the narrow gap might scare the life out of us was proving highly accurate. After weighing the odds, we decided to go for it.

The entrance was 70 feet wide and lined with house-size boulders. Jaja pulled down the jib, and I started the engine. That way, we had more control of the boat as we passed through the opening. I kept one eye glued to the depthsounder and one eye focused ahead. Jaja stood on the bow rail staring into the murky depths in front of us, scanning for underwater hazards. We motorsailed so close to some of the rocks on shore that it looked as if we could touch them. Fortunately, the water remained deeper than 20 feet, and the surface was smooth in the narrow gap. The danger was actually quite low, but it would be foolhardy to assume this in advance. In the end, it was the sudden proximity of shore on either side of the channel that proved disorienting.

Slowly, the main body of the loch opened up in front of us. I felt my muscles relax. Nevertheless, we held some of our jubilation in check. We would still have to go through the cut again when we left in a few days' time.

Because Loch Maharabhig is surrounded by land, we felt like we had just sailed into a mountain lake. Rolling hills of gray rock interspersed with green and purple bracken encircled us. Shaggy sheep dotted the terrain, and our kids tried to get their attention by "baa-ing" loudly.

The photocopied chart showed several small deserted bays with good depths for anchoring. However, when we inspected these bays, none of them seemed large enough for *Driver* to swing on her anchor without going aground. We didn't feel like messing around with lines to shore, or with second anchors to prevent the boat from swinging, so we looked at other larger bays around the loch. But these were either too exposed to the blustery south wind or else too deep. Typical. Eventually, we dropped the hook in a calm anchorage in the lee of some cliffs across from an island called Eilean Thoraidh.

We were finally on our own, anchored in an isolated bay, swinging to the breeze, enjoying total privacy. No houses or boats were in sight. We had not anchored in a deserted bay for over a year, not since we explored Iceland's Glacier Fjord region on the northwest coast. That area was a national park dominated by waterfalls and festooned with wildflower meadows. Before striking out for the Arctic Circle, we spent a week walking the hills and rowing along the quiet, deserted shorelines.

Cruising sailors frequently enjoy "anchoring out" to avoid the expense and commotion of tying up dockside. In Iceland and the Faroe Islands, there are very few places in which to anchor safely. There are plenty of harbors, but these are chock full of docks and quays. Anchoring in these busy ports is unsafe because commercial vessels can easily run down a boat at anchor. There are few natural harbors in either country. The best natural bays, such as Reykjavík, Akureyri, and Tórshavn, are devoted to commercial shipping, fishing, and tourism industries, which are crucial to the local economies. Most of the other harbors where we tied up–Flateyri, Grímsey, Seydis Fjord, Fugla Fjord, Ejde–were not natural harbors and would have provided marginal protection without the addition of substantial, man-made breakwaters. Luckily, dockage in Iceland and the Faroes was free. We were charged for tying up in Scotland, but we usually had the alternative of anchoring in one of the many protected, natural anchorages.

Secluded anchorages are pleasant for other reasons, too–not just as a means to avoid payment. Away from the towns, time is pleasingly irrelevant. By choice, our life on board is slow paced. Towns, on the other hand, infect us with nervous energy. In Loch Maharabhig, it took us a day or two to unwind and to remember that every minute doesn't have to be organized.

As soon as we ate lunch, we prepared to row our dinghy ashore. I designed and built our 10-foot fiberglass dinghy myself so that it would safely bear our weight. It could actually hold five full-grown adults and still row easily. Another way we slowed our pace of life was by not using an outboard engine on the dinghy. An outboard would demand maintenance. This would eat up time and dig into our budget. Also, with an outboard engine droning away, conversation would be impossible. We have some of our best family times rowing around quietly in our dinghy, listening to shoreside noises and to the rhythms of nature.

The afternoon we arrived in Loch Maharabhig, we roamed the hills with sheep that grazed among heather and gorse. We discovered a rocky beach nestled in the lee of some cliffs that made a good playground for the kids. They scurried about, lifting stones looking for sea creatures. The sun beat down for a generous number of hours before it started raining again.

We stayed in the loch for several days waiting for the weather to break. Rain squalls came at intervals, and the temperature dropped to around 50 degrees Fahrenheit–damp and unpleasant. Once again, we lit the diesel stove. The thrill of summer that we experienced in Stornoway was washed away, just as the rain washed the salt spray from our cabin windows. From the tops of the surrounding hills, we saw the rough conditions on the open water. The notion of bashing to windward with seasick kids was more than we could bear. Maybe we were tired of hardship. Maybe we lacked a goal.

After three days of rain, we began to reexamine our itinerary. We still had time to cruise the west coast of Ireland and cross the Bay of Biscay ahead of the autumn gales. The Tropics were looking better and better. A beachy Christmas. No more snowsuits, no more hats, mitts, and rubber boots. Instead of cold, wintry rain, we could enjoy warm, tropical rain. Instead of burning 800 gallons of diesel a year to heat our cabin and run our engine on the often windless seas, we could indulge in other ways.

Our destination was still up in the air because our application to spend the winter in Denmark was denied. The reason for the denial: We had lived in Iceland for a year already. It made no sense to me that a year in one country could affect a year in another, but the immigration officer at the Danish Embassy met my protest with typical bureaucratic obstinacy. Over the phone, I could literally hear the heels of her shoes digging into the floor under her desk.

"We're tourists," I argued. "We will live on our boat and spend lots of money. The grocery stores will love us."

"No. We will not give you a visa."

"Why not?"

"Those are the rules."

There were many rude things I wanted to say to her, but I held my tongue. Petty gratifications–such as mouthing off at bureaucrats–are generally counterproductive. I walked away from the phone booth wondering if my restraint was a sign of increasing maturity or increasing laziness.

The rain dried up on the third afternoon, but the adverse winds persisted. We grabbed the chance to visit the fishing and sheep farming community called Marvig at the head of the loch. We hauled up *Driver*'s anchor, motored a mile, and reanchored nearer to the village. Later, we dragged the dinghy up the stone beach amid piles of abandoned fishing nets, fish traps, broken buoys, and rotting rowboats.

Marvig was everything we imagined an Outer Hebrides village to be. A single-lane road ran up the steep hill from the wharf and snaked between sparse homesteads before disappearing over a flat ridge. We followed the road, pushing Teiga in her dilapidated stroller. Chris and Holly walked with springy steps in their new sneakers. The day was still gray with a threat of more rain. We should have worn boots and brought raincoats.

The hillsides were green and rocky, well manicured by the sheep. Post-and-wire fences stood intertwined with ancient stone walls, the construction of which seemed too perfect to have been made using random rocks. The stones fit together snugly–like Legos. In my imagination, I saw myself heaving stones year after year, breaking my back to clear my fields. I grew fatigued looking at the walls and thinking about how much work it took to build them.

Our kids tried to chase the sheep, and Jaja and I still "baaed" involuntarily. Three farmers were shearing sheep in a pen near the crest of the ridge. Using special scissors whose handles were attached by a spring instead of a pivoting screw, the Old Boys worked quickly and silently. They courteously stopped when we offered a hello, touching the brims of their dirty caps with their scissors. Every quarter-mile, a stone house with a slate roof occupied a section of cultivated land, bringing order to the chaotic landscape. There were kitchen gardens, clotheslines, goats, cars, and crumbling stone sheds. However, we did not see any children's toys–no swings, bikes, or anything colorful. All the clothes on the lines were adult-size.

We continued for another mile with the wind in our faces, happy to be moving. After mounting another ridge and seeing a large expanse of heather and rock, we decided to turn back. We were overcome with lethargy. Where was the energy that we had in the Faroes? Our walks ashore were becoming fewer and shorter. We suspected that we were beginning to suffer the repercussions of traveling without a specific destination. We picnicked behind a large boulder and fueled up on coffee, chocolate, and fruit juice.

Back at the dinghy, Jaja and I sat on the round rocks. We finished the coffee in our thermos and let the kids play on the stony beach. They squealed excitedly and danced around, pretending they were being pinched by small crabs. Actually, it was the poor crabs that were being tortured. A small pickup truck drove down the hill to the wharf and discharged four men. The three Old Boys we had seen shearing sheep smiled, but the other man was younger, about our age, and he ignored our intrusion. He launched a water-logged rowboat and paddled out to a 25-foot wooden fishing boat. A choking cloud of blue smoke erupted from the exhaust when he fired up the engine.

The Old Boys waited patiently on the wharf smoking hand-rolled cigarettes. Jaja and I summoned up the courage to talk to them. They spoke Gaelic among themselves, and fluent English–clipped and fast–to us. We had no trouble understanding them.

"Hello," Jaja said.

"Aye, and hello to you," one of then offered cheerily. "Seems as if your wee duckies are at home on a beach. Glad I'm not a crab today." Chris, Holly, and Teiga were still lifting stones and giggling.

"They're born to it," Jaja said.

"Is that your boat anchored round yon point?"

"Yes, it is," Jaja replied. "She's been our home for two years."

"Saw your flag. Sailed her up from America have you?"

"Yes," I answered, "but we've just recently come down from Iceland."

"Iceland? Well that's a wee bit away from America."

"That's for sure." There was a pause in the conversation. I ventured another comment. "This is our first trip to Scotland, and we think it is very beautiful."

One of the Old Boys spat on the ground. "Well, this part of it is, anyway."

"Going fishing?" Jaja asked.

"Nay. Goin' out to collect our sheep from the island next to your boat. Time to shear 'em. We could leave the wool to fall away on its own, but I don't like my animals lookin' like rag dolls. It's a disgrace."

"Can't you sell the wool?"

"Nay. T'ain't anyone who wants the stuff anymore. We wouldn't break even for the trouble it'd take to get the wool t'market. We only shear 'em, like I say, out of respect." I looked at the farmers' clothes. They were wearing synthetic fleece jackets.

Our suspicions were confirmed when we asked if there were many young people in Marvig. Most had gone. There was nothing much in the village to hold them. The fellow who was getting the boat–the son of one of the men–had returned to the Outer Hebrides with his family. He made a living farming salmon in the large, floating pens that were anchored in a corner of the bay. We thought of Flateyri in Iceland, another town that had a falling population. There were no easy answers. It took fortitude to accept a simple lifestyle when greater opportunities existed elsewhere.

The Old Boys said they would never leave Marvig. One of them smiled kindly. "We're just old dogs, born to these islands. This is our place, but we don't blame the young folks for going. Everyone should have a chance to move toward what he wants. Grab a piece of life before life passes you by."

After the kids went to sleep that night, Jaja and I stayed awake discussing our cruising options. We agreed that it was, indeed, time to reach out and grab something–before the summer passed us by. We wanted to be moving toward a challenge, something to give the slow days at anchor more value. Drifting through the summer rain with thoughts of the approaching rainy winter was uninspiring.

When Jaja and I are unfocused, we tend to fall back on the "knowns" in our life. Spain was a safety net because we had been there and knew what to expect. Back then we were single–into the first months of our relationship. Our raw love needed no destination. Following the sun was enough.

Jaja and I each took a sip of Grand Marnier. We swirled the sticky liquid on our tongues, then let it run down our throats. Lingering twilight lit the midnight skies, and *Driver*'s cabin was painted in subdued tones.

Jaja said, "Remember how the light affected us when we arrived in Reykjavík? We couldn't get enough of it. I remember sitting in the cabin like we are now with the sunlight pouring through the ports."

"Those first weeks in Iceland were some of the best we've had on this journey," I said. "Dreams behind us, dreams in front, dreams off in the distant future. We've reached the "distant future" part now. What's next? A rainy winter in some northern European town? Or back to the Tropics?"

"I'd like to stay in Scandinavia for a year," Jaja said. "I think we'll be disappointed if we go south. Leaving Iceland was like finishing a very good novel. It's hard to start the next one. Our minds are caught up in the last plot, the themes, and the characters."

"After I read *One Hundred Years of Solitude*, by Gabriel García Márquez," I said, "I couldn't touch another book for a long time," I knew Jaja also loved that story. "Remember the wayward South American gypsies? The crazy schemes of José Arcadio Buendía? And the sweltering passion of his family? After that book, all others seemed contrived. I'd start a new novel then put it down after 20 pages."

"But there is always another good book," Jaja said. "You start out skeptical, then become engrossed. New themes evolve; you discover new characters and new surprises. If we go back to the Caribbean, we'll wonder what our hurry was."

Light rain pattered on deck, and a small gust made the rigging hum. Teiga sighed deeply, and we both tensed, expecting her to wake up. Luckily, she dozed off again. We relaxed. Chris usually slept like a log. Holly was a sleep-talker. When she dreamt, we frequently had a good chuckle at her clearly spoken, yet incomprehensible sentences. She still spoke Icelandic in her sleep.

I dug out the small-scale chart that covered the waters from the Faroes to Norway and south to Denmark. We stared at the printed coastlines. Great Britain looked like a big, well-defined island. Denmark took the form of a fragile spur on the shoulder of Europe. The Norwegian coast was a gnarled, unlimited tangle of islands and fjords. It would take a lifetime to see it all. What a challenge!

I said, "I know we planned to sail in northern Scotland for the rest of the summer, but look at the Norwegian coast."

Jaja traced her finger over the chart. "Who knows what will happen next year? Maybe this will be our only chance to see Norway. If we speed up our time in the Highlands, we could spend a few weeks sailing up the Norwegian coast."

I made a quick measurement with the dividers. "It's about 700 miles to Bergen. If we push, we can be there in under three weeks."

We let the numbers hang in the air. Jaja poured another dram of liqueur into our mugs.

I sipped. "That will give us all of August to explore Norway." Facetiously I added, "I have a feeling the scenery will be more inspiring."

Jaja sipped. "I was thinking we could winter over in Sweden or Norway instead of Denmark."

I nodded. Denmark was also not out of the question. We were denied an extended visa, but we knew we would get a two-month tourist visa on arrival. If we wanted to stay for the winter, we could reapply from within the country. Often, rules governing visas contain gray areas that provide flexibility to cruisers who live aboard. Saying "no" to a piece of paper is the most natural thing for an official to do. We could go to the immigration counter in person, plead our case, belittle our pride, and fight bureaucracy for a chance to stay.

Jaja took our empty mugs and washed them in the sink. I rolled up the chart, turned off the cabin light, and got ready for bed.

"Why don't we let a place pick us for the winter?" I said. "I'm sick of trying to be so organized, and the thought of a paper chase in Denmark nauseates me." We were out to see the world, but the only waves we wanted to make were the ones in *Driver*'s wake.

"On to Norway, then?" Jaja asked.

I smiled in the half-light and used Jaja's favorite line: "Like a herd of wild turtles."

THE ISLE OF RHUM in the Inner Hebrides is well forested and mountainous. We anchored in a bay called Loch Scresort, then rowed ashore wearing full foul-weather gear and sea boots.

Jaja rowed. It was her favored role dating back to our *Direction* voyage. She liked the exercise. Curiously, the sight of Jaja rowing the family had amused many a male cruiser over the years. If I was rowing to shore alone, to fill the water jugs perhaps, a fellow cruiser might wave hello and offer a good natured salutation. When Jaja rowed with the kids and I as passengers, nine times out of 10 the same guy would say something like: "Yeah! That's what I like to see, mate! Put the women to work!"

On our trip to shore at Rhum, the rain poured down. We passed several boats en route, but any unflattering comments were lost to the screaming wind. Over the years, Jaja had trained me to hold my tongue when this type of remark came our way.

"Let 'em have their jollies," Jaja would smile, slyly. "No use dropping down to their level and skinning your knuckles."

Kinlock Castle stood prominently at the head of the bay. Nearby was a campsite crowded with nylon tents. Near the beach, a pathetic fire was surrounded by slumped figures wearing ponchos. The campers extended their hands toward the fire to collect the scant warmth. They looked like real-life statues in a real-life fountain. Jaja and I had fantasized once about backpacking and camping across the Scottish Highlands. I regarded the hikers skeptically.

"Remind me never to go camping in Scotland, Jaja."

"Yeah, but who comes to Scotland and expects sun?"

"We did."

The next morning looked the same as the day before. Rain and low clouds. *Driver*'s cabin was warm, free from condensation, deck leaks, and drafts. I thought of the campers in their soggy sleeping bags.

We were bound for Tobemory, roughly 25 miles away on the Isle of Mull in the Inner Hebrides. In the guidebooks, Tobemory looked interesting. There was a scotch distillery tour for the parents and a miniature railway for the kids. Jaja also needed to do laundry, and she fantasized that we would find a laundromat.

During the night, strong winds surged down the mountains of Rhum, causing *Driver* to pull hard on her anchor chain. In the morning, the forecast called for several days of small-craft warnings due to a stalled low-pressure system. We were stuck again. Sailing to Tobemory would be foolish. The distance was relatively short, but a portion of the passage would be wide open to the North Atlantic.

We sat in *Driver*'s cabin listening to the wind. During our shore excursion the day before, we had walked the perimeter of Kinlock Castle, which was actually more of a mansion than a castle. It was private, closed to the public. The nearby children's park was muddy, and the trails ranging inland were boggy. We wondered what we would do all day on board. Games, coloring, reading, music, cooking, eating, washing dishes. We were getting cabin fever.

Most of the locals we met tried to convince us that the waters around northern Scotland are some of the roughest in the world. Currents, shoals, incessant attacks of low-pressure systems, unpredictable winds. We were promised some very dangerous sailing. We are used to locals' telling us that their stretches of coastlines are the worst–probably because they see the weather at its worst. Their gloom-and-doom reports are meant in good faith, but if we take them at face value, they could undermine our confidence. The locals gave the impression that northern Scotland always has bad weather. We examined the charts, studied the pilot books, then interfaced local warnings with our own observations. We felt we had come a long way. We now had years of experience.

But sometimes experienced people still do foolish things. While the rain bucketed down and the wind howled, we hoisted the anchor and tied a second reef into the mainsail. Peering at us through their cabin windows, other cruisers shook their heads. We sailed out of the harbor, confidently bound for the Isle of Mull. All we wanted to do was get to Norway as quickly as possible.

We stayed close to the shore of Rhum to remain in the protected lee for as long as possible. Close in, the wind was fluky with many lulls. The jib and mainsail would fill, then sag, as the wind came and went. Suddenly, a roaring gust rolled off 2,500-foot Askival, the highest peak on Rhum. We saw it approaching–a dark splotch on the water–giving us ample warning to ease the mainsheet before it hit. *Driver* heeled under the blow, took a wave over the bow, then found her feet again. We kept on. The kids watched the action from the companionway, warm and dry in the shelter of the dodger.

Another gust. Ease the mainsheet, steer the bow a little closer to the direction of the wind, and luff the jib to spill some wind. In the ensuing lull, steer away from the direction of the wind and trim in the sheets again. Everything was under control.

Then, without warning, a hurricane-force downdraft bowled into us. *Driver* was thrown on her side–onto her port beam. There was such tremendous force on the mainsail that I couldn't free the mainsheet from the cam-cleat to spill the wind. Jaja clung to the windward lifelines, her legs hanging in midair parallel to the crazily tilted deck. I dropped the tiller and mainsheet and gripped the backstay with all the strength I possessed. The kids were plastered like swatted flies against the inside of the dodger. We stayed over, the mast down to 80 degrees from perpendicular.

For the first time ever, I saw the lifeline stanchions on the low side disappear under water. Water also covered the cabin windows on the leeward side. Then the impossible happened. Water flowed into the cockpit. The wind exerted tremendous force on the sails and pinned us down. After a slow four-count, *Driver* righted herself gracefully. Fortunately, both Jaja and I were wearing safety harnesses. We could have easily been washed overboard during the knockdown, and our harnesses would have been our only ties to the boat.

I jumped below to check for damage. All 250 books in the kids' racks had gone flying. Cassette tapes had become airborne. Pots and pans, charts, pencils, dividers, settee cushions, and pillows–things we thought would never move–were strewn around the cabin. I lifted the bilge to check the patch; it was watertight. I also looked to be sure that the engine was still on its mounts.

On deck, another gust roared in the rigging, but Jaja had uncleated the mainsail in time. I went onto the foredeck to check the mast and sails. The spreaders were straight, the sails were sound, the rigging was intact, and the mast was in column. The only casualty was the top section of the two-part mast that we used in our dinghy when we sailed it. I was peeved at the loss. Allowing stuff to fall overboard is just plain sloppy seamanship.

Secretly, Jaja and I both hoped that the other would chicken out first. Unfortunately, when we set out on a passage, be it three miles long or 3,000, neither of us likes turning back. In fact, I can think of few instances when we have ever done so. After four miles, we reached the end of the Rhum. A short, steep surge was wrapping around the point, making *Driver*'s bow plunge up and down. Unable to remain in the lee of Rhum any longer, we headed toward Mull and into the dreaded section of exposed ocean.

Our course took us close to a low, windswept scrap of land called the Isle of Muck. For safety's sake, we would have preferred that our course took us farther away from the island. However, we had trimmed *Driver*'s sails in tight, and we could not point any closer to the direction of the wind. With the sails close-hauled like that, we sacrificed some forward speed in order to point "higher" (closer to the wind direction) and a little farther away from the island. As we pounded over the breaking seas, we felt as if we were standing still. The current, the 30-knot onshore wind, and the force of the waves conspired to push us onto the island. At the critical point when Muck lay dead to leeward of us, we were less than a mile away from it. I clenched my jaw as I remembered the Langenes Peninsula. Here we were on another lee shore. If we experienced any sort of gear failure, we would be driven ashore within minutes, crushed against the rocks. Visibility was poor, and through the rain, all we could see were the rocks on Muck that looked like tombstones. We were committed.

Time stood still. Rain and salt spray blew under my hood and trickled down my neck. I ignored it. I sat on the low side of the cockpit, my mind focused. The wind was trying to destroy us by creating rough seas, yet the breeze was also trying to save us by powering the sails. I was hand-steering to take advantage of any fluctuation in the wind. In the gusts, I allowed the boat to "round up" and point closer to the direction of the wind. This allowed me to steer a course a little farther away from the island. At the same time, it caused our sails to luff, or flap, slightly and spill excess wind. When each gust was over, I would "fall off"–alter course away from the wind direction– and this would fill the sails with wind again. I sent impulses to the tiller, encouraging *Driver* and the wind to work as partners to save us.

The end of the island was in sight–the place where we would regain some sea room. I held my breath as we approached the point. Spray exploded high into the air as the waves collided with the rocks. It felt like we were walking casually past a spooky graveyard on a stormy night. We climbed the seas at a near crawl. Ever so slowly, like a fading, ghostly illusion, Muck disappeared behind us. We made it by the skin of our teeth.

I let out my breath and held the same course for the Point of Ardnamurchan at the entrance to the Sound of Mull–another obstacle for us to round. It was critical for us to clear the headland on one long tack. If not, we would be forced to tack back and forth through the "eye" of the wind. With her stubby bulk, *Driver* would not make much forward progress tacking in these strong currents and rough seas. We had to keep *Driver* pointing high, yet moving purposefully. We had eight miles to go.

Jaja retreated below to lie with Teiga. Chris and Holly lay on the settees. We turned off the diesel stove because the strong wind backed up the stack and filled the cabin with noxious fumes. When I looked below, all I could see were piles of blankets. The cabin was cold and damp.

After the knockdown, I put Chris in charge of watching the bilge. He gave regular reports. Soon after clearing Muck, he stormed into the companionway and yelled that we were sinking. I lashed the helm and dove below, expecting the worst. But the patch was holding, and there wasn't much more water in the bilge than usual. I dipped my finger into the bilge and tasted it. No salt. Just the oily taste of condensation. Every time the boat rolled, what little water there was ran up and back along *Driver*'s shallow bilge. I surmised that, mesmerized and slightly scared, Chris had imagined the worst. I told him everything looked fine in the bilge and that he should get some rest.

Three miles to go. The image of the headland showed clearly on our radar screen. Our GPS indicated that the course we were actually making gave us a safety margin of just 10 degrees on the compass. It was going to be close. I steered by feel, as well as by sight. I became one with the sails and the seas. I literally willed *Driver* to make headway. I squeezed out every possible ounce of forward motion. My jaw was sore.

According to the tide book, we had the current with us. The mists cleared slightly, and I could see the lighthouse marking the Point of Ardnamurchan standing solitary and forlorn. I could also see another squall approaching to windward–a black cloud, heavy with more rain and wind.

Like the Isle of Muck, the Point of Ardnamurchan was a lee shore; the wind was blowing us onto it. Moving forward and turning back were both risky. It was a precarious situation, and we needed every resource just to maintain equilibrium between us and the headland. More than once this day, we had willingly put ourselves in a situation where luck could influence the outcome. For instance, nature was capricious, and man-made components that seemed indestructible could break without warning. There were 50 ways that the mast could fail and come crashing down. If we needed the engine to save us, there were 100 ways that the engine could malfunction. We were on our own, bracing our nerves against the possibility of a problem. A whole lifetime of experience and planning could pivot on the unpredictable. There's no doubt that we learn to know ourselves when we round life's headlands.

For 20 minutes, the outcome was in the balance. My will against the will of nature. *Driver* is a well-found boat, but I played all manner of scenarios in my head, anticipating possible problems and analyzing how to cope with spur-of-the-moment emergencies.

If the mast breaks, we will be blown ashore quickly. Anchoring will be the last option. It's too rough and too deep. If the broken mast is dragging in the water still connected to the boat by the shrouds, I will have to go below, grab the big wire cutters, and cut the mast free so we can try motoring. Or would it be better to let the mast drag in the water to slow our drift and then radio for help?

Rounding the point represented safety. I could see the "safe zone" just ahead. Momentarily, I wondered why we humans feel compelled to test the outer limits of this zone. Maybe there's some corner of our brains that is exercised and titillated by going beyond the normal realms of security.

As I changed course to round the point, I felt the built-up tension inside me subside. Gradually, my stress was replaced by a feeling of fulfillment. After what seemed like an eternity, we finally ran safely downwind into the Sound of Mull. Jaja sensed the change in *Driver*'s motion as I altered course, and she and Teiga came up from below into the dodger. Chris and Holly were sound asleep.

"I just put the kettle on." Jaja said. "I'll make you a coffee in a sec'."

"Thanks."

Time took on meaning again as we surged towards another calm haven.

THE HARBOR AT TOBEMORY WAS CROWDED. The historical buildings on the foreshore had been restored and were painted bright colors–picturesque at the base of a steep, green hillside. Large Victorian houses lined the ridge behind the town.

The anchorage was awkward. It was a big harbor, but the shallow places were full of boats. The rest of the good anchoring spots were filled with visitors' moorings that were already occupied by other cruising boats. We surveyed the scene, watching our depthsounder and getting a feel for the available swinging room. If we stayed as close as possible to the other boats, we could anchor in 60 feet of water. Farther out, the depth plunged quickly to 75 feet. Although some of the boats hung on chain rodes, most were on rope. We envisioned a middle-of-the-night anchor drill if the wind shifted. It would be a nightmare if boats stretched out their anchor ropes and started banging into each other. We would worry about that later.

I put the engine in reverse, and Jaja let our anchor and 200 feet of chain slowly rattle overboard. We went back, and back, and back–way too close to the boat behind us before the anchor finally caught. I realized that we had underestimated the depth. I told our new neighbor (who was watching us angrily from his boat) that we would reanchor. Despite our assurances, he continued glaring.

We took our time grinding up the chain with our manual anchor windlass on the bow. It was backbreaking work that highlighted the advantages of an electric windlass, which we didn't have. We spelled each other after every 30 strokes of the windless handle. One stroke recovered one foot of chain. Meanwhile, Chris, Holly, and Teiga came on deck and danced around with delight. Chris loudly passed judgment on the boat behind us saying its spreaders were bent (they were). Holly and Teiga sang songs at full volume. Child opera. They were ecstatic to be in. I hated to spoil their fun, but I had no choice.

"Hey, you guys aren't wearing life jackets. Put them on, or go down below. You know better."

"But Daddy, it's so calm! And both you and Mommy are on deck! Life jackets are too awkward."

"Do I have to start making threats?"

"OK." All three kids sulked below.

"Jaja?" I said miserably, feeling like a rogue.

Jaja was laughing. "What is it, my big mean husband?"

"Never mind."

Ashore in Tobemory, we ate pizza and French fries and drank sodas. We topped off the meal with ice cream. We secretly believed our kids liked foul-weather sailing because they could rely on our sympathies afterwards and get anything they wanted. We walked along the crowded footpath and ducked into shops, amazed that only eight hours earlier we were getting thrashed under the cliffs of Rhum. Was it even the same day?

We thought back to our morning departure. Leaving Rhum because we were impatient was not high on our list of intelligent decisions. Usually, we wait for good weather almost to the point of paranoia. One thing is certain, *Driver* is a great boat. She is strong, dry, and forgiving. Going out and getting beaten up had the sole virtue of uncovering weak points in the boat's systems. So far, there were none.

I considered the three C's of seamanship: Confidence, competence, and common sense. Too much of one and not enough of the others can threaten our safety. We took heed.

Chapter Eleven

*A real cruiser is someone who spends all day
lost in a foreign city looking for spare parts.*

WHEN JAJA AND I WERE KIDS, the Loch Ness Monster was the first thing that came to mind when we sighted something mysterious in the water–whether it was in an ocean, a lake, or a birdbath. To get our kids excited, we had begun talking about "Nessie" back at the Isle of Rhum.

"Mommy? What's a Log's Nest Monster?" Chris asked.

Jaja laughed. "The Loch Ness Monster? You mean, we've failed to teach you about the greatest con...uh, the greatest controversy of all time?"

We bought a few books about the monster in Tobemory and read them aloud to try to build a little tension. It worked. As we motored and sailed the 40 miles between Tobemory and the entrance of the Caledonian Canal, the kids saw ghoulish shapes in every wave, and mystery in every floating log.

Ben Nevis, Scotland's highest mountain, hovered impressively in the smoky mists as we arrived at the Corpach Basin at the southern end of the canal. Not only were we headed for the heart of the fabled Highlands, we were going to sail *Driver* on Loch Ness and experience one of the 20th century's greatest myths.

The Caledonian Canal isn't like the large commercial canals of the world. The Panama Canal, for example, requires even small cruising boats to carry a pilot on board. In Scotland, we would tend our own lines and navigate across the lakes at will. Opening hours for the locks were 8:00 a.m. to 6:00 p.m. Some cruisers spend weeks exploring the lakes and canals, visiting secluded areas. Our original idea was to spend at least a week on the canal, but we were infected with Norway fever. The fee schedule is based on the number of days you wish to spend on the canal. It is possible to transit the Caledonian in two days if you don't have to wait for boat traffic. We paid the equivalent of US$160 for the basic three-day plan, which included free berthing each night anywhere on the canal system.

FORT AUGUSTUS IS A PICTURESQUE Highland town, reputed to receive the highest rainfall anywhere in Great Britain. It was built alongside a series of five locks that ascend the hill like a giant fish ladder. We went upward all day. The next morning, we would begin our descent toward the North Sea. We were halfway across Scotland.

We passed the day with the crews from three other cruising boats as our vessels rose through 14 locks. We discussed the rain–which had fallen steadily for a week–and told bad jokes. Not long after we secured our lines for the night, a crew of four Swedes and two other cruising couples knocked on our hull and said they were headed for a warm, dry pub and few pints of frothy stout. Did we want to go?

We thanked them but declined. All day, Jaja and I had enjoyed looking at the misty, Highland mountains and the smooth, silvery lakes. We wanted to stay outdoors to drink in the pure, clean air. The idea of entering a smoky pub lounge was asphyxiating. Anyway, after an idle day, Chris, Holly, and Teiga were raring to go, and we had promised to take them exploring. We set off in high spirits looking for anything that would be of interest.

JAJA SPOTTED A SIGN advertising an exotic animal farm. A brochure on the placard boasted real live reindeer, pigs, fowl, sheep, goats, and horses. We walked down a narrow, muddy pathway following wooden arrows that were nailed haphazardly to trees. At the entrance gate, a stocky woman wearing an apron and a dirty yellow sou'wester collected the fee.

Because of the weather, most of the animals were hiding in their enclosures, oblivious to our visit. Some exotic pigs lolled in the mud, just like ordinary pigs. The kids also saw exotic looking chickens with frilly white plumage. We hurried them along when they spotted a not-so-exotic dead chicken sprawled in a watering trough.

"He's just sleeping," I fibbed. I had always been a Monty Python fan.

Holly looked at me compassionately. "I'm sorry Daddy, but I think the chicken is dead."

The reindeer was impressive. His antlers were furry, and he looked to be in good health. The kids fed him their apple cores. It was also feeding time at the sheep pen, and since we were the only tourists mucking about, the kids were able to feed the four, exotic black lambs using baby bottles. Children feeding baby animals almost always creates ecstasy on both sides.

As we walked back to *Driver*, I realized we had been in Scotland for almost two weeks and hadn't heard anyone play the bagpipes. How was that possible? As we passed a pub, we thought we heard pipes inside. But alas, it was just a CD with Neil Young doodling on the harmonica. So close. We looked through the wet, beaded windows and saw our cruising friends sitting at the smoky bar. They raised their glasses high in salute.

At 8:00 the next morning, we entered the first descending lock. We became canal pros. Jaja and Chris would stand on the rim of a lock holding *Driver*'s docklines. They would literally walk the boat from lock chamber to lock chamber while I stayed at *Driver*'s helm. The locks were about 120 feet long and 25 feet wide. During our transit, there were usually three or four other boats in a lock chamber with us, but a few more could have squeezed in easily. The lock keepers who operated the mechanized gates were friendly, and they made no effort to rush us.

The canal was built in the late 1800s so that commercial ships could avoid the treacherous waters off Scotland's north coast. Now the canal is used primarily by pleasure craft because its locks are too small for today's commercial vessels.

The locks are also a big tourist attraction. Gawkers wandered around in the rain, pointing at the boats, and taking pictures. Now we appreciated why the creatures at the exotic animal farm hid in their pens when they saw us coming.

AFTER MUCH ANTICIPATION by our young crewmembers, we steamed triumphantly into the fabled Loch Ness. Fog swirled around us, creating an aura of mystery.

"I see it!" Chris shouted. "I see the monster!"

"Where?" the girls shouted. "Where?"

"Oh, it just went under again," Chris smirked.

"You're lying, Chris."

"No I'm not, Holly. It had two blurry humps. Just like the photos in our book."

Loch Ness is 20 miles long and one mile wide. At 900 feet, it is the deepest lake in Europe. We anchored about three-quarters of the way along the loch in a shallow bay near the ruins of Urquhart Castle. We went ashore in the dinghy and walked for a mile along a busy road to the Loch Ness tourist attraction.

The kids were enthralled. They climbed the "lifesize" monster statues, watched video presentations, and asked a million and one questions. The old wives' tales were hyped in one area of the exhibit, and they were destroyed scientifically in another. Chris, Holly, and Teiga were disappointed to learn that the whole thing was a hoax.

I was intrigued by the results of some of the research done while searching for the monster. Scientists had taken core samples from the lake bottom. Instead of finding evidence of Nessie, they found traces of radioactive fallout from the meltdown at the Chernobyl nuclear power station in the Soviet Union a decade earlier. Monstrous occurrences come in many forms.

At the northern end of Loch Ness, we tied to a floating dock near the gates of the Dochgarroch locks. In the morning, we would descend toward the northeast coast of Scotland to the shores of the North Sea. There, we would stop in Inverness–a real metropolis with a population of 50,000. We needed supplies before going to Norway, and I hoped we would find everything on our list.

Not far from *Driver,* there was a memorial to the lock keeper's three-year-old son who had fallen into the lock chamber and drowned. I looked at Teiga, who was the same age. Over the years, we have caught flak from individuals who think we are careless to bring our kids offshore. But we try to be extremely cautious, vigilant parents because the possibility that our kids could drown faces us nearly every day.

"Why did the little boy drown, Daddy?" Holly asked.

"He probably wasn't wearing a life jacket," I said.

"Oh."

I SLIPPED MY CREDIT CARD into my wallet. With Chris in tow like a dinghy, the two of us set off to scour Inverness. I needed to buy a rebuild kit for the head and a new diaphragm for the galley sink pump. We were out of oil and out of filters for the engine. I was also looking for new drill bits, a tube of marine silicon, a piece of Lexan for a deck hatch, some hose clamps, a spare 12-volt fuel transfer pump for the day tank of the heating stove, sail twine, sticky-back sail tape, a liter of white polyurethane paint for the dinghy, and some cheap paintbrushes for epoxy.

The largest chandlery in Inverness had some of the engine items, and a trip to three smaller chandleries filled the gaps. A do-it-yourself center supplied the drill bits and brushes. I never found the fuel pump we needed. The people at the glass place laughed when I asked for Lexan. They said if I ordered it, I could have a piece in six weeks. It was my turn to laugh.

There were no sailmakers in Inverness, so we had to go without twine and sail tape. I had never heard of the company that made the polyurethane paint we found. I bought a liter anyway, hoping for the best. It took me two days to cross the items off our list. Sometimes it's like that.

We always marvel at how much work it takes for us to leave land. In Oriental, it took 1 1/2 years to refit *Driver* so we could go to sea. Now we faced relatively short hops from Scotland to the Shetland Islands to Norway. Even to get ready for these short passages–to find the parts and supplies we needed–was like looking for needles in a very large Scottish haystack. Scotland offered more marine supplies than we had found in many other parts of the world, but our search made us remember that the cruising life is not just a big vacation. It also involves work and the constant maintenance of our floating home. Our "treasure hunt" in Inverness also reminded us that we are never completely independent of land. The trick while cruising is to be as resourceful as possible, fabricate and fix as much as you can, and judiciously search out and purchase the rest.

Together, Jaja and I scoured the secondhand shops for books. For a couple of dollars, we could fill a plastic grocery bag. After a few days of hunting, we had over 150 "new" books. We donated some of our old books to the same shops to make room. Holly would read anything. She literally absorbed books and didn't mind that many of them were outdated. She laughed at the cheeky British slang, but crikey! Her everyday speech became preposterous. Jaja and I discovered some bloody good stories. We also found some that were simply frightful.

Upon our return home, Jaja asked Holly and Chris a rhetorical question. "What would you rather have: Hundreds of new books, or a TV?"

Chris groaned. "TV is so boring. All you do is sit there staring."

Holly brightened up. "Do you know what my secret wish is, Mommy?"

Jaja held her breath. "What?"

"I wish that there were libraries in every anchorage."

Jaja smiled. "So do I."

INVERNESS ENTERTAINED US WELL. In addition to searching for the stuff we needed, we went on a castle tour, touched base with our families in the States, gave coins to a busker playing the bagpipes (who looked like Neil Young), worked on the boat, did the laundry in a washing machine, and saw an outstanding circus theater for kids.

All that was left was to plunder the Scottish "aisles." There was the Isle of Veg, the Isle of Tins, the Isle of Pasta, and the Isle of Rice. There was also the Point of Attraction: Alcohol. Armed with a two-page shopping list, we began our assault.

Grocery shopping is our least favorite chore because most aspects of food are a hassle to us. Food represents the biggest slice of our budget. Food requires hours of preparation and hours of cleanup. When we put a meal on the table, often the kids won't eat it. Food clutters the lockers and demands that we carry utensils with which to eat and cook it. More than one-quarter of the interior space on *Driver* is dedicated to its preparation and disposal. Cooking would have probably been more fun if we didn't have to do it several times a day.

We have experimented with elaborate recipes to please our palates, but the preparation and cleanup usually overshadow the thrill of consumption. Jaja once found a recipe for cheese fondue in our Better Homes and Garden paperback cookbook. I remembered the fondues my mother created using several different cheeses and breads. I explained how the bread turns soft after it is dipped in the fondue–how it had slid down my throat and warmed my stomach. Jaja closed her eyes in delight, and the kids dreamed about refusing something new.

I offered to make this exciting dish. But we didn't have any real cheese, so I melted processed cheese in a saucepan then added beer because we didn't have white wine or vermouth. Stir and simmer. We also didn't have any bread, so I popped a bowl of popcorn. We stuck the puffy kernels on ordinary forks and dipped into the "fondue." The popcorn disintegrated immediately in the cheesy goo creating a coagulated mess. I had unknowingly discovered a viable alternative for underwater epoxy.

We unloaded our food at the cash register in Inverness. That was the easy part. We still had to put the food into boxes, transport it to the marina, negotiate the docks, heft it aboard *Driver*, pass it down the companionway, and stuff it into lockers. The logistics seemed overwhelming, but the rewards were far reaching. When *Driver* was fully stocked, it meant that the next adventure about to begin. Food, fuel, and water. I reflected that nothing is more satisfying than an ocean-ready boat.

The total food bill was probably equal to what the checkout girl made in a month. But we were headed to Norway where food was reported to be worth its weight in gold. We needed to stock up in advance. The cashier apologized for the five-foot-long receipt as if it was her fault, then asked if we were throwing a big party. I said that our kids just ate a lot. I asked for transportation back to the boat, figuring we were entitled to some sort of reward for spending a fortune.

The store manager graciously loaned us Iain, a young, red-headed Scotsman. We made a train with our four overloaded shopping carts and helped each other over curbs and potholes back to the marina. Iain also helped us heft everything into the cockpit. When I offered him a tip for his good-natured assistance, he obstinately refused to take any money. He said getting out of the store for a half-hour and into the hot sun was payment enough. A real Scottish lad.

I handed everything down the companionway to Jaja. The cabin filled rapidly under the deluge of groceries. The first chore was to stow 250 cans without dinging the woodwork. We stacked the cans in the settee lockers–on their sides like cordwood–with the labels facing up for easy identification later on.

Then we stowed the dry provisions. Raisins, oatmeal, and peanuts come in cylindrical containers that wasted space. We repacked those things in good quality, zipper-locking plastic bags so that they would stack efficiently. We also removed extraneous cardboard cartons from products that were packed in plastic inside. We put paper sacks of sugar and flour into zipper plastic bags–not only to retain freshness, but also to contain possible leaks in the paper sacks.

We stowed and sweated. Great Britain was having a mid-July heat wave. The sunshine streamed through *Driver*'s open hatches conjuring up memories of the Tropics. It was the hottest day we had experienced since leaving Bermuda. We felt lucky to have such good weather for provisioning. Rain can turn everything into a rusty, soggy mess. We wore bathing suits below to help us stay cool.

Once more, we thought about turning south to follow the sun instead of continuing north to the Shetland Islands and Norway. The blazing sunshine had revived our spirits. Weather greatly influenced our mood because we were outside so often. But we had become actors in our own play, unable to change the script. Norway beckoned.

THE SUNSET AT 10:00 P.M. was fiery red with shafts of blazing light escaping from behind heavy clouds. As the last rays faded, we motored into the protected inner basin at Wick Harbor, 80 miles north of Inverness at the northeast corner of Scotland. We prepared to tie up to a 50-foot, rusty fishing boat.

We drifted slowly with our engine idling. A fat man drinking beer sat in an old Land Rover on the jetty. When I began to secure our stern line to the trawler's solid steel stanchions, he rolled off the front seat of the vehicle, tottered to the edge of the jetty, and began yelling instructions.

"Hey!" he called. "Hey, city boy! Use the friggin' cleats!"

I shouted back sarcastically. "So, it's all right if we tie here, then?"

"Of course it's bloody all right! *But use the cleats.*"

I saw no stern cleats on the trawler. There were only pipes, winches, stanchions, and hawseholes. I ignored the fat man and began rewrapping our stern line around a hefty steel beam that supported a row of overhead blocks. I was surprised by the man's shouts. Fishermen, who make a living from the sea, live in a different world from cruisers who seek only pleasure. The usual exchange is silent antagonism. Iceland and the Faroes were the first places we ever visited where fishermen approached us on equal terms and befriended us. We figured we were back in "civilization" where there are more cruising boats, and more chances for the old antagonisms to reappear between those who do–and those who don't–make their living from the sea.

Jaja jumped onto the deck of the trawler and began tying her line to the massive bow cleat. I was halfway through tying a bowline when the fat guy leaped with surprising dexterity off the jetty onto the fishing boat.

"Didn't I say for you to use the friggin' cleats?"

"*What* friggin' cleats?"

"It's under them nets, city boy."

I was losing my patience and hollered at Jaja to cast off her line. The pile of nets covering the cleats probably weighed 500 pounds, and I wasn't about to try to move them. "The heck with it Jaja, let's move."

"Now, now, now," said the fat man drunkenly, "No need for you gettin' uppity. You can tie to the beam. Only, better let me do it. Doubt you can even tie your own friggin' shoes."

The guy made a sloppy hitch then went onto the trawler's foredeck to "assist" Jaja. He berated her for doing a bad job of cleating our bow line, then told her to undo it and try again. Jaja smiled. Typical of her even temper, she walked away laughing.

"You yachtsmen are all a rum bunch o' friggin' sailors," he observed.

I was suspicious. If the fat man didn't like us, why was he darting around helping? I took a chance. "You want a beer?"

He took the canned Guinness without saying thank you, but his demeanor instantly changed. He sat on the nets casually. "This here is me brother-in-law's boat," he said calmly. "We'll be goin' out tomorrow."

"What time?"

"Seeing how tomorrow is Sunday, be about noonish."

As we chatted, humanity began to ooze through his tough, abusive words. He was like an angry bulldog who needed a good scratch behind the ears.

"Thanks for your help tying up," I lied.

"Anyone gives you trouble, you tell 'em to talk to ol' Glennis here. You tell 'em I said you could tie up."

After he drove away, I retied our stern line.

The harbormaster came around on Sunday morning to give us a key to the showers. When I mentioned we weren't leaving until Tuesday, he said we could pay on Monday. He was wearing a suit and tie, and his family was in the car. Nevertheless, he took us on a quick tour of the bathrooms, showed us how the showers worked, how the lock on the door operated, and how the toilets flushed. After showing us a better place to tie up, he told us which bollards to use.

After he left, I turned to Jaja and grinned. "People sure are helpful around here."

DENSE FOG ENVELOPED US physically and mentally. We were in a void– motoring with our sails up. Despite the lack of wind, the sea was rough and confused. *Driver* rocked and rolled, pitched and yawed. To make matters worse, our electronic autopilot broke shortly after leaving Inverness. Our other self-steering, the windvane, would not work in windless conditions. So we hand-steered. Without any visible landmarks, we were forced to stare at the compass continuously. This tested our patience and sapped our energy. *Driver* was wallowing grotesquely. Even a split second's distraction at the helm caused us to fly off course by 20 or 30 degrees. We were headed for the Shetland Islands, 140 miles northeast of Wick.

The hours passed, and we saw nothing but fog and birds. Ships and other craft slid past anonymously on the radar screen, some as near as a quarter mile.

Sumburgh Head, the southern point of the Shetlands, showed bold on the radar. Warned by the pilot book, I gave it a six-mile berth to avoid the wicked tidal overfalls. The fog became thicker, the light gray sky turned dark purple, and it began to rain heavily. The drops created silvery splashes almost two inches high on the smooth sea, making the water brighter than the sky. Then the wind started to blow, sending rain into my face and down my neck. After 16 hours of heavy fog, Jaja and I were both mentally exhausted. Our moods matched the dense weather.

As we entered the channel leading to Lerwick Harbor, I double-checked our position. We had plotted our track on the chart using fixes from our GPS and by triangulating landmarks on the radar screen. The radar proved the existence of land, the GPS confirmed it, and the depthsounder backed it up. Still, my tired mind harped on the "what-ifs." Fog eats away at your psyche because without visual reinforcement, all sensory input is bent out of kilter. Disorientation breeds fatigue, and fatigue is the father of navigational mistakes. I forced myself to rely on our electronics because under the circumstances, they were more reliable than my tired brain. Entering an unfamiliar harbor is difficult enough with good visibility.

The Vikings cultivated the Shetland Islands 500 years before Columbus first spied the New World. Now they belong to Great Britain. With its stone architecture and narrow cobbled lanes, the town of Lerwick has a pleasing Old World feel. But I wondered how the Vikings would have perceived the constant automobile traffic and the "modern" buildings. What would they think if they saw a row of telephone booths or a traffic light?

I was standing in one of those phone booths with a dirty receiver jammed against my ear. I was calling the factory in England to order a replacement bearing for the broken tiller ram on our electronic autopilot. I was on hold. While I waited, I marveled at the number of teenagers and young adults with odd bits of polished shrapnel sticking into their pierced eyebrows, noses, and lips. If a Viking saw them, he would really wonder.

Finally, I talked to a salesman. I praised the autopilot. I wanted to make it clear that I wasn't complaining; the piece had just worn out. Over the phone, we figured out the part number. Then the representative gave me the phone numbers of several independent dealers that sell the autopilot in Britain.

"Call one of them," he said. "If they don't have the part in stock, they can call me. I will send them the part so that they can send it to you."

"That will take weeks!" I said. "Listen, I'm in transit. Can't you send me the part today? Please?"

"Sorry, but I will not undercut my dealers."

"I see. But it's OK to screw your customers?"

He hung up.

I called the factory again, asked to speak to someone in customer service, and relayed my problem to a friendly voice named Sally. She asked for the part number, my credit card number, and a mailing address. She said she would hand carry the part to the mailroom and send it express mail. The part arrived 36 hours later.

Frequently, the only way to succeed in the age-old cruisers' quest for parts is to find kind people who will help you. I vowed that I would bend over backwards in the future to help fellow travelers whenever the opportunity arose.

THE LAST PROJECT before we could slip our lines and head to sea was to fill our empty propane bottles. Our galley stove uses propane for fuel. Cold food and no coffee were simply not options for our passage to Norway. I took the bottles to the main gas plant, a few miles from the town center. They sat on the counter like buoys.

The guy in charge frowned. "These look like American cylinders." he said.

I nodded.

"They're also rusty," he added with a sneer.

I nodded again. I had been meaning to scrub off the rust.

"Well, I got some bad news," said the gas man. "The boss strictly forbids us to fill foreign cylinders. Says it's against the law. Can you believe it? I won't even mention what he thinks about rusty bottles."

I nodded and reached out to take our bottles away.

"Not so fast," he said. "Not so fast, mate."

"Why? What's the problem? There's no law against asking, is there?"

"Course not. It's just that I also got some good news: The boss is in Jaypan this week on holiday. Come on, I'll fill 'em up. You really should have scrubbed the rust off, though."

We carried the bottles out back, and he asked if I knew what weight the cylinders should be when they were full. I didn't. He filled the bottles to overflowing then tipped out a little of the liquid gas to make them safe.

"That should be good enough," he said.

"I've got my family on the boat with me."

"Have it your way then." He tipped out a little more liquid.

Later, I related my "propane success story" to Jaja.

"Now that we have a destination and more focus, things seem to be going our way," she said intuitively.

THE MORE WE FOCUSED on Norway, the more our feelings of aimlessness disappeared. We had more energy. We had a purpose–something to strive and plan for. Our excitement infected the kids, who were literally bouncing off the walls inside the cabin. We were on a new high.

Cruising has more reversals of fortune, more emotional ups and downs than shoreside life. Living in a house, such as the one we rented in Oriental, resembles being moored in a calm harbor. The wind occasionally blows, creating a bit of chop. However, the floor stays predictably level and the anchor stays firmly set. Cruising and being on the move resembles sailing over ocean swells. There are the stunning crests where you are on top of the world, and there are deep troughs in which your view is obscured and the water threatens to drown you. Up and down. Up and down. Day after day. Always a new sensation.

DURING THE EIGHT DAYS we waited for optimum conditions to cross the North Sea, our dreams of Norway intensified. A pleasant giddiness infiltrated our thoughts. We dreamed of a pristine landscape with mountains, fjords, and vast open spaces. Going to Norway seemed as natural as drawing our next breath.

As we left Lerwick Harbor, the low clouds and drizzle, which had hung over us for days, began to dissipate. The clearing sky turned the sea into a vivid blue avenue. The wind blew at 12 knots from the northwest. I hoisted full sail, and *Driver* galloped along at 6 knots toward the land of trolls and codfish.

Thirty-two hours after our departure from Lerwick, the orange glow of early evening lit the Norwegian coast. From the sea, the low coastal islands blended with the snow-capped inland ranges. The scenery resembled a smooth, impenetrable wall of painted colors. The chart contradicted the illusion, however, showing fjords, passes, and hundreds of islands. As we approached land, the first line of coastal reefs slowly became defined. The land took on depth and dimension. Although we were paying close attention to our navigation, *Driver* seemed to know instinctively the way to safety. We sailed on. Jaja soon spied the lighthouse guarding the entrance to Kors Fjord. Beyond the lighthouse, the intricate but well marked channels beckoned.

When the land came abeam of us, the colors seemed all wrong. The green foliage gleamed yellow with reflected late-day sun. The blue sky shone green. White boats and seagulls appeared orange. We steered *Driver* cautiously up Kors Fjord away from the open sea, enjoying the ever-smoother water. Soon we were landlocked. Like Loch Maharabhig in Scotland, we felt as if we were sailing on a big lake. Another hour under way brought us to a tiny anchorage called Litenvika. Jaja let the anchor rattle over the side into the cold green water of this quaint cove, which was just 12 miles from the city of Bergen. All motion finally ceased.

The evening air was crystal clear and still. The mooring lines on the wooden fishing boats were slack. All we could see from *Driver* was an impenetrable veil of leafy trees and the hard lines of peaked roofs. The five of us sat in the cockpit, whispering, snacking on popcorn, and absorbing our first impressions of Norway.

Sound traveled supernaturally. A screen door squeaked open, then banged shut. A baby cried. Someone was chopping wood. Someone else guffawed. Our senses were heightened, as they had been when we made landfall in Iceland.

"How does it feel to be in Norway?" Jaja asked the kids.

"It's exciting." Chris said.

Teiga jumped up and down enthusiastically.

Holly was thoughtful. "I feel like I just walked into a storybook."

I looked around. It felt as if anything was possible.

Chapter Twelve

When Jaja and I named our boat Driver,
we obviously didn't expect a leisure cruise.

HIGH-SPEED CATAMARAN FERRIES, cruise ships, mega-yachts, trawlers, sailboats, speedboats, cabin cruisers, and converted fishing boats all crowded the inner basin in Bergen. It was a mob scene. The occupants of the speed-boats had lowered their canvas dodgers. Oiled bodies and burned flesh gleamed everywhere. Music blared from hidden speakers. Beer cans glinted in the sunlight.

Pleasure boats, rafted four deep, were tied bow-to-stern along the visitors' wharf. We were lucky to find an open spot against the wall. Within a half-hour, two small cabin cruisers were laying alongside *Driver*. Even though the crews of those boats had to walk across our deck, we liked being on the inside. For one thing, it was easier for our kids to go ashore.

I had called ahead on our VHF radio to notify the port captain of our arrival and to ask if he could notify customs and immigration. When we enter a country for the first time, we must stay aboard until the authorities have examined our passports and boat registration papers. We waited.

"When can we go ashore, Daddy?" Chris asked.

"Soon."

"How soon?"

"The port captain said customs will be right down."

"But when exactly?"

"The port captain monitors VHF Channel 12," I chided. "Why don't you give him a call and ask?"

"Daddy..."

From our cockpit, we had a commanding view of the city. On our side of the basin, Bergen's historic buildings had been converted into tourist shops and apartments. The other side looked more urban with shopping centers, department stores, and restaurants. The sprawling central market at the head of the basin was jammed. People were everywhere.

Buses, cars, and taxis threaded their way through the throngs. A steady stream of gawkers filed by *Driver*, all asking the same question: "Did you sail that boat all the way from America?" After patiently replying at least 50 times, I took down our American ensign. We were bushed and wanted to enjoy the day. It was hot in the cockpit, and we luxuriated in our sweat.

Bergen is famous for rainfall. Moisture moves across the North Sea and is trapped by the mountains. Gravity pulls it down as rain. The fellow aboard the cabin cruiser next to us said it had been raining all year and that this was the first taste of summer for everyone. The coming days were supposed to be even warmer. Luck was on our side.

An hour later, I radioed the port captain again and asked about the customs and immigration officials. Apparently, the arrival of an overseas car ferry had the officials on the run. The port captain suggested that we go to the ferry terminal to find them. With our passports and boat papers in hand, we locked up *Driver* and set off toward the commercial docks.

If you cruise in Northern Europe, you will get used to visiting isolated anchorages and big towns in the same day without becoming disoriented. I remembered waking up in the quaint cove at Litenvika just six hours earlier. The flight of birds and a solitary barking dog were the only "commotion." During the passage from the Shetland Islands, it occurred to us that the winter of quiet solitude in Iceland had sent us inwards emotionally farther than we had imagined. Now, however, the mob scene in Bergen barely fazed us. We were coming out of our shells.

The ferry terminal was bedlam. A long line of vehicles snaked off the ship. The windows of the vehicles were rolled down; the roofs were loaded with camping gear. Uniformed officers, who were trying to see into the shadowed interiors, posed questions to the drivers. At least one person's hand was hanging out the window of every vehicle–clenching a cigarette between fidgety fingers. A security guard stopped us at the main gate. He said that customs and immigration would be busy for some hours.

"Don't worry about it," he said. "They are not strict with overseas cruisers. Do you have anything to declare? Alcohol? A weapon? No? Can you come back in the morning?"

Gladly.

AT THE TOURIST INFORMATION CENTER in town, Jaja collected free brochures and learned about a cable car that took tourists to a high plateau with a good view of the sea and the inland mountain ranges. When the kids heard us discussing the cable car, they began to jump up and down. "Oh, please, please, please, please, please?"

"Well..."

We waited 10 minutes on a busy street corner for the shuttle bus. There was no line at the cable car depot, and within minutes, we were being carried up the side of a mountain. After living so long at sea level, the quick ascent in a box with windows felt strange. Everything looked crooked. We felt tilted down, the mountain looked tilted up, and the horizon was in the wrong place.

"Mommy? What if the cable breaks?" asked Holly.

"We'll probably die," Jaja said.

"What if the power goes out?"

"We'll get stuck," I offered.

"Would we die if we fell out a window?"

I smiled. It's natural to ask questions. It's the way our minds work. Every activity in which we involve ourselves has a certain element of danger. Asking a flood of questions is an acknowledgement of risk. After we mentally chew on the given parameters of a new threat, we usually have three choices– accept the risk, reject it, or compromise.

We find it an odd human quality to participate in a risky activity simply because everyone else is doing it. Driving a car at the speed limit on a narrow highway, for example, has to be one of the most dangerous everyday endeavors that we "civilized" animals have devised. What's the hurry? Why do we have to go so fast? Why risk our lives going to a dentist appointment? Another peculiarity of human nature is to have unquestioned faith in a total stranger who is approaching head-on in his car at suicidal speed. What if he falls asleep and swerves into your lane? What if a tire blows out? Passing another car is like sailing around an imposing headland on a lee shore during a gale. On a busy road, you might pass 60 cars in 10 minutes. That's a lot of "headlands." Jaja and I have more control over our lives on *Driver* than we do ashore.

The warm mountain air was soothing, and we spent a couple of hours wandering along well-trodden paths. It was a relief to do something completely unrelated to sailing so soon after an ocean passage. Chris, Holly, and Teiga hopped, skipped, jumped, and talked nonstop. Before descending in the cable car, we stopped at the visitors' center, ate ice cream, and admired the view of the sea. The sun deck was crowded with Norwegians, many of whom were drinking bottled water out of plastic cups and eating a brown substance that might have been cheese.

The next morning, I returned alone to the ferry terminal. It was Saturday. The harbor was quiet, the roads empty of cars and people, the terminal deserted. I thought of Reykjavik. Arriving in that city at the end of our passage from Bermuda was one of the most satisfying landfalls we had ever made. We had earned the right to be there. Bergen, on the other hand, was exciting but felt like a way station en route to something else.

The customs office was quiet. After I filled out a simple one-page form, the agent thumbed through our passports, returned them, and gave us permission to cruise in Norway for three months. He was unconcerned that we had arrived the day before.

"Do you need to put an entry stamp in our passports?" I asked, leery of the apparently lax entry procedures. I knew from past experience that this could be a bone of contention with other immigration agents. If we had to change our plans, for example, and wanted to leave the country by airplane, there would be no proof of our arrival. Airport officials can be sticklers for procedure. The customs document I had filled out only gave *Driver* permission to be in Norwegian waters.

The official thought about it. "The immigration agent isn't in yet. So don't worry about it."

"But..."

"I'm kidding. It's really not a problem."

I walked away thinking that a country like Norway, which was nonchalant about customs and immigration procedure, was our kind of place.

Three large city blocks in the middle of Bergen had been converted into a pedestrian walkway with gardens, fountains, and sidewalk cafés. Every 100 feet or so a sweaty busker entertained a small crowd of coin-shuckers. Young kids rode their skateboards with whoops and shouts. Smiling adults with briefcases cruised around on roller blades. Little kids in fancy strollers held shiny balloons, while brisk well-dressed women held expensive looking department store bags. I counted at least 10 people with camcorders taping the scene at any given moment. The energy of the place was similar to Bermuda, or the EPCOT Center in Florida. All that was missing was a big black mouse with funny ears and white gloves. The pulse was exhilarating, not irritating– partly because we knew we would soon be enjoying quiet bays and anchorages.

Our general itinerary was to sail as far north as Ålesund, a town 170 miles up the coast from Bergen. We wanted to visit Geiranger Fjord, a spectacular gorge carved by the glaciers. The vertical mountains that ring the fjord looked outrageous in the tourist brochures, and we thrilled at the thought of sailing *Driver* there. We wanted to see as much as possible before turning south for the winter.

FOR US, THE NORWEGIAN COAST was a dream come true. Thousands of offshore islands and rocks create wide channels, sounds, and narrow canals, which allowed us to navigate without ever having to confront big, ocean waves. Chris, Holly, and Teiga were in heaven. We could go 30 miles and never see a wave larger than a fishing boat wake.

Ever since the Faroe Islands, when the milder weather had begun to inspire outdoor activities, Chris and his bosun's chair had become a single entity. As soon as he woke up and finished breakfast, Chris would put on his life jacket, run onto the foredeck, adjust the height of the chair, and spend the rest of the day suspended. If we were motoring on calm seas, he would "fly" from bow to stern around the mast. If the sails were set, he would hang with his feet dangling over the water or lie against the mainsail on the windward side. Sometimes he would tie the chair to the backstay and sit comfortably and quietly 10 feet above the cockpit, observing the world.

Holly and Teiga watched their older brother with envy. It was only a matter of time before they, too, wanted "swings." One calm afternoon while we were motoring, I dragged my tools into the cockpit and made two more bosun's chairs from scrap wood that I had rescued from a dumpster in Lerwick. I hung Holly's new chair from the spare jib halyard on the foredeck, and Jaja hung Teiga's over the cockpit where we could keep an eye on her. *Driver* looked like a training platform for a circus. When other boats passed us, the crews stared in astonishment.

It was a relief to finally experience the hot days of summer. Although the frequent dead calms were disappointing, we motored diligently northward. The days blended together in a blur of mountains, small towns, and empty anchorages. After the light morning mist cleared, the afternoons were sunny. By the end of a solid week of fine weather, we stopped worrying that each warm day might be the last.

One afternoon, while passing through an area of narrow channels and small islands, we put the fenders out and tied *Driver* alongside a protected 10-foot-high rocky cliff. It was a natural wharf. After looping our mooring lines around low pine trees, we climbed ashore and explored barefoot. The scratchy pine needles felt alien to our pampered feet. We lounged on hot, black rocks and let the sun burn our pasty white shoulders. Later, Jaja did the laundry, I changed the engine oil, and the kids played naked in the dinghy getting soaked–yet staying warm.

Having grown up in Seattle, I could remember summers when June and July were cold and rainy, creating weeks of misery. Then August would come, its relatively hot days making up for the whole year of gray clouds and drizzle. Jaja and I recalled winter days in Iceland, and the chill in the Faroes. Iceland was supposed to be cold. The Faroes had been warmer than Iceland, which made them seem like a veritable paradise. We wished for even warmer, drier weather in Scotland–which for the most part didn't materialize.

Yet to our surprise, now that we had experienced a succession of sunny days in Norway, the cold seemed like a faint memory. We liked the advantages that remote, cold-weather locations offered, but a hot day also had its virtues. The sun melted the hard edge of our ambitions and replaced those schemes with languid acceptance. Going to Geiranger Fjord seemed like enough. of a challenge to bite off for one summer.

IN SEVERAL LOCATIONS along the Norwegian coast, bold headlands jut defiantly through the splay of rocky islands. Vessels rounding these headlands are obliged to transit the open sea. One of the most notorious headlands is called Statt. Like Langenes in Iceland, a semipermanent gale rages there all winter. Even in summer, strong winds can howl unabated for days. And like the area around Langenes, various current systems collide in the shoal waters off Statt.

Because of the unpredictable weather and the severity of the conditions even during a moderate blow, many Norwegian cruisers who travel up the coast end their wanderings at Statt. Favorable conditions might entice them to make an easy rounding of the headland, but adverse winds could cause endless delays when cruisers try to return south. Whether or not they had rounded Statt, every Norwegian sailor we talked to warned us to be careful.

A traditional jumping off point for the northbound passage around the headland is an island called Silda. We tied *Driver* to the visitors' floating dock inside the quiet well-protected harbor and put the equivalent of US $5 into a locked box at the head of the dock. A narrow, tree lined road wound through the village passing well-maintained wooden houses and dilapidated workshops. Outdated fishing gear lay piled in organized heaps everywhere–nets, buoys, bent propellers, rusty engines, and rotten wooden skiffs. The village had probably not changed much over the decades.

A muddy path led around the back of Silda and provided a beautiful view of the sea. At 3 1/2 years of age, Teiga was turning into a good hiker. We did hold her hand, however, when we climbed the steep parts. If her short legs became tired, either Jaja or I would hoist her to her familiar position on our shoulders. Of the three kids, Chris was the best walker because he was the oldest and had years of practice. He was as young as Teiga when we lived aboard *Direction* in Northern Australia. Yet he would tramp through the insect-ridden Aussie bush like an aborigine.

To the north of Silda, the sun blazed low in the sky, and a slight haze turned the atmosphere the color of a lemon. The sea looked polished with neither ripple nor swell, and it mirrored the yellow sky to perfection. The headland of Statt protruded boldly in the distance. The bluish peninsula sloped down from the coastal mountains and ended in the characteristic blunt snout. I had seen 100 other headlands just like it.

By the time we returned to the harbor, the sun had dropped below the mountains, and the shadows were chilly. I lit the diesel stove. We grabbed clean clothes, soap, and towels and headed back to town where showers were available at the school. The girls sang as they washed. They had discovered that luxuriating under hot water was a fair compromise for the inconvenience of having to get wet. The shower ran on the honor system. We put $2 worth of Norwegian kroner into a pink plastic piggy bank next to the unlocked door.

While we were at the showers, a 40-foot German cruising boat docked near us. It had come down from Kristiansund–about 120 miles north of Statt. The crew wanted to visit a group of Norwegian islands called Lofoten, about 100 miles above the Arctic Circle, but they were also determined to sail the entire way up and down the coast without using their engine. Because of the calms, they ran out of time and fell short by hundreds of miles.

Choosing to sail everywhere on the Norwegian coast is an admirable goal. With little wind in the coastal channels, you should be prepared to look at the same mountains for days on end. I am too impatient to be a good light-air sailor, and because *Driver* was loaded with provisions, she was too heavy to be a good light-air boat. We spent most of our travel time motoring–seeing new sights at the expense of diesel consumption and noise. Distances in the north are vast; summers are short. We realized that this might be our only chance to see the Norwegian coast.

The Germans were the second set of cruisers to mention the Lofoten Islands. In Lerwick, we met the crew of a Swan 72 that had just returned from Lofoten. They raved about the steep mountains, the many anchorages, the fortitude of the people, and the anachronistic feel of the small towns. Lofoten sounded like a dream. We decided to research the region when we got to Ålesund, the town we would visit after rounding Statt.

ON MY 36TH BIRTHDAY, we woke before sunrise to catch the north-going tide around the headland. It was another lemon-meringue morning. Heavy dew coated our decks, and drips from the shrouds and mast bombarded us as we untied our lines. We powered slowly out of the harbor while the kids slept. The wind and sea were dead calm. As soon as we cleared Silda's northern point, we set a course toward the empty horizon bordering Statt. The sky turned blue as the morning matured, and by the time we reached the headland, the temperature hovered near 70 degrees Fahrenheit.

The kids awakened relaxed. Except for the droning of the engine, there was no indication that *Driver* was several miles from land. After breakfast, the kids came into the cockpit looking fresh. Their hair gleamed from the showers of the previous day.

"Happy birthday, Daddy!" From behind their backs the girls brought out hand-drawn cards and a paper folder that they had decorated with metallic ink. They had been busy. Inside the folder were many drawings and construction-paper collages. Chris presented me with a hand-drawn picture of *Driver* showing me at the helm holding a coffee cup; a big yellow sun shone from the corner. While Jaja steered, the kids and I went below and taped the creations in the V-berth for display. Homemade gifts are the best of all.

We hugged the point closely and marveled at the calm sea–motionless against the jagged rocks. We could have dropped the fenders and tied to the tip of the infamous Statt.

"Happy Birthday," Jaja said, pointing to the calm water tickling the rocks.

I nodded. "A present the whole family can enjoy."

We motored for several more hours on the remarkable, windless sea to the protected inner basin at Ålesund. It had been a very respectable 52-mile day.

The next morning at a bookstore, we thumbed through several coffee-table books on northern Norway. We found page after page devoted to the Lofoten Islands. Thousands of years before, when glaciers had covered Norway, the tops of those islands remained free of ice. After the glaciers receded, the island peaks–which had not been scoured by the ice–were still sharp and jagged. Old fishing towns, such as Reine and Henningsvær, were dwarfed by stunning mountains. Houses painted red with white trim dotted the shorelines, high jetties rimmed the harbors, and double-ended varnished fishing boats floated like full-scale models of perfection.

The photos had an enticing, magical quality. Months later, when the storms of winter–and the storms of a wintry bureaucracy–were raging, we would remember that day in the Ålesund bookstore as our point of no return. While looking at the photos, we had a strange feeling that we had been to Lofoten before. The names of the places in the Lofoten group meant nothing to us, but the look of the mountains triggered succinct, tactile emotions that made the hair on our necks bristle. We couldn't shake the urge to go there.

Before traveling to Iceland, none of the photos we had seen of that country had such a strong effect on us. It wasn't until our first evening in Akureyri that we felt a weird tingle of distant recollection. Standing on the jetty in Akuryeri under the pristine sky next to the large schooner, we felt that the mountains at the back of the fjord looked familiar. We were sure we had seen them before. In a movie, perhaps? Or *National Geographic* magazine? What could explain our overpowering desire to live within sight of those peaks for an entire winter? I looked at the mountains in Akureyri every day during our winter aboard and never grew tired of their quiet dominance.

The Lofoten Islands are 500 miles north of Ålesund if you travel inside the coastal islands and reefs. That distance was equal to a return trip to Inverness, which now seemed half a world away. A direct offshore passage to Lofoten would shorten the distance to around 350 miles. With fair winds, we might complete that passage quickly, perhaps in 2 1/2 days. Our original plan was to stop at Ålesund and then turn south. Why did we want to continue going north with autumn knocking at the door–especially since we had no idea where to hole up for the winter?

To give ourselves time to mull over the potential change in our itinerary– and our newest challenge–we set sail for the headwaters of the mighty Gei- ranger Fjord, over 60 miles inland from the coast.

The Norwegian fjords can be dangerous for small boats. We had read about the violent *fallende vind*, a sudden explosion of cold air that rushes down the steep mountains, felling trees before it. The crews of old-time fish- ing dories lived in fear of this "falling wind," which strikes the water almost vertically. The wind didn't capsize the dories; it pushed them under! Straight down. These dangerous williwaws are most common when a strong wind is blowing from the east. Fortunately, we had moderate westerly winds. *Driver* sailed up the gorge with her jib and mainsail set wing 'n wing. Perfect sailing.

At the headwaters, we anchored *Driver* on a sloping shelf using two anchors with six-to-one scope on each of the rodes. Although the day was warm and calm, there was no telling what the wind might do in the narrow, mountainous chasm as the day matured. Better to play it safe.

Wearing jeans and sweaters, we set off early the next morning to hike in the mountains. The path went practically straight up. By 11:00 a.m., it was so hot that we stripped to our underwear. Teiga sat on my shoulders during the ascent, singing happily. Chris and Holly talked nonstop, oblivious to the strain. Jaja and I panted. The view from the ridge was worth the sweat. We could see the dark green waters of the fjord snaking back toward the ocean. Off to the side of the bay, almost invisible, *Driver* looked miniscule, alone at anchor. So small.

I RECALLED AN AFTERNOON aboard *Direction* sailing in a brisk breeze on the Indian Ocean. The swells coming from the Southern Ocean were like immense hills. *Direction* would ride high on the rim of one swell, then slowly settle down into the trough–into a chasm of blue water. We would sail up the next gentle face, catch a glimpse of the horizon, and then slide into a watery landscape again. The duration between swells was 50 seconds. These were monster waves compared to our tiny vessel. During the five-second view from the top of one swell, I saw a huge ship far in the distance. I watched its progress for 10 minutes. The ship was approaching us and would pass very close. When it was a mile away, I hailed it on our VHF. While we waited for a reply, Jaja and I watched the tanker battle the gargantuan seas. The bow rose high. Then like a slow-motion movie, it plunged completely under. Water gushed halfway down the decks, and spray flew over the bridge. We heard a reply to our radio message.

"This is the captain of the *Exxon Warrior* to the sailing vessel *Direction*."

I bid the captain a good afternoon and commented on his motion through the seas. I said, "My four-year-old son would like to know your overall length." You have to be specific when asking the size of a ship. If you ask how "big" the ship is, the answer is usually given in tons.

"Eight hundred fifty feet," came the reply.

We chatted about the weather and where each of us was headed. Then he asked for our position. I was dumbfounded. Was the guy blind? By then we were very close, about 500 yards away on his starboard beam. I told him.

"I don't see you," the captain replied. "Let me get my binos." There was a long pause. Then he shouted into the microphone. "Jesus Christ!" he said. "Is that you? How long is your boat?"

"Twenty-five feet," I answered.

"Jesus, man! Are you insane?"

I looked at *Driver* from under the canopy of pines above Geiranger Fjord. Just a fleck on the water. What drove us to challenge vast oceans? Was it our simple–yet extreme–lifestyle? Perhaps that was it. We like visiting places that are extreme, yet down to earth.

While we continued to look down at the fjord, the tentacles of Lofoten attached themselves to our brains. We wandered through the pine forest discussing the ramifications. Wasn't it foolish to continue northward? It was already August. We could only expect a few weeks more of settled conditions before the fall gales began their attack. Wasn't that cutting it a little too fine? By September, it was conceivable to get stuck in port for weeks waiting for a good forecast to travel down the coast and back around Statt.

Why were we tempted to go to Lofoten so late in the season? Because a few strangers had mentioned the islands? Because the mountains looked beautiful in photographs? In part, we were enticed by the aura of the north. Our nine months on Eyja Fjord in Iceland changed our vision of the cruising life. In the high latitudes, we found unique privileges and a special spirit. Jaja and I were eager to return to the far north where the values of the people ashore reflect the values we seek afloat. We wanted one last look at the northern reaches before turning south for the winter.

We reminded ourselves that the Lofoten Islands–500 miles away–were relatively close. If we turned south thinking we would visit them the following summer, chances were we would never return. We might always regret not trying now.

It was the same old story.

CHILDREN ARE DRIVEN by motives they often do not understand. They beat around the bush toward obvious conclusions, and react to new situations with candid naïveté. As we roam through childhood, similar situations keep cropping up with minor variations. By the time we reach young adulthood, we start to understand and anticipate the patterns of human nature. When we become adults, we are "armed" with our accumulated wisdom. But sometimes as adults, we still mask our true motives with cunning self-deception.

That day at Geiranger Fjord, we may or may not have recognized that we were headed for Lofoten. At the time, we told ourselves it would suffice to just mosey up the coast another hundred miles or so to see what was there. Deception at work.

"The islands on the way to the next harbor at Kristiansund are supposed to be radically different from what we've seen so far," I suggested.

"Really?" Jaja said. "Well, we'd be fools not to check it out. It's only another day or two away."

"That's right! And we would still have plenty of time to turn south."

Before setting out from Ålesund, I arranged to have our mail sent to Kristiansund. We had received no correspondence for three months. Jaja called her sister Valerie, who organized our affairs in the States, and asked if she would send our mail via international courier–an extravagant measure but the only practical choice. Regular airmail was unreliable and could take weeks. We didn't have time to wait.

The wind began howling as soon as we left Ålesund. We had gone only 10 miles when a gale warning was issued over VHF Channel 16. Hot air over the land was sucking in cooler air from the sea, and an unexpected "dry" tempest was brewing. We ducked into Terøya Island, found a safe place to anchor behind a stone causeway, and spent two days listening to the north wind scream. Despite the gale, there was not a cloud in the sky. Brilliant sun filled our cabin with intense, cheerful light.

It was too windy and chilly on deck for bosun's chair acrobatics, so the kids lazed below. They were very mellow; I think they enjoyed having a break from "chair mania." I taught Chris how to use my soldering gun, and he spent hours destroying a cheap radio bought at a secondhand shop in Scotland. Later, with a little more practice, he resoldered the wires of a broken cabin light.

I thought of the 80 miles separating us from Kristiansund. The protected inshore route wound its way among steep mountains, low islands, shallow reefs and sandbars. There was only one unprotected section, north of a village called Bud, where we would have to make an open-sea passage. According to the pilot book, this area is the most dangerous place on the Norwegian coast. And it wasn't even a headland. It was a low, rocky strip of land that looked perfectly harmless. But there are many reefs near that part of the coast, and shoals that spread out to sea for 10 miles. Strong currents set over the area, creating strong tide rips. I thought about what we had seen in the Faroe Islands and was resigned to wait for settled conditions. Summer was waning quickly. It was possible that our trek north would soon be finished.

WE STOOD ATOP A HILL behind the harbor at Bud looking seaward, scrutinizing the fabric of whitecaps and swells washing over the "most treacherous" section of the coast. Unless conditions improved radically, it would be too rough to set out the next morning.

There are two routes by which you can negotiate this 16-mile stretch. Technically, the least hazardous course is straight out to sea for four miles, then due north well away from the reefs and rocks along the coast. However, this way you pass over a vast underwater shelf that causes dangerous tide rips. Even in settled weather, the sea can be lumpy. If the wind pipes up, the area becomes dangerous in minutes.

The alternate inshore course snakes between hundreds of wave-swept rocks and reefs. It is a shorter route, and the small islands and large reefs diminish the ocean swells. On the chart, the meandering reef route seems to be adequately marked with metal poles. But if the wind increases suddenly, even these protected waters could become rough, making navigation extremely hazardous. The pilot book recommends that only experienced sailors attempt the inshore route and that only large well-found craft take the offshore course. We wondered where we and *Driver* fit into this scenario.

Back on the dock, a fisherman who spoke English said the wind was supposed to die out by morning.

"I'll believe it when I see it," I said conversationally.

He asked, "You going the offshore route or through the reefs?"

"Thought we'd try the reefs."

The fisherman pursed his lips. "I wouldn't recommend it."

"Oh?"

"You have to be experienced to get through without hitting anything. If you stray off course or lose your way, you'll be in a minefield of reefs. Most foreign cruising boats take their chances and stand well offshore."

At sunrise, I climbed the hill to check the sea conditions. Peering through the binoculars, I whistled in disbelief. There was not a breath of wind; the whitecaps and swells had vaporized. The sea could have been a peaceful mountain lake. I ran down to *Driver*. Jaja was brewing coffee.

"We need to leave immediately," I said, out of breath. "It looks like a silver platter out there with an invitation card on it saying, '*Driver* go North.'"

Starting the engine no longer woke the kids; they were used to casting off early. If anything, the engine lulled them to sleep. It was a good thing the kids were sleeping. We would need to concentrate entirely on our navigation. We slid out of the harbor bound for the reefs north of Bud.

When the first barrier of low windswept islands blocked our path, I questioned the wisdom of negotiating the inshore route. However, the dead calm allowed us to proceed very slowly under power. A narrow gap soon opened up, and Jaja steered between the rocks. Now I understood why this route was so dangerous in strong winds. In some cases, we passed within 10 feet of rocks. A moderately strong breeze could have blown us off course and put us aground, even under power. Sailing would have been impossible.

In the distance, we spotted a rusty metal pole with two small rocks next to it. Behind it an island curved like the back of a cartoon whale. On the chart, I found the symbol for the marker, the rocks, and the Moby Dick island. Check, check, and double-check; we were exactly where we thought we were. One of the gravest mistakes an inshore navigator can make is to assume he knows his location without confirming his assumptions with solid references.

The metal poles were about 10 feet high, three inches in diameter, and painted black. They were nearly impossible to distinguish against the black rocks. Even when we used binoculars, the poles were difficult to see. While scanning for the next marker, I took a quick look out to sea. Although there was no wind, the white, peaked waves of a wicked tide rip spiked the air about two miles outside the reefs. Fortunately, the water around *Driver* was glassy.

Another marker, another reef, another island. Go straight, make a dogleg to port, aim for the rock that looks like a dented Volkswagen. Converting a chart's two-dimensional limitations into three-dimensional reality took patience. The Norwegian navigation charts were precise, and any mistakes would be caused by our negligent interpretation of them. We picked our way with determination.

After an hour, we relaxed; everything was going well. Jaja and I didn't want to put the whammy on our morning by admitting the truth, but we were enjoying this life-size maze. Our minds were focused–tuned to the same wavelength.

"Do you see the next marker?" I would ask, lowering the binos.

"No."

"See the green patch on the blunt rock?"

"Oh, there it is. The marker's just a finger's width to the right of our forestay."

"Bingo. To play it safe, swing to port about five degrees."

"How's that?"

"Perfect."

There would have been a more exciting tale to tell if a gale had come up, pinned *Driver* on the reefs, and threatened her with breaking waves. But the sky overhead remained cloudless, the sea stayed impossibly flat, and the kids slept. Not all challenges are accompanied by white-knuckle tension.

Three hours later we left the coastal reefs, ducked back into the magical waterways of Norway, and continued up a broad, landlocked channel toward Kristiansund. The kids finally woke up, and the real day began.

IN KRISTIANSUND, we discovered that miracles do happen: Our mail was waiting for us. There were many letters from Adda and Gudni, and from other friends in Iceland. We had bank statements, new credit cards, and contracts for two articles that a sailing magazine had purchased. Suddenly, there was grocery money for the next three months. The most exciting letter, however, was from a book publisher who had caught wind of our voyage.

"We would like you to write a book about cruising aboard a small boat with children," the letter began. It was a provocative offer.

We strolled along the streets of Kristiansund with our minds full of ideas: A book proposal, a request for more magazine articles, plus an offer to write stories for a well-known Web site. Would we be able to write a book while cruising? Our time was already filled just operating and maintaining our floating home. Moving many miles every day sapped our brains and suffocated our creativity. What's more, our future plans were uncertain. Where were we going to live for the winter? And, how soon would we arrive at our winter haven?

Everything hung in midair. With too many loose ends beginning to fray, we needed to commit to at least one decisive action. We needed to strive for something tangible.

"Jaja?" I let a moment's silence hang provocatively. Then I spoke with a smirk. "What do you say we wander up to the bookstore and look at the navigation charts for Lofoten?"

LACK OF RAIN and plenty of sunshine inspired us. But the wind continued to blow from the north. Was it giving us a message? Should we run before it and go south? It would be wonderful to sail with a tail wind. Instead, we doggedly fought our way north against the wind–up the rocky channels and sounds under power. We did not have time to spend extra hours tacking back and forth into the wind, and there was no reason to go offshore and pound into the oncoming seas. So we stayed inshore covering mile after mile–48 miles a day,

50, 65, 72. Day followed day. The Norwegian coast slid by in a blaze of colors and textures.

Time became pleasantly irrelevant. One hour under way was no less taxing for us than 10. We developed the second wind that long-distance runners often speak about. We felt neither pain, nor hardship, nor boredom, nor stress.

Pushing hard to click off the miles in Scotland had distressed me. What was different now? Was it our appreciation of the remaining good weather as the season waned? Or was it because we were driven by something that was greater and larger than we were?

In his famous novel *N by E,* author Rockwell Kent writes of his ill-fated journey to Greenland in 1929 aboard a 33-foot cutter. In the opening chapters, he ponders the name that the skipper had chosen for the boat–*Direction.* Kent says that there was:

> ...something foreboding about her name...ominous...The name, a proclamation of man's will, was an encroachment on the special and sole virtue of the gods...Call your ship Daisy, or Bouncing Bess–and the sun of life will sparkle on your course where fair winds drive her laughingly along.

When I named my 25-footer after the boat in my favorite sea story, I did it consciously. At that time, before I met Jaja, I needed all the direction in life I could get. I didn't want the gods to smile. I wanted them to test me.

We rejoiced in the number of northbound miles covered each day. The kids delved into a world of camaraderie and complacency so solid we knew that they had achieved a new level of maturity. They were well behaved and kept themselves occupied. They giggled and made up stories while hanging in their swings. It reinforced our belief that low-stress parents have low-stress kids.

The perpetual light of summer, which shed useful illumination past 10:00 p.m., had a profound influence on us. Jaja and I got up at 6:00 a.m., long after the sunrise, got *Driver* under way, then enjoyed about three hours of solitude together before the kids woke up. We talked a lot about the book project.

On the morning of August 20th, we crossed the Arctic Circle. It was a meditative experience. The first time we crossed that magic line–north of Iceland almost exactly one year earlier–we heralded the event as one of our life's greatest achievements. We brought the kids on deck, and Jaja and I drank a toast. But now, we didn't even bother waking the kids. We wondered if all goals were just fleeting moments of ecstasy that dimmed with the passing of time. What about next year's goals, we wondered. Would they also become bleached like a red shirt hung in the sun too many times?

After seven solid days of motoring and sailing, we reached the city of Bodø. Twelve hours later, a low-pressure system moved over the area bringing torrential rain and strong onshore winds–a precursor of the autumn gales to come. Fortunately, the town dock was protected by a mast-high breakwater, which deflected the ocean waves. Nevertheless, spray flew over the wall and dissipated in a white mist that hung over the marina.

While waiting for the weather to moderate, Jaja restocked our food lockers and entertained the kids. I serviced the engine: New oil, new filters, new seawater impeller, valve adjustment, and a test of the thermostat. We topped up our fresh water and diesel.

Three days later, the wind and rain magically vanished. By noon, the sun was shining through broken clouds. The forecast called for light winds, possibly deteriorating into another gale later that week. Summer was already "going south." I calculated how long it would take us to cross the 50 miles of open water to Lofoten. I calculated the tides and estimated the hours of darkness when it would be difficult to see the dangerous shoreline of our landfall. I figured if we maintained hull speed, we would arrive with an hour of daylight to spare. A half-hour later, we were under way. Our destination: An island group at 68 degrees north latitude.

WE CLEARED THE REEFS near Bodø and aimed *Driver* across the open sea to the village of Reine on Moskenes Island in the Lofoten group. While we motored, Teiga played on her cockpit swing, and Chris and Holly hung suspended in their personal bosun's chairs. A swell undulated underneath the fabric of the sea, but the water's surface was like silk–smooth and unrippled.

From their privileged position five feet above the deck, where the wind suppressed the noise of the engine, Chris and Holly played games that involved their imaginary figures Pot and Mary. These characters had magical powers and went on long adventures. The stories the kids invented had enduring themes, but the children wove in new concepts based on the books that Jaja had recently read aloud. The *Borrowers* series of books about little people living in England had a big influence on the kids' imaginations, and our recent acquisition of the *Narnia* series by C. S. Lewis had opened up vast new imaginary realms.

Jaja and I kept an ear half-cocked to the kids' story lines to see what was going on inside their heads. It pleased us that violence, although present in their dialogs, was not a mindless fascination. The kids' imaginary creatures and heroic good guys sought harmony, not aggressive dominance. Maybe our kids were naïve by 1999 standards, but once lost, innocence can never be recaptured.

The color of the sea between *Driver* and the mountainous island of Moskenes was yellow and red. It looked like we were motoring across the surface of a ripe mango. To the north of Moskenes, the Lofoten Islands continued in a jagged line, merging with the hazy blue mainland over 60 miles away. To the south, the mountains sloped away, ending at a low group of islands and reefs called Røst. The wicked, swirling currents between Moskenes and Røst had been the inspiration for the story *Maelstrom* by Jules Verne.

We had less than 10 miles to go when the sun slid behind the peaks. The backlit mountains were in deep shadow, while we were blinded by rays of light. In the high latitudes, the sun doesn't set straight down. It glides laterally along the horizon in a slow, coasting descent like a shooting star. The jagged peaks tried to block the golden rays, but the sun doggedly slid sideways, reappearing again and again between the ridges that stood up like tines on a fork. Finally, the sun dropped below the lowest valley, and the spectacular sunset was over.

Without the sunlight in our eyes, we began to see features on the shoreline–lighthouses, buildings, and telephone poles. Soon we picked out the entrance, made a dogleg around a pile of black rocks, and motored slowly into Reine Harbor. We located the floating visitors' dock, dropped the fenders over the side, prepared the lines, and came to a halt alongside. Chris shut down the engine. The harbor was as quiet as the night sky.

We sat in *Driver*'s cockpit awed by our surroundings. On the nearest foreshore, a row of traditional red-painted fish houses sat atop pilings that were encrusted with sea growth. Picturesque wooden fishing boats, ripe with the scent of the sea, bobbed on moorings and crowded against private jetties. The sky was colored in gradations from red toward the west to purple higher up, and finally, to black overhead.

On the south side of the tiny harbor, a rock wall rose vertically from the beach to a height of 1,800 feet. The opposite northern shore was dominated by a line of sharp peaks. It seemed like we had been dropped into a gorge. A slight breeze blew through the rigging, and the decks were damp with dew.

Our minds were clear and sharp. We felt as if we had just arrived home. Jaja stood with her elbows resting on the boom staring at the fading colors of the sunset and at the black outline of the razorlike ridges.

She was meditative. "Dave? I think we've found our winter haven."

Chapter Thirteen

Sometimes you just have to go for it.

1 AWOKE TO SUN streaming into the cabin. The open hatch over our bunk admitted the cool morning breeze, which mixed with the dry, warm air coming from the diesel stove. The day held promise–a vacation feeling. After all the miles we had traveled since leaving Bergen, we felt as if we could finally take a breather. Had we really found our winter haven?

Jaja yawned. "I wonder what Reine looks like in daylight?"

Before I could say anything, she rolled over, pulled the comforter up to her chin, and returned to sleep. Then I, too, slipped back into a delicious slumber.

The next time we awoke, it was nearly 10:30 a.m. Holly was reading a book in bed, and Chris was in his bunk listening to music through headphones. Teiga was still asleep.

"Mommy! You're awake!" Holly said.

Chris was less diplomatic. "Can I have breakfast?"

Within minutes Jaja was dressed and in the galley.

"French toast!" Teiga said, opening her eyes at last. "My favorite!"

While the kids ate, I walked to the public phone at the head of the dock and called the weather bureau. Another low-pressure system with heavy rain and moderate southwesterly winds was due to hit us in 36 hours.

I returned to *Driver* and shared the forecast with Jaja while I ate my breakfast. We had been planning to go for a long walk.

"Instead of walking," she said, "let's take advantage of the nice day and explore the inner part of Reine Fjord on *Driver*."

After weeks of putting miles behind us, it was a novel experience to go for a lazy day-sail. A fair breeze was blowing, and *Driver* moved easily through the water with her mainsail and big jib pulling. A few aluminum skiffs whizzed by. They were loaded with kids wearing life jackets and holding fishing poles. Several small wooden fishing boats drifted over shoals, their crews jigging for cod. Everyone waved as we sailed past.

Our kids played on their swings, then trailed fishing lines behind the boat.

"Where are we going?" asked Holly.

"Back to the same dock in Reine," I replied.

"Really?" Holly said incredulously.

"Really," Jaja answered.

Usually when we are cruising, every forward mile is brand new, and unfamiliar anchorages add spice to our experiences. I realized that we seldom sailed anymore just for the fun of it. The usual motive was to advance our position along a line on the navigation chart within a certain time frame. Ironically, the simple thrill of sailing had been one of our original motives for going cruising. Now it seemed as if we often let sailing become another form of mindless transportation–like driving a car.

In the south arm of the fjord, on a grassy peninsula backed by sheer cliffs, we saw a small homestead–four tiny houses, several outhouses, and two large storage buildings. The place was called Tennes on the navigation chart. As far as we could tell, no roads connected it to the outside world. Tennes looked deserted, and we wondered who had lived there. Jaja and I fantasized what it would be like to winter over in such a remote and picturesque location. We were sure the scenery would be enough to fill the long days of isolation. The black cliffs and sharp peaks were like cogs that meshed perfectly with the gears of our imaginations.

As we lazed around on deck letting the fluky winds determine *Driver*'s course, we began our usual decision-making process. Should we stay in the Lofoten Islands over the winter? The climate was a major consideration. On the down side, the clothesline over our diesel stove once again would be loaded with snowy garments. In the winter darkness, our solar panels would stop producing amps. Filling our water tanks would be a constant battle. The advantages would include the northern lights, the inspiring view of snow-covered mountains on blue-sky days, and the pleasure of gathering with friends on stormy evenings.

Once again, we were drawn to the values we found in the north. We wanted to explore the untamed, unspoiled, natural surroundings; we wished to gain an appreciation of the heartiness and endurance of the people. The Norwegians we had met so far were patient and good natured–similar to the character of our Icelandic friends.

"In Iceland, we thrived living aboard in a cold climate," Jaja said. "We could easily do it again."

I laughed. "I remember a conversation we had not two hours after leaving Akureyri. It went something like: 'Now that we've lived aboard in a cold climate, wouldn't it be great to do something different?'"

"I know, but now that it's been warm for so long, don't you miss the feeling of winter? Coming into the warm cabin during a snowstorm, the sensation when the sun returns, and a gathering of friends on a dark day?"

Unlike me, Jaja can easily make "radical" choices. It is her default setting. My brain, on the other hand, has to be programmed for each new situation.

Should we stay, or should we go? Our conversation skirted theoretical precipices, roamed over sun-drenched meadows, slipped on icy rocks, and lounged in windless hollows. Up and down, round and round we talked. We had heard about an English couple who had wintered in Bodø; some Germans had spent five years somewhere in Lofoten; and American John Armitage, coauthor of the *Norwegian Cruising Guide*, had spent several years living aboard in northern Norway. Apparently, getting permission to stay was not a problem.

I thought about our summer. In four months we had covered 2,500 miles and stopped in 48 anchorages. During the entire trip up the coast from Bergen, we had secretly regretted every mile we traveled north because we knew that shortly we would have to turn and head south for Denmark. If we stopped now, we could forget about the return miles and luxuriate in the cozy feeling of a safe harbor until spring. Best of all, we could avoid a paper chase in Denmark. Maybe we should stay.

When the choice among various options is not clear, I must arm myself with facts. Unfortunately, adventure is usually not compatible with logic. For every argument that justifies an "extreme" action, there is a parallel argument that discourages it. Many times, you just have to take a chance and worry about the consequences later. Wintering over in the Arctic was one of those times.

"Let's do it," I agreed. "We'll figure out the technical problems as they come along. This place is too good to pass by."

When we told our kids that we would stop for the season very soon, Chris became thoughtful. He understood the implications.

"Will we have to go school again?"

I chuckled. "I'm afraid so."

"I can't wait to go to school," Holly said. "I had so much fun last year."

"Well, we'll give it our best try," Jaja said. "As soon as we find a place to live, we'll ask the school if you can attend."

Chris sounded concerned. "What if I don't like my teacher this year?"

"Everything will work out," I said. "Be optimistic. Think to yourself, 'What will my teacher be like?' Not, 'I hope I like her.'"

Chris and Holly were not afraid of learning Norwegian. Learning Icelandic had given them confidence. They also remembered the friends they had made in Akureyri and looked forward to meeting a new group of playmates.

Back at the now-familiar dock in Reine, we sat in the cockpit watching the colors of the sunset blend and shift. We were awed by the beauty of the region and felt satisfied with our impromptu decision to stay. Linked with my enthusiasm, however, was a stomach-thumping dose of reality. We would be dropping into an unfamiliar town where we didn't speak the language or understand the social customs. We needed to find doctors, dentists, a school, a safe place for the boat, and marine services.

Driver was our ultimate concern. If our home was safe, we were safe. That evening, we examined sketches in the Norwegian coastal pilot book searching for harbors with good protection from every wind direction. We also looked for towns that offered services related to the fishing industry. The presence of these services usually indicated a thriving community. A prosperous town will attract young people. Young people have kids, kids need schools, and busy schools attract good teachers. A town full of kids also means good medical services. A young population looks to the future; a forward-thinking town usually possesses a strong community spirit. We were looking for more than a quiet place to keep the boat until the next summer. We wanted to meet and begin to understand the people, the way we had in Iceland.

A BRISK BREEZE blew rain on our backs. *Driver* raced along over a lumpy gray sea on a beam reach. With icy spray flying over the deck, it felt like late autumn, not late summer. We were headed 40 miles north to Svolvær, a town of about 3,500 people. It was the first place on our list of possibilities for a winter harbor. If Svolvær were "the place," then our summer cruise would end that day. The thought gave us mixed emotions. Living in a state of constant forward motion is an alluring lifestyle. Everything is new; every day is fresh and exciting. Stopping after a long period of travel is a relief, but it nearly always gives us a feeling of loss.

At the end of our circumnavigation aboard *Direction*, we cruised up the Intracoastal Waterway, the inland waterway on the U.S. East Coast. It had taken two months of searching to find Oriental, North Carolina. We felt like Goldilocks: *This place is too big, this place is too small, this place is too flat, this place is too congested. And finally–this place is just right.*

Winding down and coming off our ocean high was part of the search process. Cruising on *Direction*, we had coped with seasickness, storms, bureaucracy, and the threat of midocean illness. Living ashore represented different inconveniences: A steady stream of bills, backed-up plumbing, a loud stereo next door, yard work, car repairs. While living ashore, we often felt pinned down. We couldn't pick up the anchor and move to a quieter street when the neighbor's dog barked at 2:00 a.m. A storm at sea will eventually blow itself out. The dog might live for years.

In Lofoten, the winter weather would pin us down. If we grew tired of the snow and the darkness, we would be stuck until spring. We remembered the logic we had used in Iceland: *If we can't stand the climate, we can leave the boat and fly somewhere warm.* We laughed. That line of thinking had grown old, like a worn out coat that we couldn't quite part with. We knew we wouldn't exercise the option, but it was comforting to remember it.

Driver sailed sprightly into Svolvær Harbor. Near the end of the breakwater on the cement walkway, a 12-foot-high bronze statue of a cloaked woman was temporarily roped in place. Her pedestal at the seaward extremity of the breakwater looked as if it was still under construction. As we sailed past, Jaja went on deck, doused the sails, and prepared a bow line. Five minutes later, we tied to the visitors' pontoon in the heart of town. What would we look for when we stepped ashore? We trusted our instincts to guide us.

After lunch, we wandered into the central square. The kids ran in circles. They sensed our energy and excitement. On the main street, all the shops were occupied, the windows were clean, the displays modern. We walked by chandleries, hotels, pubs, and two major banks. There was a clothing store, a paint store, an electronics shop, a bookstore, a toy store, and a hardware store. Svolvær seemed to have it all. Teiga spotted a large white sign cut out in the shape of a molar.

"Mommy! They even have a dentist!"

"Obviously a dentist with a sense of humor."

We said "hello" politely to everyone we saw, and people said "hello" back. Shopkeepers were courteous. We continued ambling through town toward the marina and past the public library. There was no marina office, so we went to a nearby hotel to inquire about paying for our slip. The friendly proprietress told us that the marina was a co-op venture built by volunteers. Her husband made several calls on our behalf and then told us that we could tie to the end of B Dock.

The grammar school was a three-minute walk from the marina. School had begun the previous week, but it was Saturday, so the playground was empty. Chris, Holly, and Teiga grabbed swings and started flying. Jaja and I peered into the classroom windows. Everything looked tidy and well organized. The view from the schoolyard included towering peaks: 1,800-foot Fløya, 2,000-foot Blåtinden, and a rock pinnacle called the Svolvær Geita. The bases of the mountains were less than a half-mile away. About five miles away across the channel from town, the distinctive 2,500-foot peaks on Stormolla Island dominated the horizon. Svolvær looked like Reine, only on a larger scale.

Before committing ourselves, we wanted to see if the staff would allow Chris and Holly to attend the local school. Other than that, the town was stunning, thriving, and friendly. A broad asphalt sidewalk led from the school to the town center, which exhibited a strong potential for ice cream. We crossed the main road, skirted an empty lot, and then stopped in our tracks next to a new brick building surrounded by scaffolding.

"Hey Jaja!" I yelled. "Look! They're building a new post office!"

IT TOOK TWO WEEKS for Chris and Holly to adjust to the routine of getting out of bed promptly for school. At first, they were angry. They argued that all summer we had encouraged them to stay in bed as long as possible. It's tough being a kid.

Although we had dropped into the school unannounced, the staff welcomed our kids enthusiastically. They looked forward to having two English-speaking students. Soon we met Chris's and Holly's new teachers. We invited them down to *Driver* for coffee.

The next evening, Chris's teacher Anne Brit Schultz sat in *Driver*'s sunny cockpit and watched as her two sons swung high on the bosun's chairs under Chris's careful guidance.

Anne Brit chuckled. "Christopher inspires so much confidence that I have decided not to worry." Her son Håkon, a year older than Teiga, hung suspended a few feet above deck level with one hand on the mast. His face was split by a wide grin. Stian, a year older than Chris, pushed off the shrouds expertly with his feet and swung around casually.

"A natural," I said.

"We have a spare bicycle in our garage," Anne Brit offered, "which Christopher is welcome to borrow." When Chris heard that news he rappelled to the forestay, then did a triple spin while flying to the backstay. Anne Brit laughed. "I guess that means he accepts."

The following day, Holly's teacher came aboard. Svolvær was still enjoying sunny weather, and we lounged comfortably in the cockpit drinking coffee and eating snacks. Bjørg brought her three kids with her, and they, too, received the bosun's chair initiation. Later, Bjørg's youngest daughter Emma, age 10, took Holly by the hand, and they wandered down the dock toward shore. When they returned, Holly was in high spirits.

"Mommy! Emma said she would loan me her old bicycle. Is it all right?"

We looked inquisitively at Bjørg, who smiled and nodded.

"Yes!"

When the sun dipped below the mountains at 8:00 p.m., the cool sea air quickly displaced the day's warmth. We retreated into the cabin, which still retained the heat of the day.

Bjørg said, "I think it is fantastic the way you are living with your children. You are giving them so much. Holly is an asset to my class. Already, the other pupils are using the few words of English they know to make her feel welcome. They are so curious about Holly and all the places she has been. I think almost all of the kids wish they could live on a sailboat."

EVERY FRIDAY, we prepared *Driver* for cruising so that we could cast off as soon as Chris and Holly stepped aboard after school. We had gone from world cruisers to weekend sailors in the blink of an eye.

In preparation for one outing, I asked Chris to fill the water tanks with the dock hose while I went to town on an errand. When I returned, the hose was hanging over the side still running, and no one was on deck. I stepped aboard and heard Jaja whispering to the kids in the cabin.

"Here comes Daddy. You girls let Chris tell what happened."

I descended the companionway steps into the cabin. Chris was sitting in a corner of the settee with his head buried under his arms.

I was alarmed. *"What happened?"*

"Chris has something to tell you."

Thinking the worst, I asked, "Did he break the word processor?"

"No." Jaja laughed. "It's nothing like that."

Convinced that nothing else too terrible could have happened, I waited impatiently. I hate a long prelude to bad news.

Chris stammered, "I...filled...the...diesel...tank...with...water!"

I looked at Jaja. "He didn't."

"He did."

"You didn't." I said to Chris.

"I did."

I knew for a fact that the 110-gallon tank was half-empty.

"How much water did you add?" I visualized pumping out the tank, and I wondered where in Svolvær I could find a legitimate place to dump water tainted with diesel.

"I only added about two minute's worth," Chris answered.

"So you realized your mistake and stopped before the tank was full?" I was greatly relieved. "Well, Chris, there is hope yet."

We conducted an experiment. We stuck the dock hose into an empty water jug and let it run for two minutes to measure the approximate amount of water that Chris had poured into the diesel tank. Thankfully, the water pressure in the hose was low, and two minute's worth of water amounted to less than five gallons. Using a six-foot length of copper tube at the business end of a hand bilgepump, I reached the sump at the bottom of the diesel tank where water accumulates. I pumped five gallons of water into a cheap, folding plastic water jug that Chris held steady. I had used the copper tube many times before to extract condensation from the tank.

"So Chris," I said after we had finished. "What lesson did you learn today?"

He took his time answering. "Uh...next time you ask me to fill the water tanks...uh...I'm going to make Holly do it."

I wasn't sure if I should praise my son's logic or admonish his impertinence. As we motored out of the harbor, I made Chris monitor the glass bowl on the fuel filter/water separator as if his life depended on it.

GETTING AWAY each weekend was good for morale; it was part of our winding-down process. Settled weather gave us a string of sunny weekends. Out of habit and curiosity, I noted the weather and sea conditions between Svolvær and Denmark on a regular basis. Storms raged off Statt churning up the waters of the North Sea. If we headed south at this late date, we would have a difficult passage. We figured the good weather at Svolvær was a sign that wintering over in Lofoten was the right choice. What we didn't know was that the autumn sun was like a wolf in sheep's clothing. It enticed us to relax in a quiet "pasture" while other "wolves" lurked not far away.

One Friday night in an empty anchorage, the air temperature was a tantalizing 52 degrees Fahrenheit. We reclined comfortably on deck, watching the neon green of the northern lights flicker overhead. Being warm and seeing the aurora borealis was an exhilarating combination. I recalled our dockside observations in Akureyri when the polar nights robbed our body heat and cut the time we could spend outdoors viewing the spectacle. Now, as *Driver* bobbed placidly and tugged gently at her anchor, the northern lights reflected on the still water like a tropical sunset. Gone was the urgency to experience the phenomena before succumbing to frostbite.

"Do you think they're seeing the northern lights in Iceland right now?" Holly asked.

"Maybe," Jaja answered. "I wonder what Adda and..." Before she could finished her sentence, the entire sky exploded in a whirl of violet, yellow, and green. It was impossible to take it all in at one glance. If you looked to the east you missed the fire in the west. And the sky to the north differed from the sky to the south. I tried to focus on one part of the show. As in life, you can achieve a deeper appreciation by focusing on one point of interest rather than trying to absorb as much as possible. Children are more apt to see the world as a blur of events, unable to take it all in–as if they were standing on a merry-go-round. Adults, on the other hand, can focus if they choose.

"Look over there!" Chris shouted.

"And over there," Holly said.

Teiga was more relaxed. "I like all of it."

"It looks like the green and purple swirls are dancing," Holly said.

Saturday morning dawned clear and blue. Our percolator gurgled reassuringly, filling the cabin with the aroma of coffee. Steam rose and fogged the cabin ports. Fresh coffee revived memories of my childhood camping trips when the early morning chill was chased away by this time-honored adult drink. I tried sips of coffee as a kid. But I didn't start drinking the stuff until I was 19 years old after someone handed me a cup of steaming French roast.

"Yuck," I exclaimed. "It tastes like burnt wood sap!" But the aroma filled my sinuses, and the late-afternoon caffeine jolt gave me an unexpected burst of energy. By the end of the week, I was a confirmed coffee drinker.

I poured the coffee and handed a cup to Jaja. The kids were asleep, so the cabin was blissfully quiet. *Driver* swung slowly on her anchor line, pushed by a silent breath of wind. Sunlight entered the cabin ports and roamed over the interior woodwork like a spotlight. As the boat swung, the sunlight cut a path across Jaja's eyes, and she tipped her head back to enjoy the moment. Then the sun moved on. It glinted on the stainless steel stack of the diesel stove. The metal looked dull in the bright light, and I made a mental note to ask Chris to polish it the next time the stove was cool.

SPEAKING IN SUBDUED TONES, Jaja and I broached a topic that had surfaced many times during our early morning conversations while anchored along the Norwegian coast. The idea actually originated back in Iceland. Ever since Halli mentioned Svalbard, the group of islands at 80 degrees north latitude. Jaja couldn't shake the place from her mind. She was determined that we should sail *Driver* to Svalbard the following summer.

I was against the idea. "Our boat is too small, Jaja, and it will be too cold. I can appreciate the allure of traveling deeper into the Arctic, but I can't imagine taking *Driver* to such an extreme location with the kids." Suddenly, I realized I was using the old worn-out argument.

Jaja grinned. "You said the same thing about Iceland."

I reiterated the hazards. Winter pack ice surrounds the island group until May, and icebergs are common year-round. In all our high-latitude cruising, we had never actually experienced icebergs and sea ice. The weather around Svalbard can be very unpredictable, with snowfall at any time. For a few months each summer, the pack ice retreats from the west coast of Spitsbergen, the main island. This allows "safe" navigation into many of the fjords. But the ice can return without warning, trapping unlucky or inattentive mariners.

Jaja countered that despite its high latitude, Svalbard experiences relatively mild weather by arctic standards. The northern islands in the group are less than 600 miles from the North Pole, but the average summer temperatures still "soar" to the high 30s. "Sailing to the island of Spitsbergen will give us a glimpse of the deep Arctic from the deck of our boat, Dave. We might see whales, walrus, millions of birds, even polar bears."

We had read that 70 percent of Svalbard is covered with glaciers, many of which melt into the protected fjords. We spoke with several Norwegian cruisers who had made the journey on sailboats not much larger than *Driver.* They raved about the beauty. None of them, however, had brought along three crewmembers under the age of 10.

I sighed. "When I think about going to Spitsbergen, I can only visualize the tactical problems: Getting reliable weather forecasts, figuring currents, coping with fluky winds, and the constant threat of not finding a good anchorage at the end of a long day. My brain is numb. Cruising between Iceland and Norway was hard enough. Going to Spitsbergen's west coast would be even harder."

I took a sip of coffee and looked at the sun shining into the cabin. It was another beautiful day. Despite my reluctance to go farther north, I let my mind consider a few ambitious thoughts. Then I mentally kicked myself as my more cautious side took over.

"We've just arrived in the Arctic to spend the winter aboard, and already we're planning to go farther. Shouldn't we focus on the next few months instead of planning for the distant future?"

"Yes, I suppose so," Jaja said. "But here in Lofoten, we're within striking distance of the Svalbard group. The southern fjords on Spitsbergen are only 650 miles away. It seems a shame not to try to get there, especially after we've spent so much time getting here. I'm worried that if we don't at least think about Spitsbergen, something unplanned–something we really don't want to do–will fill the gap instead."

I sighed, then took a sip of coffee. Jaja had a gift for seeing the big picture. "But..."

"You actually want to go," Jaja said compassionately. "You just don't know it yet. I think if we went, it would be the greatest thing we ever did."

"The goal to top all goals?"

"We'll never know unless we try." Jaja tried to sound casual. *"Anyway, it's just an idea."*

As AUTUMN PROGRESSED, the days grew shorter and shorter. Svolvær is located at 68 degrees, 14 minutes north latitude. On December 5th, the sun drops below the horizon completely and stays there until January 6th. On the winter solstice (December 21st), there would be less than four hours of dim blue twilight–assuming the sky were clear. We had been eager to witness the dark winter days in Akureyri, and we felt the same anticipation in Svolvær. We had learned to appreciate the darkness just as we had thrived on the perpetual light of summer. Now we were headed into a winter with even longer periods of darkness each day than in Akureyri. While it may be difficult for others to understand, we felt privileged to be facing such a dark season.

At the marina in Svolvær, we moved from the exposed end of B Dock to a more secure slip on D. The new slip belonged to a man who had recently sold his boat, and he let us use his space for the equivalent of US$15 a month.

Driver barely squeezed into the berth. With less than eight inches clearance on either side, there was just enough space for our fenders.

Burning candles to save electricity during the winter in Iceland was an exotic experience, but one candlelit winter afloat was enough. In October, I bought an extension cord to plug into shore power at the marina. I snaked the cord through a dorade vent on *Driver*'s deck and into the cabin. I plugged four clipon lights into the cord. The 220-volt electricity, which is standard in most of Europe, was supplied through a coin-operated meter on the dock. It cost us a meager 75 cents a week. By using our electric lights, we could illuminate our lives for as many hours as we wished without worrying about depleting our 12-volt batteries. *Driver*'s cabin became bright and cheery—a shining refuge as the days darkened.

When the ground froze in late October, the water tap on the dock was turned off. With no serious ice in the harbor, however, we could motor to the fuel dock and fill *Driver*'s water and diesel tanks whenever we wanted. Unbelievably, the Gulf Stream reaches its long fingers even this far north and prevents the seas surrounding Lofoten from freezing. Pack ice and icebergs are unheard of anywhere on Norway's west coast. Fishermen ply the waters year round.

Applying for visa extensions was the last thing we needed to do before settling in for the winter at Lofoten. In my cover letter to the immigration department, I emphasized that we had the financial resources to support ourselves without having to seek employment in Norway. I provided an itinerary and stated that we would live in Svolvær aboard *Driver* until May. Then we would sail up the Norwegian coast to Nord Kapp. In June, we would make the passage to Spitsbergen. We included bank statements and several credit-card transactions to prove we were solvent. The staff at the local immigration desk photocopied our passports, boat papers, and bank documents. Then they sent the package to the main office in Oslo for processing. The local officials said they would notify us in about three weeks.

Jaja and I pondered what we should do if our application were turned down, but we didn't put much energy into the conversation. The Icelanders had let us stay, and I recalled the nonchalance of the officials in Bergen. We had discussed applying for an extension soon after our arrival in Svolvær, but with two months remaining on our entry visa at that time, it seemed pointless. We applied for an extension in mid-October, two weeks before our cruising permit was due to expire.

In preparation for the snow, ice, and gales to come, I removed *Driver*'s sails, stowed them on deck under the dinghy, and affixed thimbles and shackles to our dock lines to prevent chafe. *Driver* was battened down for the season.

WE HAD ENCOUNTERED MILD SLEEPINESS when the sunlight began to fade in Iceland, but for some reason, fatigue hit us 10 times harder in Svolvær. By mid-November, our muscles felt leaden, and our eyes were heavy with drowsiness. Darkness fell at 2:30 p.m. The clock said, "stay awake," but our circadian rhythms said, "go to sleep." Each day, the period between 3:00 p.m. and our kids' bedtime at 8:00 p.m. was a grueling, coffee-saturated stretch. Mild depression accompanied our lassitude.

Jaja said she hadn't been so tired since her last pregnancy.

My heart began pounding. "You're not...you know..."

"I don't think so."

"*What do you mean you don't think so?*"

"Well, it's impossible, isn't it?"

Even though we were sleepy, the onset of darkness produced feelings of complacency that completed the cycle of light. Summer was a time of urgency, a time to be outdoors in the nearly perpetual sun. Winter was a season of introspection, a recharging time. It was satisfying to sit indoors and not feel guilty for "wasting" the day. We knew from experience that November's fatigue would lift eventually–like a fog at sea.

In a way, I liked the dark, rainy days of late autumn because they were more conducive to writing. Jaja and I began hacking out an outline and some sample chapters for the book. We continued to write magazine articles and mini-stories for the sailing Web site. I chuckled to myself when Chris filled the diesel tank with water because such moments helped fill our notebook with Web-story ideas.

We exchanged many letters with Adda and Gudni in Iceland, and they always managed to cheer us up. One day we received this one from Adda:

> Dear Friends: This is to inform you of the tragic news that we ran out of toilet paper on October 8th, 1999, at exactly 2:45 p.m. This means that if 72 toilet paper rolls last for 153 days, the average use is 0.47 rolls per day for the household. Therefore, the average daily use of toilet paper for each person is a little under 0.12 rolls. Which means that on a yearly basis, one person would use about 43 rolls. In our next letter we will continue and calculate the price...

I wrote a facetious letter back to Adda to inform her that her calculations were biased against men. When I was a bachelor on *Direction,* one roll of toilet paper would last a month. That figure changed overnight to one roll per week when Jaja moved aboard. According to Adda's statistics, men use the same amount of toilet paper as women. I knew this to be untrue.

Toilet paper had been the cause of one of our first disagreements on board *Direction.* Years ago, Jaja and I were reprovisioning in the Cape Verde Islands in preparation for our transatlantic crossing to Barbados. *Direction*'s larder was almost bare, and we needed to buy a substantial amount of food. Unfortunately, the banks in the capital city of Praia were on strike. All we had were travelers' checks and about $120 in bills. The black market would not take the checks, so we had to make do with the little cash we had. Needless to say, we were facing a lean ocean passage in the food department.

We wheeled a rusty shopping cart around the dusty supermarket in Praia. All we could afford were the basics: Rice, pasta, flour, and a very cheap local delicacy–canned tuna. We agreed that we would buy no "luxury items" such as chocolate, peanuts, sugar, coffee, tea, powdered milk, or dish soap. I went on a foray to find baking powder, and when I returned to our shopping cart, there were three rolls of toilet paper resting comfortably on top of the rice sacks.

"Toilet paper is a luxury item," I said haughtily. "We have plenty of paper-back novels aboard that will suffice for this one passage."

Jaja smiled seductively. "Toilet paper is a basic, Dave. Didn't you know?"

"No," I faltered, "I didn't know that. Um, can't we make do with one roll?"

Smiling, Jaja lifted a roll of toilet paper. Underneath was a jar of instant coffee.

Bribery.

TO HELP OVERCOME our November weariness, we took long walks with the kids. The cold air revived us physically and spiritually. During a Sunday stroll at Kong's Lake, about two miles from *Driver,* we crossed paths with a quintessential Viking. She was a tall, striking blonde with sparkling blue eyes and a powerful bearing. She smiled at us warmly.

"My name Gry Falch-Olsen. You must be Dave and Jaja. Your son Christopher and my son Edvart are classmates. Would you like to come up to our house for coffee? My husband and I have been wanting to meet you."

We followed Gry to her house, which backed into a steep mountain on one side and overlooked the lake on the other. During our walk, we learned that she was a teacher at the high school and that her husband Stein Alsos was the dentist who had the molar-shaped sign in town. Their two-story house was painted traditional colors–red with white trim–and it had a turf roof. From the top of their driveway, the family could see the reef-strewn sea to the east of the Lofoten Islands. Beyond the reefs, the coast of mainland Norway 40 miles away showed as a jagged smudge.

Gry and Stein joined us in their upstairs living room. Their three boys, ages 5, 9, and 12, played downstairs with Teiga, Holly, and Chris. The walls of the living room were covered with tasteful art–pen and inks, oils, and watercolors. Most of the colorful images were Norwegian scenes showing golden summer landscapes, blue winter scenes, verdant mountains, and hard-working commercial fishermen.

Noting my interest, Stein said, "Some of my dental patients are young art students. I accept their work instead of their money."

"Lucky for them," I said sincerely.

"No," Stein chuckled. "Lucky for me. My living room wouldn't look as beautiful covered in bank notes."

Outside, huge flakes of snow began to drift down lazily. Soon, a squall bent the pine trees next to the house.

"Looks like we found shelter just in time," Jaja mused.

Gry said, "I can't imagine what it's like on a boat with kids now that it's winter. At one time Stein and I dreamed about the cruising life."

Playfully Stein said, "But at that time we had visions of white sand, not white snow, and we didn't have kids."

Jaja laughed. "Dave calls this our midlife cruising crisis."

"We were in a rut," I explained. "Cruising in the Tropics with our kids was great, and it sustained us for many years. But we needed a new challenge."

Gry smiled. "Don't most American men just buy expensive red automobiles?"

I laughed. "This cruise was actually Jaja's inspiration."

"Then that's lucky for you," Stein joked. "Many women would have taken a lover."

It was not surprising that we had much in common with our easygoing hosts. Couples who have the same number of children often forge automatic bonds. Our conversation roamed along humorous paths as we drank coffee and ate homemade goodies. One special Norwegian pastry is called *lafse* bread. The batch we ate had been baked from scratch by Stein's mother. It was an effort to not be a pig and eat it all myself.

In between mouthfuls, I asked, "Have you lived in Svolvær for many years?"

"I grew up here," Stein said, "And Gry was born eight miles away in Henningsvær–a town full of beautiful women." He winked. "We both left Lofoten to go to university. After we married, we lived the exciting city life in Oslo, but deep down we longed for the rich, natural surroundings in Lofoten. We returned about 13 years ago, and our oldest son was born soon after."

"Even though you grew up with it," I asked, "does November's darkness bother either of you?"

"No," Stein admitted. "It's a part of us, just like living on a boat is apparently a part of you. You accept it, so it's not a hardship." He raised his eyebrows.

"*Touché.*" I said.

Stein lowered his voice and continued with mock seriousness. "The consensus around town is that you and Jaja are completely insane." He wrinkled his nose and nodded. "I just thought you should know."

I laughed. "Perhaps we are."

"No, I disagree," Gry said adamantly. "You and Jaja know what you want, and you are determined to have it. People sense your perseverance, and they admire you. It's only for conversational purposes that they say you are insane." She laughed.

"Yeah," Stein said facetiously. "Tomorrow at the office I will have to be careful not to say anything nice about you."

"Could be very bad for business," I grinned.

ONE OF OUR FAVORITE walking routes took us across the bridge to Svinøya Island, then along the quiet road to the end of the breakwater.

The bronze statue of the cloaked woman, entitled the "Fisherman's Wife," was mounted on a pedestal. The figure stood looking seaward, her cloak pressed to her body by an eternal wind. Her left hand was raised in front of her face to shield her eyes from the elements. Her posture was relaxed, as if she were accustomed to scanning the horizon for her man's return. Or perhaps she had her hand raised woefully to wave farewell one last time before the dark seas of fate made her a widow. The Fisherman's Wife symbolized the Lofoten fisheries. Our kids called her the "Lady".

One dark afternoon in late November, when gale-force winds were driving sleet horizontally, we stood on the breakwater looking out to sea. A gargantuan ground swell was pounding the rocks, sending spray over the Lady. With our noses jammed in our collars, we imagined conditions on the open ocean. We visualized what it would be like on board–wind screeching in *Driver*'s rigging, huge waves pounding against her hull.

Back at the protected marina, *Driver* greeted us. She was rock steady. Her rigging and hull were unaffected by the conditions offshore. Contentment filled our hearts. We would not have to deal with ocean storms for many months. Conversely, the knowledge that we *would* venture onto the ocean the following spring gave value to the winter that we would spend at the dock. Safe in port, with time in the bank, we felt like millionaires.

Chapter Fourteen

Challenge and adversity can hone your character,
like a whetstone on a knife.

A THOUSAND YEARS AGO, when the Vikings began to "cruise" the high
latitudes, they spoke a language called Old Norsk. During their wanderings,
they settled in Iceland, and Old Norsk became the Icelandic language. Due
to Iceland's isolated location and its countrymen's desire to retain the purity
of their language, Icelandic has remained nearly unchanged to this day.

Chris and Holly worked hard in school to learn Icelandic. Their mouths
wrestled with entirely new combinations of vowels and consonants. They
found it easier to learn Norwegian. They only struggled for a couple of
months, and by November, they had the hang of it. Their Icelandic language
skills gave them a head start with Norwegian, the same way knowledge of
Latin helps someone learning a Romance language. It also helped that Chris
and Holly were young, because kids absorb everything like sponges.

Jaja and I found it difficult to "absorb" *any* Scandinavian language.
After our failed attempts to learn Icelandic, Jaja wanted to make a serious
effort with Norwegian. She enrolled in a language class taught to refugees.

Most of the students occupied dorms in the next town. They took a bus
to Svolvær three times a week for the mandatory language program.

Jaja was motivated to learn, but most of her classmates were uninter-
ested because they didn't want to be in northern Norway. They couldn't
fathom why Jaja, who was from a country they dreamed about, would
choose to live on a cold, dark island in the Arctic.

"Why are you in Svolvær when you could be in the United States?" they
kept asking her.

Jaja's heart went out to a young Iranian woman who asked, "Why is it
always dark here? Is there no sun in Norway?"

What a transition. Hot desert to arctic winter. Jaja tried to imagine what
it would be like if she were evacuated to Iran during midsummer and had to
wear a chador veil and learn the Farsi language.

Jaja was able to comprehend the new sounds and the word chains of the
Norwegian language fairly easily. The Middle Eastern refugees–who spoke a

language that sounded as if they were continually trying to clear their throats—had to learn both new sounds and a completely new alphabet.

To help the class memorize numbers, the teacher conducted bingo games. Jaja reported that her classmates were only half-listening and that they talked amongst themselves instead of participating. When the teacher announced that the winner of the game would receive a bar of chocolate, their interest increased miraculously.

At least it was better than winning a paint set.

THE MARINA IN SVOLVÆR did not have facilities, so we went to the indoor swimming pool twice a week for a swim, a sauna, and a shower. In between, we washed our hair over *Driver*'s sink.

We missed the outdoor pool complex at Akureyri. Sitting up to our chins in hot water on dark mornings with snow falling gently around us had been very agreeable. At night in the pools, we frequently watched the northern lights. The pool in Svolvær was lit by fluorescent tubes. It was noisy, and the water was tepid. We welcomed the liquid diversion and the exercise, but it wasn't the same as swimming outdoors.

Chris, Holly, and Teiga also longed for the hot pools in Iceland. However, they adapted more readily to the cooler Norwegian swimming pool. Jaja and I remembered swimming when we were kids in mountain lakes that would have preserved ice cubes for several hours. Children seem to be immune to cold water. We youngsters never understood why our parents preferred to sit in the sun on lawn chairs. Now we knew.

If fresh water had been readily available on the dock in Svolvær, we would have boiled it in pots on the diesel stove and bathed aboard *Driver*. When we had sufficient fresh water, our routine for taking an onboard shower was simple: We added boiling water to a bucket of cold water until the desired temperature was reached. Then one of us would pour the water over the other with a saucepan. The water would drain into a shallow well under a teak grate in the cabin floor. For disposal, we would pump the gray water into a bucket using a hand bilgepump.

There were no laundromats in Svolvær. At first, Jaja did laundry by hand using the hose on the dock. After the dock water was turned off, she washed clothes in the sink at the marina clubhouse. Then Bjørg introduced her to Allis, a good friend who owned the Anker Brygge hotel and docks at the main harbor.

"I've heard all about you," Allis said. "I have three boys in Holly's class."

"Oh, you have the triplets. I can't imagine that—and all boys too," Jaja said, with admiration.

"I can't imagine hand-washing clothes and linens for an entire family," Allis said. "You're welcome to use the washer at Anker Brygge whenever you want." Here was another kindness from someone we had only just met.

On Tuesday nights, Chris and Holly played handball, a popular European indoor game that is a cross between basketball and soccer. There were about 30 kids on their team, and they spent hours running wild in the gymnasium. Even Teiga was welcome. She played with the other little brothers and sisters who came for some recreation on the dark, autumn afternoons. I assisted the coach every other week by chasing lost balls and by parroting instructions using hand signals.

The last week of November, Chris and Holly went door to door to raise money for their handball team. Carrying flashlights and wearing reflective orange shirts, they left *Driver* excitedly to sell candles and packs of holiday paper napkins. At least it wasn't toilet paper.

Jaja and I had sold scout cookies and raffle tickets as kids. We recalled how it felt to knock on a stranger's door and mumble practiced words. We admired our kids' gumption for trying to speak a new language to strangers. Chris and Holly were proud to be part of the team.

A half-hour after the kids left on their selling debut, Jaja and I were startled out of our reverie by a knock on the side of *Driver*'s hull. I poked my head out of the dodger and saw a policeman standing on the pontoon.

"Are you David Martin?"

"Yes." I panicked instantly. "Is there an emergency with our children?"

"What? Uh, no."

Completely baffled, I returned below and told Jaja that a cop was coming aboard. The young officer struggled down our companionway and settled onto a settee in the main cabin. He carried a roll of damp papers in his hand.

"Hey, it's warm in here," he said.

"It's home," Jaja echoed.

He had a perfect command of English and got right to the point. "We have been in contact with the immigration office in Oslo."

"Oh, thank you! Did you bring our visas to us?"

"No, not exactly. I'm here to inform you that your application to stay in Norway has been denied. I'm sorry, but you have seven days to leave the country."

I was stunned. "But..."

The cop continued. "If I could get you to sign this document and to note the time that I have served it, I'll be on my way."

I scrawled my name with a pen. "But, we can't put to sea now! It's winter! It's dark! It would be madness!"

"You'll have to speak with the immigration department tomorrow. According to this document," he said holding up the another paper, "you have a chance to appeal the decision."

"But..."

"I must go."

AFTER THE POLICEMAN LEFT, our walls of serenity began to crack, and within seconds, our Norwegian high collapsed. We could only visualize black clouds scuttling over angry seas. Our ears were roaring as if we were standing next to a waterfall.

"This isn't possible," Jaja had despair in her voice. "Next Tuesday! Leave by next Tuesday!"

We were at a loss for words and let silence hang in the cabin. We both felt hunted. We had playfully entertained the possibility that the visa could be denied, that we would have to leave Norway and go somewhere else. Now our jokes about getting kicked out were about to become reality.

Jaja continued. "You know what? I don't care about us. I'm worried about Chris and Holly. In two weeks, it'll be Holly's birthday. She's already making plans. And what about the class Christmas parties and the first handball tournament? We can't leave Svolvær, Dave. They'll be devastated."

"We can't tell them anything," I said, "until we've had a chance to discuss it with immigration tomorrow."

"This sucks," Jaja said.

"Yes. This sucks big time."

"I guess we should have applied back in September when we first arrived," Jaja said.

"We agreed there was no use asking until our visa was up."

"Looking back now, it seems like a dumb idea."

"But all we're asking for is a tourist visa extension!" I was practically shouting. "We don't want a work permit. When have we ever had a problem getting a tourist visa extension?"

We studied the documents the policeman had left. One of them stated that we had to leave, and the other–the appeals form–stated that we might have a chance to stay. Both were written in Norwegian; it was hopeless.

Chris and Holly tramped noisily down the dock. In high spirits, they burst into the cabin talking a mile a minute. They stripped off their rain gear, left it in a wet pile on the cabin sole, and continued talking wildly. They had sold all but two candles and napkin packs. We told them we would sell one to my mom in Seattle, and Jaja said we would buy one ourselves.

"We can't wait until next Tuesday," Chris said.

"That's when we get to hand in our money," Holly finished.

Jaja asked, "Did you guys have any problems?"

"Well, the first door we knocked on was answered by a really old lady."

"We couldn't understand everything she said."

"But I think she told us to go away."

"I think she also said that we were charging too much."

"The next house said they didn't have any money."

"The house after that didn't have change."

"Most of the houses had lights on inside, but no one answered the door when we rang the bell."

"We learned to keep ringing the bell until someone answered."

"That usually worked."

Jaja looked at me and shook her head.

After Chris and Holly had gone to school the next morning, we loaded Teiga into her stroller and walked to the police station. The immigration office was on the second floor. The two women in charge were polite and spoke English, but they were not able to translate the Norwegian legalese in the documents. We asked their opinion about the decision forcing us to leave. They agreed that the denial didn't make sense. When we asked about the appeal, they suggested that we file immediately as an act of faith.

We left the police station feeling slightly hopeful, but we couldn't let go of the thought that we might actually have to put to sea in December at 68 degrees north latitude. We tried joking that we could sail back to Iceland. Iceland wouldn't turn us away. If we left Tuesday, we could spend Christmas with Adda and Gudni. To hell with the Norwegian authorities. If they didn't want us to stay, we would just leave. Screw 'em. Forget the appeal. We weren't going to play their damn game.

Then we thought of our kids. We owed it to them to at least try. We wandered around town in a state of mild panic wondering what to do. So much for escaping rules and regulations. By going north to find a town with a freedom of spirit, we had put ourselves into a precarious and potentially dangerous situation. Going to sea in December was unimaginable.

BACK IN AUGUST, during the first week of school, a parent-teacher meeting was scheduled for Holly's class. Naturally, the meeting would be conducted in Norwegian. Nevertheless, Holly's teacher encouraged Jaja to attend. The best way to learn about the school and to meet new friends was to attend local functions.

"Do you want me to go?" I asked, holding my breath. After a summer of relative isolation, I knew I wasn't quite ready for the PTA.

"No, I'll do it."

I was vastly relieved, and the realization that I was off the hook gave me courage. I said, "Are you sure? I don't mind going."

Jaja started laughing, and gave me a hug. "Dave, you're a crummy liar."

Jaja returned to *Driver* in high spirits a couple of hours later. The parents had greeted her warmly. Coffee was served, and homemade cakes were passed around. At the start of the meeting, Holly's teacher Bjørg had introduced Jaja to Edd Meby, who spoke excellent English. He helped Jaja understand the discussions about homework, field trips, class parties, and some finer points of the curriculum.

Edd, who we later learned was the subeditor of the local newspaper *Lofotposten*, explained that in Norwegian schools, children remain with the same group of classmates from first grade until they graduate. This arrangement not only gives the children a sense of stability from year to year, it also allows the parents to become well acquainted and work together for the kids.

At the meeting, Jaja also met Ragnhild Tennes, who had a son in Holly's class and a daughter in Chris's class.

"I suppose we'll be eating cakes together often," Ragnhild said to Jaja, with a keen sense of humor. Ragnhild had brought a large basket of homemade cinnamon buns.

The next afternoon we ran into Ragnhild at the library, and Jaja introduced us.

"I am not a sailor," Ragnhild confessed. "I grew up in Oslo, and my family spent most of our holidays in the mountains. But my husband Svein grew up on the sea near Reine, at the southern end of Lofoten."

"Reine was the first place we saw in Lofoten," I said. "We spent an entire day sailing in the fjord. What a magnificent area to be from."

"You've been there?" Ragnhild said. "Maybe you saw some houses built on the peninsula called Tennes. That's my husband's family name."

"Tennes!" Jaja said. "We sailed right by it. In fact, we wondered what it would be like to live there all winter."

"Then you'll have to meet Svein. He grew up at Tennes and lived there until he went to university. No one lives there now; all the old folks have either passed away or have moved closer to town."

Ragnhild taught an advanced English course to Norwegian adults. She shyly asked us if we wouldn't mind giving a short talk to her students. "It would give them a great chance to get some practical experience," she said.

The following week, we talked to her students about our travels on board *Direction* and *Driver.* Someone made a cheesecake, coffee was served, and we interacted easily for about an hour. When we finished the discussion, the class applauded and presented us with a book of Lofoten wildlife photography and Norwegian poetry translated into English. In parting, Ragnhild said that if we ever needed anything, we only had to ask. With full stomachs and with a genuine feeling of community spirit, we bid everyone farewell.

That talk seemed like light years ago. Now we did need help. Jaja walked up to Ragnhild and Svein's house to ask for assistance in translating the papers that denied our visa. We had to discover the reasons for the negative decision rendered by the Utlendingsdirectoratet (UDI), the central immigration office in Oslo. By law, Ragnhild read, we were not allowed to extend our visa while traveling in the country. If we wanted to stay for longer than three months, we had to apply while we were in our home country–the United States of America. Technically, we were not allowed to file an appeal from Norway, either. However, there was some vague mention of exemption due to "just cause." In our opinion, we had just cause, so we wrote a new, more specific, letter to be included with the appeal.

In the letter, we reiterated our buoyant financial situation and estimated how much currency we would inject into the local economy during our nine-month stay. We detailed our plans for the following summer, and we mentioned that we were writing a book about our travels and needed time to collect information about Norway. We hadn't actually received a book contract to sign yet, but Jaja and I were hopeful. In the letter, we highlighted the dangers to be faced at sea on a small boat with three kids. I wrote that if we were forced to leave, our only course of action would be to sail back to the States, a distance of 3,000 miles. I stressed that winter was hardly a time to make such a journey.

Jaja and I reasoned that since we had already committed a faux pas with our visa extension, it would be wise to file the appeal immediately to try to straighten things out. In our letter, we reminded the UDI that we had originally come to Norway for a short time but that we wanted to stay because we liked the country so much. The following morning, the local immigration office in Svolvær faxed our appeal to Oslo.

IN EARLY DECEMBER, Svolvær received the first major snowfall of the season. The roads were covered by an even whiteness, roofs looked like thickly frosted gingerbread houses, bare trees bowed under the load, and the familiar drone of snowplows echoed off the mountains. The snow brightened the dark landscape and reminded us of our low-stress winter in Akureyri. Once again, *Driver*'s deck was covered with frozen precipitation, and we could hear flakes hissing on the hot stack of our heating stove.

We had experienced eight months of snow-covered decks in Akureyri, and now, after a short summer, we were buried again, headed into another winter. Snow had become very familiar. One difficulty we did not anticipate, however, was untying our frozen dock lines in order to cast off and motor to the fuel wharf. I would pound on the lines with a hammer, and Jaja would pour kettles of boiling water over them. The prospect of putting to sea made me wonder what it would be like handling our sails if the sheets and halyards were frozen.

The first week of December was also Christmas craft week at school. Each day during school hours, the students moved to a different classroom. Many of the projects were similar to the crafts that Jaja and I had made as kids. There were winter snow scenes made from cotton balls and glitter, ceramic elflike creations that usually broke on the way home (and had to be glued back together), and of course, the ubiquitous candle display made from plaster of Paris and shiny tree ornaments.

Interspersed with these "fun" crafts were traditional northern Norwegian crafts that had evolved over the centuries to fill a real need. In one room, Jaja volunteered to help make *toving,* a woolen felt which is still used for slippers, boot inner liners, and mittens. In another room, the kids made sweet drinks using frozen hand-picked summer berries. They also made hard candy and traditional Christmas cakes and cookies.

In Akureyri, we had been able to choose which holiday craft projects we wanted our kids to make. The school in Svolvær was more ingenuous. The students were expected to complete every craft–more projects than in Akureyri–and to sell us all their finished crafts in a pretend store. The profits went toward the class budgets.

Our Christmas preparations in Akureyri had been filled with carefree exuberance. We remembered the night we bought the fake pine garland at Blómval and stopped in a rustic café for hot chocolate and cappuccino. The peaceful snow slid down the shop windows, gathered in little piles, and absorbed the glow of colored lights. Our first weeks in Akureyri had been difficult because we were working out the bugs of living dockside without electricity or a freshwater hose. By Christmas, we had conquered the unknowns.

Looking back, we realized we had approached the Icelandic winter with calm reserve, and our modesty had been rewarded. In Norway, we were overconfident and relaxed through the autumn. Now the gate at the tollbooth was closed, and we were fumbling in our pockets for exact change.

Jaja and I sat in *Driver*'s dark cabin one evening after the kids had gone to bed listening to wind-driven snow that skittered through the rigging. "You know what my dad used to say," Jaja said half-seriously, half-mockingly. "Life's not fair."

"We need to cheer up," I said unenthusiastically.

"If it were just you and me, Dave, I would put to sea with no hesitation. But it's not fair to our kids. They've made a big effort to learn the language and make friends. They'll be heartbroken if we have to leave."

I nodded. "We'll do our best."

FREE TIME IS A PERK of the cruising lifestyle. Lucky thing, because without a car in which to go shopping, or a handy washer and dryer standing ready in the basement, we spent hours each week accomplishing basic tasks. Time is like money: If you have a surplus, it's easy to spend, and when it's in short supply, life miraculously goes on. In Svolvær, we were aware that we had more free time than most of our friends, so we tried to tread lightly and not to overstay our welcome. We knew that people who live ashore, especially if they have children and jobs, find that their days are filled. We experienced this ourselves in Oriental, North Carolina.

When cruising, it's difficult to initiate shoreside friendships in a foreign culture. If we come on too strong, a gate of suspicion might swing shut in our faces. But play the passive roll, and no one will know we exist.

In Svolvær, we had a head start making friends because of some well-timed publicity. A few days after Jaja attended the parent-teacher meeting, *Lofotposten* published a two-page story about us. During the interview, which focused on our sailing adventures, we praised Lofoten and highlighted our reasons for choosing to stay. Within days, individuals who read the story approached us. Nodding acquaintances became chatting ones, and as we continued to see people around town, at the school, and at other friend's homes, our social base widened.

Although temporarily satisfying to the ego, publicity has its ups and downs. We were flattered that other people were interested in us and in our lifestyle, but publicity also contradicted our goal of leading an unobtrusive life. In the extreme regions where we chose to cruise, however, publicity gave our seemingly outlandish lifestyle some credibility. The media stories showed that we were a family–whose members, like everyone else, had birthdays, dentist appointments, daily triumphs, homework, tantrums, dreams, and disappointments.

The articles we wrote for sailing magazines provided a different sort of publicity. We welcomed the income, but sometimes I felt hypocritical. Our lifestyle was simple, and our boat was low tech. It made me a tad uneasy to see our stories squeezed between glossy advertisements for expensive boats and state-of-the-art electronics. I worried that would-be cruisers on tight budgets might become discouraged that they could not go to sea without all those things. On *Direction*, we learned that the basic necessities are a sound boat, a few charts, a timepiece, and a sextant. Confidence and self-sufficiency are the important things, but they can't be bought. They are acquired through experience.

EXCEPT FOR TALKING with Ragnhild and a few other close friends, we kept our immigration problems under wraps. We were distraught, but until we had definite word from Oslo, there was nothing we could do. We also continued to keep the dilemma secret from Chris and Holly. Teiga heard some of our conversations, but she was too young to understand.

By the end of craft week, we relaxed a little. The wheels of bureaucracy could move slowly, especially around Christmastime. We figured the appeal would not be considered until January.

This fantasy lasted until the next Gestapo-like knock on our hull. A different uniformed officer came aboard, and Chris and Holly stared at him with big eyes.

My mouth felt sticky. "I hope you have brought us good news?"

"No, sir, I'm afraid not. Your appeal has been denied."

"Damn! Why does bad news travel so quickly?"

"Well, sir, I can't answer that. I'm here to inform you that you have seven days to leave the country on your own. Otherwise, we will have to escort you out."

"Do you understand the implications of our having to leave on our boat at this time of year?"

"I agree that the UDI's decision does not make sense."

"Of course it doesn't make sense! Even the..."

"Dave!" Jaja had a pleading tone.

I took a deep breath. "Sorry," I said to the cop. "You're just the messenger. Look, you'd better leave. I'm not in control of my words at the moment. I'm sure I'll regret everything I say if you don't go."

Jaja followed the officer into the cockpit and thanked him for coming down.

Chris and Holly followed the exchange in silence.

"Why are they making us leave?" Holly asked.

"We have followed the rules incorrectly," Jaja admitted, "so they are not going to give us a visa extension to stay for the winter."

"Will we be here for my birthday?"

"I'm afraid not."

"What about the handball tournament?" Chris asked.

"No."

"But the craft sale is after the tournament. What about all the things we made for you?"

"We can get your teachers to give us everything before we go."

"But you're supposed to buy them!"

"What about Christmas?" Holly asked.

"Look, we'll go to immigration tomorrow to talk to them. But we're not making any promises. It looks like we may to have to go."

"Where will we go?"

"We haven't decided."

"Should we tell our teachers and our friends?"

"Not yet. Let's wait until we talk to immigration."

We had not experienced such a sickening feeling since we discovered the hole in our hull during the passage to Iceland. Our current situation wasn't life threatening–at least not yet–but it jarred our confidence to the roots. All week we had been preparing mentally for departure, but the possibility that the appeal would succeed had taken the sting out of our imaginings.

Jaja and I sat awake long after the kids had gone to bed–drinking wine and discussing our options in a new light. They were no longer hypothetical; they were real. The most obvious option was to put *Driver* "on the hard" for the winter, fly to the States, return in the summer, and sail north to Spitsbergen. Simple. There was only one problem. We didn't have a home in America. Where would we live? We are a big crew. We could have "landed" on our families for a couple weeks, but never for six months. We could rent an apartment, rent a house, or buy a trailer, but a temporary move to the States would disrupt our kids incredibly. They would have to make new friends and start attending a new school in midterm. Flying to the States and renting a place would also cost a small fortune.

Sailing back to the States was almost impossible. The only practical route was to sail due south to the Shetland Islands 600 miles away. With reasonable winds, we could make it in four days. But I had been watching conditions closely. The unstable winter weather wasn't consistent for even 12 hours, let alone the time it would take us to make the passage. Low-pressure systems intensified, stalled, skidded, and merged with other lows. The best compromise would be to hug the Norwegian coast, pay close attention to the weather, and then duck into a dark, unfamiliar harbor at the first sign of adverse wind.

The possibility that we would be forced to leave was a grim reminder that the cruising life is not oriented around security. Cruising is a transient existence in which problems often negate creature comforts. Cruising also encourages, and sometimes requires, spontaneous decisions. We tried to remind ourselves that such decisions–for example, deciding on the spot to spend the winter in Lofoten–don't always work out for the best.

OUR FIRST CHRISTMAS TOGETHER–in 1988–had arrived triumphantly at the end of a brutal, weeklong passage. *Direction* had been anchored at Gomera in the Canary Islands when a mid-Atlantic gale sent a dangerous surge into the small harbor of San Sebastian. We tried to ride out the ground swell, but conditions were predicted to deteriorate. The gale was tracking straight for the Canaries. Worried that we might be trapped in the unprotected harbor by strong winds and even larger waves, we put to sea to eliminate the risk of *Direction*'s dragging her anchor and being smashed on the beach. We set out in a moderate breeze for the Cape Verde Islands, 600 miles to the south.

We thought we could outrun the southeastern edge of the low-pressure system, but a spur of the gale caught *Direction* and whipped her for 24 hours. The first night, white water broke over the decks and filled the cockpit ceaselessly. *Direction*'s tiny hull was tossed violently, subjected to new levels of abuse. Jaja and I lay below huddled on a settee. It was too dangerous to stand watch on deck.

The storm finally blew itself out, and we continued toward Isla Sal in the Cape Verdes. Two days before making landfall, a storm in the Sahara Desert kicked up a pall of fine red dust, which was carried hundreds of miles offshore by the wind. The dust was so thick that it obscured the horizon like fog. Our sails turned red, and the rigging wire appeared to be coated with cinnamon. The Sahara Desert collected on deck in piles, like drifting snow. With no horizon, the sextant was useless. We sailed southward blindly, ignorant of our position.

On Christmas Day, we still had not sighted land. Night was fast approaching. Soon we would have to drop the sails and stop moving forward–just to be safe. The ocean currents in the area were unpredictable; there was no telling where we would end up if we kept going. We had already sailed 200 miles without a sextant sight.

At 4:00 p.m. as we peered into the red mist, the faint image of white surf emerged dead ahead. We changed course and sailed parallel to the thin line of gray beach. An hour later, we stumbled upon the harbor breakwater at Palmeira. I was awed. Considering that we had been dead reckoning for 36 hours, the odds of finding the dust-shrouded island had been 1,000-to-one. We set the anchor, drank a bottle of Portuguese wine, and collapsed into bed.

Now Jaja and I sat in *Driver*'s cabin in snowy Svolvær and drained our wine glasses. We might also be "celebrating" our next Christmas at sea. Instead of hot dust obscuring the skies and coating the sails, snow would be swirling into little drifts on deck and coating the rigging like frosting. I shivered at the thought.

THE LADIES AT THE IMMIGRATION DESK in Svolvær were as surprised as we were about the turn of events. They had been confident when the appeal was filed. They had assumed that because of our unusual circumstances, we had "just cause" for being allowed to stay.

With the refusal in hand, they confirmed that the appeal had been denied solely because regulations prohibit filing while we were in Norway. They said the only solution was for us to go to the States, send in the appeal again, and wait for the answer.

"How long would that take?" Jaja asked hopefully.

"Up to six months, if they give you priority."

"What if we leave Norway to file the appeal and it gets turned down?"

"Then you would not be able to return to Norway for one year. After that, you could return on another three-month tourist visa."

"But that would be next winter! We'd be back in the exact same predicament!"

"Yes."

"Look," I said. "Do the crowd at the UDI realize that our boat is our only home, and that it's also our office? Do you think you could call the person in charge of our case and talk to him on our behalf? Maybe plead a little?"

"Could you please tell the UDI," Jaja said emotionally, "that when Christmas morning comes and they wake to a warm house, we'll be in the middle of the ocean with our children."

The ladies agreed to try.

WITH HEAVY HEARTS, we prepared *Driver* for sea. I bent on the frozen mainsail, removed the diesel engine injectors for servicing, topped up the batteries with a charger plugged into shore power, inspected the rigging, and checked that we had the necessary navigation charts. I had recently received an up-to-date Year 2000 nautical almanac from the States. I faxed Hailing Port Services in North Carolina asking them to send *Driver*'s newest documentation decal via express mail. Jaja made several runs to the grocery store to buy food for a month at sea. *Driver* was in good shape; we were mental wrecks.

The sun had already dipped below the horizon for the season. If we put to sea, we would have zero hours of sunlight on the first leg. I wondered what it would be like to stand watch with 20 hours of darkness and just four hours of scant twilight. A new moon was on the way. For the first time in my life, I was genuinely scared to go to sea.

At the immigration office the next day, we learned that because our appeal was technically "illegal," no one had been assigned to our case. No one had even read our letters. No one sitting in that plush office in Oslo had any idea what he or she was putting us through. The immigration ladies were trying to speak with the department head in Oslo, but apparently she was out of town until the following Monday or Tuesday. We were supposed to be out of the country by Wednesday.

It was an anxious weekend.

On Monday afternoon, Jaja was in town with the kids, and I was aboard *Driver* trying to concentrate on writing. A brisk knock on the hull made my stomach sink. The policeman standing on the dock wouldn't come aboard, but he said quite sincerely that we were entitled to legal council and that the attorney at the police station wanted to see me. Jaja and I had read in a cruising guide that the local authorities could grant asylum to ships. I hoped for the best and cycled down to the station in the dark while big snowflakes fell from the sky. My bicycle was a real winner. Earlier in the season, I had pulled it out of Svolvær Harbor at low tide. After scraping away the barnacles, it took half of a can of WD 40 to make the wheels spin again. After that, the bike required no further restoration except new brake cables.

I sat in a stark office answering routine questions to which I was certain the attorney already knew the answers. I looked around as I spoke. Floppy disks were stacked haphazardly on a bookshelf. There were mountains of files on the desk, and sticky notes hung from all available surfaces. I was losing my ability to be friendly. All we wanted was an extension on our tourist visa to get us through the winter. We were being hassled over a technicality.

The attorney reiterated that qualifying for the visa wasn't the issue. The problem was that we had not followed the rules. We had filed our application from within the borders of Norway. I mentioned that Jaja and I hadn't filed the appeal, it had been filed on our behalf by the local immigration department across the hall.

"Why did you come to Norway?" the attorney asked, changing the subject.

"Have you read our cover letter? It explains it all perfectly well." I knew the guy was trying to help, but it felt as if he were treating me like a criminal. I was on guard for reasons I didn't have time to analyze.

"You say you will be spending foreign dollars in town, yet your kids are using the school system for free."

"The headmaster welcomed our kids to the school when we asked permission last August. We pointed out to him that we were not taxpaying Norwegian citizens, but he said that every child in the world is entitled to an education. If you have questions about this, you should ask him."

Jaja had already informed the staff at the school about our problems, in case they became involved inadvertently. The headmaster was supportive and said he would vouch for us.

The attorney made a new sticky note and affixed it to his desk lamp. He said, "Tell me, why do you think you should be allowed to stay in Norway?"

"Look. We're tourists. We *wanted* to stay because we like it here. Now that it's winter, we're stuck. Taking my family to sea at this time of the year would not be wise."

"You have stated that fact plainly in your letter." The attorney held my steady gaze. "It's on that point, incidentally, that we are forced to intervene. We agree that it is too dangerous for you sail your boat during the winter, especially with your family." Then he paused.

I didn't like his tone of voice or his stare. They gave me the first indications of what was coming.

He said, "If you attempt to leave Svolvær Harbor on your boat with your family, we shall be forced to stop you, confiscate the boat, sell it, and use the money to reimburse the cost of deporting you."

My mouth was way ahead of my brain. "You won't have to worry about that because we'll leave during a blizzard, and you'll never see us go." My face was burning. Who the hell was this chump to tell me what I could and couldn't do?

"Young man, you are in a lot of trouble. You will not be allowed to risk the lives of your family and be a burden to our coast guard."

I had nothing to say.

He said, "My advice is for you to engage a lawyer. I think you are in deeper than you imagine."

"Can you recommend one?" I certainly wasn't going to ask him to represent us.

"I'm not allowed to do that."

"So what am I supposed to do? Spend a day knocking on doors? You must know someone in town who would be able to help us." I felt like saying, "not someone like you," but this time, I wisely held my tongue. Small miracle.

"Off the record, I can recommend an ex-colleague of mine. Her office is in the town center." He gave me directions and said he would phone ahead. I left his office wondering whose side he was on.

I DASHED DOWN the snowy street. I was going to hire a lawyer–my first lawyer–and I was disappointed that Jaja wasn't with me to share the experience. I waited 20 minutes in the waiting room. The longer I waited, the less triumphant I felt. Events were crumbling all around us, and I felt especially stupid for smart-mouthing the police attorney. Would I ever learn? I was shown into a tidy office with a splendid view of the harbor. I shook hands with attorney Ingrid Sollid. She went straight to the point.

"I've spoken with my former colleague, and he's outlined the problem."

"Do you think you will be able to help us?"

"I'll try. I have a trial date tomorrow in Tromsø, and I won't be back until Thursday night. I'll ask my secretary to inform the UDI in Oslo that I have taken your case and that they are not to proceed until they hear from me at the end of the week."

"We are supposed to leave by Wednesday," I said. "The police attorney threatened to deport us if we don't leave. He even threatened to confiscate our boat if we try going by sea."

Ingrid laughed. "Did he say that? Well, they won't do anything. In fact, I don't believe they have the legal right. How can I get a hold of you?"

"You can fax me at the library." I gave her the number.

"Don't worry about a thing." She looked at her calendar. "Come back here Friday at two o'clock. Bring all the documents you have."

"What will this cost?"

Ingrid smiled. "So far, nothing has happened, so it won't cost anything."

"I mean..."

"Don't worry about it yet. I will see you Friday."

I went back onto the street feeling bewildered. I had just engaged a lawyer. I felt a sudden burst of confidence knowing that at least we had a chance to fight back.

The snow stopped falling, and it felt good to be outdoors after sitting in the warm offices. The streets were covered with tightly packed, smooth snow–a condition that made cycling almost predictable. The lights from the buildings made the snow sparkle and the surrounding mountains glow. Svolvær was a winter wonderland. I felt lucky to be there on this night riding my bike under the dim stars that appeared between flurries. I knew we had to pull ourselves together and not let the immigration thing consume us. I thought that *any* good news would help.

On my way back to the marina, I stopped at the library to check for messages. A five-page fax lay waiting. I read it, smiled, stuffed it into my backpack, and hurried home.

Jaja had been worried. "Where have you been? Your bike was gone, so at least I knew you hadn't slipped on the dock and fallen into the harbor."

I detailed my meeting at the police station. Jaja rolled her eyes when I mentioned sailing away in a blizzard.

"Dave!"

"I know, I know. The guy had my hackles up. He was almost provoking me."

"Now what do we do?"

"We, Dave and Jaja Martin, have enlisted the services of a lawyer."

"You're kidding! Who is he?"

"He's a she. Ingrid is a savvy woman. She's no-nonsense, friendly, and very busy. She has a gorgeous diamond-and-platinum necklace and set of earrings that you would kill for. She doesn't think she can do anything to sway the decisions of the UDI, but she is determined to try. Oh, some good news. Because of Ingrid we don't have to leave on Wednesday."

Jaja visibly sighed. "Are we going to get to stay through Christmas?"

"We won't know anything until Friday." I pulled the five-page fax out of my pack and handed it to Jaja. "Here, check this out."

She started reading. "Hey! It's the book contract."

"We did it, Jaja. Included in the deal is an advance on royalties, a laptop computer, and a printer. We're in business. The advance will probably be enough to pay Ingrid."

Jaja gave me a stop-being-so-cynical look.

"I'm just trying to see the bright side."

Jaja shrugged.

The next morning, we signed the contract and faxed it back. Now all we had to do was write the book. We wondered what we had gotten ourselves into.

JAJA, TEIGA, AND I sat quietly in Ingrid's office while she answered a telephone call. We looked out the windows. The snow wasn't falling vertically; it was blowing sideways. When she hung up, Jaja asked Ingrid if she could stall our imminent departure until January 1st, so we could salvage Christmas and New Year's for our kids. Ingrid said that an immigration officer had finally been assigned to our case and that she needed to talk to this person. We would have to wait until the following week for answers.

"I'm sorry," Ingrid said. "At this point, we'll just have to be patient."

It was another long weekend.

On Saturday, we walked out to the Lady. The sky was overcast, snow threatened, and a deep ground swell was pounding the outer rocks. Three years earlier, a storm with hurricane-force winds and gargantuan seas flattened the breakwater. The seas were so large that houses around Lofoten, which had stood on rocky promontories for decades, were swept away. The sea has no rules.

We stood at the end of the breakwater looking seaward. Black clouds covered the sunless horizon. It would be fully dark very soon. Cold gusts were kicking up whitecaps, forcing us to bury our faces inside our jackets.

Holly turned to Jaja, "Mommy? Do we really have to go out there?"

We had decided not to hide anything from our kids. "I hope not, but maybe."

On Sunday, we went walking in the mountains.

On Tuesday, there was a fax from Ingrid. She had been in contact with the UDI. Later, when we met in her third-floor office, she said, "The UDI is going to let you stay in Norway until January 31st."

We were elated, "So they're processing our appeal now?"

"No. They are not. They are giving you time to make arrangements. I told them that they cannot force you to leave with only a week's notice. They also now understand that you have children who should not have their Christmas ruined." Ingrid smiled.

"Do you mean to say that there is no chance we will be allowed to stay through the winter?" I asked.

Ingrid shrugged. "They are holding firm, saying that rules are rules. They will not permit you to file for an extension inside the borders, nor will they allow you to appeal that decision inside the borders. They are adamant that you must process the paperwork from your own country."

I asked, "Can't we fly somewhere closer? For instance, Sweden? England? Or Denmark?

"Unfortunately, the rules state that the applicant must apply from a country in which he has citizenship or from which he has a residence visa. You may not file from a country in which you have only a tourist visa."

Around and around it went. We thanked Ingrid profusely for getting us the extra time and then asked for an accounting of our expenses.

She waved her hand in the air apologetically. "No, I have done nothing except make a few phone calls." She stood up. "Let's get together after New Year's. There's nothing further to be done with the holidays coming up."

The news that we could stay for Holly's birthday, the handball tournament, the craft sale, Christmas, and New Year's took the edge off our growing fatigue. Jaja and I both looked haggard and felt sick with worry. Even the kids felt our depression. Knowing we could stay, albeit temporarily, helped on the surface, but the fire of doubt burned in the pits of our stomachs. We were caught in a terrible limbo–a no man's land. It was difficult being festive when we knew we were still going to have to make some harsh decisions. Conditions at sea in January would be worse than in December.

Chapter Fifteen

*It's tough to hold firm to your ideals
while wading through a sea of strife.*

THE CRAFT SALE AT THE SCHOOL was a huge success; the gym was packed. Buying only the crafts their own children had made, each parent carried a bulging plastic bag. At Holly's class table, she presented us with an angel made of Styrofoam and gold cloth, a construction-paper winter scene, a hand-decorated jar of bath crystals, and a large white Christmas stocking made from woolen *toving*. Holly took our money, bagged everything up, and handed the cash to Bjørg. The routine was similar at Chris's table.

Anne Brit beamed. "The children are so proud today!"

Chris had focused on ceramic projects. He sold us a dozen tiny elf figurines, several cups, and a flat clay disk that had bulging eyes, stringy hair, and a wide smile. The ceramic things were delicate, and I wondered silently where we could stow them safely on *Driver*.

While I was paying for Chris's creations, I bumped into Stein. He was buying stuff from his son Edvart. The din was deafening, so we shouted at each other.

"In America," Stein teased, "don't they call this extortion?"

The following week, Jaja and I joined the grammar-school kids in a procession to the Svolvær Lutheran Church. Inside the airy chamber, we listened to 250 pure voices singing Norwegian Christmas carols accompanied by the full-size pipe organ. The children's innocent, lilting tones infused our hearts with warmth. For about an hour, we forgot about the UDI.

Here was evidence of the extraordinary attitude of the local children and adults–just one of the many reasons we had been drawn to this wonderful region. In an old fishing area such as Lofoten, where ocean storms have been stealing fathers and sons for generations, Christmas was an inward time–a time for families and friends. Shop windows were decorated modestly, stores did not blare Christmas carols, and there were no Santas ringing bells on the street corners. Few houses had outdoor Christmas lights. The subdued atmosphere was unfamiliar to us. Our American instincts sought millions of colored lights, the Christmasy voice of Bing Crosby, and a hundred imitation Santas walking around *ho-hoing* like cheerleaders. Christmas in Lofoten had value. It was a time to relax, a time to enjoy friendships. The spirit of the community was a force that needed no electrification or colorful baubles. We could *feel* the Christmas spirit.

Sitting there on the stark wooden pew, amid singing children and teachers, I felt a surge of hope. Jaja, Holly, Chris, Teiga and I were a unit, a force that could wield great power if we channeled our energy outward. At that moment, the wheels of bureaucracy seemed as meager as the gears in a cheap pocket watch. I looked at Jaja and stared deep into her green eyes.

She felt it too.

FOR US, CHRISTMAS DAY had always been a family time, a time to lie around in pajamas. Except for the one Christmas in the rented house in Oriental, North Carolina, we had spent all our Christmases on board away from social gatherings. Christmas was a day for Jaja and me to forget about being adults. It was a time to be a kid with the kids.

To compensate for the stress caused by our problems with the UDI, Jaja and I violated our rule of limiting the number of presents we bought for the kids. In a world favored by instant gratification, less is often more. In Svolvær, however, we appeased our guilt for involving our kids in our immigration troubles by drowning them with toys. We went overboard.

During our years of cruising, we had learned to watch for presents year round. We never knew, for example, where we would be at Christmas or what we could buy there. We knew what our kids liked, so when we saw something appropriate, we bought it and stashed it away. We used some of these things for Christmas presents. We doled out some on birthdays. Sometimes, we used our stash for "nice guy" awards. On *Direction*, we kept a bag of small, inexpensive toys wrapped in colorful paper. We gave them to the kids during passages to help relieve their occasional restlessness. At sea on a small boat with babies, buying an hour or two of quiet time with a cheap gift gave Jaja and me the opportunity to recharge–a gift to us more valuable than gold.

On *Driver,* the backs of our clothes lockers were crammed with an impressive inventory of goods. We were a floating toy store with something for all ages. The toy store in Svolvær was also well stocked, and we added needlessly to our shipboard booty. We were helping the local economy far more than we had estimated in our letter to the UDI.

Keeping stuff hidden from three kids aboard a 33-foot sailboat is a trick. Undoubtedly, Chris, Holly, and Teiga had an inkling that the lockers in our V-berth held more than just clothes. However, they kept their distance. They were confident that We-the-Parents would divulge the contents at opportune moments; we trusted them not to peek in the lockers. Faith travels in circles.

Doing anything secretly on board took timing, so wrapping the overabundance of gifts in Svolvær was a challenge. On Christmas Eve, we waited until well after midnight to begin, so that our crew would not wake up and catch us in the Santa act. We pulled everything out from hiding and covered the settees with the toys, games, and electronic things. There was even stuff we had forgotten about.

We started by making three equal piles. Normally, we would have removed "select stuff" to save for later, but on this particular Christmas, our excitement knew no bounds.

"Give it all!" we exulted.

In the wee hours of Christmas Day, we wrapped, sipped liqueur, threw a towel over the exposed booty when a child stirred, sipped more liqueur, ran out of tape, ran out of paper, and ended up using aluminum foil for wrapping. As well as the presents we bought, there were packages from our families. By 2:00 a.m., a heap of colorfully wrapped boxes covered the entire cabin sole between the settees. The stockings were stuffed and hung. With whispered exclamations of, "I think we overdid it this year," we collapsed into bed.

BEFORE DRIFTING OFF to sleep, I thought of the loot covering the cabin sole and wondered where in the world we would stow it before going to sea. Something would have to go. That, I knew, would cause great angst among the younger members of the crew.

On *Direction,* our 25-foot wonder boat, we had minimal space for a growing family of four. We regularly traded books and toys with people we met. We wore our clothes to threads; we didn't bother with shoes. Although culling our worldly goods became a way of life, it was never one of our favorite activities.

The lack of space on *Direction* also forced us to keep the number of galley implements to a bare minimum. We had a can opener, a sharp knife, a big pot, a small pot, a frying pan, and a couple of mixing bowls. Although we had more storage space on *Driver,* we exercised the same economy toward "kitcheny" things. After all, a rum bottle works fine for a rolling pin. And who really needs a garlic press? By limiting the number of "unnecessary" items such as extra cutlery, excess plates, and superfluous bowls, the lockers remained uncluttered and the sink empty of dirty dishes.

When we go cruising, it's tempting to bring as much of "the house" as possible. Over the years, we have seen every sort of household appliance aboard other cruising boats: Blenders, food processors, electric mixers, bread makers, rice makers, and coffee machines. All these need to be driven off an inverter, an electronic device that converts the boat's 12-volt DC battery current to household-type 110-volt AC current. It takes copious amounts of 12-volt power to run an inverter. By using appliances in an effort to simplify cooking, the boat's battery charging system needs to be more complicated (and costly) so that it can handle the load. Since we have often met cruisers who complain about being bored, all those time-saving appliances seem to be a paradox. For us, the joy of cruising is reaping the rewards of its inherent simplicity.

Driver has more space belowdecks than *Direction*, but like dust, possessions quickly filled every nook and cranny of the larger boat. We faced our most challenging culling exercise when we moved out of the rented house and onto *Driver*. During our 18-month stint ashore, we had tripled the volume of our possessions. We had acquired cars, bicycles, baby strollers, roller skates, two guitars, tons of books, clothes, shoes, and enough toys to satisfy 10 children. I had the most toys of all–a sizable inventory of hand tools and spare parts for the boat. Scrutinizing the worth of our junk by its size and by the frequency of its use was an irksome task. We had to ask ourselves which would be more fun–collecting a garage full of material objects or sailing to Iceland.

Logic does not necessarily ease the pain of reality. Chris, Holly, and Teiga reacted emotionally when we asked them to give up some of their worldly possessions so that our belongings would fit into the boat. Holly had learned to read at age four, and she knew every title of the hundreds of children's books we owned. Chris was a budding junkman, and he had fashioned a 12-volt city using old electrical parts from *Driver*. The kids had Lego creations, stuffed animals, and boxes of miscellaneous debris. Jaja took the children into their rooms and asked what they would like to keep and what they could part with. She explained that they would have to give up something so we could move on board.

They gave Jaja a blank stare. "We like all of it."

Even 18-month old Teiga clung fast to her cherished possessions.

Jaja was in a quandary. "We've given them most of this stuff, and now we are asking them to get rid of it. It's not fair."

We gave Holly and Chris a big box for the stuff they could keep, and several more big boxes for the items we would store at my mother's and stepfather's house in Seattle. My mom had very generously offered us a basement closet in which to keep things that we couldn't take to sea. Over the years, we had shipped a variety of items to her for storage, and apparently, the closet was nearly full. As time passed, we lost track of what was in closet. Nevertheless, it was comforting to know our possessions were there–whatever they were.

Jaja saved our kid's artwork, their homemade crafts, and some souvenirs. Unfortunately, the majority of the "safekeeping" boxes were destined for the Salvation Army. It's tough being a parent.

Jaja and I began culling our own stuff. We had helped our kids come to terms with their belongings, but we adults still had a mountain of worn out bric-a-brac. A yard sale seemed the best way to pass along our things to "good homes." We advertised the sale with the come-on statement that everything would be dirt cheap. Even Chris and Holly rummaged in the safekeeping boxes that lined our hallway and salvaged some items for the sale–in hopes of earning some pocket money.

The yard sale was a dismal affair highlighted by moments of misery. Customers pawed over our treasures with repugnance–as if the goods were rotten vegetables. It was hard to admit that our personal belongings were worthless. The sale reminded us that the value of "stuff" exists only in the eye of the beholder. That night, I stole surreptitiously across town in our van, which was crammed with unsold chattel. I unloaded everything into a large commercial dumpster. Good riddance.

The next morning on our way from the house to the boat, we cruised past the dumpster. We recognized a half-dozen of the previous day's shoppers rooting through the smelly steel box, triumphantly rescuing our discarded treasures. Jaja and I wondered if we would ever understand the human race.

We began moving our stuff aboard *Driver* in Oriental the week before her christening party. All we needed to simplify the process was a nice half-mile-long conveyor belt from the house to the boat. As we stowed, we were reminded that there is a considerable amount of space inside a sailboat hull. The hallway at the house was jammed with boxes. It took many trips in the van to make a dent. We carried load after load below into the cabin–where it all neatly disappeared.

Then, with an imaginary grinding of gears, the process of filling *Driver* with goods came to a shuddering halt. I looked in dismay as Chris and Holly dragged a large, green garbage bag out of the van. It was full of stuffed animals.

"I think you have confused *Driver* with a certain biblical boat," I said. "Look, I'm sorry guys, but some of those synthetic pets will have to stay ashore."

"But Daddy!"

"Bulk," I said. "Sheer bulk."

Jaja stepped in to mediate. "We'll find room."

I examined the bag and made a quick estimate. "But Jaja, 50 creatures? The kids seldom played with those things at the house."

"We have 63," Chris corrected. "I counted 'em this morning."

"Dave?" Jaja said, "I'll make a deal with you. Let the animals file aboard, and we'll buy you a bottle a rum."

"Mount Gay?"

"The one-liter size."

"All right. Move 'em along."

AFTER OUR LATE-NIGHT wrapping spree, Christmas morning in Svolvær came quickly. As in Akureyri one year earlier, we feigned sleep in the dark cabin while listening to Chris's, Holly's, and Teiga's discussion about the arrival of Santa.

"Chris?" Holly whispered. "Get your flashlight."

"It's broken. Remember? That's one of the things I asked for."

"Borrow Daddy's."

"You borrow it. It's your idea."

Holly crawled out of her bunk and fumbled for the flashlight, which was stowed at the bottom of the companionway ladder. "Here, Chris. You turn it on."

"OK."

Through squinted eyes, we watched the beam of light play over the pile of wrapped gifts and along the cabin walls where three bulging stockings hung suspended from reading lights.

"Woooooooowww," all three of our Christmas connoisseurs exclaimed simultaneously. The light was quickly extinguished. Then the only sound was wind blowing in the rigging. The cabin was pitch dark again.

I could feel Jaja grinning.

"Got'em," I whispered.

It had taken weeks of subtle suggestions and cunning remarks to make our kids think of asking for the stuff we had already purchased. They were shy to ask for more than one or two things because they knew Santa didn't like greedy kids. They also knew that Santa wouldn't bring them an impractical gift (something enormous like a trampoline or a horse). Our kids had an undying faith that Santa would bring them exactly what they wanted, so they didn't worry about making a list. It was easy for Jaja and me to mold their desires to what we had already bought and stashed. But every year we had the same apprehensions; we hoped our kids liked what they would soon be opening.

Teiga was almost four years old, and she was consumed by the Santa Claus myth. If Holly and Chris had figured "it" out, they weren't telling. After all, letting go of a childhood conviction is difficult. I often felt guilty perpetuating Santa Claus because the end result is the disappointing discovery that life is ordinary. Learning that there is no big, jolly fellow who gives you cool things for free can be a life-altering letdown. Children take a step toward maturity when they discover that the magic is really their parents' doing.

The next step is for children to learn how to acquire what they want by earning it. Through this, they discover that the value of something is often determined by the time or money expended in its pursuit. Sometimes you must even pursue and hold onto intangibles such as personal ideals, lest they become valueless myths.

A STIFF NORTHEASTERLY BREEZE had been blowing through the marina all night, kicking up a slight chop. *Driver* pitched uncomfortably. The wind shrieked and made the boat heel over. I had a sobering mental image of conditions offshore. Understandably, Jaja and I were apprehensive about going to sea in January. Not only did we face the threat of storms and dangerous waves, but ice might form in the rigging. Iced rigging could cause *Driver* to become top heavy and possibly capsize. I also worried that blowing snow would fill the long, vertical groove in the mast. The plastic sail slides that hold the mainsail to the mast travel up and down in this groove. If they were blocked by ice or snow, we might not be able to adjust the height of the mainsail to reef it during a storm.

The previous, innocent Christmas in Iceland seemed light years away. I recalled the quiet fjord, the ice thumping the hull, and the contented feeling that we were safe in port until spring. Whenever I thought about our battle with the UDI–which was about 30 times an hour–the illogical motives of bureaucracy made my blood boil. We should have felt snug and cozy in Svolvær. Instead, we felt like vagabond tramps in a holding cell. "Stupid" was the only word to describe the situation. Jaja and I were stupid for not researching the rules, and the UDI was stupid for acting as if we were a threat to national security.

Of all the alternatives, leaving *Driver* in Svolvær and flying to the States was the safest and most responsible action–especially considering our children. On the surface, abandoning *Driver* made rational sense. Deep down, however, it felt wrong. Very wrong. As the hours wore on and the days passed, the right course of action became very clear to us. If forced, we would go to sea as a family. That included the five of us and *Driver*.

The wind remained strong and steady throughout Christmas Day. We adjusted physically to the motion caused by the chop. The sky was overcast, the air was damp, and the temperature was a fraction below freezing. The arrival of the day's scant twilight at 10:00 a.m. was followed all too soon by darkness at 2:00 p.m. We had no reason to go outdoors, and every reason to stay in the cabin. We ate roast lamb, drank hot chocolate, finished pot after pot of coffee, and loosened our belts to accommodate more. We did puzzles and played with the new toys. It was our best day in weeks–all was quiet on the northern front.

The time between Christmas Eve and New Year's is a special week in Svolvær. It's called the "quiet time," and the shops are only open for a few hours on certain days. We visited friends and invited them aboard *Driver*. In between, we spent peaceful family evenings on the boat.

In Norway, Father Christmas does not have the same awe-inspiring reputation that he enjoys in other parts of the world. Santa is mainly for kindergarteners. He gives out candy around town, usually a week or two before Christmas, and then his job is finished. The presents under the tree are given by family and close friends. In Norway and Iceland, Christmas Eve is the magic moment for kids.

The evening meal on the 24th is a formal yet intimate occasion that is shared with relatives. Children are not allowed to open their gifts until the plates have been cleared. One child is given the job of picking a present, reading the to/from tag out loud, and handing it to the proper person. Everyone watches the lucky recipient open his gift.

"I can't imagine waking on Christmas Eve morning," Holly mused, "knowing that I had to wait *all day* before I could open the presents under the tree."

"Why do they do it that way?" Chris asked. "Why not open the presents first thing?"

"It's the custom," Jaja said. "It's what everyone is used to."

"I like our way better," said Holly. "I like waking up full of anticipation, but I like knowing that I don't have too long to wait."

STEIN AND GRY INVITED US to their house on December 26th to eat lamb's back, a traditional Norwegian meal. Visiting them was always a treat, and Gry was an excellent cook.

When we arrived, another couple was trying to keep pace with two mobile toddlers who looked like fraternal twins.

"These are our neighbors Kari and Thorvardur," Stein said, with a grin. "We only invite them over at Christmas." He put his hand to the side of his mouth and whispered loudly. "Charity."

Kari picked up her little daughter, walked over, and punched Stein on the shoulder playfully. With mock anger, she said, "Stein is a terrible, terrible man. Never believe a word he says."

Gry came out from behind the stove and gave Jaja and me a hug. "Welcome, welcome! Hello, Holly and Teiga. Where is your brother?"

"Downstairs with Edvart," Holly said.

"These are for you guys," Thorvardur handed each of us a bottle of julé øl, a strong, 7 percent beer that the Norwegian breweries only produce at Christmastime. "Merry Christmas."

"Thorvardur brought the beer tonight," Gry said politely.

"Oh yes, that's right!" Stein said, slapping his forehead with mock recollection. "The beer! I knew there was another reason why we invite them at Christmas."

"How old are your twins?" Jaja asked Kari.

They just turned one," she replied.

Holly reached her hands out timidly to the little boy. He took them, and Holly very carefully walked with him a few paces across the living room.

"Hey! He likes you," Kari said. "He doesn't go with just anybody."

Moments later, Gry came in carrying a large platter of lamb served with sweet summer berries called *moltebær.* *"Vær sa god!"* Everybody come and eat!

As soon as we sat down, Stein poured some akvavit, a fine, grain alcohol flavored with caraway seed. He passed around pewter shot glasses.

"To Dave and Jaja," Gry said raising a toast.

"Yeah," Stein added facetiously. "Yankees go home."

Jaja laughed. "You probably have friends at the UDI."

"I keep sending them bribes to make you leave, but you're still here."

"You need a lawyer," I suggested.

Stein laughed. "It seems that your lawyer Ingrid is too good. Maybe that's the problem."

Kari and Thorvardur had puzzled looks on their faces, so we explained our predicament.

"Oh, that's so unfair," Kari said. "They can't make you go at this time of the year!"

"Is there any way we can help?" Thorvardur asked.

"Not at the moment," I said. "But thanks for asking. The wheels of bureaucracy are sitting idle for the time being."

Stein said, "Did you know that Thorvardur is Icelandic? He has probably filled in his fair share of immigration papers. Of course, he solved all his immigration problems by marrying Kari, who's Norwegian."

I said, "So, one option for staying is that Jaja and I should each marry a local?"

Stein nodded. "For example."

Jaja's eyes lit up "Marry a tall, handsome Viking? What a good idea!"

On that note, all the adult's glasses were topped up with red wine. The kids got soda.

"To the Vikings," Stein said. "Skoal!"

"Skoal!" The kids all made a big show of banging their glasses together like grown-ups. No one broke a glass, but a lot of soda was slopped on the tablecloth. There was a moment of silence while everyone sipped.

Thorvardur said, "I hear you guys lived on your boat in Akureyri."

"Yes," Jaja said "What town are you from?"

Thorvardur laughed. "I'm not from town. I'm from a place. It's a small fishing village on the Snæfellsnes Peninsula called Hellnar."

Jaja was surprised. "Really? We were there last year. What a mysterious place!"

"My father and uncle built wooden boats," Thorvardur said. "We enjoyed some of the best cod fishing in Iceland."

"Did you ever meet the Icelandic author Haldur Laxness?" asked Jaja. "He made Hellnar famous in his book *Under the Glacier.*"

"No. Laxness spent three summers in Hellnar prior to writing that book, but I was too young to remember any of that. He interviewed my parents and the other family members, though."

After dinner, all the "big" kids went downstairs and began playing rambunctiously. The adults stayed at the table drinking cognac and coffee. The twins fell asleep on their parents' laps.

Stein said, "My parents have a cabin about one kilometer down the road from us, not far from Kari and Thorvardur's house. My dad said you are welcome to stay there for the remainder of the winter if you like. Or, you can just "vacation" there until the hounds come barking."

We took advantage of the offer and stayed there during the rest of the holiday. The cabin was surrounded by pine trees, and we luxuriated in the quiet forest. It was grand to chop wood, build roaring fires in the potbellied stove, and go skiing right from the front door.

"I bet staying in Tennes for the winter would be like living in this cabin," I said to Jaja.

"Except it would be even more isolated–and darker, since the sun is hidden behind the steep mountains there until March," she answered.

About 100 paces from the cabin's back door, a cold, dark outhouse stood like a sentinel. Its only source of illumination was candlelight. Once, during a chilly, half-asleep nocturnal visit, I was inspired to pen this limerick.

> *There once was an outhouse in Norway,*
> *With dangerous ice in the doorway.*
> *I slipped when I entered,*
> *Rolled my eyes and surrendered,*
> *Then fell on my butt in a sore way.*

ACCORDING TO THE NEWS, the world far away from the outhouse was gearing up for Year 2000 computer malfunctions, which would be caused, supposedly, by software that couldn't read the 2000 date. It also seemed as if many people were waiting expectantly for the end of the world. We read that television networks from the United States would provide up-to-the-minute, around-the-world coverage of the midnight celebrations on New Year's Eve. This would also provide the networks with a chance to record the possible chaos from computers going haywire.

The Norwegians aren't quite as crazy about New Year's fireworks as the Icelanders, but they run a close second. Every grocery store, sports store, and gas station sold large rockets, small rockets, and variety packs. We bought a few dozen rockets and justified the expense because it was the Year 2000. Early in the afternoon of New Year's Eve, rockets began whizzing through town on projectories that threatened unwary pedestrians. It was nearly dark all day, so fireworks made a show at any time. The rockets extinguished themselves on snowy metal roofs and frozen lawns.

At 9:00 p.m., we left the cabin and trekked toward town to watch the festivities. It was cold. The air temperature was around 20 degrees Fahrenheit, and a stiff breeze lowered the wind chill to inhuman levels. We crunched down the icy single-lane road pulling Teiga on her sled. Chris and Holly skipped effortlessly, energized by the prospect of midnight fireworks. They remembered the thrill of New Year's in Akureyri and couldn't wait to experience it again.

On the road, we met Stein and Gry, who invited us to tag along to a neighbors' house. We joined the party on a balcony and drank hot, spiced wine called *glögg*. The children, who greatly outnumbered the adults, filled their cups from the nonalcoholic bowl. Candles and torches flickered in the wind making the pure white snow dance with a yellowish cast. Bottle rockets screamed through the dark trees. Kids tossed snowballs playfully, while laughter rose and fell in the crisp air.

Norwegians love to sing, and this occasion definitely inspired song. Accompanied by a trumpet, a saxophone, and a trombone, adults and kids filled the night with harmonies passed down through the generations. The singing ended when the *glögg* bowls ran dry.

"We will be going from house to house partying until midnight," Stein said. "We'd love to have you to join us."

"Thanks," I said, "but we promised Chris, Holly, and Teiga that we would watch the fireworks display in town close-up."

"You'll be able to see it from here," he said.

"I know, but they have their hearts set on being in the thick of things."

Stein flashed a knowing smile.

"OK," I said, "Jaja and I want to be in the middle of it, too."

As we walked to town, our thoughts roamed back to Iceland. How was Knútur's party going this year, we wondered. What were Adda and Gudni doing? How many million kronur's worth of fireworks were the citizens of Akureyri shooting off? In Iceland, our good cheer had been buoyed by deep satisfaction; we had survived almost half the winter intact. In Svolvær, we weren't exactly melancholy, but we had just completed an intense year of sailing. Now with the immigration department breathing down our necks, we felt the need for family unity. We felt happy to be out in the fresh air, on our own nocturnal adventure, anticipating what the coming year would bring.

"Look at the sky!" Holly remarked. "It's covered with stars. Daddy, do you remember that night sailing to Iceland?"

About 10 days out of Bermuda, the clear, moonless sky allowed us to view an awesome spread of stars. The Milky Way appeared as a brilliant white path, rivaling telescope photos I had seen in books. It was hard to believe that this band was our own galaxy viewed on edge. During daylight hours, earth's light-diffused atmosphere limits what we can see in the heavens. During that clear night, we sensed the vastness of the cosmos and felt the insignificance of our existence. Planet Earth felt like a ship sailing through a sea of glowing islands.

Jaja and I have spent a lot of time on the open sea. We've seen hundreds of night skies free from the glare of civilization, but that night en route to Iceland had a unique, pristine quality. I tried to awaken Chris, but he was out cold. We roused Holly easily, and she sat with Jaja and me in the cockpit wrapped in a blanket.

"This is a special night," I explained.

"Can you take a picture of it?"

"No," I said, "not from the moving boat. Anyway, seeing the stars is only part of the experience. Your feelings as you look at the stars are important, too."

Now as we walked down Svolvær's back roads to town, Holly said, "When I look at the sky, I feel as if I can do anything. It feels like, like..."

"Like there are no boundaries." Jaja whispered.

"Yes. That's it exactly."

PEOPLE GATHERED IN THE CENTER of Svolvær for the annual fireworks extravaganza. Like Jaja and me, many of our friends and acquaintances had been drawn to the carnival-like atmosphere. People drank, sang, and danced in the streets. Bundled-up children slid on their sleds and ran around energetically. Teenagers clustered in dark corners.

Suddenly, the stars were obscured by the magenta glow of the aurora borealis. It felt incongruous to be standing on a town street waiting for an artificial display of light while the northern lights skidded across the sky like a waking dream. No one seemed to notice. We felt like yelling, "Look up everyone! You're missing something more amazing than rockets!"

Workmen set up what looked like a 15-foot-long bicycle rack with a dozen metal tubes welded to it. The rack served as the launching stand for the do-it-yourself pyrotechnics. At 10 minutes before midnight, the crowd swelled, and rockets were being launched from the rack nearly nonstop. Other people were setting off explosives between buildings. The fireworks landed on rooftops and splashed into the harbor. Our kids were entranced. I set off several of our own rockets from the launching tubes. They shooshed up and exploded lustrously overhead.

"Daddy, set off another one!"

Some idiot tried to launch a four-footer by standing it up in a sewer grate. At the last second, just as the fuse ignited, the rocket fell over. It blasted off like a cruise missile, but horizontally about three feet off the ground. Miraculously, it missed everyone in the crowd before exploding in a shower of sparks over the harbor. Another rocket also took off at an angle and landed aboard the local ferryboat tied to the town dock. With a robust, echoing BOOM! sparks spilled from the openings along the ship's side.

Now five and six rockets were going off simultaneously, and dozens of fountain cones spewed sparks. Chris, Holly, and Teiga were waving sparklers wildly. A misfire exploded under a taxi, giving the illusion that the vehicle was in flames. At midnight, fishermen's parachute flares were landing in the crowd, rockets were going off 10 at a time, and another misfire–burning red and yellow–flew between my head and Jaja's. We were standing shoulder to shoulder. It didn't seem possible that both of us remained unscathed.

"Happy New Year!" I shouted.

The central square was a blaze of sparks, drifting cardboard debris, and falling wooden sticks. We had no way of knowing if computers were failing worldwide, but there was enough chaos right here to give a fair imitation. The noise echoing off the buildings was deafening, and we could barely see through the smoke. A guy on a rooftop with a megaphone was telling people to stop launching rockets, but the crowd didn't quiet down for some time. Teiga held her hands over her ears, but Chris and Holly were grinning. Over the protests of our two pyrotechnic-loving offspring, we hurried away from the "danger zone."

No longer charged with excitement, the kids admitted that they were freezing. Jaja and I also had numb feet, cold fingers, and a deep chill. Because it was late, we did not want to trek all the way back to the cabin in the woods. We headed home instead. *Driver*'s cabin never felt so warm and inviting. The Year 2000 had arrived.

ON JANUARY 7TH, WE RECEIVED A FAX from Ingrid inviting us to her office. We settled into chairs and noticed that her demeanor was somber.

"The UDI said they will allow you to fly to Denmark so that they may process the appeal."

"Did they say how long it would take?"

"About three weeks."

Jaja said, "I know we suggested that we travel to a nearby country while the visa was being considered, but isn't leaving just a petty formality? If they're going to give it to us, why not just give it? Anyway, can we be sure they'll *really* grant us the visa?"

"No."

"So then we would be stuck out of the country and away from our boat." Ingrid nodded. "Yes."

Jaja and I glanced at each other. "No," I said, turning to look at Ingrid. "We aren't going to put ourselves in that vulnerable position."

She smiled. "If you had accepted their terms, I would have been surprised. I'll tell them you refuse." Ingrid grew serious again. "My professional opinion is they are not going to give you this visa on your terms."

Jaja and I felt the same way. In fact, we had come to Ingrid's office prepared to tell her about our plans for departure. There had been plenty of time for us to scrutinize every alternative–from flying away to sailing away. After weighing the pros and cons, Jaja and I realized we could not make the decision based only on hard facts. To gain a clearer understanding, we elevated our decision-making to a more abstract level–a level that included our aspirations and ideologies.

We had set out from the States on our boat with our kids to have an adventure. We had successfully fought the trials of preparation and departure. We had survived storms, midocean hull damage, and the derision of others for choosing to spend the winter in Iceland. We had coped with winter darkness, freezing temperatures, foreign languages, rough coastal sailing, and countless landfalls. We had sailed our boat to Lofoten by choice, and we had bungled the rules. Now the UDI was another challenge to be met–another headland to be rounded. If we packed up and flew away on a jet, it would be admitting defeat. Instead of fighting the bureaucratic storm, we would be abandoning ship.

I detailed our plan to Ingrid. "Since we must leave by the 31st, we've decided to go next week. That will give us two weeks to travel down the coast before we have to leave Norwegian waters. We will slip past the Fisherman's Wife in the darkness and let her bid us farewell."

Ingrid gave a noncommittal nod. "I have been trying to get some sort of backing from the weather service, or even from the coastal radio station in Bodø, stating that it is unsafe for a small boat to go down the coast. However, no one is willing to stick out his neck on your behalf and speak against the UDI."

"I wouldn't expect them to."

"Everyone I've talked to thinks the situation is absurd," Ingrid confirmed.

I nodded.

"Give me a few more days. I'll contact you."

Two days later, I was back in Ingrid's office.

"I've contacted the weather people again. They still won't commit themselves. I've talked to the police here in Svolvær again. They won't commit to anything, either. The UDI officials are not going to change their minds. The only thing I can suggest is that we take your story to the media."

The idea had crossed our minds, but Jaja and I were hesitant to go public with our troubles. We were worn out with the ordeal and also a little embarrassed. We had become immune to false hopes.

"Do you really think it will help?" I asked.

"Maybe." Ingrid said honestly. "Anyway, it's your only hope. At this point you have nothing to lose."

"How do you want to go about it?"

"I will call the UDI agent in charge of your case and tell her that we are going to contact the newspapers. I expect she will do nothing, but I must follow protocol. Come back to my office this afternoon, and I'll let you know the outcome."

I returned several hours later.

Ingrid was brisk. "I was not able to speak with the officer in charge, but her staff were unconcerned about our plan to contact the media. I will set up everything with the national papers. Perhaps you could go down the street and talk to *Lofotposten*."

"What should we say to the reporters?"

"Just tell your story. The journalists can contact me for legal details. Remember, this is a last-ditch measure. I don't have any idea how it will turn out."

AT 4:00 P.M., we received a knock on our hull. Eli and Torstein, the two journalists from *Lofotposten* who had interviewed us after our arrival in Svolvær, came aboard and settled themselves comfortably in the cabin. They had already called Ingrid. Armed with the facts, they cultivated our emotion. It didn't take much coaxing.

Prior to Eli's and Torstein's arrival, Jaja and I had discussed what point of view we should adopt with the media. We had already come to terms with going to sea, so we would talk about that. We planned to keep it simple.

"We aren't fighting for a visa to stay in Norway," Jaja explained. "We are fighting for the right to stay in Norway while our appeal to stay is processed."

I said, "If it takes until summer before the appeal can be processed, we will be ready to go, and the outcome won't even matter. If we have to sail away from Norway next week to file the appeal from another country, we won't be coming back to cruise the coast because we will have already left."

After the interview, Jaja took the kids to the swimming pool. While they were gone, a husband-and-wife team of freelance journalists from Måson Media in Svolvær came aboard *Driver*. I was apprehensive to do the interview without Jaja at my side, and I tried to put them off until she returned. However, John Inge and his wife Vibeke were on a deadline. I provided a version of our story similar to the one we gave to the *Lofotposten* journalists.

When Jaja returned, I told her about the interview. She panicked.

"Oh my God, Dave! What did you say?"

"Don't worry about it," I said soothingly. "I was on my best behavior. I actually thought about what I was going to say before it came out of my mouth."

Jaja looked doubtful.

The next morning, January 12th, page one of *Lofotposten* carried a large photo of us. A long, comprehensive story followed on page two. Ingrid came down to the boat at 8:00 a.m. If she was frustrated because we didn't have a telephone, she hid it well.

"There was no time to fax you," she said. "Two journalists who represent the national paper *Dagbladet* will be in my office at 10:00 a.m. They are flying here from Tromsø. And this afternoon, three more journalists will be flying up from Oslo."

"This is it, isn't it?"

"So far, I'm pleased with the amount of interest."

Events were unfolding quickly, and we were beginning to have apprehensions. Would people read the newspaper stories and think our case was justified? Or would we be perceived as fools? By going public, we had laid ourselves open to ridicule and derision.

We went out for an enjoyable lunch with the journalists from *Dagbladet* and then spent the afternoon with them. We talked about our previous travels on *Direction* and how we had never had an unreasonable reception by any government.

We went on to say that even Australia and New Zealand, which had fairly severe immigration laws when we were there, bent the rules when it came to cruisers who needed to wait out the season or who needed to make repairs. We held firm to our resolve. If necessary, we would sail away into the stormy January seas.

Later that night, the well-known Norwegian sailor, author, and political columnist Ragnar Kvam, Jr., arrived from Oslo. His flight had been delayed by a snowstorm, and the four-hour journey had taken 10 hours. He came aboard *Driver* with the other journalists from *Dagbladet*.

Ragnar spoke out against the Norwegian government, saying he was embarrassed that his great seafaring homeland was treating foreign sailors with gross indifference. A few years back, Ragnar had cruised from Norway to the Pacific Ocean on his 38-foot sailboat. He had also lived aboard for two winters in Alaska. He spoke of the goodwill that the Americans showed him. Of all the places in the world, he pointed out, we had chosen to live in northern Norway. He was incensed that the compliment we paid to his country had been rebuked. What kind of message was that? What did that say about Norway? He reiterated that he had flown all the way to Lofoten to stand up for his principles and to speak out against the government he believed was acting unjustly.

In the course of our conversations, we learned that Ragnar passed through the Panama Canal aboard his boat in 1989, just one day after we went through on *Direction.* We both crossed the Pacific the same year and met the crews of many of the same cruising boats along the way. It's a small world.

After the interview, the journalists suggested we go out for a beer. All I wanted to do was go to bed. Being a Wednesday, only a few pubs were open, so we went to a local bar called the Styrhuset. It was filled with smoke, but thankfully, the music was subdued. We didn't have to shout to make conversation.

Svolvær-based journalist John Inge was already there, and the five of us took a booth. We drank countless pints of strong lager and stayed until the place closed at 2:00 a.m. I staggered drunkenly back to *Driver,* negotiating the icy streets with care. I poured myself into bed. Jaja was warm and inviting.

"How was your night out with the boys?" she asked sleepily.

"It was all right. We had some good laughs. But I kept thinking of you here alone. I would have rather stayed home."

"I know," Jaja said. "When they suggested going to the pub, I could see all you wanted to do was collapse."

I chuckled. "That was 4 1/2 hours ago, and now I'm wide awake." We lay silently for a moment. Corn snow was pelting the canvas dodger. We had become connoisseurs of snow sounds, and the dodger acted like a microphone.

"The journalists were having a good time," I observed. "Their interviews were finished. I was having a hard time joining the beer-guzzling camaraderie because our situation hasn't changed."

At 6:00 a.m., we got up to prepare for journalist Olga Stokke and her photographer. Both of them worked for *Aftenposten,* Norway's largest newspaper. Tired and slightly hung over, I went outside and shoveled a 200-foot-long path in the heavy snow–all the way from *Driver*'s dock to the parking lot. I tried telling myself that the exercise would clear my head. It didn't work. After just a few hours of sleep, I felt even more tired.

The interview with Olga lasted three hours, but it felt like a fleeting moment. We had much in common. As the morning wore on, we stopped being interviewer and interviewee and became mutual friends. We shared many of the same philosophies on life, our humor was well matched, and we admired each other's accomplishments. Jaja and Olga also discovered that they both loved books. We learned that Olga had written a story about Ragnar Kvam many years before, and it was partly due to that story that Ragnar had met his wife. The seemingly careless paths that led each of us to Lofoten had unfathomable connections.

All day, we were greeted by local well-wishers who had been reading the articles written by the journalists from Måson Media, *Dagbladet*, *Lofotposten,* and *Aftenposten.* We were treated with admiration, not with the derision we had feared. We could walk through town without feeling embarrassed.

At 3:00 P.M., just before closing, I went to the library to check for messages. There were none. I continued down the street another two blocks to Ingrid's office, climbed the stairs, and entered the reception area. I wanted to thank her for successfully orchestrating the visits from the newspapers.

When I walked in, she was reading a single-page fax. When she saw me, she was genuinely surprised.

"How uncanny that you're here! I've just received this from the UDI." She held the fax in the air.

"Oh?" My pulse began to race.

In a matter-of-fact tone Ingrid said, "You may continue to stay in Norway until they decide whether or not they will accept the appeal."

"You did it!"

"No, I've done nothing. They have made a nondecision, really. They say they need time to reconsider their first decisions."

My head was still numb, and I nodded in slow comprehension. "So they might still make us go."

"No, I disagree. I believe they will do nothing. I think the remainder of your winter will be unprovoked. They won't dare make you leave now."

I thought of all the newspaper stories that trumpeted our precarious situation–that the government was forcing a family with three children to put to sea in winter. We knew the UDI wasn't forcing us to go to sea. That was our choice.

I shook Ingrid's hand. "You must take credit for this decision. Thank you."

"You're welcome."

I went straight to *Lofotposten.* Eli was in her office, and she offered me a seat.

"The UDI has backed down," I said, "We can stay for the moment."

"Wonderful!" With a reporter's discipline she grabbed a notepad and began asking questions. "Are you going to celebrate tonight?"

"Probably not. I'm too tired. Maybe tomorrow. Anyway, we haven't actually won anything; they've only decided not to make a decision. But yes, I'm ecstatic that we can stay a little longer."

"What does Jaja think?"

"I'm headed home right now to tell her."

Just then, Ragnhild and Gry entered the office. Unknown to Jaja and me, they had written a petition that asked the Svolvær Town Council to intervene and let us stay in port through the winter. They had been working hard all day and had collected hundreds of signatures. When they heard that we could stay, they beamed. I also learned from them that the kids in Chris's class had written a letter to the King of Norway begging him to let "Chris and his family" stay in Norway. The community was on our side.

I walked slowly through gently falling snow back to *Driver*. The town was eerily quiet, which made it easier to think. I thought about the people of Svolvær. Five months before, we had been total strangers, and now they were fighting for us. We had never anticipated a community coming to our aid like this, and we would never be able to thank everyone who had taken our side.

I opened the dock gate with my key, slid down the snowy ramp, and ran toward *Driver*. Using energy I didn't know I had, I hopped effortlessly on board over the lifelines. I was grinning from ear to ear.

"Jaja!"

ON THE 25TH OF FEBRUARY, more than a month after going public, we received an official-looking letter from the UDI. Our pulses raced, and a feeling of doom settled over us. Despite Ingrid's assurances that the UDI would leave us alone, we reserved a tiny bit of skepticism just in case. We hoped to sail for Spitsbergen in June when the weather was favorable, but we took nothing for granted. If the UDI forced us to leave the country at the first hint of summer, Spitsbergen would still be locked in ice. In that case, we would sail south and find adventure elsewhere.

I looked at the letter. "Should we open it?"

"I think it will be OK," Jaja reasoned. "If it were bad news, the police would have already come knocking."

Jaja ripped open the envelope, extracted the one-page letter, and began deciphering the foreign words with help from her English/Norwegian dictionary.

I couldn't help myself. "What does it say, Jaja?"

Jaja was nodding positively as she deciphered, and a smile spread across her face.

"For God's sake," I asked. "What does it say?"

"Hang on, I'm almost done."

Sitting there, I could feel the churning seas exploding against storm-ravaged rocks, feel the backlash of wind swirling under high cliffs, feel the...

"We can stay in Norway for two years," Jaja blurted out.

"What?"

"The UDI has given us a two-year cultural visa." Jaja put down the letter. "This is unreal."

Ingrid had discovered the cultural visa. It allowed artisans to live in the country so they could absorb the culture and spread knowledge about Norway around the world. Our book contract had arrived at the 11th hour.

I was stunned. By holding tight to our ideals and our dreams, we had shaken off the iron grip of bureaucracy. Stormy January seas be damned! The last time we felt this good was the morning Teiga drew her first breath.

We rushed to Ingrid's office. "You've won the case," I said shaking her hand. She had received favorable publicity in all the papers, and now the case had a rock-solid conclusion. I was happy for her.

"I never believed they would do anything," she said distractedly.

"You have our mailing address," I said making an obvious allusion to payment.

Next, we hustled down the street to the immigration office. This time, the glass doors at the police station were not foreboding. We climbed the staircase without the feeling of dread that accompanied our earlier visits. We entered the immigration office triumphantly. Ten minutes later, with passports legally stamped, we were free to explore Norway, and to ponder the rich irony of the UDI's decision.

We cut across Svolvær's central square, walked by familiar shops, said hello to familiar faces, and skirted familiar snowbanks. Our hearts felt so light they threatened to lift us off the ground.

As I walked, my mind retraced the path that had brought us to this day in Lofoten. Cold Iceland, the lofty Faroes, damp Scotland, and dry summertime Norway. It was tempting to berate the UDI for all the agony they caused us. But I realized that our anger would be defensive. We knew that people often get angry when they are caught doing something against the rules, no matter how petty those regulations are. It was our fault the mess began, so I tried to be fair and reign in my mental criticisms.

As for the citizens of Norway, who had come to our rescue and backed our position with real words and sincere actions, it would be impossible to thank them enough. If we hadn't bumbled our way into the jaws of bureaucracy, we might never have fully understood the compassion of the Norwegian people. The great seafarers had not let us down.

Chapter Sixteen

In every friendship, you leave a little of yourself behind,
and you gain a little of the other person.

Skiing is a big part of Norwegian culture. It has been said that Nordic babies are born with skis on their feet.

"The poor mothers!" Jaja remarked.

Holly and Teiga borrowed cross-country skiing gear for the winter from the Tennes family, and Chris borrowed equipment from his friend Edvart. After school, our kids skied in the marina parking lot or down the snowy sidewalk toward the fire station. Chris and Holly helped their little sister when a ski came loose or when she toppled over.

"Teiga!" Chris cajoled. "Did you fall on your nose on purpose? If you wanted to eat some snow, sticking your head in a snowbank isn't the easiest way to do it!" Teiga would laugh at the comments. She would forget about her latest wipeout, struggle to her feet, and carry on. Jaja and I were seldom far away, but we tried to stay out of sight. When our kids thought they were "alone," they pulled together and coped with difficult situations much better.

When we skied as a family, we trekked 20 minutes to Lake Svolvær where we could cross-country ski for miles on the flat snow-covered ice. There were also trails leading away from the lake into the surrounding mountains. On fair-weather weekends, hundreds of folks on skis, including many children, would use the lake as a starting point for exploration. We were particularly intrigued by the *pilks*: Five-foot-long fiberglass toboggans that looked like miniature kayaks. Two short rods connected each pilk to a harness around a skier's hips. Pulled by the skiers, these sleds carried babies and children too small to ski. The children sat propped up like dolls, wrapped in sheepskins and wearing down one-piece suits and wool hats.

"Oh Daddy!" Holly and Teiga crooned in unison. "Can you buy a pilk?"

I chuckled. "You guys are too big and heavy."

"No! It would be for our dollies! They don't weigh much."

Our mode of transportation from the boat to the lake was a small sled called a *spark*–the Norwegian word for "kick." A spark has long metal runners, a stout handle, and a wooden seat that can carry two small kids. Either

Jaja or I would place one foot on a runner and propel the sled with the other foot, as if pushing a scooter. We were able to move at surprisingly high speeds on the snow-packed roads and sidewalks. Going downhill could be dangerous, though, if we didn't brake with our feet.

When the first snow fell in December, we saw people whizzing around town on their sparks. Jaja was enthralled.

"We should buy one of those, Dave. What a great mode of transportation!"

At first, Jaja and I shared one spark. Sometimes we went "sparking" just for the fun of it, but mostly, Jaja used the sled for hauling groceries or laundry bags and for ferrying kids. I used it for transporting propane bottles and boat supplies. If the conditions were just right, however, Holly and Teiga would squeeze onto the seat, Jaja and I would each stand with one foot on a runner, and Chris would stand behind, holding onto us.

One day during Christmas break, we were doing our family "spark-balancing act" on a back road near the cabin when Thorvardur passed us in his van. He waved and pulled over.

"You guys look like circus performers!" he laughed.

"We've finally found the answer to our transportation needs," Jaja said.

"I have several sparks in my garage. There's an adult-size one for Dave and a youth-size one for Chris. Stop by the house any time and pick 'em up. They're yours for the winter."

In January, just a few days after our adventures with the Norwegian press, we entered Chris, Holly, and Teiga in the annual Svolvær cross-country ski "races." We "sparked" our kids and their skis to the town soccer fields near the lake for the first of 10 weekly sessions.

Children between two and 14 were eligible, and almost the entire grammar school was there. Every child wore a special numbered shirt, which made him or her feel part of a team. The number, however, was used only for identification at the start. The event was designed to bring kids together in healthy, low-stress, outdoor recreation. It also got them in shape for the downhill ski season. Parents milled around in groups drinking coffee and helping the smaller kids. Overhead stadium lights illuminated the course. At the end of each race, every kid got a bun and a hot drink; there were no winners or losers. When the program ended in April, each kid received a trophy.

Stein had organized the races for many years. Each week, he stood at the starting line and one by one, called out all 250 names on a bullhorn. Two-to-five-year-olds skied one lap around the upper field. Then Stein would move to the lower field to start the older kids, who skied several laps.

Every kid got his moment of glory:

"Number 29, Sunniva Johansen. Ready, Go!"

"Number 30, Marit Krane Meby. Set, Go!"

"Number 31, Teiga Martin. Get ready, Go!"

Every week I marveled at how smoothly the event operated. There was no shoving or pushing, no impatience or grumbling. Whether it was snowing, blowing, or clear with northern lights, the kids waited for their names to be called and set off with proud determination. One evening, I reflected that Norway has always had a strong national ski team–part of the country's core identity. I looked at the two-year-olds propped up between their parents' knees, balanced like dolls on narrow skis. Here were champions in the making.

When he finished calling numbers on the season's first day of "racing," Stein wandered back to the clubhouse for a cup of coffee.

"How are you getting home?" he asked. "Do you have a ride?"

"Thanks," I said, "but we're proper Norwegians now. We have two sparks."

"You're a bunch of crazy Americans," Stein joked. "Proper Norwegians have heated cars."

SNOWFALL IN SVOLVÆR during the winter of 1999-2000 was nearly as heavy as the record-breaking snows that fell in the region a couple of years previously. In contrast, we heard that Akureyri was experiencing its driest winter in many years. How ironic that we had been buried in snow the winter we spent there. Perhaps we bring snow with us. Gudni showed his disappointment in a letter. He reported that the mountains near his hometown Grenavík were nearly bare and his new snowmobile was sitting unused in the front yard. In a return letter, we teased him and told him to bring his snowmobile to Lofoten.

Looking back, we were glad we experienced copious snowfall and thick harbor ice during the winter we spent aboard in Akureyri. Otherwise, it would have been like sailing in the Tropics without finding white sand, clear water, coconut trees, and hot sun. Our expectations would have been cheated.

Many people in Svolvær were upset by the smothering snow, which was nearly seven feet deep. They were constantly scraping car windows, shoveling driveways and roofs, and plowing roads. The town budget for snow removal was nearly depleted. But other individuals like us cheered. Snow enabled us to use sparks for transportation, and it encouraged healthy, outdoor recreation for our kids such as sledding, building snow forts, and of course, skiing.

The heavy snowfall also meant weeks of gray clouds. Technically, the sun began rising above the horizon on January 6th, but we didn't catch a glimpse of it until the 19th when some low rays gleamed through a crack in the clouds and bathed the world in an electrifying glow. Then, as a snowsquall approached from the north, the sun turned the flakes orange, making the town and the mountains look like a computer-generated image.

On February 8th, we saw clear blue skies for the first time in the Year 2000. When we arrived in Svolvær the previous September, we were warned that there could be weeks of constant cloud cover.

"That's not a problem," I said knowingly. "I grew up in Seattle."

On that first clear day, the third-grade students in Chris's and Holly's school marched through town to the top of the Svinøya Island Bridge where they sang songs to the glimmering sun.

> *Now the sun is shining on the windowsill,*
> *Hey! The sun is shining for you and me!*

Having experienced winter darkness once before, we were able to view our experience at Svolvær in a new light. It felt as if we were reading a good book for the second time, finding different nuances. We remembered how we felt at Akureyri when the light started to return. Instead of wishing the sun would come back more quickly, we savored the dark afternoons and cultivated the peaceful feelings of winter. Soon enough, the summer light would instill in us a feeling of urgency.

THE DAY AFTER THE SUN made its appearance, I sat in front of our new laptop computer and listened to wet snowflakes beating against the dodger. I sipped some coffee, poised my fingers over the square white keys, and tried to fill the inquisitive screen with words. It was 5:00 a.m. The family was still sleeping. At 6:00 a.m., I would pour Jaja a cup of coffee–her usual wake-up ritual.

I looked at the blank screen. Jaja and I had roughed out the themes and concepts for the book. It was my job to put them into words. After I wrote a section, Jaja would interject her philosophies, clarify information, and organize my thoughts. We had a well-honed system. I wrote in the first person, but Jaja and I shared the "creation."

For me, writing was like navigating with a sextant. I always had a mental destination in mind, but I didn't always know the exact course to that place. Nor did I know how soon before an idea or a memory would rise above the horizon. Sometimes, my mind was cloudy, and I could only recall disjointed images. Then, to help fill the gaps, I would mentally retrace our wanderings and let geographic associations sharpen my recollections.

This morning my brain was asleep, so I looked around the dimly lit cabin hoping for inspiration. I studied the various dings and scratches in the paint, and I scrutinized the worn places on the varnished cabin sole. The wear and tear provided a historical record and gave the cabin character.

How had events changed *our* character? Before leaving Oriental, North Carolina, our goal of sailing to Iceland had been the impetus for every decision we made and every action we took. With that feat behind us, it was difficult to recall the tensions we had felt at the beginning of our cruise. Some of the things we worried about before the passage to Reykjavik seemed like trifles now: Could we cope mentally with the climate? Would we be able to handle the rough coastal sailing conditions? Would *Driver* hold up? Where would we spend the winter? Was our heater adequate? The cold no longer fazed us. Snow was as familiar to us as white sand had been in the Tropics. Now Chris and Holly were bilingual in English and Norwegian. We were writing about our journey to Iceland, instead of planning for it.

Spitsbergen was the new challenge. Despite our northern wanderings, we had never experienced sea ice. We could read about ice and talk to others who had dealt with it, but until we came face to face with glacial debris and "the pack," we would never know what it meant.

When Jaja and I began ocean sailing over a decade earlier, like any novices, we had a limited cache of experiences on which to draw. Our horizons expanded slowly. We conquered each obstacle as it came along, and our list of "achievements" grew. A little mental headway in one situation gave us confidence in another. We not only tested the limits of our physical capabilities, we tested the mechanical limitations of our two floating homes.

During my teenage years, when my father sensed my troubled adolescent insecurities, he stressed that everyone had a forté.

"Find the thing you do well and build on it," he said. "Personal achievement—no matter how unconventional—will give you the confidence to succeed in other, less familiar arenas."

I began to pay attention to the events in my life. Was I good at math? Science? Geography? Not really. How about guitar playing? Art? Abstract thinking? I was interested in some of these things and had some ability but no astounding virtuosity. Was I really good at anything?

During this evaluation period, I became deeply involved in sailboat racing on Seattle's Puget Sound. I crewed on all types of boats from small dinghies to 50-footers. At 14 years of age, I was generally the youngest crewmember. So I paid attention, tried not to make the same mistakes twice, and most importantly, kept out of the way. I learned about racing rules, sail trim, tactics, and how to jury-rig almost anything. By the time I was 16, I was as experienced as many of the adults. Unfortunately, this heady knowledge had a harmful affect on my personality. I developed the unpleasant habit of loudly questioning shipboard authority. I became a know-it-all.

During these coming-of-age trials, I discovered my forté: The ability to think clearly and find a quick solution to any shipboard "crisis"–medical, tactical, or mechanical. I could call up past experiences in a flash, examine options, project, and even inventory in my mind the available tools and materials. My "calculations" included estimates of how long each option might take to carry out and how effective it would be in the long run. I would go into a sort of trance–during which, time slowed down–and I would feel all my energy focused liked a laser beam. It was a marvelous sensation to be able to respond decisively to mini-crises, and the realization provided a great boost to my self-esteem.

In my 20s, when I began rebuilding *Direction* for my voyage around the world, I had an unwavering faith in my ability to think clearly when chaos reigned. Deep down, I knew that no matter how bad things were at sea, I would find a way to come out on top. It wasn't arrogance that soothed my nerves, it was a deep-seated faith in my abilities.

After a decade of cruising together, Jaja and I had a large repertoire of experiences. Storms, near groundings, electronical failure, illness, infection, cash flow difficulties, childbirth, and bureaucracy. Our ambitious cruising sometimes put us into precarious situations. We did not seek trouble, but we did prepare for it. We researched weather patterns and ocean currents, and we read accounts of others who had traveled before us.

The ice in Spitsbergen posed another challenge, like the challenge of coral reefs in the Tropics. I navigated *Direction* across hundreds of miles of reefs in the Pacific Ocean using only a sextant and a digital watch. The risks included nighttime darkness, cloud cover, and invisible currents–all of which hampered the effectiveness of celestial navigation in these hazardous waters. We were extremely cautious in the Pacific. We knew our limitations and were aware of the risks.

Atoll-hopping on *Direction* was challenging, but the beaches, the warmth, and the freedom from having to wear heavy clothes were some of the rewards of tropical cruising. Spitsbergen has the added danger of ice and cold, but with round-the-clock light, we would be able to see hazards. And we felt that *Driver* was the right boat for the icy "playing field." As we had discovered in Akureyri, her steel hull was very tough. I remembered how the ice in the inner basin would act like a large battering ram smashing into the hull. The ice would break while the hull remained undamaged.

I TOOK ANOTHER SIP of coffee. In 30 minutes, the family would begin to wake up. I turned back to the computer screen seeking inspiration. Nothing.

Once again, my eyes roamed the cabin until they came to rest on a large ding in the cabin sole near the companionway. I remembered how I had inflicted that "wound."

When our refit of *Driver* was finally finished, we brought the boat cushions onboard. We had made burgundy covers during the winter. We kept the cabin closed for a week to allow the final coats of urethane varnish and polyurethane enamel to dry. It was a sweltering day in August. When Jaja slid back the new companionway hatch, the toxic aroma of paint wafted out and hung like a portrait in the still, hot air. It was the scent of success, the cologne of completion. If art is life, then we were really living.

The combination of white paint, slick teak trim, and the richly colored cushions caused a mind-blowing transformation in the cabin. As if by magic, we forgot the hectic process of rebuilding the boat. The thousands of hours, the strain on our family life, the drain on our savings. The refit was nearly over; the voyage was about to begin.

Eighteen-month-old Teiga walked cautiously across the varnished maple cabin sole. Chris and Holly explored their new bunks. Jaja and I drank coffee, careful not to mar the shiny surfaces. Whispers of air and shafts of light reached through the open hatches and made the paint in the cabin shine. This was home. The cabin would be the place where each new day began. It would be our sanctuary at sea, our hideaway at anchor. Its image would follow us to sleep when we switched off the lights.

That first day, history was already making her mark. Our bare feet challenged the urethane. Our coffee cups left minuscule scratches. Our bodies were making unseen abrasions in the upholstery. I had spent two months painting and varnishing the raw wood of *Driver*'s new interior. It was difficult to watch the "bumps" of life already marring the gloss.

Later that week, I was working under the companionway, checking the alignment of the coupling between *Driver*'s engine and the propeller shaft. It was a hair out of adjustment. I loosened the engine mounts and was slowly levering the engine with a crowbar when I accidentally bumped a large wrench, which I had set nearby on the galley counter. The heavy tool flew into the air, did a half-twist, and landed prongs-down on the varnished cabin sole. The wrench left two accusing welts in the sole as a reminder of my carelessness. It was the first of many dings to follow.

When Jaja saw the dual craters in the sole, she spoke wryly in the third person, as if she were reading aloud from a book. "And she was glad, because she wasn't the one who dropped the wrench."

I WAS STILL SITTING in front of the computer. Jaja was packing the kids' school lunches and organizing their clothes. My mind was caught in a whirlpool of memories, and I knew I would make little progress on the book this morning. I thought of *Driver*'s maiden voyage from Oriental down the East Coast to Florida. In South Carolina, we began looking for our old boat *Direction*; someone told us that she was berthed near Charleston. Seeing the boat again would undoubtedly conjure up all sorts of memories. I wanted to sharpen those mind pictures before our passage to Iceland.

We finally found *Direction* in a backwater marina. She looked forlorn and deserted. When we sold her the previous year, it had been a relief to stop maintaining her, and to have money from the sale to help pay for *Driver*'s refit. But as time passed, nostalgia crept into our hearts.

When I spotted *Direction*'s mast through the binoculars, my heart began to pound. Jaja tightened her grip on my shoulder.

"Let me look," she asked quietly.

Chris and Holly were fidgeting with excitement. We set *Driver*'s anchor, climbed into the dinghy, rowed across the wide channel, and tied to a dock at the marina. The bright sun reflected off the metal hardware on the boats in the slips. Jaja and I chuckled as Chris and Holly bolted down the dock, their life-jacket straps trailing behind them. Teiga was in her usual position, straddling Jaja's hip.

Chris hopped aboard his first home in a familiar way and shouted, "Look how small she is!"

I peered below, incredulous that we had lived in that miniscule cabin. There, we celebrated Christmases and birthdays, and knew fear, love, and freedom.

Holly asked, "Daddy? Why does *Direction* seem smaller now?"

I shook my head. Did we really sail this boat around the world? I sat in the cockpit. *Direction* represented something significant to each of us.

My dad bought this same Cal 25 new in 1971 when I was seven years old. He named the boat *Martini*, and it became the family's weekend and vacation escape vehicle. Since I wasn't motivated to pit myself against my studies, my dad sensed that I might benefit from pitting myself against myself. He gave me the boat when I was 21 years old. My "higher education" began when I tore *Martini* to pieces and transformed her into a small offshore cruiser. When I finished the refit, I renamed the boat *Direction* and set out to conquer the world.

Now I watched seven-year-old Chris running around on *Direction*'s deck like a maniac. I was the same age when my father bought the boat. Did I look like Chris does now? Was the circle complete?

I remembered our family's first outings aboard *Martini* on Lake Washington in Seattle. I was scared to death that first season. As long as there was no wind, I thought sailing was great. But as soon as the sails filled and the boat heeled over, I would cling to the windward rail and scream.

"We're gonna tip over! We'll drown!"

My dad would smile. "Naw, we'll be fine, Davey, just fine. The Cal 25 has a positive righting moment, so it won't tip over. It says so in the brochure."

At age nine, my parents enrolled me in a sailing program where I conquered my fears aboard a 14-foot sailboat called a C-Lark. Three thousand miles away in New Jersey, Jaja's father was teaching her to sail in a 14-foot boat called an Albacore. Jaja recalled her first season on the water more fondly.

"Daddy, make the boat heel over more!" she would plead.

My early sailing experiences remained vivid in my mind. The apprehension I felt as a child made me meditative as an adult. Halfway through our circumnavigation, Jaja and I were in the middle of the Indian Ocean getting pummeled by an 11-day gale. One night, I stood on deck between sail changes, oblivious to the howling wind that screamed in the darkness. I recalled the frightened young boy on Lake Washington. I could hardly believe that now I was crossing the Indian Ocean on that same daysailer. Did I really used to cling to the rail when I was seven and scream with fright?

"Earth to Dave."

"Huh?" I looked up. Jaja was trying to get my attention. The sun was shining, *Direction* was tied to a dock near Charleston, and the boat was owned by a stranger. "We shouldn't have sold her," was all I could say.

Jaja rubbed her hand on *Direction*'s deck. "I know."

THE BURST OF FEBRUARY SUNLIGHT in Lofoten was just a teaser. Spring was still a long way off. The sunny break was followed by several more weeks of gray skies and constant snowfall. During this "inward" time, I dove into my computer, and progress on the manuscript accelerated. But I also found myself thinking more and more about sunny, tropical sailing days aboard *Direction*. These "flashbacks" eventually infiltrated the manuscript and wove themselves into the book's main themes.

Then one Saturday morning, we awoke to glistening, spring sunlight. The varnish in *Driver*'s cabin shimmered; the white paint sparkled. Our upholstery looked a little aged, but it, too, seemed to glow.

It didn't take us long to cast off. By 11:00 a.m., the engine was ticking as we motored from Svolvær toward a small cut called Troll Fjord about 10 miles north of town. The brilliant March sun warmed my face as I sat in *Driver*'s cockpit with my foot on the tiller. There was zero wind. Chris and Holly giggled as they hung on their chairs near the mast. Teiga and Jaja were busy with a coloring book. Jaja would look at the page, orient her crayon, and then lift her face to the sun and color with her eyes closed.

"Mommy, you aren't staying in the lines!" Teiga complained.

The sky was blue, the sea was blue, and the land was white as far as the eye could see. The ice and snow on *Driver*'s deck was melting in the direct sunlight, but it remained dry and solid in the shadows. It was our first "cruise" since October. And it was going to be our first encounter with floating ice–however minor–while under way.

The entrance to Troll Fjord is only 300 feet wide. The scenery was spectacular. The north wall is over 1,000 feet high and is capped by icy mountain peaks. The south wall is lower, but meager only by comparison. Frozen waterfalls were sandwiched into snowy mountain chutes. Steep, craggy ridges were topped by intricate rock formations. The cliffs were separated by narrow mini-valleys. About a mile long, the fjord widens into a small round bay at its inner end. When we entered this bay, we felt as if we were at the bottom of a bucket. Everywhere we looked–except back toward the narrow entrance–was straight up.

The afternoon sun had warmed the snow and ice at the top of the north wall–in contrast to the somber frozen south side that was in shadow. As *Driver* passed through the narrowest part of the entrance to the fjord, we heard a crack like a shotgun blast. Falling ice tumbled around us. Pieces splashed in the water near the rock wall. The venturi wind blowing in the entrance whipped small ice particles around like dust caught in a miniature tornado. Cantaloupe-size ice chunks bobbed in the water, but *Driver* sliced through them easily with her knifelike bow. I was pleased that our bow pushed the ice out and away from the boat. It didn't scrape along the hull as I had feared. I mentally filed this information for future use.

The sun touched the inner bay of the fjord softly. The bay was large enough that we could avoid the falling ice if we stayed in the center. Near the back of the fjord, 30-foot icicles clung to the bottom of a frozen waterfall and dripped into the sea. The "photo op" was too tempting to ignore. Jaja hopped into the dinghy with the camera, and I maneuvered *Driver* under power to a position in front of the waterfall. Crack! A small avalanche cascaded over the frozen falls. I heard Jaja's exclamation above the sound of the thumping engine.

"Wow, Dave! Did you see that?"

After the photo session, we turned off the engine and drifted, immersed in the scenery–the creaking ice, the frozen beauty. We had cruised to Troll Fjord in the autumn, but the mountains didn't have the same aura without their blankets of snow.

The cold air falling from the steep icy walls made it feel as if we were inside an old-fashioned freezer, which needed to be defrosted. I shivered and pulled up my hood. Despite the cold, we couldn't get enough of this fabulous place.

We left Troll Fjord reluctantly. It wasn't safe to spend the night there because of the unsettled, transitional weather at this time of year. We moved to Gullvika, a cove surrounded by mountains on the island of Stormolla, about eight miles from Svolvær. Gullvika was one of our favorite anchorages. I got up at midnight and peered outside hoping for a glimpse of the northern lights. Instead, snowflakes were landing on deck like silent paratroopers. I woke Jaja so we could both watch the feathery flakes "invade" our floating home. The flurries moved on and were replaced by stars that winked at their own reflections on the mirrorlike water. We crawled back under the warm comforter and talked about Spitsbergen. We didn't worry about the sound of our voices. At this late hour, nothing short of a 10-megaton explosion would wake the children.

A year earlier, I had only vaguely heard of Spitsbergen. It was "up there" somewhere, near the top of the globe. In my imagination, I saw a group of explorers with ice-encrusted beards wearing down-filled parkas and dark sunglasses. They stood on a snowy plain under a blue sky next to a flag that was whipping in the breeze. As we learned about Spitsbergen, we realized it offers much more than a full-page photo in *National Geographic* magazine.

Spitsbergen has a varied environment–each location seems to have its own character. And there is abundant wildlife–birds, land animals, and sea creatures. The photos we saw of mammoth glaciers and high mountains, particularly in the northwestern area, bore a striking resemblance to the mountains of Lofoten. There were many bays and dozens of potential anchorages. It seemed as if summer in Spitsbergen could be heaven, except for one major drawback–ice.

Some years, the pack ice retreats from the west coast of Spitsbergen as early as May and presents a minimal threat to coastal navigation during the summer. Other years, the pack barely retreats at all. It floats off the coast menacingly, clogging the fjords at whim.

Even if the pack retreats, the drifting chunks of ice that break off the glaciers are a constant threat. We heard about a crew who anchored their boat in a quiet bay for the night only to be roused hours later by floating glacial ice banging against their hull. After a slight windshift, a vein of bergy bits had infiltrated their protected cove. The crew was obliged to raise the anchor and move to a safer location several miles away.

Every location, despite its hazards, also has its perks. Around-the-clock light would be a bonus in Spitsbergen. Even if we had to move *Driver* during the wee hours, we would not have to grope fearfully along an unfamiliar coast in the dark. I remembered running down Iceland's east coast the previous May during "nighttime" snow flurries when there was still enough light to see. Nature is often well balanced. The cold saps your energy, but the perpetual light gives a big boost. In an extreme place like Spitsbergen, we would need all the "natural" help we could get.

ON MAY 17TH, WE CELEBRATED Independence Day, the anniversary of the day in 1905 when the Norwegians dissolved their union with Sweden. It felt like summer had finally arrived. The five of us walked to the grammar school wearing T-shirts, jeans, and sneakers. We purposely left our coats behind and didn't feel cold. It was strange. Only the week before it had been snowing. Arctic weather is very unpredictable.

Grades one through 10 lined up on the school playground behind the marching band and the town politicians. Two kids held each class banner, which was supported at the ends by wooden poles. Chris was chosen to be a banner bearer, and he waved to us happily. At 11:00 a.m., the parade marched down the main street toward the waterfront and the town center.

Spectators waved hundreds of red, blue, and white Norwegian flags. A full-size flag flew from almost every house. The spring green of budding trees, thawing grass, and recently dormant shrubs contrasted with the red flags as far as the eye could see.

In the central square, we stood in the bright sunlight chatting with friends and looking expectantly at a raised podium. It was amazing how many faces we recognized in the crowd. Just nine months ago, they all would have been strangers.

Bjørg stood nearby with her students. She waved, and we walked over to chat. Jaja asked her why so many people were standing in line outside the nearby convenience store.

"Ice cream," Bjørg answered. "It's traditional for adults to buy their kids ice cream after the speeches."

"What a long line," I remarked.

"Join us for ice cream at my house, so you don't have to go through that misery," she said.

"Thanks," I said. "I'll remind my kids of that when they start nagging me for a cone."

A member of the town council approached the microphone and began speaking rapidly in Norwegian. Soon everyone was laughing. Jaja and I had difficulty following the speech. What was going on? What was he saying?

This time–unlike orientation day at Brekkuskoli in Akureyri–the roles were reversed. We asked Holly to translate.

"Oh, he's just telling us about the coming year," Holly said casually. "You know, things like that."

"Things like what?" Jaja wanted to know.

"I'll tell you in a second," Holly said politely.

I caught Jaja's eye and smiled.

Norway is a proud nation. On Independence Day in Svolvær, women and girls, from grandmothers to babies, wear the traditional Norwegian costume: An ankle-length, dark blue, wool skirt with a matching vest and a white blouse. Each outfit is hand-embroidered with an intricate pattern of flowers and adorned with silver buttons and a silver broach. Men wear suits and polished shoes. Many boys wear neckties. Jaja and I felt out of place wearing jeans. We thought about the July 4th celebrations we had experienced in the States, which were often oriented around baseball, barbecues, and beer. In Norway, it is against protocol for women to drink alcohol while wearing the national costume.

We followed our noses to Bjørg's house a few hours later. The succulent smell of *bacalau*, a traditional dish made of dried cod, wafted out the front door, down the driveway, and into the street.

"Welcome! Come in!" Bjørg greeted us with a big smile and a hug. We took off our shoes at the door and joined the party. The kids raced off with their friends, and we sat down with the other parents.

Stein came over and gave us each a big hug. Earlier, he had been one of the speakers in the town center. Formally dressed, he stood on the podium with his five-year-old son Isak perched on his shoulders. Although we didn't understand much of what he said, the crowd reacted with periodic laughter.

Stein had changed into running shorts and a T-shirt, in contrast to the other guests who were still dressed formally.

"You look like you're ready for American Independence Day," Jaja laughed. "You're wearing *our* national costume!"

"I'm just trying to make you feel at home," Stein said.

"You just want to get a tan," I teased.

While sitting outside on the deck soaking up the precious solar rays, we felt privileged to have such good friends. They had taken us into their hearts, accepted us, and allowed us to become part of their lives. In turn, they and their children had become a very important part of our lives. I looked around. Everyone was animated, laughing and talking. Jaja got up and came over to me.

"I'm having a nice time, but I'm sad deep down," she whispered. "I have a big lump in my throat."

I nodded dully. "I know what you mean."

"I was remembering that first parent-teacher meeting in Bjørg's class-room," Jaja said, "when Edd translated for me. I can't believe we're leaving all our good friends."

"*Vær sa god*!...Come and eat!" called our hostess from across the veranda.

Kids appeared out of nowhere and jockeyed for positions at the heavily laden outdoor table. In addition to Bjørg's exquisite bacalau, there were sal-ads, breads, sweet cakes, and soda for the kids.

The kids finished first, excused themselves politely, and began racing around the yard playing tag and hide-and-seek. Jaja and I sat comfortably, at peace with the world. Why did we feel the need to leave? Hadn't we found our "place" at last?

Bjørg was an honest friend. We had shared many dinners and picnic lunches together during the previous year. She said she was both sad and angry that we were leaving. We had arrived in Svolvær out of nowhere, she had made a place for us in her life, and now we were moving on leaving that space empty.

Gry urged us to stay. "You and your children have a place in Svolvær," she said. "Edvart can't understand why you're leaving when you seem so happy here."

The next afternoon, we would cast off our dock lines and continue our journey. Our journey toward what? Were we moving toward adventure? Or away from commitment? What the heck were we looking for, anyway? Would we always keep moving? We had experienced many of the same feel-ings when we left our good friends in Akureyri. Leaving was becoming more difficult each time.

JOURNALIST OLGA STOKKE flew to Lofoten from Oslo to write a follow-up story about our departure. The last time we met was under the pall of gray winter skies and obstinate bureaucracy. This time, we sat in *Driver*'s cockpit bathed in warm sun and surrounded by mountains that showed traces of renewed springtime life. We were in a reflective mood as we reminisced with Olga over our experiences of the past winter.

"What amazes me the most," Olga said, "is how positive you are regard-ing the whole ordeal with the UDI. Many people would be bitter."

"It was our fault to begin with," I said. "At the start, we were angry because we stupidly put ourselves in such a vulnerable situation. But in the end, we were overwhelmed by the support given to us. The town took us under its wing and fought for us. Also, we met many kindhearted individuals from all over Norway, whom we wouldn't have met otherwise. The press was especially sympathetic."

Olga asked, "What is your fondest memory of Lofoten?"

"Listening to the children singing in the church at Christmas," Jaja said. "Their pure voices filled us with hope during a difficult time. Those kids are Norway's future. What a lucky country."

Olga said: "Considering the amount of time and energy you spent wrestling with bureaucracy, you were still able to do a lot of things this winter."

"This winter was a good lesson in living for the moment," Jaja said. "We looked at life differently because there was always the possibility that we might have to leave. Instead of putting things off, we tried to do it all."

"Like obtaining the sparks in December?" Olga asked. "Most tourists wouldn't have bothered–especially if they though they might only be able to use them for a week or two."

"The spark was my automobile this winter," Jaja laughed. "I used it every day to transport kids, groceries, and laundry; sometimes all at the same time. But mostly I wanted to experience moving around town on a sled. It seemed so exotic."

After the interview, I went to the post office, checked our mail one last time, and filled out a form requesting that future mail be forwarded to the States. I was puzzled; we still had not received a bill from Ingrid. I walked across town, up the stairs to her office, and shook her hand.

"As you know," I said, "we are leaving in a couple hours. Uh, we have not received a bill for your services."

"That's because there isn't one," Ingrid said.

"What?"

She smiled. "It's all been taken care of."

I was dumbfounded. I didn't know if I could cope with her kindness. "You can't do this! We never intended...I mean, what about...?"

Ingrid dismissed my protest with a casual wave. She smiled, "Have a pleasant journey to Spitsbergen."

"But..."

"And give my best to Jaja and the kids." She shook my hand and returned to her office.

I walked slowly down the stairs and stepped onto the sidewalk. I took a last look at the central square. What a town.

THERE WERE AT LEAST 20 KIDS on board *Driver* when I returned–Chris's and Holly's classmates. They lined the deck and sat on the main-boom like sparrows. John Inge, our journalist friend from Måson Media, had been hired as Olga's photographer. He climbed *Driver's* mast to the first set of spreaders and began taking pictures of the scene. Parents and friends stood on the dock. Jaja and I went around saying goodbye.

All sorts of clichés can fall out of our mouths when we leave our friends: *"I'll miss you. I'll be thinking of you. I've had a really good time. You'll have to come visit us next. Don't forget to write. This has been a special time."*

Poets such as Wordsworth and Tennyson could weave an emotional web of farewell with deft, flowery words. For us regular folks, however, starting a farewell with, *"O friends of mine that I have known..."* would sound pompous and would definitely confuse the situation. So we tend to stick to commonplace expressions–words that don't quite reveal our real emotions.

If a farewell contains the right kind of emotion, I think everybody knows it. Words are unnecessary. Sometimes it's best to just be quiet and wave. Let your eyes be the transmitters and receptors of goodwill.

At 6:00 p.m., I fired up *Driver*'s engine. Unlike our departure from Akureyri, we set a specific time for leaving. At least we remembered to do something right. The visiting kids scrambled onto the floating dock, which began to sink beneath the weight of the well-wishers. Earlier that morning, we had turned *Driver* around so her bow faced out of the marina slip. From past experience, we knew that the odds of having a problem when backing out–a more difficult maneuver than going forward–increase geometrically with each pair of eyes that are watching us.

We gave each friend a final hug and whispered what felt like inadequate words of thanks and farewell. It was because of these friends that our winter had been so rich. These people *were* Svolvær. We would miss them terribly.

Everyone was uncharacteristically silent. Even Stein, who usually had a repertoire of wisecracks, sat mute on the bow of the neighboring motorboat with John Inge.

With a final wave, Jaja cast off our lines, and I slipped the shift lever into forward gear. I waited for *Driver* to move, but she remained rooted in place. For an embarrassing moment, I thought I had forgotten to untie a dock line. When I looked astern quizzically, everyone laughed. A half-dozen of Holly's and Chris's friends were holding onto our self-steering windvane, which hangs off *Driver*'s stern. I increased the engine RPMs and began a playful tug of war.

Finally, the kids on the dock lost their grip on the windvane, and amongst roars of laughter, *Driver* was free. We waved, and our friends waved. We could see everyone's face clearly. There was Gry and her three sons. Kari and Thorvadur held the twins while their 14-year-old son stood close by. We saw Edd–with his daughter on his shoulders–standing next to his wife. The Tennes family, Bjørg and her three kids, Anne Brit, and many others waved goodbye. As the distance increased, the magic thread that connected our hearts to theirs parted. Suddenly, we were on our own again–a family on the move–and part of us felt very empty.

We motored out of the marina, passed under the Svinøya Island Bridge, and moved slowly down the main harbor while we took a last look at the town that had welcomed and supported us. Kari and Thorvardur drove to the end of the wharf and stood waving. *"Ha det! Ha det bra!"* Goodbye! Have a good one!

We steamed past the Lady, whose raised hand now seemed to express harmony and good cheer. Thankfully, the open sea was calm, but with every boatlength we traveled, we experienced deep waves of sorrow. Chris and Holly were sobbing quietly, and Teiga had her head buried in Jaja's neck.

To help quell our sadness, we ate the food we had received as farewell gifts. The kids said they weren't hungry, but that was before they tasted the sticky buns Ragnhild made. Then they ate the coconut custard pastries baked by Edd's wife. After motoring for about 1 1/2 hours, we arrived at Gullvika, our anchorage for the first night. We needed to unwind, to let our sadness play out. We ate homemade fish cakes for dinner accompanied by a bottle of white wine. We went to bed early finding solace in sleep.

For us, the sad farewell had annihilated the thrill of departure. We knew from experience, however, that the sadness would soon be replaced by good memories–and by the demands of voyaging.

We were headed for the ice.

Chapter Seventeen

"The journey of a thousand miles must begin with a single step."
–Lao Tzu, Chinese philosopher, 6th century BC

*D*RIVER PLOWED THROUGH steep-sided seas. Her 10-ton bulk, which makes her lethargic in light air, was an asset now that we had 30 knots of apparent wind screaming across the deck. *Driver* wasn't thrown around by the waves as a lighter boat would have been. Her displacement made the motion onboard more comfortable and allowed us to steer a somewhat straighter course. *Driver* is a good sea boat, and we were blasting along toward Spitsbergen like a humpback whale headed for its mating ground.

I stood on deck in my red foul-weather gear, gripping the shrouds for balance. *Driver* was heeled at an angle; the starboard rail was almost in the water. The boat lifted and fell, pitched and yawed rhythmically. The sea was playing familiar games with our progress. I looked toward the bow, released my grip on the shrouds, and started moving across the foredeck. I didn't look at my hands or feet. I focused on nothing, yet saw everything. My body absorbed the motion, and my instincts assimilated the constantly changing angles and planes in which I moved. I knew if I kept my actions fluid, I could achieve a sense of nonmotion, the same way a skier can absorb the bumps of a mogul field by keeping his knees loose and bent. In a few simple bounds, I crossed the 14-foot distance, grabbed the forestay, and perched on the bow rail. Safe.

I tugged on my 20-foot-long safety tether to gain a little slack. Then I tightened the lashings that kept the anchors from clanging annoyingly in their bow rollers. I also added an extra sail tie to the big jib, which was lashed to the lifelines near the bow. After completing my chores, I took a moment to appreciate the unique perspective from the bow.

Looking aft, I saw that the pleasing curve of the small jib matched the shape of the double-reefed mainsail. The two sails were sheeted in as far as possible, and they worked together magically to propel us through the water. I knew the scientific reasons why a sailboat defies logic and why a cruising boat can sail as close as 45 degrees to the direction of the wind. Nevertheless, I was always delighted by the "trick" of sailing upwind.

Back in the cockpit, I hunkered down on deck outside the canvas dodger. Driven by the wind, salt spray blew aft from the bow, continuously drenching the whole boat. All at once, I felt *Driver*'s bow lift...lift...then plunge aggressively into a large wave. Instinctively, I ducked behind the lee of the dodger and pressed my head against the wet canvas. A fraction of a second later, what seemed like a ton of water slammed on deck and washed over my back. I held on and let the deluge pass.

I glanced at the thermometer mounted on the backstay–34 degrees Fahrenheit, slightly below average for June 16th. As long as the temperature didn't drop any lower, ice in the rigging shouldn't be a problem. Then I poked my head into the dodger and looked at the compass. My heart sank.

Jaja, who was sitting in the companionway, spoke my thoughts. "The angle of the wind hasn't changed. It's still pushing us toward the coast."

I sighed. We were less than 15 miles from Sørkapp, Spitsbergen's dangerous southern cape. The wind was not cooperating. It was blowing from the northwest–from the exact direction we wanted to go. Since a sailboat cannot go directly into the wind, it must zigzag back and forth–first on one "tack," or course, then on the opposite tack. Sailing to windward is like hiking up a switchback trail. You gain elevation while walking a greater distance. On our present tack, we were being pushed toward a very inhospitable shoreline. We could not point away from the coast because we could not steer any closer to the wind direction. The only solution was to come about onto the opposite tack and steer away from shore.

The waters at Sørkapp are shoal, rocky, and prone to severe tide rips. In gentler conditions, we might have sailed within, say, five miles of shore. But not today. The noon weather forecast warned of winds increasing to 35 knots ahead of a cold front. It was best to keep dozens of miles of open water between *Driver* and the land. I made preparations to come about, or to "tack," as the maneuver is sometimes called.

Currently, we were sailing about 50 degrees from the "eye," or direction, of the wind. Our wind angle was not as small, or as close, as it would have been in calmer conditions. Now, for every two miles *Driver* sailed, she made less than one mile toward our destination. Hornsund Fjord, the closest protected anchorage, was 60 miles away. With a tail wind and following seas, we could have been there in nine hours. Now, with these screaming headwinds, it was going to take at least 20 hours. I looked at my analog watch, noted the position of the secondhand, and counted the number of waves passing under *Driver* during a one-minute period. Then I did a little mental arithmetic. Instead of crashing over an estimated 6,400 waves, I figured *Driver* would be abused by 13,000 watery crests before we made landfall.

Tacking *Driver* is more difficult on the open sea than tacking her in protected waters. On a smooth bay, I might push the tiller over slowly and watch the bow move easily through the eye of the wind. The mainsail would luff, or flap, casually, and the big genoa jib would flutter gently against the mast as it passed from one side of the boat to the other. As soon as the genoa sheet was pulled in, *Driver* would glide across the bay on the opposite tack without much loss of headway. Tacking can be nearly effortless when the sea and wind conditions are mellow.

Tacking in steep seas and near-gale-force winds, on the other hand, creates pandemonium. I poked my head into the companionway and hollered, "Plug your ears and hang on. We're tacking."

I disconnected the windvane self-steering and held the tiller. I steered *Driver* over the face of a swell and felt the boat accelerate down the back side. Just as we reached the bottom of the wave and began to climb the next face, I pushed the tiller hard to leeward. As *Driver* rose up the wall of moving water, the bow turned across the eye of the wind. The mainsail luffed and flogged like a banner snapping in the wind. It sounded like 1,000 bullwhips all cracking at once. As *Driver* turned, the wind started to fill the jib on the opposite side. I released the jibsheet and let it run. Immediately, the jib began to luff. With two sails shaking at once, it felt as if the mast would come down. Chris told me later that it sounded like a helicopter was landing on the foredeck.

Normally, *Driver*'s forward momentum would help her to begin moving on the opposite tack. This time, the force of the wind and the seas on her bow stopped her dead in the water. The wind filled the mainsail on the new tack, but we had not yet pulled in the jibsheet. The jib was still flogging–streaming out perpendicular to the hull. Without adequate sail power, *Driver* stopped dead, wallowing broadside to the seas and unable to point up closer to the direction of the wind.

I wrapped the jibsheet around the winch and started cranking to trim the sail. Suddenly, I looked to windward. A monstrous green wave raised its ugly head–higher and higher. Just before it broke, I saw daylight through the thin, dancing crest. Thousands of artists have tried to paint that translucent water at the point just before it dissolves into foam. Few have succeeded.

With unfortunate timing, *Driver* rolled heavily toward the wall of water. The flat side of the wave met our flat-sided steel hull with a resounding, WHOMP! The impact was so loud that Chris sprang up from belowdecks to see what we had hit. Standing water rolled across the deck and over my sea boots.

I wasn't worried about the integrity of the boat because past experience had shown us the strength of *Driver*'s steel topsides. Soon after we bought her, I probed a suspicious looking blemish in the side of the hull with an ice pick. It was amidships, about 18 inches above the waterline. It took me five minutes of digging to uncover a dimple in the steel hull that a previous owner had filled with epoxy long ago. The steel was not pierced–just bent–but the crater was deep enough to hide a golf ball.

Several months later, after I had removed the interior of the cabin, I located the dent on the inner surface of the hull. I figured if I pounded the protrusion hard enough from the inside, I could flatten it out. I gripped the handle of a five-pound sledgehammer firmly, planted my feet, took aim, and let go with a swing that would have impressed any major league baseball player. The resulting THONG! was sizzling. I screamed involuntarily as my eardrums reverberated from the shock waves. Outside, dogs barked, and porch lights came on. When I recovered my senses, I examined the dent. Nothing had changed. Except for the loss of some paint, the dimple was completely unscathed. Later, I refilled it with epoxy.

After we recovered from the monster wave, Jaja held the tail of the jibsheet, which was wrapped around one of the winches on deck, and I ground the winch with the handle. Around and around and around. The sheet came in slowly. Finally, we pulled in the billowing sail until it was no longer luffing. *Driver* gained headway and once again, began to move forward over the seas.

I reset the windvane, tidied the lines, and took a breather. I was sweating. Except during moments of heavy activity, I needed many layers of clothing to stay warm in the chilly air. That day, I wore rubber boots with one-inch-thick fleece insulation, a one-piece fleece jumpsuit, a wool sweater, a wool hat, and insulated waterproof gloves. Over all of this was a one-piece, foul-weather suit with built-in flotation. The thin, internal flotation foam also acted as insulation. Moving around was cumbersome, but at least I was warm.

AFTER THE TACK, I stood watch for several hours–warm and dry inside the dodger. The kids were out for the night, and Jaja was dozing with Teiga in her arms. At 10:00 p.m., I put my rain gear back on and stood in the cockpit scanning the horizon. One of the thrills of sailing in very high latitudes is the total absence of darkness. Even at midnight, the sun burned yellow and bright, high above the wave tops. The perpetual light of summer was upon us.

The texture of the sky had been changing all day. At noon it was overcast with snow flurries. At 3:00 p.m. the sky cleared. By 5:00 p.m., the wind began to blow hard. Now the clouds on the windward horizon were purple and maroon, and the sea was steely black. Judging by the signs, conditions would get worse before they got better.

We sailed for another hour. At 11:00 p.m., the windspeed increased a notch. I straightened my safety line and waded along the soaked, pitching foredeck. I dropped the jib, lashed it, and returned to the cockpit. Instead of making five knots and pounding through the cold, arctic seas, we were crawling along at 2 1/2 knots with only the mainsail up. The motion and noise had diminished because we were moving more slowly. Jaja and I were very tired. It made sense to lower the jib and reduce sail until the wind and seas moderated. It was a relief to stop pushing, to let the wind blow and allow *Driver* to bob around. We were 30 miles off the coast with plenty of sea room, and on our new tack, we were headed toward empty ocean.

I slid down the companionway and shed my sodden foul-weather gear. A fresh gust of wind whistled in the rigging. The wind was increasing. Good thing I lowered the jib. Otherwise, I would be on deck now fighting to lower and control the flogging canvas. Jaja climbed the companionway ladder and perched in the dodger to look for ships and ice. Despite our seemingly remote location, we had seen several enormous fishing trawlers that day. We also knew there were supply ships and cruise ships in the waters off Spitsbergen during the summer.

Floating ice was an even greater danger. Stray chunks called "growlers" floated low, or just under the surface. They could be as small as oil drums or as big as trucks. To appreciate how invisible a growler can be to a sailor, look at an ice cube in a glass of water. Now shake that glass to create a "storm." The crew of a coast guard ship in Norway told us they had once seen a growler 20 miles south of Sørkapp that was 40 feet in circumference–flat as a squash court and clear as urethane. If *Driver* struck ice, it would be like hitting a reef. Fortunately, we had around-the-clock sunlight, which increased our chances of spotting ice–or for that matter a ship–in time to avoid a collision. Our slow forward speed gave us additional time to notice dangers.

I stretched out on the settee in the main cabin and felt the weight of fatigue. We had been at sea for only 3 1/2 days, but it seemed like many, many more. Despite the favorable weather forecast when we departed from the Norwegian coast, the first two days had been extremely rough, almost dangerous. The constant threat of gales and ice, the cold temperatures on deck, and the implications of our extreme northerly location sapped our energy reserves.

IT WAS A LONG "NIGHT". Jaja and I took turns staring at the empty seascape from the shelter of the dodger. The weather was very unstable. Snow flurries and wind squalls alternated with broken clouds that allowed the yellow sun to stab our tired eyes. The surface of the sea alternated blue, gray, and black. Wave tops crumbled and slapped the hull. Spray often sounded like sand thrown against the dodger. Time crawled. Ten minutes felt like an hour, and an hour felt like a half-day.

Driver was bobbing along at 76 degrees north latitude. The windvane self-steering held us on course, and only the small triangle of the triple-reefed mainsail propelled us. Our slower forward speed provided a welcome respite. On the down side, we weren't making much headway toward our destination. Nevertheless, reducing sail felt like the right decision.

Another squall. Granular corn snow whizzed through the air, made staccato "ticks" against the dodger, and collected in feeble piles around the deck. The next breaking sea sluiced it all away. The temperature wavered a hair above freezing. Hornsund Fjord, our destination, is locked in ice for eight months of the year. Presumably, the water would be open by now. But our worries would not end when we entered the fjord and anchored. Drifting glacier ice could threaten *Driver* at any time, and polar bears could attack as we walked on land. I thought of the large-caliper rifle that was resting in the V-berth. It didn't feel like the Year 2000. It felt as if we were living in some forgotten time battling an endless gale and headed into a wilderness full of wild animals.

I tried to release the tension in my shoulders. "Relax," I told myself. "We've done our research. We have official permission to visit Spitsbergen. We have studied ice safety. We have the right clothes, enough food, all the charts. And we have a gun."

Leaving Svolvær had been the first step in our journey to Spitsbergen. But most of our preparations took place 10 days later in the Norwegian town of Tromsø. I tried to shore up my confidence by remembering our final week there.

TROMSØ IS A MODERN CITY of 50,000 people located 150 miles north of Svolvær. It's touted as the Paris of the north–with enough bars, sidewalk cafés, and restaurants to comfortably seat the entire city population at any given moment. Distinguished by several reputable educational institutions, Tromsø boasts the northernmost university in the world.

Tromsø Harbor is typical of most Norwegian ports. There was no place for us to anchor, but the marina was new, with floating aluminum docks, and it was inexpensive by American standards. For the equivalent of US $7 a night, we had showers, a coin laundry, fresh water, and electricity. We were also in the heart of the city. Most of what we needed was within walking distance.

For centuries, Tromsø has been a jumping off point for expeditions to Spitsbergen's west coast. Whalers, explorers, trappers, and rescue teams provisioned in some of the same buildings that border the winding city streets today. Near *Driver*'s berth was an arctic museum devoted to the history of Spitsbergen. We wandered through the exhibits studying old photos, vintage clothing, outdated radio equipment, varnished wooden skis, reconstructed trappers' huts, and displays of flora and fauna. Even Chris, Holly, and Teiga felt the aura of adventure that wafted, foglike, through the quiet halls.

Polar bears are a featured attraction at the museum–as common as palm trees in a tropical scene. Taxidermy bears added a feeling of reality. Bearded trappers in old photos dragged white carcasses on sleds. In recreated camp-sites, polar bear furs lay about like sacks of copra.

Guns were a common denominator in the vintage photos of Spitsbergen and in the recreated camps. Guns for killing. Guns for protection. Every man carried a gun. Neither Jaja nor I had any useful experience with guns. As teen-agers, we had both shot BB guns and .22 caliber rifles at targets. As adults, we were antigun fanatics. When Chris and Holly were small, we refused to let them play with toy guns. We even removed the guns from some toy Lego fig-ures they received one Christmas. We do not believe that pretending to shoot one another is a very civilized pastime for our children.

If we were going north aboard *Driver,* however, our attitude about weap-ons would have to change. Spitsbergen is home to well over 3,000 polar bears, which puts visiting yachtsmen at a disadvantage during meal times.

Chris and I visited a gun shop in Tromsø. I felt wildly out of place and very hypocritical wandering with my son in that house of weapons. I exam-ined the guns, naïvely wondering which one would work for us. How could I ask about guns and not sound like a total novice? Maybe they wouldn't sell me one. Then what would we do?

I harbored a mental image of a typical gun shop owner–at least 300 pounds with tattoos, mirror sunglasses, and a dangling cigarette. I pictured myself approaching the counter nervously while he scowled and said, "Wha'choo want, boy?"

Thankfully, my stereotype image was wrong. The proprietress of the store was a kind-looking woman, slim, dressed in jeans and a blouse. I felt the strength of her Nordic personality immediately. In answer to my inquiry, she informed me that as a foreign tourist, the law prohibited me from buying a gun. However, considering that our destination was Spitsbergen, the law allowed me to rent one to protect ourselves against bears. Poachers were jailed, but tourists were allowed to shoot in self-defense.

The one question that I anticipated came quickly.

"Do you have a gun license in the United States, sir?" she asked.

"Uh...no."

With her eyebrows raised high, she asked, "How long did you say you wanted to rent the gun for?"

"Two months."

She licked her lips. With controlled nonchalance, she picked up a calcula-tor, added a few figures, and shrugged her shoulders. Next, she hollered into the back room. A giant of a man emerged carrying a gun case. He placed it on the glass counter and opened the lid, revealing a well-worn rifle called a High-lander .308. It used bullets measuring 2 3/4 inches long. I gaped. This was no .22. It was an awesome gun, big enough to kill a charging polar bear.

The woman smiled at my reaction. "Are you familiar with guns, sir?"

"Yes," I hedged. "I've had lots of experience with guns."

"But Dad," Chris blurted out. "I thought you said you didn't know the first thing…"

The shopkeeper gave Chris a keen look and chuckled to herself. I filled out some paperwork and handed over a $100 deposit. She gave me a temporary gun license. Now that the gun was mine, I decided it was safe to ask a few questions, such as, where did the bullets go? I tried to sound knowledgeable by using words like *cartridges, ammo chamber,* and *trigger mechanism*. Thanks to watching John Wayne movies as a kid, I could act like a real pro.

The woman patiently answered my questions, then made a suggestion. "As soon as you get to a secluded place, perhaps you should do some target practice."

I smiled. "Good idea."

I strutted toward the door carrying the gun in its slick black plastic case. When I hit the sidewalk, I felt about two inches taller and extremely conspicuous. I wondered who was more naïve–me or the shopkeeper.

Back in *Driver*'s cabin, I opened the case and examined our newest toy. I showed Jaja how it worked, and together we gave a brief lecture to our kids on gun protocol.

I said, "You kids are never, under any circumstances, to open the gun case, or play with the bullets." I felt like a rogue. Bringing the gun aboard made me feel tense and uncomfortable. Jaja and I knew our children would not disobey us and touch the gun, yet it was disconcerting to disrupt our placid lives with an object that required strict rules.

The open gun case dominated the cabin. We all stared at it.

"I hope we don't have to shoot a polar bear." Holly said uneasily.

"The gun is for protection," Jaja said without much gusto. "We'll only shoot a bear if we have to. Hopefully, we can scare a bear away by firing the gun in the air."

"But what if the bear doesn't go away?" asked Holly.

"If we feel that a bear is going to attack us, we'll have to kill it," Jaja said.

"I guess if the choice is between killing a bear or being eaten by one, I'd rather kill the bear," Chris said.

Jaja and I exchanged glances. What had we gotten ourselves into?

THE TROMSØ HARBORMASTER was a retired Norwegian ship captain who spoke English with a Scottish accent. He had read in the newspapers about our plight with the UDI, and he scowled at the recollection.

Jabbing his index finger in the air, he said, "If you'da been here, in *my* harbor last winter, I would've given ye Port of Refuge and told those bastards in Oslo to piss off. Makin' ye go to sea in January. I've never heard such a load of rubbish."

He told us where to shop for boat parts, and kindly offered to drive us around. We bought new basic rubber boots for the whole family and added thick wool insoles for warmth. With heavy wool socks, our feet would be warm enough for walking on shore. Going crazy and buying expensive specialty gear did not make sense. If we started feeling cold we would return to *Driver*'s warm cabin and make another trip to shore later.

After two winters aboard, we were well supplied with cold-weather clothing, so we did not need to buy any other items to wear. The kids still had their insulated one-piece snowsuits, which we had bought new at the beginning of the school year in Svolvær. Our biggest chore was stocking up with groceries. Fortunately, the store was less than a five-minute walk from the boat. Jaja laid in a good supply of food, but didn't overdo it. Spitsbergen is a tax-free zone, and despite its remote location, grocery prices at the settlement of Longyearbyen were reportedly less expensive than in stores on the Norwegian mainland.

While Jaja shopped and stocked in Tromsø, I researched the legal requirements for cruising in Spitsbergen. This was a once-in-a lifetime chance to visit the island group on *Driver*, and we did not want spoil our arrival with incorrect or incomplete paperwork. We had already suffered enough bureaucratic acrimony. The Svalbard group of islands is under Norwegian jurisdiction, but anyone can land and live there, even without a passport. The hitch is that you may not stay for long unless you have a prearranged place to stay and enough funds. Since *Driver* was our home and since we had ample savings, these were not issues for us. Nevertheless, I wanted to be sure that there were no special regulations for cruisers. I phoned the tourist information office in Longyearbyen and learned that before the governor's office would issue a cruising permit, we needed to acquire rescue insurance. The local rescue organization in Longyearbyen was ready and willing to save lives, but obviously they had been burned enough times to require proof that the people being rescued could pay the bill. Costs for a rescue could run into tens of thousands of dollars.

To determine the dollar value of the insurance coverage we would need, we had to supply the administration staff at the governor's office with details about *Driver*, our crew, and our specific cruising itinerary. Up to this point, we had only a vague itinerary in mind. We knew we could make it to Hornsund, the southernmost fjord, but beyond that, we planned to wing it, depending on weather and other circumstances. Unfortunately, such an indefinite plan was not going to get us a cruising permit.

We spread out the navigation charts. For the first time, we scrutinized each area we hoped to cruise. According to the insurance regulations, our premiums would increase as we moved farther north away from the central rescue station at Longyearbyen. How far north did we actually want to go? The distance up the west coast of Spitsbergen from Hornsund to the northernmost fjords is about 200 miles. It isn't a great distance, but we remembered our first summer in Iceland two years before. We had moved slowly and waited for good weather. In Spitsbergen, we might be trapped in port by weather, or the pack ice might descend and restrict our options. We also had to think about the return trip. For every mile north, we would have to cover a mile south.

Our eyes roamed over the charts: Bellsund, Isfjord, Kongs Fjord, Magdalene Fjord, and Smeerenburg Fjord, to name just a few. And smaller fjords branched off each of these major cuts in the coast. There were anchorages galore. Our eyes focused on the extreme northwest coast, on a small island called Amsterdamøya. It was located at 79 degrees 45 minutes north latitude.

We looked at the chart in silence. The kids played noisily around us in the cabin. Holly and Chris argued about which of their Lego boats was best suited for a journey to rescue Pot, who was trapped in a crystal river chasm. In recent months, Teiga had joined the ongoing imaginary game about Pot and Mary, but today, she lost interest as her brother and sister hammered out minute details for the rescue. Pot's faithful bird-servant, Pummelmump, insisted on using his jet boat cruiser (which had retractable thrusters), but Holly argued for the pirate ship. Chris said there would not be enough wind for the pirate ship, and Holly said there would not be enough fuel for the jet boat.

"Hey, I know!" I said, "Why don't you sail the pirate ship to the river, and then use the jet boat to make the rescue!" All three kids gave me such a tiresome look of childish contempt that I got up to make coffee. I thought the matter was finished, until Chris started telling me all the reasons why he thought my idea was impractical.

While the kettle heated, I looked out the cabin windows. The Tromsø waterfront reflected an air of history. Double-ended varnished fishing trawlers rafted against the main wharf, the foreshore gleamed with traditional architecture, and the narrow city streets served as a reminder that automobile traffic didn't exist when the town first began to grow.

I turned off the gas and poured the boiling coffee into our cups.

Jaja held Teiga on her lap, and they were looking at ice charts in the pilot book. "You know, we've come so far these past two years, it seems like a waste not sail to the limit. Don't you think so?"

"What's on your mind?" I held my breath.

"This is our chance, Dave. If we stop at Amsterdamøya Island, which looks like it lies about two miles off Spitsbergen's northwest coast, we can pick our weather to make a day-sail to the edge of the pack ice. It would be cool to sail *Driver* above 80 degrees north."

I handed Jaja her coffee and looked at the pilot book. On average, the summer pack ice hovers around the 80th parallel–just 15 miles north of Amsterdamøya. Some years it recedes as high as 83 degrees north. Other years, it never leaves the west coast of Spitsbergen at all.

My pulse began to pound. I could feel the pull of 80 degrees north. I felt like a climber contemplating how it feels to stand on the summit of Mount Everest, the highest point on earth. If we ventured to the pack ice aboard *Driver*, we would be sailing to the northernmost position on the planet that a small boat can reach. I wondered out loud if we would ever be satisfied with last year's achievements.

"I hope not," Jaja answered quickly.

"Yeah, neither do I." Everything seemed to be leading us to this final, northern goal–finding *Driver* in the back of a boatyard during an innocent Sunday afternoon drive, the refit accomplished on a ridiculously tight schedule, leaving Bermuda, wintering in Akureyri, our last-minute trek up the Norwegian coast, Lofoten, the UDI.

Taken at face value, going to the edge of the pack ice on *Driver* sounded outlandish. But I knew that as we sailed north, our perspective would change. We would become comfortable with our surroundings, and more knowledgeable. Gradually, we would learn to "read" the ice and the local conditions, and to gauge the right time to hole up or move on.

Back in Iceland, when Halli proposed sailing *Driver* to the Svalbard group, I thought the trip sounded impossible. Now in Tromsø with all the facts before us, it didn't seem quite so daunting. About 20 to 30 cruising sailboats visit Spitsbergen each summer. We even heard of a 35-foot fiberglass catamaran that had made the trip. Back in Svolvær, when we mentioned our desire to sail to Spitsbergen, Gry told us about her great-grandfather who had sailed a 20-foot open boat to Spitsbergen at the turn of the century. On board were his wife and their three-year-old child. They arrived safely and even spent the winter ashore in a small hut. Compared to their tiny wooden craft, *Driver* was a battleship.

Most cruising sailors head for the Tropics in search of a warm paradise. When someone speaks of the South Pacific, it's natural to think of hot sun, beaches, and tropical water. Cruisers are lured there because they can go barefoot and because they are reassured by the myriads of other cruisers who sail the warm waters. But few cruisers will admit that as many dangers lurk in warm seas as in cold ones. For example, coral reefs claim numerous boats each year. Other risks include cyclones, 10 hours of darkness each day, unpredictable surface currents, and diseases such as malaria.

In comparison, the dangers posed by ice, cold, and isolation don't seem so bad. It's true that in cold cruising areas, hypothermia may slow your reactions and judgement. However, with the right clothes and an awareness of hypothermic symptoms, the cold is no more of a threat than the blazing tropical sun and the lightheaded dizzy spells that result from letting too much heat beat down on your cranium.

When friends back home hear about our northern voyages, or the winters aboard in Iceland and Norway, their response is predictable.

"It must be miserable. So cold!"

Miserable? Our thoughts turn to the friendships, the northern lights, the snow-laden trees turned orange by the midmorning sun, and the silent anchorages all to ourselves. Our children thrived in the calm, safe environment where they enjoyed complete freedom.

I drained my coffee cup and set it down on the chart table next to the cruising permit application and accompanying forms for Svalbard. I knew if we wanted to go to 80°north, we would have to take it slow. One step at a time–same as always.

Nonetheless, I was still apprehensive. I hoped that the closer we sailed to the pack ice, the less intimidating it would become. "To the ice then?" I asked.

Jaja smiled.

THE NEXT MORNING, I faxed our itinerary to the governor's office in Longyearbyen. It stated that we intended to cruise the west side of Spitsbergen Island between Hornsund and Amsterdamøya Island. The official reply came back quickly. Based on the facts we provided, they calculated that the cost of a worst-case, full-fledged rescue–if we needed one–would not exceed $17,000. They gave us two options. We could pay 10 percent ($1,700) in cash, which would purchase a two-month, nonrefundable insurance plan from a carrier in Longyearbyen. Or we could post a bank guarantee for the full amount of $17,000 dollars, which was nearly equivalent to our cruising budget for an entire year.

Neither option was attractive. The $1,700 insurance policy did not cover loss of life, nor property loss or damage. It did not cover medical expenses. It merely compensated the coast guard in the event of a rescue operation.

Jaja said, "What it boils down to, Dave, is whether we stake $17,000 and rely on our gut instincts and inner resources, or whether we follow modern convention, buy the insurance policy, and allocate responsibility to others."

I chuckled. "That pretty much sums it up, doesn't it?"

Regardless of price, a rescue insurance policy was a mental crutch that could potentially alter our psychology in an emergency. Obtaining the insurance would be an admission that our cruise to Spitsbergen was too much for us to handle on our own. On the other hand, if we did not buy the insurance and put up a cash stake instead, were we taking excessive chances? Would the fear of paying rescue costs alter our decision to accept help–even if calling for help happened to be the most logical option?

"Let's say there was no such thing as rescue insurance, or even a rescue team," I said. "Would we still go to Spitsbergen?"

"Of course we would," Jaja replied.

Buying insurance was not going to make our journey safer. We would still be on our own in a vast, rugged region. How we dealt with emergencies was merely a matter of perspective. It didn't take us long to make our choice. Providing the bank guarantee was the decision most in character with our past experiences.

I contacted our financial advisor in the States, who faxed a letter to the governor's office in Longyearbyen confirming that $17,000 would be available in our account between June 15th and August 15th. Two days later, we received notice that our cruising permit would be waiting for us upon arrival in Longyearbyen. We also received permission to cruise the waters south of Longyearbyen en route to the settlement. Now all we needed was a good weather forecast before leaving the Norwegian coast.

WE DEPARTED FOR SPITSBERGEN from Honningsvåg Harbor on Magerøy Island, about 120 miles north of Tromsø. Magerøy is host to two important capes. The first is the well-known Nordkapp, a magnificent, bold headland frequently touted as the northernmost point in Europe. It attracts tourists from all over the world. Geographically, however, the northernmost point is a low, unimpressive peninsula called Knivskjelodden. It's about three miles west of Nordkapp and juts three quarters of a mile farther north.

The previous summer, during our journey up the Norwegian coast from Bergen, we had wanted to sail *Driver* around both Nordkapp and Knivskjelodden. At the time, it seemed like an impossible goal because it involved a 1,200-mile coastal journey just to get there.

Now, sailing around the two "most northern" points of Norway was only a small step in our continuing voyage. Our perspective was changing again. New horizons stretched before us–along with perhaps some of the greatest challenges of our lives.

After waiting nearly a week in Honningsvåg for the right weather conditions, we were rewarded with a reasonable long-range weather forecast: 15- to 20-knot winds from the starboard quarter with continued clear skies. I telephoned the ice prediction center in Tromsø and learned that satellite images showed open water in the main fjords in Spitsbergen. The water surrounding Sørkapp was also free of icebergs. It was time to go.

We stopped at the dock in Honningsvåg to top up our diesel and water tanks. The fuel guy asked where we were headed. He looked at *Driver*, then at our small kids, and shook his head.

"Spitsbergen? Better you than me, bud."

We shrugged off the not-so-cheery farewell, aimed our faces at the sun, and thought positively. We were aware of the risks we were taking, but we also knew we had thousands of miles of cruising experience to draw upon. All the fuel guy saw was a young family on a small boat.

Honningsvåg Harbor is on the south coast of Magerøy Island. After 1 1/2 hours of motoring into light, fluky winds, we picked up some breeze at the northeast corner of the island. I raised the sails, switched off the engine, and set a course for Spitsbergen. Only 425 miles to go.

Eight miles away on our port beam, Nordkapp hovered regally in the clear air. Its 800-foot-high summit is flat, but the sheer, blunt end of the headland was awe inspiring. Beyond it, Knivskjelodden tapered off into the sea. We wanted to sail close to these capes to get an intimate view of our latest milestones, but the 15-knot easterly wind fought with the west flowing current. There was no reason to subject ourselves to a potentially dangerous tide rip, so we stayed five miles off. By midnight, the Norwegian coast and islands had disappeared below the horizon, but the sun still blazed high in the sky, lending the impression that it was midafternoon. We bathed in the golden rays of perpetual arctic light.

By morning, the sky had clouded over, and harsh 30-knot easterlies replaced the easygoing 15-knot winds that had accompanied our departure. As the wind increased, I reduced sail over a span of several hours. First, I reefed the mainsail, then the jib. Later, I reefed the main again, removed the medium-size jib, and replaced it with the smaller one. The seas were long and steep, streaked with white foam and unforgiving to our stomachs. We were all seasick. The temperature on deck hovered in the low 40s, so I cranked up the diesel stove. The temperature in the cabin rose to a balmy 75 degrees. It's less stressful to barf when you're warm.

The weather forecast at noon revealed that the weak high-pressure system, which was supposed to have prevailed for several days, had shifted position slightly and merged with a distant low-pressure area. The wind was predicted to blow 30 knots or more for at least 36 hours. Despite the forecast, there was no turning back now; the wind was blowing us away from the Norwegian coast.

THE CURRENTS BETWEEN Norway and the Svalbard group can be tumultuous and complex. The dying Gulf Stream comes up from the south, splits, and sends tentacles every which way. Some of the Gulf Stream current continues north, some veers east, and the rest swirls in large eddies. The sea bottom is also irregular. These factors, combined with the strong easterly winds, created a sea state disproportionate to the strength of the wind. To further confuse things, a long ground swell was rolling in from the southwest. It met the steep, easterly-flowing waves at an angle, creating even greater mayhem.

Driver continued on course at hull speed, even under reduced sail. We had finally lowered the mainsail altogether and lashed it to the boom, which left only the small jib flying. The sweeping seas were large and confused, but for the most part, not dangerous. The real problem was the periodic appearance of massive tide rips. Like mythical beasts or furies, these rips would engulf us every 30 or 40 minutes. During these times, we felt true fear–while also wondering how the rips could possibly occur at such regular intervals. When one of these monsters had us in its jaws, we were under siege for several minutes. Our watery world was filled with dangerous chasms, towering peaks, and liquid avalanches. *Driver* would enter this arena and be battered grotesquely.

These tide-driven seas *were* dangerous. The roar of breaking waves was deafening. They lifted *Driver*'s transom and sent her surfing down the crests at top speed. Then she would plow headlong into the next watery wall, stop dead in her tracks, and get knocked over. Surf broke over the deck; *Driver* lumbered under the weight of the Barents Sea. If we peered out from the dodger, the view defied reason and experience. These waves made the seas we had experienced on Iceland's east coast look like small harbor chop.

During these periodic attacks, I was tempted to drop the jib and deploy the sea anchor. Our sea anchor is a sort of cloth parachute about 10 feet in diameter that trails astern just below the surface at the end of a 400-foot length of 5/8-inch nylon line. When deployed, the "anchor" bites into the water and checks most of *Driver*'s forward speed. Instead of climbing capriciously over the peaked waves and falling into the troughs, the anchor would allow *Driver* to ride the waves more slowly and safely, and to become part of the surface tapestry of the sea.

Despite its potential advantages, I was reluctant to deploy the sea anchor. Reducing our forward progress could crush our morale. At least we were putting miles behind us. Another consideration was personal comfort. The jib dampened the rolling motion. True, we were pounding and lurching, but the motion was tolerable. If we lowered the jib and rigged the anchor, *Driver* would roll from gunwale to gunwale like a metronome on water skis. Life in the cabin would become untenable.

After each tide rip ended, we sailed on relatively "normal" seas. Each time, I was relieved that we had not opted for the sea anchor. Then we would plunge into another tidal maelstrom. Once more, we would agonize over what to do. Life on the edge. It lasted 32 hours.

Shortly before we departed from Svolvær, we debated whether we should invest in a sea anchor. We would be sailing into the deep Arctic where conditions could turn nasty very quickly, and we thought that despite the cost, it was time to add this piece of equipment to our gear inventory.

I walked to the commercial fishing supply store owned by Thorvardur to see what he had in stock.

"Here's one," he said. "Just the right size for *Driver*. You can have it."

"It's too expensive." I said. "I can't accept this as a gift."

"But you have to," Thorvardur laughed. "I'm giving it to you." He continued to press the anchor's yellow, vinyl storage bag into my reluctant arms. "If you have a sea anchor, you'll feel prepared for your passage to Svalbard. Even if you never use it, just knowing you have it might ease your mind if conditions turn nasty. If peace of mind is all this anchor brings, then that is the best gift I could ever give you."

During the bad times on the passage to Spitsbergen, I strained every mental fiber assessing the sea state and the severity of the most recent knockdowns. I worried constantly whether conditions had exceeded what was ultimately safe for us. But the onslaught always stopped just moments before I decided that it was time to deploy the anchor and slow down. We thought of Thorvardur often; the peace of mind his gift brought allowed us to push on.

Despite the rough-and-tumble abuse, *Driver* made incredible progress. We covered 275 miles in two days–well over halfway to Hornsund Fjord. Although the wind and seas began to subside, more bad news was ahead. The new weather forecast predicted that a low-pressure trough, ahead of a high-pressure system, was expected to sweep across the area, bringing northwesterly winds. We would have to sail close-hauled–close to the direction of the wind–to reach Spitsbergen. It meant that we would fight the waves rather than ride them.

When the low-pressure system arrived 12 hours later, the windspeed fell to zero and the temperature dropped to 33 degrees. It began to snow. The seas remained steep and sloppy while various wave trains fought for superiority. The surface waves, pushed by the old easterly wind began to give way to the new wave train that marched ahead of the predicted northwest winds. In an effort to put some miles under our keel before the headwinds arrived, we started the engine and motored toward Sørkapp.

Later that same afternoon, after the northwest wind had begun to fill in, we undertook the thunderous tack and steered *Driver* away from Sørkapp's deadly coastline. Soon afterwards, I lashed the jib on deck and left only the reefed mainsail up. Jaja held a vigil in the dodger checking for ships and looking for growlers.

The "night" stretched into eternity.

AROUND 4:00 A.M., I awoke from a nap. Jaja was perched in the dodger with her head resting on her forearm. Her index finger was hooked through the handle of a mug of tea. She lifted her head and took a sip. Apparently the warm liquid revived her. She sat up straight and spent a solid minute scanning the horizon through the dodger's clear plastic windows. Satisfied that there were no dangers, she put her head back on her forearm.

The pristine light filling the cabin indicated a clear, blue sky. *Driver*'s motion was less intense, and the wind sounded as if it had moderated. I got up very slowly. My sore spine felt as if it were made of glass.

Jaja sensed my movement. "The wind is dying down by the minute," she said, dully. "And the clouds are starting to evaporate. It's turning into a beautiful morning."

"Want to get some sleep?"

Moments later, Jaja stretched out on the settee. I made a cup of coffee. What a night. The GPS indicated that we were 40 miles from Hornsund Fjord. We hadn't made a great deal of progress in seven hours. But at least we hadn't lost ground.

The coffee gave me strength. I went on deck to face the chilly morning sun. Moving cautiously, I untied the lashings holding the jib and hoisted the sail. *Driver* took off like a horse escaping through an open stable door. I relished the renewed, lively motion. Later, I shook a reef out of the mainsail and checked our compass course. It was a happy moment when I finally threw the helm hard over and tacked the boat back toward the coast of Spitsbergen. I trimmed the sails and watched our speed increase to about 5 1/2 knots. We were still sailing as close to the eye of the wind as *Driver* would go, but thankfully, we were right on course for Hornsund Fjord. My good humor returned as I anticipated landfall that same afternoon.

The day before, we had searched in vain through the murk for signs of land–even though Sørkapp was less than 15 miles away. Today, we gazed around us in awe. To the east toward the coast, the dark blue sea and sky were split by a line of jagged white mountains that trailed off to the north. Turquoise ice betrayed the existence of glaciers.

The clear air amplified my senses. I felt a tangible connection to our position on the earth's surface. The charts and the GPS indicated our geographical placement, but I actually *felt* our remote latitude. We were nearly on the top of our planet, high above the rest of humanity, looking down on world events.

My senses were also skewed in another way. Less than 10 miles to the north, I saw several steep islands where our navigation chart indicated empty sea. I panicked. Were they icebergs? Or had I made a crucial error in navigation? I double-checked our GPS position, and I asked Jaja, who was preparing breakfast, to come on deck and look.

We stared to windward uncertainly. Where were we? It took many minutes of checking before I allowed myself to believe that these were not nearby islands or icebergs, but rather mountains 50 miles away at the entrance to Bellsund Fjord. The bases of the mountains were far below the horizon, but the crystal-clear atmosphere created a grand illusion. Without dust or moisture in the air, the normal parameters of depth perception did not apply. Faraway things appeared within arm's reach. Even gazing at *Driver*'s decks and rigging was bizarre. The distance to the top of the mast, which is 39 feet off the deck, contradicted my visual ruler. It looked as if I could touch the masthead. Wavelets near the hull sparkled falsely, and the cloth of the sails looked magnified. Salt crystals scattered over the entire boat twinkled like finely cut gems.

The kids came on deck after breakfast and watched as we approached the coast. It was the first time in four days they had left the cabin. They soaked up the thin sunlight and spoke very little. This had been a rough passage; everyone was exhausted. We needed a solid night of sleep.

AS WE APPROACHED the five-mile-wide mouth of Hornsund Fjord, all three kids stood up in the cockpit to get a better view. Spray exploded on the rocky beaches, and the snow looked rich and creamy. The kids' queasy stomachs had long ago settled.

"I wish we could get ice cream," said Holly dreamily.

"I know," Jaja said. "But we can't buy anything for another week or so, not until we arrive at Longyearbyen. Maybe we can make snow cones instead."

At the Hornsund Fjord entrance, a tide rip made *Driver* dance wildly. After the recent conditions at sea, however, our stomachs remained unfazed by this mere, inshore nuisance. I could see smooth water ahead. "Sit tight," I told everyone. "The ride will be over soon."

When we reached the end of the rough water, I looked at my watch–5:00 p.m. We had been at sea for exactly four days, three hours.

Maybe it was the clear atmosphere, maybe it was the release of tension, or maybe it was just plain fatigue–but everything seemed surreal. Unbelievably, we were cruising at 77 degrees, zero minutes north latitude, bound for a place called Isbjørnhamna (Polar Bear Bay). We would anchor in about 45 minutes. I was exhausted, hungry, and tingling all over. The passage from Norway had tested our stamina to the limit.

The wind began sputtering in ragged gusts, then dropped completely. For the first time since leaving the fuel dock in Honningsvåg, *Driver* moved with a relatively gentle motion. Spitsbergen lay calmly before us–a panorama of snow-covered mountains, glacial snouts that nosed into the fjord, and masses of sea birds.

I fired up the engine, and we motored peacefully into the vast scenery. Ahead of us, a rocky spit of land jutted out a quarter mile. We could anchor behind the spit and be protected from the surge and low waves that were carrying *Driver* into the fjord. Then, in what seemed like an instant, clouds gathered in the mountains, and snow flurries reduced our visibility to a few hundred yards. We weren't there yet.

The girls stood on the foredeck with Jaja, who was trying to spot underwater hazards. Chris sat on his bosun's chair. The kids, chatting excitedly about the snow, filled the air with innocent noise. I begged them to be silent. I was exhausted and needed all my faculties to judge the relationships between the navigation chart and the rocky foreshore. After viewing the distant horizon for four days, the land looked deceivingly close. It felt as if we were almost on the beach, but we were probably much farther away that it appeared.

I monitored the readout on the depth sounder, trying to match the displayed water depths to the depths printed on the chart. This would help us pinpoint our position. In particular, I wanted to locate two submerged rocks in the bay without hitting them first.

I adjusted the throttle nearly to idle, which gave us just enough power to make headway. Suddenly, Jaja spun around and hollered, "Dave! Reverse! Quick! Submerged rock ahead."

I put the engine in reverse, and *Driver* stopped immediately without grounding. Good. Having located one of the rocks, we knew our position and the relative positions of both rocks. We jockeyed away from the underwater hazards, and Jaja let the anchor rattle overboard. I shut off the engine. The only sound came from gentle surf breaking on the end of the rocky point. We had found shelter for the night.

Snow drifted down steadily. With one last look around, we dived below to the warm cabin–our haven and cocoon at 77 degrees north.

Jaja and I toasted our arrival with a shot of Drambuie. Chris, Holly, and Teiga slurped hot chocolate.

"Spitsbergen," I said dreamily as my eyes closed and I fell into a deep sleep.

Chapter Eighteen

Paradise doesn't have to be warm.

*T*HE NEXT MORNING IN HORNSUND FJORD, I felt drugged with exhaustion. I stumbled out of bed, put the kettle on, and glanced out of the dodger to check the anchorage. Then I crawled back under the covers. Chris was awake. I could hear him punching buttons on his tape deck and untangling the cord to his headphones. Usually, he was the first to fall sleep at night and the first to wake up. But he liked to hang out in bed until the entire family was up and dressed. Holly was a night owl and often read into the wee hours. It took repeated prodding to rouse her in the morning.

Teiga fit somewhere in between. She had her own bunk, located below Holly's, but she usually slept with Jaja and me in the V-berth. I looked at Teiga. She was on her back with one leg resting on the gun case. The three of us slept like spoons laid side by side in a drawer. One of the most difficult transitions to boat life after living in our rented house was getting used to the cramped, V-shaped berth in *Driver*'s bow. Now, however, we had forgotten what it was like to sleep in a rectangular bed. In the Tropics, where it's hot and humid, sleeping in a cramped bed can be miserable. In cold latitudes, Jaja and I welcomed the coziness and huddled together for warmth.

We each drank two cups of coffee while we lay in bed, propped on our elbows. The passage to Spitsbergen had been tiring, and the simple act of lying still was irresistible. As the morning progressed, we resumed our normal pace. Jaja hung the kids' clothes on a line over the stove to warm up, and heated a kettle of water for oatmeal. As soon as the kids were eating, Jaja began to make a ginger cake.

Two hours later, the dishes were clean, the cabin was tidy, and the kids were dressed for the frosty conditions outside. Ashore in Isbjørnhamna was a research facility operated by the Polish government. Sailors we had met in Norway said it was a treat to visit the scientists and say hello. The cake was for them.

We loaded a daypack, launched the dinghy, and straightened a few lines on deck. Then we resigned ourselves to the inevitable task–taking the gun out of its case. Although the Highlander had been on board for two weeks, we had not yet even looked at it. Once or twice during the passage, we considered shooting the gun, but either the sea was too lumpy, or we were too tired. The time for familiarization had arrived. There were no more excuses.

Jaja tried first. Ever since that significant day in Tromsø when we acquired the rifle, the gun had become our bedmate in the V-berth. (We had no other place to stow it.) Jaja said she would defend the family. She opened the case, lifted the oiled rifle, and placed a shiny, finger-size brass cartridge into the chamber. Next, she braced herself against the backstay. With the gun on her shoulder, she took aim across the three-mile-wide fjord. There wasn't a soul in sight.

Holly, Teiga, and Chris were giggling excitedly. "Ready?" Jaja asked. The kids stuck their fingers in their ears. I watched Jaja's finger tighten on the trigger. BANG! The sound was explosive. A coil of smoke drifted on the slight breeze. The grin on Jaja's face betrayed her attempt at macho nonchalance.

"Cool, Dave. Want to try it?"

Soon after, we boarded the dinghy and headed for shore. Holding the rifle, I felt like a commando while Jaja rowed. I also felt a little ridiculous. It was difficult to take the threat of bears seriously–a result, no doubt, of watching too many Disney movies.

The beach was steep, comprised of round stones about the size of tennis balls. Grounded ice chunks–some as big as the dinghy–adorned the beach. Jaja landed between two mini-bergs. An important consideration when cruising in cold climates is the height of your rubber boots: They should be higher than the draft of your dinghy. When the bow nudged the bottom, Jaja and I stepped into the water on either side. The tops of our knee-high boots remained six inches above water level–enough to keep from filling.

I held the boat steady while Jaja carried the kids to dry land. Together, we dragged the dinghy about 20 feet up the beach–well above the high tide line–and set the anchor firmly. In the Tropics, you might be able to swim and retrieve a drifting dinghy, but in Spitsbergen, swimming in the 36-degree-Fahrenheit water would cause hypothermia in minutes.

THE RESEARCH FACILITY was a flat-topped building with many small windows. Painted blue, it was about the size of a double-width mobile home. Adjoining it was a one-story building with a peaked roof. There were several smaller outbuildings, a dog kennel, a couple of snowmobiles, dozens of rusty oil drums, a flag pole flying the red and white Polish flag, and many antennas poking into the sky. A bearded man wearing khaki pants and a flannel shirt opened the front door. He greeted us warmly in perfect English and welcomed us inside.

Jaja hesitated. "What should I do with my gun?"

As a rule, the scientist explained politely, a visitor should leave his weapon outside or in the entranceway with the bolt open to show that the rifle is disabled.

We followed him inside and shed several layers of clothes in the hall. Sunday brunch was under way in the main room. Our host pressed us to sit and help ourselves to big platters of roast chicken and French fries. Holly's eyes popped when she saw the fries. The eight other scientists beamed happily as we ate. They had been at the station for 11 months, and they welcomed our intrusion. Children were rare visitors.

"Do we really need to carry our gun all the time?" Jaja asked.

"Never, ever walk on shore without it," a young man stated emphatically. His colleagues nodded. "We've already had 86 visits from bears this spring."

As we ate, we asked many questions. The bears generally spend the winter in the eastern regions of Svalbard. During the spring, they drift to the west coast on the receding ice floes searching for seals to eat. Or else, they walk overland for the hunt. At this time of year, they are usually hungry—even starving. The males live solitary lives of hunting and wandering. The females also roam alone but are often accompanied by offspring. Two cubs per litter are the norm, and cubs live with their mothers for two years before striking out on their own. Hornsund is famous for bears. A pass between the mountain ranges leads the bears naturally from their winter habitat to the seal-infested waters of the fjord.

"If I see a bear, how do I know if it will attack?" Jaja asked. "At what point should I decide to shoot?"

"If a bear is closer than 100 feet, it's a threat. Your gun should be loaded and ready to fire. If a bear is sniffing the air, it's probably just curious, so there may be nothing to fear. If a bear approaches with its head low to the ground, swinging its head side to side, it should be considered aggressive. It may be getting ready to charge. If you have time, fire your gun once in the air. The report will often scare the bear away. But reload quickly in case it attacks."

I absorbed the scientist's information with growing apprehension. We had already read about bear attacks in a book called *A Journey to Svalbard,* by Christian Kempf, but it was far more vivid to hear about bears firsthand. Jaja and I frequently discussed what we would do if a bear attacked. The idea of an attack actually happening was terrifying. A male polar bear standing on its hind legs can tower up to nine feet high and weigh well over 1,400 pounds.

Kempf's book failed to cover one issue that interested me. I asked, "Will the flame from an ordinary distress flare–the hand-held variety, not shot from a pistol–scare away bears?"

"No. The flame will just make them curious." One of the men got up from the table. He returned with what looked like a 24-gauge distress flare pistol in one hand, and a fat, silvery shotgun shell in the other. "This is the best deterrent," he explained. "This shell contains a small explosive. You fire it, and the bomb inside travels about 30 feet. A moment later it explodes and scares the bear without causing him injury."

"I really don't want to kill a bear," Jaja said. "Maybe we should get one of those things. It sounds foolproof."

"It's not quite perfect," the scientist warned. "If the bomb travels *beyond* the bear, it might run toward you instead of away. Even if the bomb lands between you and the bear, the sound of the explosion reverberating off rocks and mountains might be confusing. The bear still might run at you. And there's no telling what a scared bear might do once it's headed your way."

"There's no easy solution," I said.

"No. The bears are the masters here. They are fearless. Do not hesitate to kill if you think the threat is real."

HORNSUND FJORD is 15 miles long, with seven active glaciers spilling into it. At the back of the fjord, three of the glaciers join together creating a continuous wall. This wall rims a large, semicircular bay called Brepollen. The glacial wall is hundreds of feet high, and a dozen miles long.

According the scientists, Hornsund Fjord had been locked in the grip of winter ice just three weeks earlier. None of them had ventured down the fjord lately, so they did not know if the water at the back of the bay was open. Apparently, it was not uncommon for Brepollen to be clogged with ice year round. From our anchorage in Isbjørnhamna, all we could see was liquid salt water stretching up the fjord.

It was tempting to laze around all day to fully recover from our recent passage. After all, we had only been anchored for 18 hours. But conditions on the fjord were calm and settled. With the unstable weather patterns in this part of the world, we wanted to make the most of each good day. We raised anchor.

Driver drifted quietly under mainsail and genoa along the south shore of Hornsund. The snow lay like a blanket from the mountain peaks to the water's edge. Puffy, white clouds leaked sunlight, allowing occasional shafts of warmth to meander down and touch our bare faces. Here and there, the same sunbeams zeroed in on a mountain slope creating blinding reflections on the snow.

"Oh!" Holly said. "Look how pretty the mountains are when the bright sun shoots down and hits them!

"Yeah," Chris agreed. "It looks like slow-motion lightning."

Soon the research station was obscured by headlands jutting into the fjord. Except for *Driver,* there were no signs of civilization. We had the entire fjord to ourselves. After a few of hours of slow going, we sighted the glacial wall that defines the back of Brepollen Bay. Too soon, we came to a barrier of fjord ice. The back of the bay was still four miles away. End of the road; there was no going farther. But it didn't matter. The wind had dropped to zero, and the fjord's surface was mirrorlike. We parked *Driver* alongside a two-foot-thick slab of floating ice as if it were a dock.

Nearby, a 1,400-foot-high rock pinnacle called Bautaen rose out of the frozen slopes. Ring seals lounged like couch potatoes on the ice, and sea birds swarmed in clouds. We had read that there were millions of birds in Spitsbergen. If we had ever thought the number was exaggerated, we believed it now. Fulmars and kittiwakes soared majestically, while auks, puffins, and guillemots flapped clumsily. Nature filled our souls with priceless riches. We took off our coats and drank coffee and hot chocolate in the dry cockpit.

We felt humble–meager compared to the vast scenery surrounding us. I thought of the noise and pollution in major cities where man reigns supreme. In cities, the ground is covered with pavement. Tall buildings block the sky, and laws, which protect humans from other humans, are necessary. Here in Spitsbergen, nature rules. Acts of stupidity or inattentiveness can extract high penalties. It made me wonder why "civilized" man feels impelled to act in a way that requires a manufactured system of authority. When civilization supplants nature, artificial laws displace natural ones.

As WE PREPARED to cast off from our ice "dock" and return to the anchorage near the research station, I spotted a polar bear strolling on the ice. It was heading right for us. Then Jaja spotted two more bears that were smaller than the first and the same size as each other.

"I bet the big bear is the mother," Jaja said, "and the others are her cubs."

I turned on the engine and powered away from the ice floe. If we hadn't been paying attention, the bears could have walked on the ice right up to *Driver* and caused havoc on deck. I filed this valuable lesson in my memory bank.

Mother bear jumped into the water and began swimming towards us. Feeling somewhat safer in open water, we slowed down the boat to get a closer look.

I was taking pictures wildly.

Jaja was calm. "I'd better get the gun, just to be on the safe side."

She went below, removed the gun from its case, placed a bullet into the empty chamber, and set the gun upright, like a fishing pole, against the stern rail. I increased the engine RPMs to hold us at an even distance from the bears that were swimming at a speed of about one knot. We told the kids to move away from the rail and stand next to the dodger. The largest white beast continued to swim after us. Our dinghy was trailing behind *Driver*, and the bear was dog-paddling 15 feet aft of the dinghy, trying to paw it. Before long, the two cubs hit the water to join in the pursuit.

Chris said, "Daddy? What if the engine stops?"

Valid point. If it did, we'd be sitting ducks for the bears. There was no wind for sailing.

Chris continued to vocalize my thoughts. "Do you think a bear could climb on deck from the water?"

Another good question. Jaja and I exchanged glances.

The bears were swimming after us energetically, lifting up their heads and growling. They were apparently hungry.

"Go get a seal!" Teiga said.

The two small bears growled in unison.

"I think they understood you," Jaja said in jest. "Their growls meant, 'small children taste better.'"

"Mommy..."

After studying the bears for 10 minutes, we motored away reluctantly. We felt we were teasing them by staying just out of reach. As the distance between us widened, the bears finally gave up the chase and swam back to the ice. Then each one completed an extraordinarily smooth, powerful leap onto the floe. Effortless.

"Wow!" Chris spoke for all us. "Did you see that?"

The three bears shook themselves like dogs and staggered off to hunt something else.

On the way back to the research station, we made a detour into Burgerbukta, a narrow bay about three miles long. On the chart it looked like a capitol Y. In the two prongs of the Y, which were each a mile long and a half-mile wide, glaciers oozed out of the high mountains into the water. We approached the eastern prong to see how close we could get to the front wall of the glacier. Although we could see the wall clearly from a distance, we wanted to get nearer. Glaciers are like works of art in an immense, outdoor gallery. In a regular art gallery, it's natural to want to poke your nose up close to a painting or a sculpture to feel the power of the artist's imagination. Likewise, we were drawn to the glacier because we wanted to experience such a gigantic creation up close.

Most of the glaciers in Hornsund were active, and their ragged, seaward edges were an unreal aquamarine color. It looked as if blue prehistoric skies had been released after being trapped for eons.

"Why is the ice blue?" Holly asked,

"Red and yellow light have long wavelengths, so they pass through the dense ice easily," Jaja explained. "Blue light has shorter wavelengths, and it gets trapped, scattered, and reflected back. The ice is actually very, very, clear. It just reflects blue light the easiest."

"The same as the sky," Chris said, looking up.

Jaja smiled. "Right!"

The sky was now cloudless, and the sun was shining above the mountains. It looked and felt like early afternoon. The sun's location due north of us and our level of fatigue were the only indications of the late hour. Energized by our surroundings and by the perpetual light, we had been running in high gear all day. Now we needed a quiet night's rest. At midnight, we dropped anchor again in Isbjørnhamna.

A light breeze had begun to blow from the northeast causing a slight chop in the anchorage. *Driver*'s stern swung toward shore–not a good situation. If the wind increased and caused our anchor to drag, *Driver* might drift onto the rocky beach before we could do anything about it. We considered standing anchor watches–taking turns staying awake to be sure conditions didn't deteriorate. But after a quick meal, Jaja and I were too exhausted.

Sleep devoured us within minutes.

I WAS AWAKENED BY ICE banging against the hull–a noise that had become familiar during our winter in Akureyri. The wind had increased slightly, and *Driver*'s bow was pitching up and down. I didn't want to get up, but I thought it wise to look outside. I reached over and picked up my watch, which was lying on the chart table: 4:30 a.m. I crawled out of bed, walked barefoot across the chilly cabin sole, and climbed into the warm dodger. My eyes felt scratchy.

On deck, the morning sun filled the world with electrified brilliance, and the wavelets blinked like strobe lights. As my eyes adjusted to the glare, I noticed that the wind direction had veered about 30 degrees. Earlier, a cluster of rocks about a half-mile away had been acting as a sort of breakwater. Now, the wind blew directly from the fjord into our anchorage.

A vein of calf ice–ice that had broken, or "calved," off the glacier–was drifting though the anchorage. Most of the pieces were football-size and posed no threat to our hull. However, I soon became aware of a more serious danger. A huge piece of ice about the size of a steel shipping container was drifting straight down on us. A collision was imminent. I jumped below and dressed–wool socks, long underwear, sweater, one-piece suit, hat, gloves, and boots.

I darted aft and grabbed an oar from the dinghy that was floating astern of *Driver*. I ran to the bow and stood with the oar, poised like a whaler holding a harpoon. Ten seconds later, I jammed the oar against the ice block to try to push it away from *Driver*'s bow. I might as well have been pushing against a concrete wall. The weighty chunk was mostly awash, and all I did was move *Driver* aside. I held the oar against the ice and slowly walked aft on deck to make sure the ice didn't bang the hull or damage the propeller. I watched it drift astern toward the beach. Before I could return to the foredeck, *Driver*'s pitching bow came down hard on a tree-trunk-size piece. The impact the ice sent shuddering reverberations through the hull and into the rigging. I pushed the offender aside. I looked forward. More big pieces were coming. We had to reanchor quickly. The next big ice chunk would reach us in only three or four minutes.

There was an unsurveyed anchorage about two miles away that looked like it would provide better shelter from the new wind direction and the drifting ice. I started the engine. Jaja was already dressed for action, and she bounded on deck to grind up the anchor chain. I found the page in John Armitage's *Norwegian Cruising Guide* that describes the anchorage. Before we sailed to Spitsbergen, I had read the book cover to cover. Now I reread the instructions for entering this bay, then went on deck to take the helm.

The wind was rising. I was positive an easterly gale was brewing. We had read about the vicious winds created when a relatively warm, dry, easterly airflow blows over the frosty glaciers in Spitsbergen. Once this wind starts, it creates a strong venturi in the mountains. We needed to reanchor quickly. It might be blowing 50 knots in less than an hour.

A half-hour later, we cautiously approached the 500-foot-wide, unsurveyed lagoon called Antonio Pigafettahamna, which John Armitage had nicknamed "Antonio's." Less than a mile from Antonio's, the towering ice-wall of Hansbreen Glacier dominated the view. The wall was ragged, like the side of a block of cheese that had been broken in half. In recent years, the Hansbreen Glacier had receded considerably, exposing this new bay. The lagoon was protected by a rocky spit–a glacial moraine that arched gracefully out from shore. I looked at the shore; it was lined with rocks. According to the guide, after entering the bay, we should proceed cautiously in dead center.

Jaja stood on the bow acting as lookout while I held the tiller and kept an eye glued to the depthsounder. "I can see bottom," she hollered over the rising wind. "What's the depth?"

"Twelve feet." I answered.

We motored slowly into the lagoon. To our right, perched on the narrow moraine-peninsula, at least a thousand arctic terns squawked and bickered. They were hunkered down practically on top of each other. Then, for reasons we could not detect, they all took flight. A mass of gray, black, and white feathers filled the air, as if the land beneath the birds had exploded. The flock circled the anchorage once, returned to their guano-covered rocks, and landed with raucous squeals.

A fresh gust of wind, stronger than all the previous ones, whistled across *Driver*'s deck. Even though we had no sails up, *Driver* heeled slightly, and I could feel the boat slow down almost to a stop. I increased the engine RPMs to help maintain headway and to prevent us from losing steerage.

"It's looking shallow," Jaja observed.

"We're down to 10 feet." The best protection in the lagoon was all the way to the rear of the bay. I knew the tide was dead low, so I decided we would anchor when the depth reached eight feet. *Driver*'s draft was six feet. That would give us two feet to spare at low water.

I looked at the depthsounder. Eight feet. We were three quarters of the way into the bay. This seemed good enough. I pushed the helm over slowly. As *Driver* turned into the eye of the wind, I made some mental calculations. At high tide, the depth would be nearly 12 feet. With five-to-one scope on the anchor chain, we would need to let out 60 feet. That meant our total swinging diameter was 120 feet, or roughly four boatlengths. I steered *Driver* straight for the eastern shoreline.

"Rocks ahead, Dave."

I threw the tiller hard over. *Driver* turned on a dime, and I steered a reciprocal course back toward the western shore. The steady 25-plus-knot wind from dead astern pushed us along rapidly. I watched the depthsounder: Steady at eight feet. I sighted a spot on the water's surface near *Driver*'s bow and kept my eye on it until that same spot was even with our stern. The distance equaled roughly one boatlength.

We had covered 10 boatlengths when Jaja hollered, "Underwater rocks! Turn!"

I spun *Driver* around. When I was certain we were exactly halfway between each rocky shoreline (about five boatlengths), and far enough away from the back of the lagoon, I signaled for Jaja to let the anchor go. The chain thumped and rattled, then played out smoothly. When 60 feet of chain had gone out, Jaja locked the windlass. With the engine in neutral, the wind pushed *Driver* back quickly.

Jaja placed her booted foot on the chain that lay between the anchor windlass and the bow roller. From experience, she could determine the nature of the bottom from the signals the chain "telegraphed" back as it stretched out on the seabed.

"Feels like hard sand," Jaja said. The wind was still pushing us back. *Driver*'s bow began to turn slowly into the eye of the wind. All at once, the bow snapped to attention, and the chain became rigid. The anchor had dug in. Then the chain gently relaxed again and hung in a graceful arc from the bow into the depths.

"It seems like a good bottom," Jaja said. "The anchor went in easily, and the chain didn't jerk or skip." When either of those things happen, it usually means the anchor is fouled on big rocks, or is unable to penetrate a gravelly or weedy bottom. At that point, the only safe action is to pull up the anchor and try again.

I turned off the engine just as the wind increased a notch and whistled even more shrilly in the rigging. The sky was dark blue without a cloud to challenge the cobalt expanse. The terns still roosted on the rocks not far behind us; we could see their feathers ruffling in the wind. Beyond the birds, out toward the fjord's entrance, the horizon was a crisp line. Sky and water. Whitecaps marched down the main body of the fjord to the open sea like sheep headed for an open pasture.

"Luck is on our side," I said, as soon as we had gone below to thaw our frozen ears and chilled hands. "Imagine trying to make a landfall today. We would have never made it into the fjord with this wind."

Jaja and I wanted to go back to bed, but the kids were ready to get up. The early morning anchoring drill had finally roused them.

"Are you sure you guys don't want to sleep longer?" I asked.

"No," Chris chirped. "We want to get up and play.

Jaja said to me, "I'm awake anyway, Dave. Why don't you try to rest a little?"

As I crawled in the V-berth, my bones felt as if they were crumbling. Another lesson learned: Don't let ourselves reach the breaking point unless *Driver* is in an absolutely safe anchorage. We were exhausted, partly because we had pushed too hard the previous day. It was exciting to be in Spitsbergen, but we had acted like kids, unable to control our desire to explore. Looking back, we should have anchored in Antonio's the previous night, instead of returning to Isbjørnhamna. The idea had crossed my mind at the time, but it was late, and we were too tired. I had judged it unsafe to enter the uncharted bay. Unfortunately, the weather had deteriorated quickly.

Antonio's is nearly landlocked, providing the foolproof protection we needed–both mentally and physically. The bay is shaped like a letter C, and the wind was blowing from the beach in the curve of the C straight out the opening. No ice could drift into the bay against the force of the 35-knot wind. I relaxed, knowing that we would be safe from ice. Let the gale rage.

IT WAS IMPORTANT to understand the "tariffs" we would be charged at each new place and to be ready to pay the going rate. We needed to avoid reaching a state of exhaustion. Because of the continuous presence of the sun, it was easy to go nonstop in Spitsbergen and to forget about sleeping. We had to be more aware of our fatigue and try to get sufficient rest. Otherwise, our judgment was likely to be affected. I thought about the coming weeks. Would we be able to pay the toll and get enough sleep? If we could, I had a feeling we were going to get our money's worth.

Jaja and I travel the world to experience the unique energy of each new locale. In the Tropics, where the constant heat can frazzle your brain, it was important to seek shade. In Iceland and the Faroes, where the tide rips tested our endurance, it was crucial to use the tide and current tables and move accordingly. Cruising in Spitsbergen was like being on an ocean passage. We could never "turn off." Therefore, it was imperative that we pace our activities and save our energy for emergencies.

We holed up for three days while the unforecasted easterly gale surged down the fjord. The sky remained deep blue, and the dazzling sun tracked overhead, never obscured by mountains or clouds. Even at its lowest point around midnight, the sun remained more than 10 degrees above the horizon. Without darkness to bookend the days, time felt pleasantly endless. An arctic summer "high" infiltrated our souls.

I woke up early on the third day at Antonio's and found Jaja sitting in the galley reading. "Have you been up long?" I asked.

"All night. I couldn't sleep; it's so bright. After tossing and turning for what seemed like eternity, I just got up. But it's all right; the anchorage is safe. I'll probably be tired enough to sleep tonight. But right now I don't feel the slightest fatigue." In his book on Svalbard, Christian Kempf stated that many people went days without sleep, then "caught up" when they needed to.

We walked ashore at Antonio's on full alert, keenly aware of the risk from bears. It was difficult not to feel apprehensive. The gun slung over Jaja's shoulder meant business. The moraine peninsula was hilly with plenty of recesses in which bears could hide. Whenever a ridge rose in front of us, Jaja walked alone with the gun ready for action. Would she find a bear? Once we tried to relax in the lee of some warm rocks to absorb the sun's rays, but it was nerve racking. We couldn't "turn off" and sit inattentively. The snow that bordered the Hansbreen Glacier was crisscrossed with fresh polar bear tracks. The pawprints were big and round–about the size of Frisbees–and they were deep.

We first encountered dangerous animals while cruising on Australia's northern coast in 1994. In the Wessel Islands, near the Gulf of Carpentaria, we saw more crocodile tracks in the sand than we could conceivably photograph. One day, we saw a 15-footer basking on some rocks 100 yards from where Chris and Holly had been beachcombing. Some might argue that sharks should be included in the "dangerous animal" category. But crocodiles and polar bears occupy a unique niche in nature. They can attack from the water while you row a dinghy, then chase you up the beach and finish you off. In comparison, the capabilities of sharks are very limited.

Polar bears have claws as sharp as kitchen knives, and they can run up to 24 miles per hour. With only one gun to defend five people, we felt vulnerable. Yet our summer would be ruined if we were seized by fear every time we stepped into the dinghy. Relax, we reminded ourselves. Just relax. We have the gun. If we keep a good lookout, there's no need to be anxious.

To help us feel more comfortable with the gun, I set up watermelon-sized hunks of ice as targets. I balanced one on a beached growler, paced off 80 feet, and scuffed a line in the sand with my boot. Jaja stood, and took aim. On her first try she blasted the ice into a shower of crystals.

The kids cheered and clapped. "Hooray, Mommy!"

I set up another chunk and fired with similar results.

"Hooray, Daddy!"

Subtracting the bullet Jaja had fired previously and the two just fired, we had 17 shells left. Satisfied that we could hit a stationary bear at 80 paces, it seemed best to save our bullets for a real emergency. The gun held five shells, and I carried the rest in a box in my pack. Twenty cartridges seemed like more than enough back in Tromsø. Now I wished I had bought more.

THE SUMMER SOLSTICE on June 21st dawned foggy with drizzle and zero wind. Jaja and I woke before the kids, warmed up the engine, ground the anchor aboard, and motored out of Hornsund Fjord. We used the radar as our "eyes."

Visibility was about a half-mile, enough to spot any ice in *Driver*'s path. Our destination was Bellsund Fjord, about 60 miles north. It was time to make some miles up the coast while the conditions were mild. Hopefully, the wind would come up later so we could sail. Until then, we would use the engine.

I reflected on the winter solstice exactly six months earlier. We had stood near the Fishermen's Wife at noon on December 21st looking southward. The sun was well below the horizon, but it created a pale glow low in the sky. The winter solstice in Svolvær was symbolic. From that moment forward, every day would bring the town closer to the return of the sun–and the thrill of perpetual light.

In Spitsbergen, we were disappointed by the suffocating, gray sky. I wanted to view the sun at midnight on June 21st. The solstice marked the apex of summer illumination–the pot of gold in the cycle of light. In Svolvær, the summer solstice was a day of celebration and bonfires–barbecues and beer shared with friends. The continuous light was a sensation worth waiting for. In Spitsbergen, we still had 18 hours before midnight. The weather could easily change before then.

While we were anchored at Antonio's, the never-ending light pouring into the cabin continued to knock our sleeping habits out of kilter. At the end of our ocean passage to Iceland, we arrived in Reykjavik during high summer. There were long hours of daylight, similar to what we were now experiencing in Svalbard. In Iceland, however, the rhythms and man-made timetables of the cities and towns kept us moving within a logical time framework. Now, without "civilization" to impose structure in our lives, we were defenseless against time. Our circadian rhythms rebelled. In the end, we discovered it was best to ignore the clock completely and to sleep and eat when we felt like it. None of us were tired until long past midnight. The kids went to bed at 2:00 a.m., or 3:00 a.m., and got up at noon. Some days we ate breakfast at 1:00 p.m., fed the kids dinner at midnight, and went for a walk at 2:00 a.m.

Jaja and I tried to catch at least six hours of continuous sleep in each 24-hour "day." Usually, we dozed at different times. This was a good arrangement because one of us could always keep an eye on the weather and ice conditions. We removed our wristwatches and moved with the flow of arctic light. We listened to our bodies. When I woke to the foggy day in Hornsund, it was almost a relief. The subdued light in the cabin matched the clock exactly: 7:00 a.m. I wanted to get going "early" to make the most of the calm conditions.

THE SAFEST ROUTE north to Bellsund Fjord was at least five miles offshore to avoid an extensive network of shoals and coastal reefs. One foul area jutted several miles to seaward off the Torrelbreen Glacier. When we reached the southern extremity of these reefs, the fog lifted revealing a textured, cloudy sky. We caught a glimpse of the glacier, an ancient beauty with an ice wall seven miles long. Intense, bluish light reflected off the glacier, illuminating the clouds directly above it.

The glacier called for a closer look. In the few short days since our arrival, we had become mesmerized by these monumental tongues of ice licking the sea. An art aficionado will prowl through galleries. We prowled around glaciers as close as safety would allow. We had become addicted to the unique beauty of each ice wall and to the feelings they conjured up in us. We drew energy from them–and an appreciation of the power of nature.

Even though it meant traveling inside the reef system, we decided to sail close to Torrelbreen. We wanted to examine every glacier in our path while we had the chance. Anything can happen during a high-latitude sailing adventure. Any number of things might cause us to cut our cruise short. Reaching 80 degrees north latitude was not a given. Just making it through each day was an achievement in itself. The thought that we might have to head back to the Norwegian coast earlier than planned–for whatever reason– always lurked in the back of our minds. This might be our last chance to sail next to a glacier.

Back in 1991, when Jaja was 7 1/2 months pregnant with Holly, we drove a friend's car around the South Island of New Zealand. We stopped at Franz Joseph Glacier on the island's southwest coast. From the parking lot, we could see the glacier about two miles away. The ribbon of gray and white ice tinged with blue looked like a dam break–or a monstrous flash flood–frozen in place. Within the solidified "river," we could see "eddies," "rapids," and "pools."

Jaja said, "It's like looking at a tornado that has suddenly frozen in mid-spin."

"Up for a hike?" I asked. Jaja's stomach was as round as a spinnaker billowing in the wind.

She laughed."I wouldn't miss the opportunity for anything. I want to look at the ice close-up. Who knows when we might get another chance to walk to a glacier?"

With 16-month-old Chris sitting in a babypack high on my shoulders, I set out with Jaja. We walked, and walked, and walked; the glacier got bigger, and bigger, and bigger. Finally, we reached a row of signs that warned tourists to stay at least 100 yards away from the dangerous ice wall. Four hikers, who had ignored the signs, were casually eating lunch about 10 feet away from the edge of the sleeping giant. The glacier rumbled–a sound that might have come from the stomach of a monster. When the glacier belched, the hikers abandoned their gear and bolted for safety, arms and legs flailing. I expected ice chunks to begin falling, but this time, nothing rained down. We were mesmerized by the wall of blue, translucent ice. It was all we could do pull ourselves away and hike back to the car.

Now it was Spitsbergen's Torrelbreen Glacier that called to us: "I'm unique! Come and see my beautiful colors and textures!"

IN ROUGH CONDITIONS, it would have been foolish to travel inshore of the reefs to see this icy marvel. Today, however, the sea was as flat as English ale. The calm wind and sea also created a sensation of eternity. We felt as if we were living inside an ancient black and white photograph. The magnetism of the ice warped our sense of judgment and pulled us in. We moved forward as if in a trance.

We closed on the glacier and began moving parallel to it about a mile off. Then, out of nowhere, the mist descended again, obliterating our view.

I laughed. "What a gyp!"

Our emotional high deflated as we continued along the now-invisible ice wall toward the northern end of the reefs. Next, we had to cut across a vast shoal between the reefs and a low headland called Cape Borthen. We weren't worried. The wind and sea were calm, providing ideal weather conditions for rounding the jutting landmass. Our chart indicated a steady 30-foot depth in the area.

Suddenly, we found ourselves moving over an underwater "minefield" of rocks, many of which were covered by about 10 feet of water. We still had about four feet of water under the keel, which is technically satisfactory. But what if there were other rocks with even less water covering them? Would we hit one?

Watching the display on the depthsounder became excruciating. The depth would trend deeper, deeper, deeper, filling me with hope. Then the depth would rise, rise, rise as we passed over another group of rocks. Reality kept coming back like bad checks bounced at a savings bank.

Jaja stood on the bow staring into the water's depths hoping to spot the shallow rocks. The cloudy skies cast a diffused glare, and glacial runoff made the water milky. Visibility below the surface was practically nil, but it was imperative to try to see the hazards.

Our Norwegian charts were "new," but they had originally been drawn using line-of-sight aerial photos and triangulation techniques. The most recent survey had been done 30 years earlier, before satellite navigation. Although the charts gave a fairly precise representation of the coast, the latitude and longitude lines printed on the chart were not as accurate as the fixes provided by our GPS receiver. Also printed on the chart, however, were conversion calculations that allowed mariners to accurately transfer GPS-derived positions to the inaccurate chart. After I added the necessary corrections, and plotted our course on the chart, I switched on the radar to double-check that everything agreed.

We should have been in deep water–but we weren't. So, either the charted depths had changed, or they had never been dependable to begin with. Icebergs were known to scrape the sea bottom, roll rocks around, and tip them on edge. A thumping dose of fear made my throat constrict. We were supposed to be in deep water, but here we were over reefs. I sat in the cockpit with my eyes glued to the depthsounder and my tongue glued to the roof of my mouth. Backtracking around the extensive reef system would cost 15 miles and about three hours. Instead, we motored slowly over the two-mile-wide bank.

Low and unimpressive, Cape Borthen was passive. Nevertheless, it was another headland to round. If we ran aground, we would be stuck. A sudden change of weather could send breaking waves over the shallow waters in minutes. We would be shipwrecked two miles from shore amid boiling surf and hidden rocks.

These morbid thoughts infiltrated my consciousness about halfway across the shoal. At that point, I knew that going forward or returning both presented about the same risks. Going back was "the known," but only by comparison. Maybe we had narrowly missed some rocks that we would hit on the way back. Going forward was "the unknown." There were sure to be additional rocks, but maybe not as many as we had passed so far. We pressed on, motoring slowly at about 2 knots. I felt like a dummy for not turning back earlier when we still had the chance.

Whenever the numbers on the depthsounder jumped from the 30s to the single digits, I took the engine out of gear and let us drift over the invisible, underwater hazard.

"We're in eight feet of water, Jaja. Do you see anything?"

"No. Just green murk."

Only two feet of water under the keel. Too close for comfort. As soon as the depth increased, I slipped the engine back into gear. For five seconds, the depthsounder read 8 feet...9...8...8...then it shot up to 15...18... 25...32. Should we motor at higher speed to get over the shoal more quickly? Or was it better to play it safe, go more slowly, and drag out the unknown?

The numbers on the depth display began shrinking again.

"Jaja, it's getting shallow again. Anything?'

"No."

I watched the sounder: 21...17...12...9...7...7...7. One foot to spare. My heart was imitating the beat of a very bad rock-and-roll CD. I took the engine out of gear.

"Can't you see anything?"

"No."

"Damn this murky water!" The minutes hung like suspended beams of sunlight in a dusty room. I could see time stretching out before me. Interminable.

In tropical latitudes, where the water is often crystal clear, it's possible to spot reefs if the quality of the light is good. At high noon, you can often "read" the bottom as if road signs are pointing the way. On the Norwegian coast, the reefs are almost all marked with metal poles. Here in Spitsbergen, the water was "unreadable," and the reefs were unmarked. Our electronic depthsounder was our only link to safety.

After 15 agonizing minutes, the depth plummeted: 35 feet...41...56...70...86...108. Finally, we had made it off the shoal into deeper water! I breathed a sigh of relief, hollered for Jaja to come back into the cockpit, and increased the engine RPMs to 2400. I watched the readout on the electronic boatspeed indicator climb to our normal cruising speed under power–5.5 knots.

Then, like a tease, the depth jumped up to 35 feet. I jammed the engine into reverse. *Driver* stopped dead in her tracks. I slipped the engine back into gear, and we motored slowly over the shallow place. When the depthsounder showed 100 feet again–which matched the charted depths–we plowed straight out to sea, away from the dangerous coast. It wasn't until we reached the 150-foot depth curve 30 minutes later that we resumed our course northward to Bellsund. Enough was enough.

I set the electronic autopilot for a northerly course and sat down in the cockpit. "Stupid," I said, "is probably a good word to describe our reef excursion."

"How could we possibly guess the chart was inaccurate?" Jaja wondered.

"I don't know. You would think that the chart, plus the GPS–with a radar backup–would equal safety. Even so, we should have turned back. That would have been the safest thing to do." Another lesson to file, I thought to myself.

"It's almost spooky," Jaja said. "It's as if the glacier was singing a siren's song, drawing us in for the kill."

"I felt it too."

I HUNKERED DOWN in the cockpit. The wind increased to 15 knots–square on the nose. The seas were short and steep; the temperature was a raw 38 degrees. *Driver*'s bow pitched up and down, sending occasional bursts of spray aft into the cockpit, splattering my rain gear.

We were motoring directly into the wind. We would just have to grit our teeth and push on to our next anchorage at Rienholmen Island in Bellsund Fjord, 40 miles away. Chris and Holly were awake, but they were semicomatose on the settees. Teiga was very seasick, snuggled in Jaja's comforting arms. Jaja was reading a children's poetry book aloud.

It was a crummy day. I looked at the blurry coast, which was partially obscured by rain. Was I having a good time? Was this the height of fulfillment? Well, not at this exact moment.

I reminded myself that for the past three days, we had enjoyed clear skies and a good anchorage at Antonio's. Now we faced a rigorous passage. Each place had its own set of checks and balances. Even in a tropical paradise, months of warm, perfect weather are followed by a season of destructive hurricanes.

I thought back to the summer of 1992 aboard *Direction*. We were sitting out hurricane season deep in the South Pacific on the island of New Caledonia. On a calm day in January, a warning was broadcast over the radio. A destructive hurricane had intensified and now was heading straight for the island. There wasn't a moment to lose. It was already late afternoon, and we had to move the boat to a protected hurricane anchorage before dark. Powered by our outboard engine, we motored at full speed, 12 miles across the lagoon toward a location we had scouted previously. The hurricane hole was located amongst a maze of shallow, winding creeks protected by mangroves.

Night fell quickly. Suddenly, it was too dark to continue up the unbuoyed, muddy river into the mangroves. We were obliged to stop and anchor in a semiprotected bend of the river, just a mile or so from the sheltered creeks. We were stuck for the night.

We could "feel" the hurricane approaching. Occasional gusts of hot, moist air blew into our open hatches as if a slumbering dragon were exhaling right next to the boat. Unable to sleep in the sweltering cabin, I checked the barometer every hour and watched the needle fall lower and lower. Something big was definitely on the way. I *willed* dawn to arrive so we could move to a safer place, but that only made the night pass more slowly.

Finally, the first rays of light touched the black clouds overhead. While two-year-old Chris and one-year-old Holly slept, Jaja and I quietly raised the anchor. The muddy estuary was full of unmarked shoals, but we conned our way through, keeping a close eye on the depthsounder. A black bruise on the shoulder of the western sky foretold of the dirty weather to come.

The entrance to the narrow creek we had discovered weeks earlier during a trial run appeared on our port side. The creek was 20 feet wide, and the mangroves bordering it reached a height of 15 feet. I turned *Direction* into the slot. Jaja and I scrambled to tie the lines to *Direction*'s cleats and around the bases of the thick mangrove trees. I was securing the last rope when the black sky unloaded all its fury. Seventy-five knot winds shrieked overhead. *Direction* heeled as if her sails were up and filling. Flying branches banged the mast and stuck in the rigging. The rain pounded. All the calm weeks at anchor were quickly being "balanced out" by the tempest. We were paying our dues.

A burst of cold spray flying across *Driver*'s deck woke me from my tropical trance. The weather in Spitsbergen seemed to change hourly. The "good" weather was balanced by the "bad" in an alternating rhythm–like waves rolling in and out on a beach. The uncomfortable conditions we were experiencing would eventually end. We just had to hold on and plunge ahead patiently.

RIENHOLMEN ISLAND was still locked in the grip of winter. Snow extended down from the high mountains to the leftover fjord ice that filled most of the cove. Fortunately, the ice was in the process of breaking up. Two-foot-thick slabs floated through the anchorage, some as small as mattresses, others as large as tennis courts. I steered *Driver* slowly between the slabs searching for a good spot to drop the anchor. The sky was overcast, and patches of mist hung majestically in the mountains, giving the panorama a fake quality like a painted backdrop.

"Daddy, is this where we're going to stop?" Holly asked.

"Yep.

"Hooray! The ice is so pretty."

The anchor splashed down. Another passage was over. The surface of the bay was calm, but the current had sent the loose slabs into silent motion. Many of them crunched by our hull annoyingly, but not dangerously, before drifting down the fjord.

We were all eager to stretch our legs. Before rowing to the beach, I spent five minutes scanning the shoreline with the binoculars, looking for signs of aggressive animals.

"It looks clear," I said.

Except for the kids, who were jumping and sliding in the snow, the only sound came from water running down from the mountains into the bay. Everywhere, small streams flowed rapidly, swollen with snowmelt. I scooped up some of the clear, fresh water in my hands and tasted it. Sweet. Using the dinghy bailer, I filled our five-gallon water jugs to replenish our dwindling onboard supply.

There was absolutely no evidence of civilization. Just nature. We felt privileged to be there. We were time travelers, alone on the planet. This was our version of paradise–one of the reasons why we cruise. It is difficult, especially as parents with three small children, to visit remote places untouched by tourism. Nevertheless, we had been able to experience what felt like untouched paradise in the Outer Hebrides of Scotland, Iceland's Glacier Fjords, and in northern Norway.

As I capped a water jug, Jaja saw a movement in the distance. She told the kids to stand next to the dinghy. They sensed the tension and obeyed instantly.

My heart started racing. I whispered, "What do you see?"

"I saw something white disappear behind that hummock over there."

Jaja raised the gun to her shoulder, took off the safety, and stood ready. I stood in front of Chris, Holly, and Teiga. I held my breath. For a moment, all I could hear was the sound of rushing water and my throbbing pulse. Slowly, the creature meandered over the hill into plain sight. Jaja chuckled wryly, lowered the rifle, and reengaged the safety. The animal was one of the thousands of white furred reindeer that roam the terrain in Spitsbergen searching for plants to eat.

"How's your pulse?" I asked.

She playfully put her finger to her wrist. "Staccato."

I felt keenly alive. My hearing and my sense of smell seemed to be operating at heightened levels. I think we humans often forget that we are animals who have a good track record for assimilating danger and adapting to whatever is happening around us. I may be an intellectual animal with a hundred and one clever tricks for justifying my existence, but underneath my "refined" facade lies animal cunning. We all have it. Con men are like vultures, preying on the unstable. Astute businessmen are ruthless hunters, like the cheetah or the crocodile. Automobile racers are like hummingbirds with lightning fast reactions. Cruising sailors are migratory birds, the wanderers, always moving through the latitudes. In fact, humans–from bums to world leaders–display all types of "animal intellect."

BELOW IN THE CABIN, Jaja read aloud from *Charlotte's Web*, one of my favorite children's stories. E.B. White's portraits of humanlike animals are gentle and calm. I *smelled* the barnyard, *sensed* the languid summer, and *felt* the characters' emotions. The kids also enjoyed White's leisurely prose. They begged for chapter after chapter.

Ice began to bump the hull. I went on deck to investigate and discovered that a semicircular piece, about the size of *Driver*, was caught on our anchor chain. I decided to help it along. Holding tight to the bow pulpit, I jumped onto the floe. It was as stable as a floating concrete dock. Using my feet, I pushed the slab away from the boat–as if I were casting off a dinghy. Then at the last moment, I hopped back aboard *Driver*.

In the distance, a patch of blue sky showed through the murk. I looked at my watch: 11:30 p.m. During the next 20 minutes, I stood transfixed as the sky began to clear. It was uncanny. The clouds weren't drifting away; they were evaporating. Maybe we would see the midnight sun on the solstice after all.

I called the family on deck, hoping the high mountains to the north wouldn't block the sun. First, it showed as a dim splotch in the gray clouds. Then as the clouds thinned, the sun became more defined. Finally, it became so bright that looking at the blinding orb was impossible. At 11:55 p.m., the last of the moisture dissolved overhead leaving a sparkling blue and white world around us.

"Woooooowwww." Holly was awestruck. The midnight sun, shining fiercely in the northern sky, blazed on the water. We could feel the solar energy heating our coats and hats. The ice, which had looked ashen on the sooty bay, now resembled inlaid mother of pearl on turquoise. A flock of male eider ducks flew by, and the sound of their feathers sounded like the whoosh of wind over tall grass.

The clear skies were accompanied by cold, dry air. Despite the warmth of the sun, the entire surface of the bay froze quickly. Suddenly, I had new apprehensions about our safety. I wasn't worried about hull damage; I was worried that the ice might become several inches thick. If ice of this thickness drifted with the tide in one enormous slab, it might take us with it. The boat would become a victim of the ice's wanderings. If the slab drifted over shallow rocks, *Driver* could hit bottom and possibly be damaged if the ice dragged her along. Through the binoculars, I could see that the ice extended more than a mile beyond our anchorage. We would have wait, but be ready to act.

The glowing sun renewed our energy levels. The kids ran on deck and swung from their chairs. They knocked holes in the ice with an oar and fished for cod. Jaja baked cookies. Sunlight poured into the cabin. At 4:00 a.m., we all collapsed. I decided that the surface ice was thin enough that it did not to pose a serious threat.

An hour later, Jaja and I were awakened by an intense scraping sound on the hull. Feeling groggy, I stood on the bow and assessed the situation. The quarter-inch-thick skin of ice was being sucked out of the anchorage by the tide, and it was trying to take *Driver* with it. Fortunately, the anchor chain remained rigid indicating that the anchor was still rooted in the bottom. The chain cut the moving ice slab like a knife, and the bow split it apart like a wedge. This gave the illusion that *Driver* was motoring forward through the ice at about one knot. A band of broken ice and water trailed behind the boat like a wake. It took about 20 minutes for the ice to leave the bay. Before going below, I watched the trailing edge depart. Silently, I praised *Driver's* steel hull and big anchor.

The outside world was blue, white, and silent. It was a shame to sleep during these calm, pristine conditions–a waste of good weather. Then it dawned on me that if nature dealt out rewards for perseverance, we had just been handed bars of gold. The anchorage was now safe for a while, which gave us the chance to recharge our bodies with sleep. I laid my heavy head on my pillow.

THE NEXT AFTERNOON, Jaja showed me Holly's and Chris's journals. Holly had written about the significance of the summer solstice and the beauty of the midnight sun. She finished her entry by quoting me: "…and Daddy told us, 'Never forget this moment.' I won't forget it."

The kids worked on their journals nearly every day. They drew pictures to accompany their written entries, and they often glued in photos, which they cut from our hoard of tourist brochures. They highlighted special memories by adding captions to the pictures. For a "summer school" project, Chris, Holly, and Teiga drew maps of the Spitsbergen coast, marking *Driver's* daily track and labeling our anchorages. Each map had a key, which contained symbols for the various birds and animals they saw. Their maps were peppered with marks depicting reindeer and seals. Jaja had compiled a list of the flora and fauna in Svalbard. From that list, the kids made charts and checked off the things they saw each day.

After a lesson on safety, Chris wrote: "Always carry a gun ashore. Look around you, stay together, and keep your wits about you. If a polar bear attacks, he'll turn you into corned beef. Never step into the gun's firing range, or you might get your head blown off."

I said, "I wish I did things like this when I was a kid. I envy our children's experiences."

Jaja agreed. "So do I."

Chapter Nineteen

"Never say no to adventure, always say yes!"
–Caractacus Potts, Chitty Chitty Bang Bang by Ian Fleming

I HUDDLED IN THE COCKPIT, clothed in many layers of cold-weather gear. Jaja came up from below. Her tightly-stretched foul-weather gear just fit over her bulky down-filled jacket. She moved awkwardly like an over-stuffed teddy bear.

"Want some hot potatoes?" she asked as she passed me a steaming bowl and a fork. The freshly baked potatoes warmed my insides immediately. They reminded me of Gudni's wonderful potatoes way back in Iceland the previous summer.

"Can I get you anything else?" she asked.

"Ten warm toes," I suggested between mouthfuls.

"I have a pair of your socks warming in the oven."

"Ahhh! My feet feel warmer already. Thanks."

We were pushing northward–away from Bellsund. *Driver* was under full sail moving parallel to the coast of Spitsbergen about three miles offshore. Wave after wave slapped against her pitching bow, as if an invisible hand were bouncing balls off *Driver*'s nose. Spray plastered the sails and rain gear, making them shine as if they had been varnished. Spume flew to lee-ward and sparkled against the dark blue sky. Sailing to windward, as close to the direction of the wind as possible, is not *Driver*'s fastest point of sail. Nevertheless, we were making good time. The northwest wind was coming off the land, and the "fetch," or distance between us and the coast was not long enough to allow large waves to form.

We sat quietly in the cockpit absorbed in our own thoughts, sheltering our bowls of warm potatoes from the cold wind and salt spray. All morning, Jaja and I had been watching the coastline pass by. Chris, Holly, and Teiga were still in bed, snuggled in their warm blankets, listening to the story *Chitty Chitty Bang Bang* on a cassette tape. When I dropped below to change my socks, the Potts family was flying in their magic motorcar over the English Channel to France. Instead of heading toward civilized territory such as England or France, we were sailing to Isfjord–the largest fjord in Spitsbergen–and the settlement of Longyearbyen.

Today, we hoped to anchor close to the mouth of Isfjord in a place called Trygghamna–"Safe Harbor" in Norwegian. The early whalers had discovered that the shape of that three-mile-long mini-fjord prevented dangerous pack ice and calf ice from drifting into the anchorage and trapping their engineless ships. It sounded good to us.

"Remember when Halli mentioned coming here?" I asked. "Imagine what we would have missed if we hadn't done it." Jaja nodded. Despite the stress and discomforts we had experienced recently, I was inspired by this clear day with its gentle seas–and by our favorable progress to windward. So far, every one of our anchorages in Spitsbergen had been special, each glacier unique. Despite the hazards, we were still energized by our voyage.

Several hours later, we sighted the mouth of Isfjord. The strengthening northwesterly winds were funneling down the entire 40-mile length of the fjord. The fetch was immense. To reach Trygghamna, we needed to traverse the 10-mile-wide entrance to the fjord. I had a feeling we were about to pay our dues for the peaceful departure from Bellsund we had enjoyed earlier that morning.

I stood on deck studying the conditions ahead of us. The water was dark blue like the sky, but the surface of the fjord was a mass of whitecaps, churned and driven by the boisterous wind.

"We're in for a couple hours of rough going," I observed. "I'd better reef the mainsail before all hell breaks loose." Jaja took the helm, then eased the mainsheet to make it easier for me to reef the sail. The flogging Dacron sailcloth snapped and cracked, and *Driver* slowed to a crawl. At the exact moment that I completed the reef, Jaja pulled in the sheet, which ran through a four-to-one block and tackle, so the mainsail would fill with wind once again. We worked together seamlessly. *Driver* picked up speed. Soon, the land at the southern side of the entrance to Isfjord was passing abeam of us. Several very tall antennas belonging to the Isfjord Radio poked the sky like sharp pins. If we ever had to radio and request an emergency rescue, those antennas would be our link to safety.

For every few boatlengths that we sailed toward the middle of the fjord, the seas increased exponentially. *Driver*'s bow soared high, then crashed into the oncoming masses of cold water. The current was flowing into the fjord, which helped us move toward our destination, but the wind was blowing in the opposite direction against us and the tide. Strong wind against strong tide is one of the worst conditions a coastal cruiser will encounter. Between the two shores of the fjord, the wind opposing the current created a horrendous tide rip. It was like watching the spiked flames of a far-off forest fire. The dancing crests of distant breaking waves seemed to block our path to Trygghamna. Turning back was not a viable option because there were no safe anchorages on the coast along which we had just sailed. To return all the way to Bellsund would take at least seven hours. We had less than five miles to go to reach Trygghamna–about one hour of sailing.

Jaja and I both saw only one option. "Let's go for it," Jaja said. "We've seen worse."

WHILE CRUISING IN INDONESIA in 1994 on board *Direction,* we were sucked into several tide rips while crossing the wide channels between the islands. Breaking seas would fill *Direction*'s cockpit and even crash against her sails. On one occasion, I calculated that seven knots of current was sucking us out to sea. During that particular maelstrom, I had to go to *Direction*'s bow to change jibs. Despite the rough seas, the wind was light. We needed a larger sail to give us more speed and help us to cross the channel more quickly.

While I worked on the bow with my back to the oncoming seas, Jaja suddenly shouted, "Dave! Look out!" I turned and stared *up* at a wall of water. With a frantic lurch, I gripped the forestay with both hands. The wave crumbled into a mass of white water and slammed into *Direction* with the force of a hundred fire hoses. The rushing water swept my feet out from under me. I clung to the shrouds and watched 18 inches of water roll along the deck into the cockpit. *Direction* looked like a kayak running through white-water rapids.

In Isfjord, the first ferocious wave train hit *Driver* like a runaway locomotive. Standing water rolled down the deck and surged into the cockpit. I fondly recalled the 80-degree-Fahrenheit air in Indonesia and how refreshing the cold sea water had felt when it rushed around my bare legs. "Isfjord" means "Ice Fjord" in Norwegian. This fact crossed my mind as a trickle of seawater found its way into the hood of my foul-weather gear and ran down my back. I winced involuntarily.

"How's the water?" Jaja asked with a grin.

"Compared to your cold feet last night? Much, much less painful."

Although the wind was partly to blame for the violent tide rip, it was also an ally. It powered *Driver* to windward. I pitied the waves as *Driver* smashed them with her steel "shoulder." Another sea crested and pounded the foredeck. I watched the knotmeter. Our speed barely wavered on the display. *Driver* continued to forge ahead.

Ironically, in the clear atmospheric conditions, it was difficult to spot the entrance to Trygghamna. We could actually see too much detail. The land appeared as a solid, unbroken line. We pressed on toward the northern shore of the fjord, confident that the entrance to the bay would reveal itself in due time. Once, as I sprang below to double-check our GPS position, I gave the cabin a cursory look. *Driver* is a very watertight boat, but given the ferocious deluge on deck, I half-expected to see a drip or two of salt water leaking into the cabin. There were no telltale trickles.

Except for the hull leak during our passage to Iceland (which we finally repaired properly in Svolvær) the only time we had taken on sea water was back in North Carolina during the first month we lived aboard *Driver*. We were motoring down the Intracoastal Waterway toward Florida when a large sport fishing boat approached us head-on at high speed. Without ever slowing down, the skipper passed way too close for comfort. As his wake reared up, I noticed that our forward hatch was wide open. I dropped the helm and ran to the foredeck. As I struggled with the hatch cover, *Driver*'s bow plunged into the enormous wake. Too late. Six inches of water skimmed across the deck like a tidal bore. Water hit my knees and shot into my face. The open hatch swallowed the rest. The V-berth where we sleep absorbed most of the deluge.

Ever since that day on the Waterway, we have been very "hatch conscious." There is nothing worse than a wet cabin, especially at sea. Nothing will crush morale faster than a soggy bunk and drenched clothes.

As we approached the one-mile-wide mouth of Trygghamna, the tide rip finally began to subside. Ahead, sheer cliffs descended into the sea. They were topped by distinctive rock formations that resembled exaggerated, abstract replicas of the mountains in Lofoten. The cliffs were broken by mini-ravines, crevices, and sea caves. Flocks of auks swarmed between the peaks–darting out over the fjord in search of food and darting back again. They flew in large groups like schools of airborne fish. We were mesmerized by the motion of the flock as it expanded, elongated, contracted, dispersed, and split to form a second flock.

"I could watch the birds forever," Holly said.

The kids were in the cockpit watching the scenery. It had been a long day for them in the cabin. In recent weeks, however, they had grown used to *Driver*'s motion and knew that the ride would be uncomfortable every now and again. They also knew the discomfort would stop eventually. We were encouraged by the children's endurance and positive attitude as they gained new levels of maturity.

Holly continued, "I'm imagining what it's like to soar over the water, turn, and dive. I almost feel like a bird."

Chris was more rooted in reality. "My neck hurts from watching," he said playfully.

"Then why don't you lay down and watch, like me," said Teiga, who had her head in Jaja's lap.

The end of the three-mile-long bay was filled with fjord ice left over from the winter–similar to the conditions we had found at Rienholmen Island in Bellsund Fjord. We couldn't anchor as far toward the back of the bay as we would have liked. Instead, we found protection to one side near a quick-flowing stream that had probably broken up the ice in that area. The anchor rattled down into 12 feet of water. Stillness.

Driver swung to the slight breeze, oblivious to the recent stresses and strains of the tide rip. For a moment, I had a fleeting, silly notion. I imagined what *Driver* would say if she could talk.

"Wow guys, that was great! Nothing like a good romp to stretch the old stringers and ribs!"

CHRIS HAD A GOOD MEMORY, especially when it involved eating treats. "Remember in Hornsund you said we could have ice cream when we got to Longyearbyen?"

"Two scoops," I said.

We had motored 35 miles down glassy Isfjord to the settlement. The conditions were so different from the tide rip the day before, that it was difficult to believe we were on the same body of water.

Holly was thoughtful. "Mommy? 'Byen' means 'town' in Norwegian, right?

"Right."

"Well, it must have been a 'long year' when they named this town."

We laughed. "Actually," Jaja said, "the town is named after Mr. Long-year. He was one of the owners of the Arctic Coal Company that was established here in 1906."

Longyearbyen is built in a valley under the visages of crumbling mountains. The settlement still thrives from disemboweling the earth. The town council is progressive and appropriates large portions of tax and revenue dollars to provide modern living conditions for the mining engineers and their families. Colorfully painted contemporary houses, paved roads, and a trendy "shopping center" cater to the 3,000 inhabitants.

The landscape surrounding Longyearbyen is plain and rocky, like a dried-up river bed. So far, it was the least interesting terrain we had seen. There were no glaciers in sight, the snow was nearly all melted, and the mountaintops were flat. The shoreline was dominated by an enormous coal-loading facility. Surrounding the facility were quonset huts, heavy mining machinery, a dilapidated fuel wharf, fuel tanks, and large, square warehouses. We vowed to finish our business in Longyearbyen swiftly and move on.

Besides coal mining, tourism also contributes to the economy of this thriving outpost. Duty-free shops offering postcards, film, camping gear, electronics, and perfume accommodate the shopping-addicted vacationer. "Local" souvenirs include polar bear skins (complete with heads and claws), sealskins, arctic fox pelts, and reindeer furs.

There were also bric-a-brac items made from various animal parts. We saw pencil sharpeners, cups, scrimshaw, picture frames, and toothpick holders all made from reindeer bone. Reindeer leather was used for pocketbooks, wallets, backpacks, handbags, and briefcases. You could also buy sealskin coats, boots, gloves, hats, and belts.

Hunting is strictly controlled in Spitsbergen, and the animal remnants for sale were the residue of licensed hunting or from the natural death of the animals. I have no moral objection to using animal products to perpetuate the human species; we certainly didn't rise to the top of the food chain wearing polyester loincloths and synthetic fleece anoraks. Aesthetically speaking, however, it saddened me to see beautiful animals converted into tacky keepsakes. I looked at a furry sealskin baseball cap and thought of the peaceful creature, a part of which had become a shoddy representation of humor. Across the cap were the words "Arctic Appreciation Club" embroidered in yellow thread.

We received a warm welcome at the administration office in Longyearbyen. Jaja gave our names to a young woman. She checked her files for our cruising permit.

"Looks like everything is in perfect order." Then she chuckled. "I read about your problems with the UDI last winter in the papers. I'm happy you were able to make it here."

"Thanks," Jaja said. "We're happy too."

"How do your children like Spitsbergen?"

"They are in awe of the birds, the bears, and the ice," I said.

"What a great experience for them. I see you plan to go as far north as Amsterdamøya Island," the woman said.

"Yes. We want to see the pack ice. If we're lucky enough, we'd like to reach 80 degrees north."

"I hope the weather cooperates for you," she said.

"How many yachts have you had to rescue over the years?" I asked, somewhat warily.

"None. The insurance is primarily for hikers and hunters, who are more exposed if unexpected bad weather hits. Sailors have a fallback because they can usually seek food and shelter on board. Unfortunately, we can't exclude cruisers from the insurance requirements because it's still possible that sailors will get into trouble. We have to protect our limited financial resources."

"We understand perfectly."

The woman continued. "On Amsterdamøya Island, you can see the ruins of an old whaling station. We only ask that you tread lightly in these histori-cal areas and leave everything intact."

"Spitsbergen is a living museum, isn't it?" Jaja mused.

The women smiled at us kindly. "Not everyone recognizes that. Just a few years ago, for example, we fined some tourists the equivalent of 4,500 American dollars for stepping ashore on Moffen Island, a very remote, pro-tected walrus sanctuary."

"How did you catch them?" I asked.

"They took pictures of themselves with the walrus, which are very pas-sive. When they got home, they showed the pictures. A wildlife officer caught wind of the photos and asked to see them. He recognized the unique landscape of Moffen Island and turned the couple in to the authorities."

The woman told us another story. Some foreign cruisers painted their boat's name, hailing port, and the date on some high rocks in the northern stretches of Spitsbergen. A ranger saw the graffiti and copied down the infor-mation. He easily traced the owners of the boat through the British depart-ment of yacht registration and verified the date with Norwegian immigration. The boatowners were fined US$4,000 to reimburse the cost of removing the paint from the rocks.

We walked out of the administration building into the sunshine and headed for the grocery store to stock up on food.

Holly asked, "Daddy, why do people paint their boat names on beautiful rock walls?" She remembered Troll Fjord near Svolvær where many people had left their marks on the sheer cliff near the entrance.

"Ignorance," I suggested. "Or ego, perhaps. Some people want the world to know where they've been."

AFTER WALKING for about 10 minutes on Longyearbyen's wide, paved main road, we reached the central shopping area. A cement pedestrian walk about a half-block long was lined with banks, bakeries, restaurants, sport shops, clothing stores and the post office.

A group of young hikers, looking disheveled and tired, sprawled near some picnic tables soaking up the thin sunlight. Their bulging packs were piled under the statue of a grim-faced miner. Some other tourists dressed in slacks, leather coats, blazers, and boat shoes were taking pictures of each other next to a polar bear statue. We identified a local inhabitant of Long-yearbyen easily; he was trying *not* to look like a tourist. His indifference was almost comical. I saw him shake his head at the picture-takers near the statue, who were fooling around and feigning attack. I can never understand why some locals despise tourists, especially when visitors keep a reasonable amount of local people employed as a result of their purchases. Perhaps the locals have been on the receiving end of too many bad-mannered tourists. Nevertheless, I liked the bear statue and made a mental note to photograph Chris, Holly, and Teiga riding on it as soon as our shopping was finished.

The grocery store was not large by American standards, or even by mainland Norwegian standards, but considering its position was at 79 degrees north latitude, it was surprisingly well stocked. It had everything we needed.

When supplying the boat before we left the Norwegian coast, Jaja had taken into account that the cold in Spitsbergen would sharpen our appetites. But we had depleted our food supplies even faster than she had calculated. The only explanation for this extra increase in caloric consumption was the intense light and perhaps stress.

Now I had a voracious appetite. Normally, I eat a light breakfast, a substantial lunch, and a light dinner. In Spitsbergen, I could accommodate four square meals a day plus snacks. I noticed that my mind seemed much clearer if I had a full stomach. The kids ate continuously in small doses. Perhaps their varied sleeping habits provided more opportunities to eat.

Our diesel fuel consumption had also increased in Spitsbergen. We used our diesel heater continuously and used the engine often when the wind was calm. We knew that fuel was available in Longyearbyen, so we didn't worry about running out. Although I had been topping up our drinking water from streams, two loads of hand-washed laundry had decimated our onboard fresh water supply. After we finished at the fuel jetty, we moved to another wharf to get water.

The harbor control office was situated at the head of the "water wharf." The harbormaster was a young Norwegian, who was accustomed to dealing with huge fishing trawlers and cruise ships. We stood on the high dock looking down at *Driver.*

"Water is expensive," he said. "I'll have to charge you."

"How much?"

"Fifteen dollars for the first five tons, and two dollars a ton thereafter."

"I only need 80 gallons," I laughed.

The young man sighed. "How much is 80 gallons?"

"Sorry," I said. "Old habits are hard to suppress. That's about 300 liters."

He asked, "Do you think America will ever adopt the metric system?"

"Not in my lifetime."

"Why not?

"It's funny," I said. "In the States, ease and convenience are considered great advantages–for instance, when you are designing a new product or marketing an existing one. Yet converting to the metric system–which is dead simple to use–is too difficult and inconvenient."

"And too expensive, I suppose," the port captain added.

"It's not easy to sacrifice today for a better tomorrow," I said. "But the longer we wait, the more expensive it will get."

"Same old story. Well, at least you're aware of the problem. OK. Water's on me today." The young man looked thoughtful. "The hose alone probably contains all you'll need."

"Thanks. You don't happen to have a weather report, do you?"

"Come in the office after you fill up, and we'll check the computer."

The hose was two inches in diameter and seemed a mile long. I stretched about 50 feet out on the wharf, handed it down to Jaja, and twisted the valve wide open. A stream of water shot out 20 feet. Jaja was nearly knocked over backwards by the thrust. With her feet braced on deck like a firefighter, she gripped the hose for dear life.

Jaja was giggling so hard she could barely speak. "Hey Dave, can you turn it down a hair?"

I pretended not to hear. "Higher?" Jaja aimed the frigid stream of water at me, but I jumped out of the way just in time.

Up in the office, we looked at the weather forecast. On the screen, we saw a map of Spitsbergen with little wind arrows pointing southward. The arrows near Isfjord had two "tails" on them to indicate wind strength.

The harbormaster studied the computer screen. "Looks like you'll have 20-knot southerly winds tomorrow."

I hesitated. "Uh, don't the arrows indicate that the wind will be from the north?"

The young man looked confused. "North winds? No. The arrows point to where the wind is coming from."

"Sorry," I said. "But, I believe the arrows indicate which way the wind is blowing."

He looked at me. "Are you sure?"

"Uh huh." I decided I could tease him. I said, "Let me get this straight. If I call you on the VHF radio for a weather update, and you say the wind will be from the east, I can expect westerlies. Right?"

The young man once again looked thoughtful. "No, that was yesterday."

Next, we checked the computer for ice conditions. It didn't look promising. The entire west coast was clear, but the pack ice hovered near the north coast of Amsterdamøya Island. Lucky we weren't trying to reach 80 degrees north today. We would haven fallen short at least 12 or 15 miles. We were a week or two away from Amsterdamøya, so there was still a chance that the ice conditions would improve.

I HAD COUNTED on completing portions of our book under way. I had forgotten, however, that bluewater cruising and creative writing are competitive activities. I tried to squeeze in an hour of writing here and there while cruising up the Spitsbergen coast, but it was futile. By the time we arrived in Longyearbyen, I put away the laptop computer. At first, I felt relieved–as if I were on a mini-vacation. But soon I began to worry. Would we fall behind schedule? The deadline, which had seemed light years away when we signed the contract, suddenly hung over us like an icy wall ready to collapse. But I knew I needed all my creative energy just to keep *Driver*, and us, safe.

This was the first time we had ever brought a work commitment with us while voyaging. Already we regretted it. Usually when we are under way, the only obligations we make are to the boat and to each other. In the past, we wrote articles for sailing magazines at the end of each cruising season while we were stopped, waiting for the end of bad weather. Our lifestyle precluded taking "jobs" with us, but, ironically, this lifestyle was the subject of the book we were writing. It was a "no-win" situation.

Why did we feel compelled to ignore the outside world? Our families, for example, were used to hearing from us sporadically. Prior to a long ocean passage, or before heading to a remote cruising ground, we made phone calls to warn our families that we would be out of touch. We sent them cards and letters along the way, but we did not expect to hear from them until our itinerary allowed it.

Was it selfishness that kept us out of touch? Or was it a survival instinct? Constant analysis of one's surroundings takes incredible mental energy, especially with children in the crew. In Spitsbergen, Jaja and I were maxed out with cooking, cleaning, childcare, boat maintenance, navigation, bear threats, ice conditions, and the ever-persistent menace of the unknown. Survival in nature means constantly being in tune with unseen challenges. Each nuance has to be assimilated. Every seemingly insignificant incident has to be cataloged for future reference. We had already made several unwise decisions. To succeed in these high latitudes, we *had* to ignore the rest of the world and focus only on events as they pertained to *Driver*. Our lives depended on it.

DRIVER RUSHED ALONG on a broad reach, her mainsail and genoa taut with the southwesterly breeze. The kids were sleeping. The sea was bouncy, but the height of the waves diminished as we entered Kongs Fjord, a 12-mile-long inlet, 50 miles up the coast north of Isfjord. Several *Driver*-size icebergs floated in the entrance to Kongs Fjord, and bergy bits–large pieces of glacial ice, usually with less than 15 feet of ice exposed above sea level–drifted in veins, moving with the current.

Jaja and I chatted casually. The idea to sail to 80 degrees north had been inspired by idle conversation back in Tromsø. At that time we thought, *"Wouldn't it be a cool thing to do?"* Since then, the idea had taken on a life of its own and had become the motivating force during our summer's cruise. We had already faced many challenges in Spitsbergen, and we had learned a great deal. Our knowledge was perpetuating itself. I suspected that each difficulty from which we untangled ourselves was a lesson in the field–training for the "final assault."

It slowly dawned on us that the entire archipelago of Svalbard was a gigantic "headland"–an enormous challenge. It was the apex, both physically and mentally, of the *Driver* voyage. Until we returned to the well-marked channels and the precisely charted bays of the Norwegian coast, we would be challenged, living on the edge.

"It's so peaceful sailing when the kids are asleep." I joked. "We can have conversations without endless interruptions."

"Yeah, I know what you mean." Jaja said. "I can actually complete an entire thought in my head! Seriously, I've been thinking about what it will be like if we reach the pack ice. I think that..."

Our reverie was broken by a call from below.

"Mommy, I'm hungry!"

"Sorry," I said. "Spoke too soon."

Jaja descended the companionway to start her day, and I continued to steer *Driver* toward our next anchorage–Peirsonhamna at Blomstrandhalvøya Island, halfway down Kongs Fjord.

According to the chart, two rocks stood like underwater sentinels guarding the entrance to Peirsonhamna. As we approached, Jaja came on deck and stood on the bow. The kids, still in their pajamas, crowded into the dodger to get a better view. When Jaja spotted the more northern of the two rocks, it reminded me of how we had conned *Driver* into Isbjørnhamna in Hornsund Fjord on our first day in Spitsbergen. Was it only two weeks ago? It felt more like two months. My eyes followed Jaja's outstretched finger, and I saw the small patch of light green water that betrayed the boulder. I steered close to it to avoid hitting the second one, which wasn't visible at all, probably due to the angle of the sun in the water.

Chris read the depthsounder display, calling out the numbers as we inched our way in.

"Fifteen feet...15...17...13...12...12...13..."

I studied the chart. The water was deep right up to the sheer rock walls that framed the cove. The head of the bay shoaled steeply to a sandy beach.

"Holler extra loud when we get to 10 feet," I told Chris. With the engine ticking away at very low RPMs, we approached the beach at a snail's pace. Jaja stood ready to drop the anchor.

I looked around quickly. The cliffs were gray, stained with white droppings, topped by lush grass. The beach was bordered by electric green moss and spearlike, emerald weeds. It was the birds that made the sparse vegetation in Spitsbergen grow with such vivid hues. They were airborne cropdusters, and their guano was the fertilizer.

Chris shouted, "11…11…10 feet!"

I pushed the helm hard over; *Driver* turned on a dime. When all forward headway ceased, I nodded to Jaja. The rattling chain echoed off the cliffs. I put the engine into reverse. *Driver* moved back, and back, then stopped as the anchor bit into the sandy sea floor. Chris turned off the engine. Silence. Except for the birds, we were alone–as usual.

The current and the northerly wind had cleared the cove of ice. If the wind shifted to the south, however, we would be exposed. Thankfully, the forecast called for light northerlies to continue for several more days. I was confident that we could rest easy for at least one night.

LATER, WE STOOD SIDE BY SIDE in the galley. Jaja was making a second breakfast for the family, and I was brewing another pot of coffee. The scenery outside seemed to gaze at us through the cabin ports.

"What a magnificent cove," I said.

"The farther we go," Jaja affirmed, "The better it gets."

"On mornings like this, it feels as if we'll get to 80 degrees north without a hitch."

"That's funny," Jaja said. "I was just thinking the same thing."

Being temporarily free from the worry of finding good shelter had given us room to dream. But still, an underlying tension persisted. We were aware of the fury that nature could throw our way, and we realized there was a good chance we might not reach our goal. No matter how hard we pushed, we could still fall short. It all depended on the whims of weather and ice.

I thought back to the obstacles we had faced during our years at sea together. All of them were stepping stones in a vast river leading to this summer's quest in Spitsbergen. The amount of time we had spent reaching this point was astounding. We had come such a great distance–mentally and geographically–since leaving the Florida coast. Bermuda was the first "stone" in this voyage.

"I wonder. Is reaching 80 degrees north just another stepping stone? Or is it the other side of the river?"

Jaja sighed. "I guess we won't know until we get back to the Norwegian coast and the next thing comes along."

I laughed. "Jaja? The next time you have an idea, could you please think warmer thoughts?"

She chuckled. "I am."

Gray skies pressed down on us the next day. The wind was zero. The temperature was about 38 degrees. The ceiling was lower than 1,000 feet, which hid the mountain peaks. A solid wall of black land encircled the fjord. Spitsbergen felt timeless.

In the 1930s, an industrious Englishman, who discovered marble on Blomstrandhalvøya Island, set up a quarry. He went bust when his European customers discovered that the marble would crack after a few years. Derelict machinery, steam boilers, tin cans, and pot-bellied stoves remained as relics of the man's broken dreams. Raw marble rocks–some as large as garbage cans–lay scattered on the barren hills. The marble was chocolate brown with threads of yellow and black. Man's history on the island was brief, but the remains of his early intrusion endured.

Despite the human "debris," nature carried on as usual. Long-tailed skuas dived acrobatically fighting with each other. Arctic terns shrieked whenever we inadvertently approached their nests. Reindeer grazed, purple saxifrage bloomed, and the continuous threat of polar bears kept us alert. Jaja carried the gun slung over her shoulder casually, the same way I carried our backpack. The gun was part of our consciousness now, part of our newest history. Even after we left Spitsbergen behind, our mental landscape would be forever marked by what the gun represented.

We hiked partway to the top of Blomstrandhalvøya Island to gain a bird's eye view of our surroundings. About six miles away, at the back of the fjord, Kongsbreen Glacier flowed down from hidden altitudes and oozed into the sea. Reflected light from the ice illuminated the clouds, transforming them from dull silver to fluorescent blue. Even on this somber afternoon, the explosive quality of light inspired awe. Glaciers represent a unique force– one that has helped shape a good portion of the earth's surface.

Once again, a glacier "called" us. The next morning, we raised the anchor and motored slowed away from the secluded bay, past the two sentinel rocks, bound for the glacier. The calm, windless conditions were ideal for exploring the ice-choked fjord. We would be able to motor close to the ice without worrying about pieces being blown into us.

At first, it was easy to dodge the large chunks. Then the ice field became denser, and the pieces floated closer together. Finally, we reached what appeared to be an impenetrable barrier of broken pieces, most of which were about two feet across. They were awash like giant ice cubes. I climbed 15 feet up the mast to the first set of spreaders to get a better view. I could see a band of open water a few hundred yards to port. If we could push through to the clear water, we could follow it like a road and motor several more miles into the fjord. Once again, we were drawn forward by the power of the glacier.

INSTINCTIVELY, I REBELLED against the idea of ramming *Driver* into calf ice in order to make headway. I thought of the iceberg that sank the *Titanic* and remembered in detail old photos I had seen of sailing ships being crushed in polar ice. But I wanted to understand exactly how well–or not so well–*Driver* would perform. It seemed vitally important for our safety. The Sunday morning calm in Kongs Fjord provided the perfect setting for "ice experimentation."

Thus far in our cruise, we had neither collided with ice under way, nor had we gotten stuck in it. But what if we became trapped accidentally? Could *Driver* make headway and escape? Could we turn? Would the ice be driven under the boat and damage the propeller? And how hard could we hit a piece of ice without damaging *Driver*'s hull or keel? It seemed like a good idea to make a safe and cautious test and to displace our fear with some facts.

Jaja stood on the bow as I steered into a wide band of small ice chunks. Like a plow turning the soil, *Driver*'s steel bow carved a path. The bow pushed the ice outward along our hull–not downward as I had feared–and left an open trail of water in our wake. The ice acted the same as the chunks we had encountered in Troll Fjord back in Norway. The propeller, three feet beneath the surface of the water, remained unscathed. *Driver* continued moving at two knots.

Next, we motored slowly and cautiously through a vein of larger chunks. We quickly discovered that the maximum size chunk that our hull could push aside without fear of damaging the propeller was two feet in diameter. Pieces larger than that were too heavy to move aside easily. Instead, they were pushed under the hull. The first time this happened, Jaja, who was standing on the bow, hollered back to me. "Neutral, Dave! Slow down." Fortunately, the ice chunk resurfaced and bumped harmlessly along the hull.

We discovered that the big hunks of calf ice–larger than five feet across–posed a real threat and that we should avoid banging into them at all cost. Many such pieces were oddly shaped and had jutting, underwater protrusions. Like icebergs, large pieces of calf ice often float with most of their bulk below the surface. If we hit one of these pieces just right, its top might be pushed away by *Driver*'s hull, but the wide base could clip the prop. If we damaged our propeller, we figured we could beach *Driver* and replace it with the spare prop that we carried for emergencies. However, with no wind, we would not be able to sail to the beach. In that case, ice moving with the currents might carry us into shoal water. It was far better to avoid hitting the big chunks in the first place.

For an hour, we zigzagged on a random course. For every boatlength *Driver* traveled, we tested, observed, and remembered. Our experience expanded. Risky endeavors such as rock climbing, flying small airplanes, ocean sailing, and deep sea diving all have a zone of predictability. We tried to determine the limits of the "safe zone" when cruising in ice. We wanted to know what was possible. Crashing through the ice wasn't as bad as we had expected. As long as our forward speed didn't exceed two knots, the smaller bits and pieces were pushed harmlessly aside.

We wanted to motor within a half-mile of Kongsbreen Glacier, but we were still four miles away when the ice pieces began getting larger and the concentration denser. I turned off the engine and let us drift, enjoying the high-latitude silence. I smiled. *Driver* seemed to bob like a wedge of lime in a vast, frozen Margarita. Chris took advantage of the calm conditions and began flying over the deck on his swing. Chris's antics made the boat rock. The mast acted like a giant swizzle stick stirring the ice around us. I smiled again.

Holly was determined to touch the ice. I took a long, serious look around with the binoculars to make sure no bears were in the area. When I was convinced it was safe, I let Holly climb into the dinghy to get a closer look. I stood in the cockpit holding the gun.

Much of the floating ice was small and flat. But there was also some relatively fresh calf ice. These pieces were large and "upright" with many projecting angles. Some were as big as *Driver*, and some were the size of our dinghy. They varied in hue from completely transparent, if the ice had been polished by the sea, to a translucent turquoise, if the ice retained a rough texture. Each piece was a unique sculpture. The pieces resembled birds, ships, lizards, ducks, and fairy-tale castles. We were floating in an art gallery admiring original works created by the hand of nature.

Holly broke off a fragment of ice with her fist and licked it like a Popsicle. With a look of disbelief, she slowly removed it from her mouth. "Mommy! I'm eating ice that's thousands of years old!"

After lunch, we continued on our tour of the wide fjord. Icebergs–some as big as ships–drifted in the deep water. Many lay hard aground on the shoals near some low islands. We headed in that direction for a closer look.

One monster iceberg was touching bottom in 318 feet of water. The color of the ice was the richest, deepest, powder blue imaginable. It was framed by a charcoal sky, which created a contrast we had never witnessed before. We wanted to touch the berg and connect ourselves to its prehistoric blueness. We approached the berg slowly, aware that at any time, a piece could break off under water and float to the surface like a battering ram, damaging *Driver* in a flash. The berg might even capsize and crush us. But we remained hypnotized by its beauty. Closer, closer. At the last moment, I put the engine into reverse, and Jaja reached out with her gloveless hand to fend off. I came forward so I, too, could feel the cold, smooth surface.

Five minutes of tension was all we could stand. I returned to the cockpit, took the helm, and powered *Driver* away from the frozen brute. I shook my head. It was foolish to touch an iceberg. And after all, it was only a hunk of ice. But diamonds are just rocks, and look what people sacrifice to get those.

FOUR MILES WIDE, Amsterdamøya Island is shaped like a pork chop, and rises to 1,500 feet at its highest point. The rocky terrain is jagged, a product of glacial action. On "mainland" Spitsbergen, two miles away, 3,000-foot jagged mountain peaks scraped against the heavens. Their ragged profiles were reminiscent of the Lofoten Islands. Both of those landscapes had been thrust upwards by geological forces. Unlike the mountains at Amsterdamøya, the tops of those peaks had remained well above the ice during the glacial age.

We lay anchored in the lee of the island, sheltered from the strong southerly winds. Looking northward through the binoculars, I could see the continuous white edge of the pack ice. Eighty degrees north was up there somewhere, but we would have to wait for more settled conditions to get a closer look. If we headed north now, the heavy south winds and the high seas might drive us into the edge of the pack.

Despite low clouds and a wind chill below freezing, we couldn't resist going ashore to see the old whaling station on Amsterdamøya. Chris, Holly, and Teiga were raring to go. Jaja had primed them with historical facts about the area, and they were dying to explore. The island was a hive of activity in the mid-1600s. According to the woman who gave us our cruising permit, we would see 400-year-old remains of earthen ovens used by Dutch whalers for boiling down whale blubber. We might even see graves.

Jaja began the long row to shore in the dinghy against the wind. The kids and I huddled low in the boat to reduce windage and to stay warm. The snowy beach was covered with enormous logs that had been carried by ocean currents from Siberian sawmills. They looked like the pieces in a giant game of Pick-Up-Sticks scattered and piled randomly. In nearly treeless Iceland, where driftwood was a valuable commodity, we heard about an enterprising man who had collected tons of it. He milled the logs into thousands of fence posts and surrounded his farm with them. Then he turned his horses loose to graze in the newly fenced fields. Unfortunately, the horses liked the taste of the salty wood and nibbled the posts to the ground in months.

Deterioration occurs slowly in the Arctic. Rainfall, which hastens decay, is almost nonexistent. Cold temperatures and relatively dry air act as preservatives. Earthen rings, about eight feet in diameter and a foot or two high, marked the location of the ancient blubber ovens. The fact that even this much had survived for four centuries, right on the beach at the water's edge, was thought-provoking.

The whalers dragged the massive carcasses onto the moraine peninsula to gut and strip them. Hundreds of whales were processed in this camp each season. The work area and living conditions must have been horrendous. Due to the layer of permafrost under the tundra, the blood from the dead whales didn't soak into the ground or run off. Instead, it lay on the surface creating lakes of blood and fluids.

Even now, the moss and grasses in these ancient "pool" areas seemed greener and lusher than in other places. We wished we could voyage back to the time of the whalers to see what it must have been like on this beach. Of course, we would not have wanted to stay long. The smell alone would have been horrific.

Having grown up in a society with modern technology and comforts, it is easy to think of our forebears with both nostalgia and a sense of condemnation. Our ancestors had a hard life, and they committed desperate acts to survive. But perhaps their underlying values were stronger. Our family chooses to live close to nature. Earlier generations did it out of necessity.

Written histories, antique furniture and trinkets, old photographs, a chat with elders. These things link us to the past. They remind us of who we are and how we got here. The people in the Lofoten Islands have embraced technology and use it as a tool to improve their quality of life–but not at the expense of the past. Everywhere in Lofoten, we saw the old mixed with the new. Traditional foods were served with imported condiments. Many people build modern houses using century-old architectural patterns and techniques. It's not uncommon to see a carvel-planked wooden fishing boat hull with an aluminum superstructure. Small children wear synthetic fleece jackets but dream of the day when they will be old enough have their own, handmade, woolen, national costume.

We ambled back to the dinghy, our heads full of "cultural insight." Suddenly, Holly spied polar bear tracks in a patch of snow. Anxiety killed our reflections. The carefree and squishy tundra now felt like a treadmill. We walked and walked, yet felt frozen in space. Our inspired conversation stopped; we no longer felt like the dominant species. After an interminable amount of time, we reached the dinghy, piled in, and headed home.

Rowing to and from *Driver* put us in an extremely vulnerable position; the crafty bears could probably swim faster than Jaja could row. An outboard engine would have given us an advantage. However, I designed and built our 10-foot fiberglass dinghy in the sweltering heat of a North Carolina summer three years earlier. When I decided to forego the outboard, I hadn't planned on meeting polar bears. It's hard to think of everything.

In the dinghy, I gripped the gun and scanned the gray water for signs of a furry head in the water. With his keen sense of detail, Chris observed that the little notched sight, which rested on the barrel of the gun, was missing. He was right. When had it fallen out? It had been there when we rowed to shore.

Great. As if the drifting ice, the unpredictable depth soundings, and the unstable weather weren't enough, we now had lost some of our scant advantage over the bears. We were used to coping with navigational issues and onboard crises, but shooting "from the hip" at polar bears ranked low in our repertoire of familiar experiences.

"Should we go back and look for the sight?" Chris asked.

I thought of the sand, the snow, and the bog we had just trudged over.

"We'd never find it." I said. I looked at Jaja and her eyes widened imperceptibly. I tipped my head back a millimeter in acknowledgement. This was a silent code that we frequently used when we did not want the kids to hear our thoughts.

"Now what do we do?" Jaja's eyes queried.

"Beats the heck out of me," my nod answered. Nothing productive was gained by our little exchange, but we felt much better for sharing our reactions.

When we reached *Driver,* the kids hopped aboard with a speed and lack of hesitation that I had never before witnessed. Jaja and I admitted that as little kids, we would sometimes leap into bed quickly, certain that "The Thing" living under our bed would reach out and grab our legs. I tied the dinghy's bow line to *Driver*'s rail. Then I leaped aboard sprightly, whipping my feet over the lifelines like an Olympic hurdler. Jaja smiled knowingly.

In the safety of the cockpit, I looked back at the shoreline. For a split second I thought I saw a furry shape disappear over the lip of the moraine beach into the shadow of a vast, rock avalanche.

"What do you see?" Jaja asked uneasily. I noticed her eyes were round again.

"Daddy!" Holly asked. "Do you see something?" Chris and Teiga came over to the rail and they all squinted into the grayish glare.

"Just a bird," I answered frankly. I looked at Jaja and tipped my head back a fraction. Her eyes went even wider.

"OK! Time for hot chocolate!" Jaja chanted. "Everybody below!"

Chapter Twenty

Your vision is only limited by how far you can see.

AMSTERDAMØYA ISLAND SITS at the entrance to Smeerenburg Fjord. Rough seas and strong southerly winds churned the sea outside the fjord. The pack ice would have to wait. The fjord, however, was protected from the worst of the weather and was calm enough for exploring. Nine miles from our anchorage, we could faintly see the Smeerenburgbreen Glacier tumbling into the water.

The southerly wind had cleared most of the fjord of small ice debris. However, some big chunks lay grounded about a half-mile from the glacial wall. With just our mainsail up, we sailed among these gnarly looking bergs. They were roughly the same size and shape as *Driver* and provided the illusion that we were moving slowly among a fleet of boats made of ice. We weren't worried. There was plenty of room to maneuver amongst the bergs. As the day wore on, the wind died, and we drifted.

The calm conditions were perfect for Chris, Holly, and Teiga. They swung on their bosun's chairs happy to get some exercise. Soon, we heard a familiar war cry.

Chris pivoted his chair to face the cockpit. "I'm hungry."

"So am I." Holly added.

"Me too!" chimed Teiga.

"But you just ate big bowls of spaghetti," Jaja said.

"I'm famished!" Chris said, quoting a line from Roald Dahl's children's book, *James and The Giant Peach.*

Holly said casually, "Do you think we could have a snack?"

Teiga started giggling. Something was up. "OK," laughed Jaja. "What is it?"

"Jell-O!" they sang, in three-part harmony.

While we drifted, Jaja boiled a pot of water and added the powdered crystals. Jell-O was the kids' favorite cruising desert. To them, it was the next best thing to ice cream. In order to speed up the cooling process, Jaja asked me to collect some ice. She covered us with the rifle while the kids and I piled into the dinghy, cast off, and rowed a dozen feet to a bucket-sized piece.

Using a Phillips screwdriver, I chiseled the ice until we filled a bowl. Free ice was a bit of an anticlimax in the Arctic, but we had learned not to take things for granted.

During the hot, humid summer of 1993 on Australia's north coast, two-year-old Holly developed an ear infection. Liquid amoxicillin, an antibiotic, was prescribed to clear it up. The runny, pink medicine had to be kept cold. We did not have a refrigeration system on *Direction* or even a simple icebox. I bought a six-pack-size cooler, placed the bottle of antibiotics in it, and kept the cooler filled with ice, which we purchased from the local pub. Two weeks' worth of ice cost more than the medicine. Now we were poking along in front of Smeerenburgbreen Glacier, and the ice was free.

While the Jell-O cooled, Jaja and I contemplated how to transport icebergs to the Tropics. If we could do it, we would become instant tycoons.

THE WATER IN SMEERENBURG FJORD resembled a wide, blue avenue leading to a grand cathedral–in this case, the glacier. The east side of the fjord was defined by steep mountains, which stretched northward past Amsterdamøya Island. In contrast, the opposite (west) shore was flat, covered with small, round boulders.

We studied the chart carefully. What we saw in print, and what we saw ahead of *Driver* were two different things. According to our chart, the rocky, western shoreline was still covered by the glacier. Even though the chart was new, it was based on survey data from 1966 and before. We estimated that in just over 35 years, the glacier had retreated over a mile, creating an uncharted section of "beachfront."

As we motored parallel to the "new" shore, we noticed that it was not straight like the eastern side. The rocky beach bowed inwards, creating a slight indentation; then it curved gracefully out again, forming a rocky point.

We had planned to anchor for the night several miles away in a large bay. But this "new" indentation tantalized us.

"Just think," Jaja mused, "if we anchor here, we can see the glacier around the clock."

I agreed. "Let's check it out. If the indentation doesn't work, we can move to the next bay."

We motored cautiously toward the rocky beach uncertain of the depths we would find. The unsurveyed indentation actually proved larger than it had appeared from a distance, and the rocky point provided surprisingly good protection from the long fetch in the fjord. Using the depthsounder, we discovered a consistent, 25-foot-deep shelf near the beach that was perfect for anchoring. Good news for two reasons: First, anchoring in shallow water made retrieving the anchor easier. Second, and more importantly, shallow water protected us from big icebergs. They would run aground before they could hit us.

We felt lucky to have found this "dent" in the shore. To the south of us, where the new moraine beach butted into the dwindling edge of the Smeerenburgbreen Glacier, a large cove offered an alternative anchorage. What's more, it was oriented to provide excellent protection. Yet it, too, was unsurveyed. It was also still covered with surface ice, left over from the winter when all of Smeerenburg Fjord had been frozen like a pond. We had experienced the same thing at Rienholmen and in Trygghamna. Many of the good anchoring spots in Spitsbergen were inaccessible until later in the summer when the ice finally broke up.

We continued to move slowly into the indentation to see how close we could get to the rock-strewn beach. When the depth reached 15 feet, *Driver* was only 20 yards from shore. Good. Deep right on in. I steered *Driver* back into 25 feet of water and made a large, sweeping circle to check the depth under our swinging radius. If the wind shifted, I wanted to be certain that we would not swing on our anchor chain and drift onto a submerged rock. The anchor grabbed instantly in the mud bottom. Jaja let out ample, 5-to-one scope. The bay was open to the east. If the wind shifted to that direction, we would be on a lee shore. However, I was confident that we could retreat safely to deep water by motoring directly away from the beach at a 90 degree angle—exactly the same way we had approached it.

HOLLY GESTURED EXCITEDLY towards the rocky point of our new anchorage.

"I think I see whales!"

We all spied their rounded backs, and congratulated Holly on her perceptiveness. I thought they looked like beluga whales. For several minutes we marveled at the creatures.

Then Chris became skeptical. "They look like rocks."

"No," Holly defended. "They're whales. Even Daddy said so."

"It *is* strange that they're not moving," Jaja said.

I took out the binoculars. Through the lenses, the whales revealed their true identities: Three smooth rocks that were uncovered by the falling tide. A slight surge spilled over them, giving the appearance of motion. I scanned the mirrorlike bay, wondering if there were more hidden rocks. Jaja and I had sounded the bottom for our swinging radius, but we did not know what hazards lay outside of this circle.

The next morning, I was awakened by the familiar sound of ice scraping against the hull. I went on deck to investigate. For some reason, the sun's glare on the water was excessively blinding. All I could see were small bits of ice bobbing harmlessly next to *Driver*'s hull.

"No big deal," I thought.

The air temperature hovered around 36 degrees Fahrenheit, but the sun's rays felt warm on my skin. The wind was still calm, and I wondered if this would be the day we would reach 80 degrees north latitude.

My pupils finally contracted allowing me to gaze across the fjord toward the magnificent glacier. I gaped. My brain could not comprehend what my eyes were telling it. Just 100 feet from *Driver*, the entire sheet of winter ice that had filled the cove near the edge of the glacier had broken loose. It was drifting up the fjord. The sheet was at least three feet thick, flat as a pancake, and had the surface area of a stadium parking lot–a monster slab that probably weighed a zillion pounds. Watching it slide by slowly, I contemplated its untold tons of inertia. Suddenly, I realized with a sickening awareness that the ice was not only drifting past *Driver*, it was also drifting *toward* us. The current was sucking the slab into the indentation.

"My God," I whispered out loud. *"We're going to be crushed!"*

In a split second, I visualized the ice slab sweeping through our anchorage. It would smash into *Driver* and bulldoze her sideways onto the rocky beach. My imagination envisioned what would happen as the keel touched bottom. We would heel over. With the ice pushing on the hull, *Driver* might be rolled on her side until the mast and rigging caught in the rocks.

The safe right-angle escape to deeper water that we had envisioned earlier was already blocked by the ice sheet. I looked toward the rocky point. Going that way was the closest and the most logical option for getting away from the drifting slab. But we would have to get there before the slab hit the point and sealed off the gap. I wondered if we dared run the gauntlet. Were the belugas the only shallow rocks beneath the milky blue water? My mind was transported back to the uncharted, rock-strewn waters off Cape Borthen, north of Hornsund. My pulse increased. I looked at the moving vise closing on us by the second. I yelled into the cabin.

"Jaja!"

Over the years, Jaja and I have learned to recognize the messages contained in the simple recitation of each another's name. We can pack a lot of meaning into a single word. Jaja bolted out of bed, put on warm clothes, and raced outside before answering.

Pointing to the approaching ice, I explained the situation. Jaja blinked against the glare and ran forward to begin levering the anchor aboard. I went below, put on warm clothes, and started the engine.

The slab was closing fast. Breathless, we took turns at the anchor windlass. My worst fear was that the anchor might catch under the ice, forcing us to abandon 220 feet of chain plus a 44-pound anchor. Fortunately, when the chain hung straight down, indicating that the anchor was directly beneath *Driver*'s bow, we still had three feet of clear water between our hull and the edge of the ice slab. My mouth was dry, and I was sweating.

We raised the anchor into the bow roller and motored slowly toward the point knowing that the beluga rocks were there somewhere under the falling tide. The depth held steady at 25 feet, then jumped abruptly. When it reached seven feet, I put the engine in reverse to bring us to a stop. We couldn't chance running aground now. Full of glacial runoff, the water was nearly opaque. Jaja jumped into the dinghy and rowed ahead to sound the bottom with an oar. *Driver* was close enough to the beach that I could see polar bear tracks in the snow without binoculars. I brought the gun on deck.

When Jaja was five boatlengths away from *Driver*, I was startled by a sickening crash. In my peripheral vision, I caught a blur of white leaping out of the water. I swung the gun around, wondering if I would be able to hit a swimming polar bear now that the gun sight was missing. I made the barrel an extension of my eye.

Then I relaxed the tension in my trigger finger. The ice slab had hit the submerged beluga rocks forcing a ragged section of ice to be thrust into the air. I looked at Jaja. She was standing up in the dinghy with an oar poised like a spear. She lowered it slowly.

"Everything OK over there?" I shouted.

She waved and resumed sounding between the rocks and the shoreline.

When Jaja's six-foot-long oar went barely halfway into the water, I swore involuntarily. Too shallow. Defeated, Jaja came back to *Driver*. With our forward escape sealed off, we had only one option—motor toward the back of the unsurveyed indentation and try to skirt behind the approaching ice-vice. Proceeding at dead slow, I glued my eyes to the depthsounder while Jaja perched on the bow and looked in vain for rocks. Our objective was to keep moving and win the race with the ice. We had to get behind the slab before it squashed us against the rocky beach like a mussel shell hit by a hammer.

I glanced upwards to rest my throbbing eyes. The white mountains stood out sharply against the blue sky, and the nunataks—mountain peaks poking out of the glacier—were perched like islands in a frozen sea. The pastel blue ice of the glacial wall rose to incredible heights, forming cathedral towers with but-tresslike supports. The towers and buttresses seemed ready to collapse at any moment, but the Gothic pieces of ice clung tenaciously. It was almost as if the glacier dared me to look away and miss the mind-blowing spectacle of ice crashing into the water.

I glanced back at the depthsounder and immediately forgot the beauty around us. Eighteen feet...16...12...9...9...8...7.5...7...6.5. With barely six inches of water under the keel, we continued to glide along gracefully, defying the odds of running aground. Suddenly, the depth shot back to 20 feet, sending a thrill through my body. But it was too soon to celebrate. Just as quickly, the numbers sank back to less than 8 feet, betraying another rock.

Five minutes went by. The depths oscillated up and down. As the ice slab drifted nearer, we were forced closer to the beach. I was too focused on survival to contemplate the insanity of our anchoring so near a glacier in the first place. Instead, I just shook my head angrily. "Of all possible moments, why did the winter ice have to break loose this morning?"

The minutes crawled by. I held the tiller steady, keeping the ice slab a scant six inches from our hull. We were approaching the rear edge of the ice–close to breaking free. Once we got behind the slab, we could turn at a right angle, away from the beach, and aim for deeper water in the fjord.

"Kill that thought," I told myself. *"We haven't made it yet."*

"Take the engine out of gear!" Jaja shouted from the bow rail.

I dove for the throttle and pulled the lever into neutral as a large piece of protruding underwater ice slammed into our hull. *Driver* lurched as if she had struck bottom and stopped cold in her tracks.

"This might be the end," I thought. The ice was now scraping against the hull. It began to push us sideways. I looked over the side to make sure no ice was near the propeller. Then I put the engine in reverse. *Driver* backed away from the slab. I glanced at the sounder: 12 feet. There was still hope.

Tentatively, I eased us forward again parallel to the ice. The depth increased to 30 feet. We were just one boatlength from the rear of the slab. Then we saw a second, enormous slab 100 yards behind the first one. Apparently, the ice sheet had broken into a few very large pieces when it started to drift. We would have to navigate the ice-clogged waters between the two slabs. There, the icy chunks were densely packed, and were bigger than the ones with which we had experimented in Kongs Fjord. We would just have to do our best. This was our chance to escape to deep water–assuming no more rocks or shoals blocked the way.

As the corner of the first slab came abeam of us, I turned *Driver* slowly and aimed toward the middle of the fjord. My mouth was as dry as stale bread. *Driver* banged into a large chunk. I caught Jaja's eye.

"Keep going," she said.

Another piece clunked into the bow and scraped along the hull. I tried to think of other cruising experiences that I could relate to the nightmare, but nothing came to mind. We had woven our way through extensive coral reefs on *Direction,* but in all our years of sailing we had never actually hit one. Our experiences this morning superseded all others. The present was unique.

"Dave! Neutral!"

My hand found the throttle in a flash, and I slipped the engine out of gear. The hull bumped the ice.

After a moment Jaja hollered. "All clear."

For several more minutes, we negotiated the scattered ice between the two menacing floes. Finally, like coming off a bumpy, dirt road onto a newly paved highway, we left the slabs and icy debris behind. *Driver* glided smoothly through ice-free water. When we found the 300-foot depth curve in the middle of the fjord, I was so relieved I felt like yelling. But I was afraid to open my sticky mouth for fear of slurring my words.

Jaja walked back to the cockpit, put her hand on my shoulder, and said nonchalantly, "Want a coffee?"

I nodded and braved three words. "Make it strong."

WE CONTINUED TO MAGDALENE FJORD about three hours away. A low, sandy outcropping called Trinityhamna Peninsula provided superb protection from the open sea, and gave adequate protection from calf ice. The anchorage was shallow, and dozens of bergy bits were hard aground in deeper water. They acted as a breakwater, preventing smaller ice from entering our cove. We felt it was safe enough to "turn off" temporarily.

The scenery in Magdalene was breathtaking. Steep mountains bracket the fjord, and at the head of the bay two miles away, the Waggonway Glacier ambles out of the mountains carelessly and wanders into the sea. Big pieces of ice were calving off the glacier almost constantly. We could hear the booming and cracking noises echoing ominously. Several minutes after each rumble, a gentle surge would rock *Driver* as if a ship had passed far away. The pieces crashing into the fjord must have been immense to send waves all the way to us.

Ashore in Magdalene, we met two rangers who were stationed in a tiny hut. They wasted no time in asking to see our cruising permit. Satisfied, they welcomed us and chatted openly. The fjord, we learned, was a well-known cruise ship destination because there was plenty of room to maneuver a large vessel. The protected peninsula made a superb landing place for the not-so-nimble traveler, and the scenery epitomized all that Spitsbergen has to offer. Ten to fifteen thousand tourists visit the fjord each year, many of whom trudge along the sandy, boggy, terrain wearing loafers, slacks, and sport jackets.

There were six rangers in the whole of Spitsbergen, and they rotated to different camps every few weeks. Magdalene Fjord was the short stick for these guys, and they couldn't wait to move to a quieter post.

"Seen any polar bears?" they asked.

"We saw three in Hornsund several weeks ago," Jaja said. "Since then, we've only seen tracks."

"How about you?" I asked.

One of them chuckled, "Thought you'd never ask. We don't get regular visits from bears in this fjord; it's a fact that upsets many travelers who hope to see them. But earlier this season, right after 1,200 tourists disembarked from a cruise ship, I saw a large male swimming on the ocean side of the peninsula. Meanwhile, the tourists were over here having a barbecue. One of the cruise ship employees had dressed in a polar bear costume, and the guests spent happy hour taking videos and photographs of *him*.

The rangers warmed to our laughter. They told us that a confused passenger from another cruise ship had asked the rangers to turn on the northern lights for a few minutes before his ship left. At least one passenger per ship asked if the midnight sun and the noontime sun were ever visible simultaneously.

Jaja and I chuckled at these stories, but then the joke was on us.

"You'll never believe what happened last week," one of the rangers said. He told us about a group of tourists standing on the hill pointed excitedly toward the water.

"Look! Look!" cried the tourists, "We see beluga whales!"

The ranger chuckled. "You know what they saw? Some rocks awash in the fjord at low tide."

JAJA AND I SAT in the cockpit sipping our fourth cup of coffee. We were motoring under a blue sky and blue ocean with calm wind and sea. If there were a better day for going to the pack ice, it existed only in our dreams. The kids played below rambunctiously. They sensed our excitement, absorbed our energy, and used it carelessly. The sound of the engine drowned out their noisy chatter.

Our desire to approach the pack ice, which could put *Driver* into another hazardous ice situation, had cooled after our scrape in Smeerenburg Fjord. There, we had been on the defensive, reacting to a brand new situation that was completely out of our control. We had felt very vulnerable. Several days of rest, however, had revived our drive to reach 80 degrees north. Now we were also prepared mentally. We knew how to operate in the center of the "safe zone," rather than tread on the perilous periphery.

Overcome by the beauty around us, we sat without speaking. The plankton-rich ocean was like a canvas reflecting the bright, indigo sky overhead. Besprinkled on this canvas, like diamonds, were bits of ice. To the north, the sky near the horizon had a whitish cast. Within a half-hour, we saw the thin, white line marking the edge of the pack ice–separating ocean from sky.

We came against the first line of ice at 79 degrees, 47 minutes north. But we picked our way around a few bergy bits, found clear water, and kept going. However, nature would soon determine the limits of our quest. A mile later we reached the solid pack.

"This is unreal," I said. "We've pushed and struggled, hoped and despaired, but here we are. It feels like a dream."

In order to see farther, Jaja and I stood on the boom. The open sea spread out behind us. The mountains of Spitsbergen commanded the eastern horizon. Ahead to the north, a "sea" of ice stretched as far as the eye could see.

A light southerly breeze blew across our faces. We climbed off the boom. Jaja raised the mainsail, and I switched off the engine. With the wind calm all day, I had relaxed. Now my senses were on alert. Was it going to blow harder? Or was this just a zephyr? I looked at the sky. There didn't appear to be any squalls coming. I checked the barometer: Steady as a rock. A northerly wind would have been ideal, because it would push us away from the ice instead of into it. If the wind increased, we would have to turn around. This was no place to take chances. *Driver* was now on a lee shore.

The gentle, five-knot southerly wind urged us on. We were happy to use the sails instead of having to rely solely on the engine. If we had a sudden problem, at least there was wind. We could sail out of harm's way.

We urged *Driver* closer and closer to the ice. The sun glinted off the pack's billions of facets, filling the air with brilliance. In a flash, my mind distilled the entire *Driver* voyage into a solitary pinpoint of thought. I remembered our seasick departure from Bermuda, when our only goal was to reach Reykjavík. Then our goal was to winter over in Iceland. Then make it to the Faroes. On it went. If someone had told us in Bermuda that we would sail to the pack ice, we probably would have laughed out loud. But we had moved one step at a time, never forgetting to dream, no matter how difficult the obstacles.

Jaja stood on deck looking ahead. "Dave, I think I see a lead."

I stepped up on deck to get a better view. The lead, or channel, split the ice as if someone had slit it with a knife. As we sailed nearer to the lead, we observed that the slit was about a half mile wide and at least two miles long. We exchanged knowing looks.

"What do you think?" Jaja asked.

"We can stop our journey here and call our summer a success. After all, we've reached the pack ice. Or, we can enter the lead and see how far north we can get. We can always turn around if it feels unsafe."

Driver bobbed along placidly, leaving a thin wake. It seemed as if she were waiting for us to make up our minds.

Without hesitation, Jaja said, "Let's enter the lead, Dave. All along we've been saying that we want to go as far north on *Driver* as possible. Imagine sailing south tomorrow and thinking: 'Gosh, I wish we had at least *tried* to go to the limit.' That would be a bad feeling to drag around with us for the rest of our lives."

"Yes," I agreed. "That would be pretty bad. Talk about choking at the last second. Compared to rounding Langenes, or conning our way around Muck, this day is almost perfect. The wind seems to be holding steady."

To be on the safe side, we made a few lazy tacks back and forth across the entrance to the lead and observed it for a half-hour. It seemed stable. As far as we could tell, the lead wasn't closing.

I looked to windward. The sea to the south was an even blue, stretching to the horizon. There were no telltale, dark blue lines indicating the approach of stronger winds. I turned *Driver* into the lead. Jaja's face was calm.

"This is it," I said. "We're nearing the end of our northern journey."

Jaja just nodded.

Driver sailed downwind under the mainsail, surrounded on three sides by frozen water. The grinding sound of ice against ice conjured images of large molars ready to chew us to bits at the first mistake. But my mind was keenly in tune with our location. My nerves felt the potential danger, but my instincts nodded approval. I comprehended the risks and understood our abilities. I *knew* we were within the "safe zone."

The outer edge of the pack ice acted as a breakwater calming even the small waves generated by the light wind. I watched the GPS readout. We had not yet reached 80 degrees north. Jaja took the helm, and I climbed to the spreaders to scan the horizon. Nothing but solid ice–an impenetrable barrier that has stopped seagoing adventurers for centuries. I shook my head. All the water that had passed under our keel, and we were going miss our ultimate goal by barely 10 miles. *Ten lousy miles.* Then my consternation gave way to satisfaction. We had given it our best shot. There is no greater achievement than that.

I climbed back to the deck. Jaja was elated. "I feel like I'm on the top of the world. Imagine, almost all of the earth's land masses are to the south of us!"

We continued sailing. Jaja called the kids on deck. She pointed to the vast whiteness surrounding us and explained that we had achieved our goal–to sail as far north as possible. The end of the lead was less than 100 yards away. The GPS indicated our position: 79 degrees, 50 minutes, one second north. *Driver* was 610 miles from the top of the planet. I thought about the time two summers before, north of Iceland, when we had crossed the Arctic Circle for the first time. Back then, we had broken a mental barrier that we thought we could never top. Now we were nearly 800 miles north of that location. Unless we were aboard an icebreaker, there was no going farther.

Four-year-old Teiga stood at the rail with the cool wind blowing through her hair. "Mommy! It's so light and sparkly!"

Gazing northwards and speaking softly, Holly thought she knew how the early explorers must have felt. "It's looks so lonely out there."

Chris argued that if he landed on the ice from the dinghy and walked fast enough, he could make it all the way to the North Pole on his own.

Jaja replied, "You know Dave, Chris might be on to something. If we welded skis to the bottom *Driver*, we could sail over the ice. Think of it. We could go to the pole!"

I held my breath, nodded noncommittally, then pushed the tiller hard over to tack us southward–back toward the land, away from the arctic light.

I ONCE READ a book about mountaineering that ended with a party of climbers standing triumphantly on the summit, waving their flags. A fairy tale ending. How did they get down? Going to the top is only half the trip. Most tragedies occur after the feat when the mind is not so keyed up, the body is weary, and supplies are dwindling.

We waited until we returned to Amsterdamøya Island that same afternoon before toasting our success. We had taken our abilities to the limit. We gave Chris, Holly, and Teiga small gifts as tokens of our appreciation. They had gone along for the ride, and their stamina and enthusiasm had allowed us to persevere. We stayed awake until the wee hours playing games, coloring, and watching the midnight sun burn yellow over the North Pole. The south wind was still mellow. *Driver* lay placidly at anchor.

The next morning, reality replaced some of our sense of triumph. We still had a lifetime of goals ahead of us. We didn't know what they were, but when one dream ends, another always seems to unfold. Could anything match the thrill of Spitsbergen? Did it matter?

I thought about our years of voyaging aboard *Driver*. We had come to love the high latitudes where the difficulties of the cold, dark, winters are off-set by the unique beauty of the northern lights or by the full moon shining on snow-covered mountains. Often you have to wait patiently for such rewards; nature doesn't deal them out lightly. There is a purity in the high latitudes that can't be found elsewhere. And there is the thrill of the perpetual light of summer. But more than anything, we admired the people we had met along the way–their heartiness and endurance, their patient acceptance of the difficult climate, and their alliances with nature.

I wondered: In later years, would we take this cruise for granted? Were we going to paste these experiences in our scrapbook and close the cover? Or would they remain part of our future? Would our old habits displace our new awareness? Or had our experiences permanently altered our way of thinking? We hoped that the spirit of the north had entered us and made us better.

So where would we go now? Would the *Driver* voyage continue? Or was this experience in Spitsbergen the finale after many years of cruising? When we bought *Driver*, we said that we would cruise on her for three to five years and then reevaluate our direction in life. The third summer was nearly over.

WHEN WE RETURNED, Rienholmen Bay was radically different from the winter wonderland we had encountered on our way north on the summer solstice. Now the hills were lush and green. It was pleasing to walk on the soft mosses and grass, to squish about in the mud. White reindeer, stark against the green fields, grazed serenely. Young calves stayed close on the flanks of their mothers, unsure of the new world around them.

We felt relatively safe, and we relaxed our guard somewhat. When covered with ice, the bay was a giant refrigerator for polar bears, with a "seal-meal" sitting on each shelf. Once the bay thawed, there were no seals to pick off, and a healthy reindeer was too quick for a bear to catch. We walked naturally without the anxiety that had accompanied our previous forays ashore. Our "quest" was now behind us. We seldom felt tired any more, and our odd sleeping habits had become second nature.

One evening, after an all-day outing, we returned to *Driver* and discovered that we had lost six cartridges for the gun through a hole in my backpack. We joked about it, laughing at our carelessness.

But our laughter was edged with consternation. *How stupid and irresponsible.*

The lost bullets became a symbolic lesson. It was surprising how easily we had accepted the gun into our lives. Only a few weeks earlier, the gun had been an alien–an awkward houseguest–always in the way, physically and mentally. We resented having to rely on it.

Now, we had made friends with the gun and felt fortunate to have it for protection. Perhaps this feeling told us something: After we totally assimilate a new idea, we will never forget it. It was then that I realized that the spirit of the north would stay with us always.

STRONG SOUTHWESTERLY WINDS persisted. We waited patiently for moderate conditions that would allow us to return to the Norwegian coast. We bided our time in Fleur de Lyshamna Bay, a protected anchorage eight miles from Rienholmen Island. For six days, we saw no sign of human life–no aircraft, ship, boat, or hiker. We were utterly alone in a vast cruising ground, already regretting our impending return to organized civilization.

Experiencing Spitsbergen is more than just absorbing the visual surroundings created by the mountains, the ice, and the animals. Time moves differently on this outpost. The mountains and glaciers seem to disarm the clock, making the days feel both timeless and ephemeral. As we walked ashore during our last days in the far north, we wondered about the unique, harmonious environment we would be leaving behind.

The ice, the animals, the weather–everything had its place. The bears hunted predictably, the ice wandered in well-worn patterns, and the weather had its seasonal fluctuations. We, too, had found a place in this harsh region. If it was sunny and calm, we stayed up all night. If it was rainy and cold, we slept. We sailed when we could, and didn't worry if we got stuck in port.

On the windward side of the low peninsula that sheltered us at Fleur de Lyshamna, the sand beach stretched for miles. It was covered with logs, fishing floats, solitary shoes, nets, thick ropes partially buried in the sand, broken plastic water jugs–the usual beachy debris. Then we stumbled upon a startling new type of flotsam.

"Neat!" Chris shouted. "I never knew computer monitors floated! It must be because of its CRT glass-tube screen. My electronics book says..."

Beachcombing had reached a new plateau. Right there in front of us in the sand represented more technology than the world had known 50 years before. People had fought battles to win this type of knowledge, and here it was, shucked off haphazardly. I wasn't sure if the cast-off monitor represented mindless waste, or if it were an omen.

I HAD BOUGHT an extra box of shells for the gun in Longyearbyen. We still had two dozen left. Knowing that we would leave soon for Norway and would no longer need the gun for protection, I set up some fishing floats as targets. A little target practice would be a good way to have fun and use up some extra ammo. We planned to save 10 shells for emergencies. Jaja and I took turns firing–practicing with the "sightless" weapon. The plastic fishing floats exploded one by one. The kids stood to one side and cheered with each hit.

Jaja took another turn. BANG! To her astonishment, when the gun fired, the wooden stock splintered into several pieces where it connected to the metal barrel near the bullet chamber. We stared in disbelief. Our one and only advantage over the dominant species in the local food chain was broken and useless.

"What if we meet a bear now?" Holly wanted to know.

Jaja and I looked at each other. Then she said to the kids, "Stay close to us."

We walked a long mile back to the dinghy as our elongated shadows followed us home. It was reassuring to spy our little rowboat pulled out of the water at the edge of our private bay. Whooping and shouting, we "skied" down the 15-foot-high sand dune that bordered the beach. We dragged the dinghy into the water, loaded the kids, and rowed back to *Driver*. I held the broken Highlander in my lap while I scanned the anchorage for swimming bears.

After the kids had been fed and the dishes washed, I drank a beer and studied the gun. My anger at the gun dealer in Tromsø began to subside; it was pointless to waste energy trying to lay blame. Why ruin our last moments in Spitsbergen with arrogant aggression?

"Take responsibility for your own actions," I thought.

Instead of luxuriating in resentment, I now viewed the shattered gun stock as a woodworking challenge. Something to pass the quiet evening. I dismantled the barrel and trigger mechanism. I took out my clamps and two-part epoxy. Then, very carefully, I fitted the wooden stock back together like a puzzle. I hung the clamped stock over the diesel stove to cure, and admired my job. By taking matters into my own hands, I had turned anger into pride.

At midnight, Jaja began to read Rudyard Kipling's *The Elephant's Child* to the kids. About the time that the Elephant Child's nose was being stretched by the crocodile, I headed on deck to prepare for our departure the following morning. On my way past the stove, I touched the epoxy on the gun stock. Still sticky. I clamored up the companionway, stepped into the cockpit, and gaped. Ten feet behind the floating dinghy, with its nose in the air sniffing the breeze, a polar bear was treading water effortlessly.

"Hey! I see a bear! Come quick!" My tone of voice made it clear it wasn't a joke.

In less than five seconds, Chris, Holly, Teiga, and Jaja were on deck. Startled by my shout, the bear became alarmed. It swam for land toward the exact spot where we had beached the dinghy two hours earlier. When it came ashore, it shook the water from its fur. Spray filled the air, and the sunlight refracted in the water drops, creating a luminous rainbow. The bear sniffed our footprints and looked around suspiciously.

Jaja was the first to speak. "I can't believe we were just there."

The bear turned and bounded up the sand dune in two easy leaps. Taking turns with the binoculars, we watched it wander down the peninsula, its nose leading it along the path of our earlier walk.

After the bear was lost from view, we retreated to the warmth of the cabin where Jaja resumed reading aloud. I closed my eyes, took a sip of beer, and lost myself in the story.

THE END.

Maps of Driver's Voyage

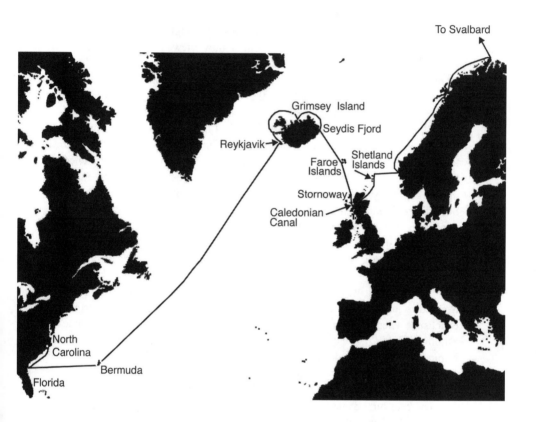

This map illustrates the route we sailed during our journey on Driver. Bermuda was our last taste of dry land before sailing 23 days nonstop to Reykjavik, Iceland. We thought that this ocean passage would be the highlight of our journey, and that reaching Iceland would be our coupe de grace. We were later proved wrong. It was just the beginning.

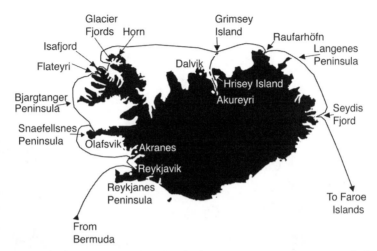

Above: Iceland has jutting headlands that pose serious navigational challenges to small boats such as Driver. However, we took our time, watched the weather closely, and ducked into the many small harbors at the fist sign of a storm. We lived on board Driver for ten months in the town of Akureyri on Iceland's northern coastline.

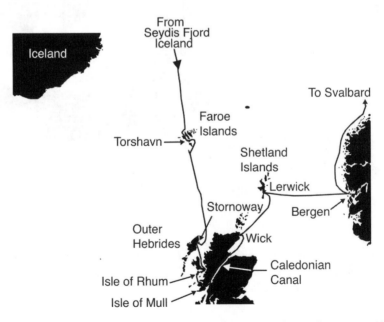

Scotland: This section of our journey was a transitional time for us mentally. With Iceland behind us, we were uncertain about where we were ultimately headed. We wandered though the waterways of Northern Scotland, searching for the "next thing".

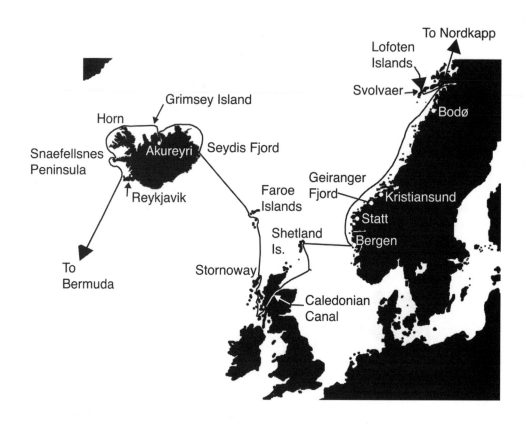

The "next thing" turned out to be sailing up the Norwegian coast. From Bergen we wandered north to the Lofoten Islands. Here, a different sort of adventure awaited us.

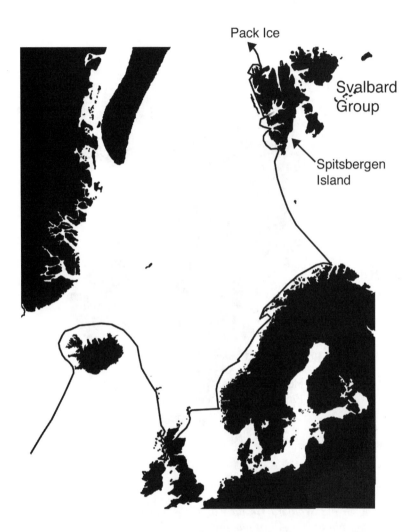

Pack Ice

Svalbard
Group

Spitsbergen
Island

Sailing across the waters between the Northern coast of Nor-
way and the Svalbard Group gave us a taste of real ocean danger.

Svalbard
Group

Pack Ice

79 50.1 N

Amsterdamoya
Island

Smeerensburg
Fjord

Magdalene
Fjord

Kongs Fjord

Spitsbergen
Island

Isfjord

Longyear
byen

Bellsund

Cape
Borthen

Hornsund
Fjord

Sørkapp

Pack Ice Limits ― ― ―

Sailing in the Svalbard Group was the pinnacle of our voyage, both mentally and physically. All of our previous sailing experiences came into focus here, and helped us to survive in this wild place.

Authors' Note

PLACE NAMES: In the Norwegian and Icelandic languages, the geographic description of a location is often included as part of the proper name. In Icelandic, "nes" means peninsula. On local charts you will find peninsulas such as Reykjanes, Straumnes, and Langenes. In Norwegian, "øya" mean "the island of." On Norwegian charts, you will find Bjørnøya ("the island of bear," or Bear Island) and Svinøya (the island of pig.) "Breen" in Norwegian means glacier.

For English-speaking readers, translating foreign place names in this book would have been a logical approach. However, if we had used English translations, readers doing further research might have found it difficult to identify the places in an atlas or on nautical charts. So, we've taken a slightly redundant approach. We've used local spellings as we read them on our charts followed by the place descriptions in English, i.e., Hansbreen Glacier and Amsterdamøya Island.

PEOPLES' NAMES: The Icelandic alphabet contains some characters that do not appear in the roman alphabet. To make certain peoples' names easier to read, we have substituted roman letters for Icelandic ones. We apologize to our Icelandic friends for the substitutions—in particular, Þorvarður (Thorvardur), Guðni (Gudni), Guðrun (Gudrun), Áþora (Áthora), and Friðrik (Fridrik).

VOICE: To make the narrative flow, we have told this story in the first person singular—in Dave's voice. However, Jaja and Dave shared equally in the book's creation.

– DAVE & JAJA MARTIN

Find Out What's Next and Stay in Touch with the Martins

Keep up to date with the Martin family! To read about other adventures, and view their striking photography, go to www.SetSail.com/Light.